To: David
Love Tammi
7/12/10

THE LOS ANGELES TIMES
ENCYCLOPEDIA OF THE LAKERS

THE LOS ANGELES TIMES
ENCYCLOPEDIA OF THE LAKERS

BY STEVE SPRINGER
Foreword by Earvin "Magic" Johnson

Los Angeles Times
1998

DEDICATION

To Alan,
Who has the talent to be whatever he wants to be,
And the good sense to know who he wants to be;
Who has shown that true magic comes from within,
And true winners don't need a scoreboard.

Los Angeles Times

Book Development Manager: Carla Lazzareschi
Editor: Mike James
Copy Editor: Steve Horn
Design: Jason Mooshagian and Chuck Nigash

ISBN 1-883792-24-X
© 1998 Los Angeles Times

Published by The Los Angeles Times
Times Mirror Square, Los Angeles, CA 90053
A Times Mirror Company

First Printing November 1998
Printed in the U.S.A.

TABLE OF CONTENTS

FOREWORD

When I was 11 years old, I went to a Piston game, sneaked into the visiting locker room by acting cool and got an autograph from the Bucks' center, Kareem Abdul-Jabbar. I walked out there like it was a dream, thinking it couldn't get any better than that. Man, was I wrong.

Eight years later, me and Cap were teammates on the Lakers. But by then, I had new dreams.

I remember, on the day I was introduced to the media at the Forum, sitting alone in the stands after everyone had left, thinking I was in a palace, listening to the cheers I knew would soon come, imagining myself dribbling the ball up and down the court, dishing off to people like Cap and Silk.

I remember walking into the empty locker room and looking at the stalls and the names above them. And then looking at my own name. I was happy and excited, and even a little frightened.

I knew it was going to be good, but I had no idea how good.

I was lucky enough to play with special people, people who were willing to leave their egos behind when it came to what I call "Winnin' Time." We had 12 egos combine for one purpose, and that was to get a championship.

I'm proud of the fact that we got five in the time I played and proud that we were able to win while also being entertaining.

"Showtime" was more than just a word to us. It was a style that set the tone for the whole league.

The Lakers have been winners ever since the days of George Mikan. Wilt and his team brought L.A. its first championship, and I'm happy we did five times as good for Dr. Buss, who spent an awful lot of money to put our club together and deserved to see results. Now it's time for Shaq and the guys to reward Dr. Buss and Jerry West with a new championship to keep that tradition going.

For 50 years, the Lakers have been about winning. That's what I'm all about too, and that's why I'll always be a Laker.

EARVIN "MAGIC" JOHNSON

INTRODUCTION

They brought glory to Minneapolis, glamour to Los Angeles and star power to the National Basketball Assn.

They were the first to bring a big league championship to Minneapolis and the first to bring big league basketball to Los Angeles.

Over the span of half a century, the Lakers have been a force in the NBA, second only to the Boston Celtics. But even the Celtics cannot boast of winning championships in three leagues.

The Lakers were the champions of the National Basketball League in the 1947-48 season, the Basketball Assn. of America in 1948-49 and, after the NBL and BAA merged to become the NBA in 1949-50, the Lakers won four NBA titles before heading west in 1960. In Los Angeles, they have added six NBA championships, covering the Forum walls with the banners of their brilliance.

They have had many of the biggest names in the game, many of the biggest games in league history and many of the league's dominating big men at one time or another. They had George Mikan, the league's first dominating big man, who led them to triumph in Minneapolis.

They had Wilt Chamberlain, the league's most dominating big man ever in terms of individual achievement, who led them to their first title in Los Angeles.

They had Kareem Abdul-Jabbar, the league's most durable big man, who helped lead them to five titles in the 1980s.

And they have Shaquille O'Neal, the league's most dominating big man of the future, if he realizes his potential.

But this hasn't been a team built solely on bulk. It has also been built on speed and finesse, on flash and dash before the smash, the team of the Kangaroo Kid and Dugie, Elg and Mr. Clutch, Stumpy and Magic and Big Game James. Their given names were Jim Pollard and Slater Martin, Elgin Baylor and Jerry West, Gail Goodrich and Earvin Johnson and James Worthy, but their skills carried them to an elite level where a nickname was all the identification required.

The Lakers have been built on daring and innovation and have always been one dribble ahead of their competitors.

They were the first to blaze a trail to the West Coast, where the NBA has thrived. They were the first to feature a gravity-defying star in Baylor, who blazed his own trail above the basket, the league's initial frequent flyer. They were the first to put their offense in the hands of a 6-foot-9 guard, Magic Johnson, who blurred the line between the frontcourt and the backcourt with a mix of talent that had not been seen in the league before.

None of this could have been envisioned when Ben Berger, a Minneapolis businessman, and Morris Chalfen, an ice-show promoter, plunked down $15,000 to buy the Detroit Gems of the NBL. For the 1947-48 season, they moved the team to Minneapolis, where the club became forever known as the Lakers.

All that $15,000 got Berger and Chalfen was a piece of paper that said they owned the team and two sets of dirty uniforms. Now what they needed were some competent players, something they couldn't expect to find on the Gems' roster considering the club had finished last in the NBL in its final season in Detroit.

Berger and Chalfen hired Max Winter, whose previous sports experience consisted of managing and promoting fighters, to run the operation. They lured 31-year-old John Kundla away from the head coaching job at St. Thomas College in St. Paul to be their coach.

The task of obtaining players fell largely on the shoulders of Sid Hartman, a sportswriter for the Minneapolis Tribune. Hartman was hardly an impartial observer. It had been his idea the year before to lure two

NBL teams to play a game in Minneapolis. The game drew more than 4,000, thus convincing Berger and Chalfen to go after a team of their own.

Now that Minneapolis had that team, Hartman, unconcerned with issues such as conflict of interest, went about the task of building up the Laker roster while still on the staff of the Tribune

Hartman got the Lakers a gem beyond anything the Detroit Gems had to offer, talking forward Jim Pollard into signing with Minneapolis. A star on Stanford's 1942 NCAA championship team, Pollard had been on an AAU squad, the Oakland Bittners, remaining an amateur so he could play in the 1948 Olympics.

But Hartman got Pollard to change his mind, and the Lakers got not only a 6-3 player, which made him one of their tallest, but a player with such jumping ability he was given the nickname Kangaroo Kid.

But Pollard was dwarfed by the man who soon arrived, the man who would put not only the Lakers but the league on the sports map. George Mikan stood 6-10 and wore glasses that made him look like a college professor. But with that height, razor-sharp elbows and a hook shot that was as devastating in its time as the sky hook would be in Abdul-Jabbar's era, Mikan soon made it clear that the only thing he'd be teaching to the rest of the league was Center 101. He quickly defined the position, setting standards that others would strive unsuccessfully to reach.

Mikan had been a star at DePaul under Coach Ray Meyer, whom Mikan credits with developing his game. Mikan then signed with his hometown team, the Chicago Gears of the NBL. In his first full season with the Gears, Mikan led the team to the NBL's 1946-47 championship. A dynasty seemed all but certain for the Gears. Instead, Maurice White, president of the American Gear Company, which sponsored the team, pulled the Gears team out of the NBL, putting it into the new league he was forming, the Professional Basketball League of America.

White's scheme went from dream to reality to rubble in less than a month, the league having gone out of business before many even knew it was in business.

White tried to shift gears again, but the NBL owners wouldn't allow the Chicago Gears back in. Instead, the team was broken up and the players were spread among the existing teams. For the first time, Berger and Chalfen were thrilled to have bought a team as bad as the Gems.

Because the Gears had finished last the season before, Berger and Chalfen had the first pick from the Gears' roster.

Whom did they select?

As fast as the pair could say, "George Mikan," they had the big man. It cost the Lakers $15,000 to sign him, big money in those days, but they got big results. The Lakers won titles in each of their first three seasons and in six of their first seven.

Mikan, who played professionally for nine seasons, led the NBA in scoring three times and rebounding once and was the most valuable player of the 1953 All-Star game. Mikan went on to briefly coach the Lakers and was later the first commissioner of the American Basketball Assn.

In their third season, the Lakers cemented the dynasty by adding two key players, Vern Mikkelsen, a 6-7, 230-pounder out of Minnesota who became the quintessential power forward before the term had even been coined, and Martin, a 5-10 point guard out of Texas, who showed as much skill in denying others the ball as he demonstrated when he had the ball in his hands. Labeled a defensive genius, Martin was an NBA All-Star seven times in his 11 seasons.

It isn't hard to understand how the Lakers were able to dominate the league in those years. In Mikan, Pollard and Martin, along with Clyde Lovellette, who joined the team in 1953, the Lakers had four future Hall of Famers.

But along with all the triumphs, there were plenty of hardships. Because for all the Lakers' early success, they were still playing in a league that was in its embryonic stage.

The Lakers didn't even have one arena they could call home. They played in the Minneapolis Auditorium, the Minneapolis Armory and St. Paul Auditorium.

They played some of their games in small towns, others in big cities where they sometimes found the stories of their games on the back pages of the newspaper. Players tried to survive on six dollars a day in meal money and get by on salaries that averaged from $6,000 to $9,000 a season.

When the Lakers won the NBA championship in 1953-54, they received a playoff share of $7,500–to be divided among nine players.

There was so little money to go around that when the Lakers won that NBA title, the only way they could get championship rings was to buy their own.

Only Mikan made any money. The highest-paid player in the league, he made $35,000 in 1953-54.

But there was no resentment from his fellow Lakers. They appreciated what he had done for his team and the league.

Still, when the Lakers arrived in New York to play at Madison Square Garden and saw that the marquee read, "GEORGE MIKAN vs. KNICKS," they couldn't resist having some fun with their celebrated teammate.

As Mikan removed his street clothes and began to dress for the game, he failed to notice that he was the only one doing so. Finally, when he had finished, he realized nobody else had removed so much as a stitch of clothing.

"OK," the puzzled Mikan was told, "that sign says you are playing the Knicks today. Go get 'em."

Playing in the era before air travel was routine for teams, the Lakers often went by train. Their long bodies crammed into spaces meant for a much shorter clientele, the players bonded. They would play marathon poker games or tell stories well into the night.

When a game in Rochester went into overtime, the Lakers didn't have time to shower and change clothes if they wanted to make the last train to Chicago and their next game. So they threw on overcoats, raced to the station and spent the night sleeping on the train in their smelly uniforms. Talk about a bonding experience.

The players often went out to dinner on the road as a team, a sight rarely seen these days when players are more likely to go out with their agents.

The kind of fun they had is illustrated by a dinner at a New York restaurant shortly after the club had moved west.

The specialty of the house was oysters. So forward Rudy LaRusso took a pearl tie pin and slipped it into one of the oysters.

When it was discovered, the players were stunned.

"You know, that oyster is legally yours," General Manager Lou Mohs said.

When one of the players reached in to feel the pearl, he was really shocked.

"Hey," he said in amazement, "this pearl has a needle sticking out of the end of it."

In the late 1950s, the laughs were drowned out by the complaints of investors. The Lakers had become a financial disaster.

In 1957, Bob Short was part of a Twin Cities group that bought the team for $150,000.

It might have seemed like a good idea at the time, but, when the debts began to pile up, Short and company began looking for a way out.

Short had hoped that the drafting of Baylor in 1958 would save the franchise. Baylor piled up the points and rebounds, but even he couldn't stop the losses, either on the court or at the box office.

When Kundla retired after the 1958-59 season, John Castellani replaced him, but Castellani had only an 11-25 record to show for his first 36 games.

In an extraordinary locker-room vote, Short asked his players to cast ballots on whether they wanted to keep their new coach. Only one player voted to retain Castellani, forward Frank Selvy.

LaRusso asked Selvy why he had voted for Castellani.

"He always played me," Selvy said.

Short replaced Castellani with Pollard, the star Laker forward who had left the game in 1955, for the remainder of the 1959-60 season.

The most memorable night for the struggling 1959-60 Lakers occurred far from any arena. It was over a cornfield in Carroll, Iowa, Jan. 18, 1960 at 1:30 a.m. The Lakers' DC-3 plane, with pilot Vernon Ullman at the controls, was trying to make its way through a fierce snowstorm.

Having lost his lights, his radio, his generator and his direction, Ullman, running out of fuel, decided to put the plane down in a cornfield. After three or four bone-jarring bounces and a harrowing 100-yard skid through the corn, the Lakers came to a merciful stop.

No harm, no foul

Joe Twit, the local undertaker, pulled up in his ambulance and told the shaken players, "We thought we were going to have some business tonight, boys."

When the players got to a phone, Larry Foust, who had been known to disappear before on his way home, phoned his wife to tell her that the team had crashed in an Iowa cornfield.

"Call me back," she said, "when you sober up."

From that low point, the Lakers rose to extraordinary heights. By the next season, they were in Los Angeles.

The team once known as the Detroit Gems had found a shiny new home. The team that had crashed in the snow of Iowa was about to take off in the sunshine of L.A.

The curtain would soon rise on Showtime.

THE LAKER TIMELINE

50 Years of Greatness at a Glance

1971-72: Team wins its first NBA championship as L.A. Lakers by defeating New York Knicks in five games. Season highlights include 33-game win streak, still the longest ever in pro sports, and record-shattering 69-13 season performance. Coach Bill Sharman is named co-NBA coach of the year.

1947: Sid Hartman, a 24-year-old sportswriter and delivery boy for the Minneapolis Star Tribune, puts together a group of wealthy Minnesota businessmen to buy the near-defunct Detroit Gems franchise for $15,000. Team gets its name from Minnesota's clear, cold waters. Team also becomes the first in the league to have its own cheerleaders, the Lakerettes. Just weeks into the team's first season, Hartman makes the deal that cements the franchise, signing 6-foot-10 George Mikan to a one-year, $15,000 contract.

1951: To counteract Mikan's scoring dominance (and inject more entertainment value in the game), the NBA widens the lane from six to 12 feet.

1958: Team finishes dead last in NBA, with 19-53 record. The reward: prize draft pick Elgin Baylor.

1957: Lakers are sold to a group of investors led by Bob Short and Frank Ryan for $150,000. Their first move was to get draft rights for "Hot Rod" Hundley.

1961: Chick Hearn, an L.A. radio and TV broadcaster, agrees to broadcast the fifth game of the Western Finals between the Lakers and St. Louis Hawks on KNX after the Lakers buy last minute air time. Though the Lakers lose the game, the team finds its broadcaster for life.

1949: First Laker game is televised, an exhibition game against the Globetrotters that the Lakers won.

1948-49: In its first season, the team wins the league championship.

1949-50: Lakers win second consecutive league championship.

1951-52: League champions.

1952-53: League champions.

1953-54: League champions.

1960: With fans defecting and losses (both on court and off) mounting, the team moves to LA. Other owners in the NBA agree only after the Lakers promise to pay the visiting teams' travel costs to the West Coast. Team moves into the new 14,000-seat Sports Arena and hires Fred Schaus as coach. Lakers lose their first home game, Oct. 24, 1960 to the Knicks with just 4,008 paying customers in the arena.

1961-62: Team again advances to the NBA championship series, but loses to Boston in overtime in the seventh game.

1986-87: "Showtime" is in fine form as Lakers win their fourth NBA championship in eight seasons. Magic Johnson is named MVP of both the regular season and NBA Finals.

1989-90: Pat Riley is named coach of the year, and Magic wins NBA MVP for the second consecutive year. Abdul-Jabbar's jersey, No. 33, is retired.

1996-97: Shaquille O'Neal arrives in L.A. amid great fanfare.

1981-82: Pat Riley named head coach early in the season and team wins its third NBA championship for Los Angeles. This is the first of nine consecutive seasons that the team will win the Pacific Division championship.

1991-92: Lakers shaken by Magic Johnson's retirement after learning that he is HIV positive. Johnson returns to play in the All-Star game and wins MVP honors. In five of Johnson's 12 seasons with the team, the Lakers are NBA champions. Chick Hearn broadcasts his 2,500 consecutive game on March 13, 1992.

1976-77: Jerry West becomes fifth head coach in the franchise's history. Abdul-Jabbar is the league's MVP.

1987-88: It's repeat time as Lakers become the first team since the 1968-69 Boston Celtics to win back-to-back NBA championships. To reach this, the team endures three consecutive seven-game playoff series, winning 4-3 series against Utah, then Dallas and finally Detroit. James Worthy is named MVP of the NBA Finals.

1997-98: Optimism about O'Neal's second year in L.A. is crushed when the team is swept by the Utah Jazz in the Western Conference Finals.

1979-80: Under Coach Paul Westhead, Laker's are again NBA champions. Magic Johnson becomes the first rookie ever named MVP of the NBA Finals as he gets 42 points, 15 rebounds and seven assists in Game 6 of the title series.

1975-76: All-Star center Kareem Adbul-Jabbar joins team and becomes first Laker selected NBA's MVP.

1983-84: Abdul-Jabbar surpasses Wilt Chamberlain as NBA's all-time scoring leader.

1988-89: Adbul-Jabbar in his last of an all-time record 20 seasons in the NBA, is celebrated during his final visit to NBA arenas during the season. Magic Johnson is named NBA MVP for the second time in three years.

1993-94: Lakers fail to qualify for NBA playoffs for the first time in 18 years.

1984-85: Lakers again NBA champions, beating Boston in the championship series for the first time in nine finals matchups against the Celtics. Abdul-Jabbar named MVP of the finals.

1992-93: Randy Pfund becomes the 10th head coach in L.A. Laker history.

1994-95: Del Harris becomes coach.

ALL-TIME LAKER LINEUP

── FIRST TEAM ──

Elgin Baylor
Forward

James Worthy
Forward

Kareem Abdul-Jabbar
Center

Magic Johnson
Guard

Jerry West
Guard

── SECOND TEAM ──

Happy Hairston
Forward

Jamaal Wilkes
Forward

Wilt Chamberlain
Center

Michael Cooper
Guard

Gail Goodrich
Guard

THE LAKERS' MOST MEMORABLE GAMES

April 10, 1962 ➤ Jerry West steals the ball from the Boston Celtics' Bob Cousy with two seconds remaining in Game 3 of the NBA Finals, drives the lane and scores on a layup to give Lakers a 117-115 victory and a 2-1 series lead. The electrifying play is the first to truly excite the L.A. fans, catapulting the Lakers into a high-profile spot among Southern California's teams.

April 18, 1962 ➤ Frank Selvy misses an open 15-foot jumper at Boston Garden with four seconds remaining in Game 7 of the finals. The Lakers lose in overtime, 110-107. Had Selvy made the shot, allowing the Lakers to triumph over the Celtics in the finals for the first time, all the years of frustration that followed and perhaps even the course
of team history, might have been been different.

December 31, 1967 ➤ The Lakers beat the San Diego Rockets, in the Rockets' first season of existence, 147-118, in the first basketball game played at the Forum.

May 5, 1969 ➤ Hurting his right knee with a little more than five minutes to play and the Lakers seven points behind the Celtics in Game 7 of the finals, Wilt Chamberlain takes himself out of the

game. When the Lakers rally to move to within one point of Boston, Chamberlain asks Coach Butch van Breda Kolff to put him back in, but Van Breda Kolff, angered over Chamberlain's decision to come out in the first place, refuses. The Lakers go on to lose, 108-106, falling to Boston once again in a series they once led 2-0.

May 8, 1970 ➤ The New York Knicks' Willis Reed, suffering from an injured right leg, limps out on the court for Game 7 of the finals, the leg heavily bandaged. An incredible wave of emotion sweeps over the arena, heightened when Reed scores the first two baskets. He doesn't play long, but long enough to inspire to team to a 113-99 victory.

January 7, 1972 ➤ The Lakers beat the Hawks at Atlanta, 134-90. It is the Lakers' 33rd straight triumph, and the last of the longest winning streak in the history of professional team sports.

May 7, 1972 ➤ With Chamberlain scoring 24 points and pulling down 29 rebounds and Gail Goodrich contributing 25 points, the Lakers beat the Knicks, 114-100, at the Forum in Game 5 of the finals to clinch their first NBA title since moving to Los Angeles.

May 16, 1980 ➤ With Kareem Abdul-

Jabbar back home in Los Angeles because of a severely sprained ankle, rookie Magic Johnson fills in at center while also playing forward and guard at various points against the 76ers in Game 6 of the finals at Philadelphia. The 20-year-old Johnson scores 42 points, including 14 for 14 from the free-throw line, pulls down 15 rebounds and hands out seven assists, leading the Lakers to a 123-107 triumph and the title.

June 9, 1985 ➤ With Abdul-Jabbar scoring 29 points, James Worthy 28 and Johnson getting a triple-double with 14 points, 14 assists and 10 rebounds, the Lakers win Game 6 of the finals, 111-100, to finally end the years of agony against Boston by beating the Celtics for the first time in the finals in their ninth try. What makes it even sweeter is that the Lakers clinch in front of the Boston Garden fans who had so long rejoiced over their failures.

June 21, 1988 ➤ Worthy picks this night and this game, Game 7 of the finals, to record his first triple-double. With 36 points, 16 rebounds and 10 assists, the Laker forward leads his team past the Detroit Pistons, 108-105, giving the Lakers back-to-back titles for the first time in their history.

THE LAKERS' FIVE GREATEST WEAPONS

2. Wilt Chamberlain's finger roll.

3. Elgin Baylor's hanging layup.

4. Jerry West's jumper.

1. Kareem Abdul-Jabbar's sky hook.

5. Magic Johnson's coast-to-coast drive.

Abdul, Paula (1963-) ➤ What other Laker Girls only dream of, she has achieved. Beginning like so many others as a cheerleader for the Lakers, Abdul went on to bridge the gap between Inglewood and Hollywood, catapulting from a spot on the Forum floor to a prominent position in the music business. She has won a Grammy Award, Emmy Awards, American Music Awards, MTV Awards, been No. 1 on the charts with singles and albums, sold millions of albums around the world and become a highly respected choreographer.

Whenever Laker Girls are asked what they expect to get out of all their dancing and yelling and sweating, they point to Abdul.

Raised in the San Fernando Valley, Abdul tried out for the Laker Girls while an 18-year-old student at Cal State Northridge. She won a spot for $500 a month and stayed for three seasons before moving on to bigger and better things.

Thus giving hope to a generation of Laker Girls.

The Laker Girls in 1992.

Abdul-Jabbar, Kareem (1947-) ➤ Lew Alcindor became Kareem Abdul-Jabbar in 1971, changing his name because of his Muslim faith.

Seven years earlier, when Cassius Clay announced he had changed his name to Muhammad Ali because of his Muslim faith, becoming the first U.S. sports figure of such stature to do so, there was a significant backlash, particularly among white America. Many refused to call him by his new name.

However, Abdul-Jabbar's decision was met by a more accepting public. Kareem means generous, Abdul means servant for Allah, and Jabbar means powerful.

At the time, Abdul-Jabbar was also starting to change his ideas about society. Particularly white society.

He didn't play basketball for the U.S. team in the 1968 Olympics because he didn't want to disrupt his UCLA class schedule and graduation timetable to compete for a country that he said was "abusing my people."

It was Hamaas Abdul-Khaalis, an old friend of Abdul-Jabbar's father, who would alter Abdul-Jabbar's perception of race in the summer of 1968.

Abdul-Khaalis, who had begun life as Ernest McGee before becoming a Muslim, was a drummer; Al Alcindor, Abdul-Jabbar's father, was also a musician.

When Abdul-Khaalis saw Abdul-Jabbar on television talking about his refusal to play in the Olympics, he asked Al if he could talk to his son.

It was a valuable meeting for Abdul-Jabbar, as he explained in his book, "Giant Steps."

Wrote Abdul-Jabbar: "The first thing he [Abdul-Khaalis] did was cure me of racism. Ever since the Sunday bombing that killed four little girls in the Baptist church in

Abdul-Jabbar's final season included a series of send-offs across the country, including this ceremony at the Great Western Forum where the retiring great was presented with a rocking chair. Surrounding his are, from left to right, David Rivers, Mychal Thompson, Orlando Woolridge and A.C. Green.

Birmingham, Alabama, when a whole lot of white people died in a tragedy–say a fire or a plane crash–I'd be happy. When Bull Connor was on the Pettus Bridge with his police dogs and cattle prods [attacking black demonstrators], I saw them on television and it left its mark. I was certain God was going to send some lightning down and sear all those bastards, and when that didn't happen, I wanted to do it myself. I would meet individual white people and like them on a personal level, but the race as a whole could die tomorrow as far as I was concerned.

" 'That's wrong,' Hamas told me. "It doesn't have to do with race… Hamas judged men and and women by their sincerity and their convictions and he taught me to deal with people not as parts of some blanket abstraction."

While Abdul-Jabbar was changing off the court, on the court, nothing changed for the 7-2 superstar center except the level of competition that he was dominating. He led the Milwaukee Bucks to the 1970-71 NBA championship, dominating in the pros as he had at every previous level.

In 1975, Abdul-Jabbar was traded with Walt Wesley to the Lakers for Elmore Smith, Brian Winters and the draft rights to Dave Meyers and Junior Bridgeman. Abdul-Jabbar was back in Southern California, where he had had his greatest basketball success at UCLA. But to repeat that kind of success, Abdul-Jabbar needed someone to get him the ball.

That someone was a 20-year-old kid named Magic Johnson, who arrived for the 1979-80 season.

In their first game together, the season opener against the Clippers at San Diego, then the Clippers' home, Johnson got the ball to Abdul-Jabbar, who scored the game winner at the buzzer.

The exuberant Johnson raced over and threw a big hug around the stoic center. Abdul-Jabbar, the hardened veteran, looked at the kid as if he were nuts.

"Hey, we got 81 more," he told Johnson, trying to prepare him for the long season ahead.

Eventually, it was Johnson who would rub off on Abdul-Jabbar. With Johnson feeding him the ball and Abdul-Jabbar shooting his sky hooks, the Lakers won five NBA titles in the 1980s, and Abdul-Jabbar became the greatest scorer in league history with 38,387 points. He was also named the league's most valuable player six times.

Abdul-Jabbar wasn't immune to criticism. There was often a perception that he wasn't playing hard, perhaps because he made it look so easy. It didn't help that he

Kareem Abdul-Jabbar stands tall against the onslaught of Mark Aguirre and Bill Laimbeer during the final game of the 1989 NBA Championship.

played in the Showtime era when some of his teammates felt he was slowing down an offense that had the potential to produce one of the greatest fastbreak attacks ever. Nor did it help that Abdul-Jabbar had an uncomfortable, awkward relationship with the media, which affected his public image as well.

Abdul-Jabbar's image is dealt with in hilarious fashion in the movie "Airplane." He is told by a young kid, "My Dad says you don't work hard enough on defense, and he says that, lots of times, you don't even run downcourt and that you don't really try, except during the playoffs."

Abdul-Jabbar grabs the kid by the shirt and replies, "The hell I don't. Listen kid, I've been hearing that crap ever since I was at UCLA. I'm out there busting my buns every night. Tell your old man to drag [Bill] Walton and [Bob] Lanier up and down the court for 48 minutes."

That moment of film did wonders for Abdul-Jabbar's image.

As the minutes ticked down in one of the greatest victories in Laker history, the 1985 title-clinching win over the Celtics, the first championship won against their hated rivals that was made all the sweeter by the fact that the game was in Boston, it was Abdul-Jabbar who was grinning and high-fiving and whooping and hollering like

Johnson so many years before.

And why not?

Abdul-Jabbar had outplayed or outlasted his opponents and critics. His was a career of excellence.

SEE ALSO • *Alcindor, Lew; Johnson, Magic.*

Abernethy, Thomas Craig "Tom" (1954-) ➤ After spending a third-round draft choice on Abernethy, a 6-foot-7, 220-pounder from the University of Indiana, the Lakers got just 6.5 points and 3.9 rebounds from him over two seasons.

So before the 1978 draft, they traded Abernethy to the Buffalo Braves, who would eventually become the Los Angeles Clippers by way of San Diego, for a second-round draft pick.

With that pick, the Lakers took 6-5 forward Lew Massey, a member of the North Carolina Charlotte team that had reached the semifinals in the 1977 NCAA tournament.

But the Lakers got even less out of Massey. He never played in an NBA regular-season game. Abernethy played three more seasons, for Golden State and finally, back in Indiana with the Pacers.

Alcindor, Ferdinand Lewis Jr., (1947-) ➤ No one—not Michael Jordan or Wilt Chamberlain or Magic Johnson—was such a good basketball player that he forced the keepers of the game to change the rules to keep him under control.

No one, that is, except Lew Alcindor.

After he dominated the opposition on the high school and playground courts of New York, leading Power Memorial High to a 95-6 record, including 71 straight victories, Alcindor came west to UCLA in 1965.

Any question about the impact he'd have on the Westwood campus was answered in his first game.

In those days, freshman were not eligible to play varsity sports, so they had their own team. In the first preseason game, the Bruin freshmen played the varsity. It was usually a feel-good game for the varsity players, a chance to break the monotony of training camp by playing in a real game, flexing their muscles a bit and

Lew Alcindor, aka Kareem Abdul-Jabbar, bats away a shot by a University of Minnesota player during the Los Angeles Classic in 1968.

testing their talent on the young guys.

But not this time. Even though the varsity was a two-time defending national champion and again ranked No. 1 in the preseason polls, it lost to the Alcindor-led freshman by 15 points.

Alcindor scored 31 points.

Finally allowed to play with the big boys in his sophomore season, Alcindor scored a school-record 56 points in his first game, against cross-town rival USC. With Alcindor at center, UCLA won the NCAA title.

How excited was the NCAA to have a new star attraction in the game? So excited it banned the dunk shot in the off-season, hoping to severely reduce Alcindor's dominance.

That was no problem for Alcindor, who had been developing a hook shot since he was in grammar school. There was no rule against that and, as it turned out, virtually no defense against what would become famous as the sky hook.

The Bruins won two more NCAA titles with Alcindor at center and were 88-2 during his career, 12-0 in postseason play.

Then he faced a new challenge. He had dominated in college, rarely facing more than one good opposing player. But at 7 feet 2 and only 230 pounds, how would a finesse player like Alcindor compete against a powerful, bruising opponent like Wilt Chamberlain? With all the tough players he'd encounter in a league where double- and triple-teaming sometimes stifled big men, would Alcindor be driven out of the middle by NBA defenses?

The Milwaukee Bucks didn't think so. They made Alcindor the first pick in the 1969 NBA draft.

By 1971, Lew Alcindor was no longer making headlines for the Bucks. Because of his religious beliefs, he had changed his name to Kareem Abdul-Jabbar.

SEE ALSO • *Abdul-Jabbar, Kareem; Chamberlain, Wilt; Holy Providence; Power Memorial; Sky hook.*

Alcorn, Gary R. (1936-) ➤ Some might look with skepticism at the 6-foot-9, 225-pound Alcorn when he stands behind the counter in his Fresno sporting goods store and tells customers he played basketball with Jerry West and Elgin Baylor and was one of the pioneers who brought pro basketball to Southern California. But it's true.

OK, Alcorn wasn't a major figure on that first Los Angeles Laker team in the 1960-61 season. He played in only 20 games and averaged 1.6 points and 2.5 rebounds before knee problems ended his brief NBA career. But he was there during the inaugural season of one of sport's storied franchises.

All-stars ➤ In all, 19 Lakers have been selected to play in the NBA All-Star game. The most frequent has been guard Jerry West, selected in each of the 14 seasons he played. Kareem Abdul-Jabbar was picked 13 times as a Laker (19 overall) and Magic Johnson a dozen.

The most dramatic appearance was probably that made by Johnson in the 1992 game at Orlando, Fla., only

Michael Jordan and Magic Johnson take a friendly breather during the 1988 All-Star game. The East, led by Jordan, won , with Jordan scoring 40 points.

three months after his shocking announcement that he was retiring from basketball because he had tested HIV-positive. Johnson was named most valuable player of the game for the second time, having also won the honor in 1990.

The Lakers whose numbers have been retired–West, Abdul-Jabbar, Johnson, Wilt Chamberlain, Elgin Baylor, Gail Goodrich and James Worthy–made a total of 63 All-Star game appearances. Three Lakers have been All-Star game MVPs: George Mikan in 1953, West in 1972 at the Forum and Johnson.

Abdul-Jabbar might have suffered through the worst and most frustrating appearance of any Laker.

It was the 1982 game at Brendan Byrne Arena in East Rutherford, N.J.

Forgetting his protective goggles at the hotel, after also forgetting to bring a warm jacket with him to the cold East Coast, Abdul-Jabbar completed a totally forgettable weekend by going one for 10 from the field and finished with only two points and three rebounds in 22 minutes. Abdul-Jabbar's West team lost to the East, 120-118.

───────────────

SEE ALSO • *Johnson, Magic.*

Allen, Lucius Oliver, Jr. (1947-) ▶ For most of his college and professional basketball career, Allen's first thought when he came down the court was to look for Kareem Abdul-Jabbar. His first goal was to get him the ball.

Allen started in the backcourt on two of UCLA's national championship teams with Abdul-Jabbar, then Lew Alcindor, at center.

Allen, who began his NBA career with the Seattle SuperSonics in 1969-70, was reunited with Abdul-Jabbar on the Milwaukee Bucks the next season.

Early in the 1974-75 season, in search of a quarterback to run their offense and handle the ball, the Lakers traded guard Jim Price to the Bucks for Allen.

Abdul-Jabbar followed Allen this time, traded to the Lakers in 1975.

Allen was a Laker for 2½ seasons, averaging 15.9 points and 5.1 assists.

But his association with the club ended in frustration. With Allen limping through the 1977 Western Conference finals because of a dislocated toe, the Lakers were swept in

four games by the Portland Trail Blazers.

Then, with the Lakers and Allen unable to reach agreement on a new contract and free agency looming just seven days ahead, Allen was traded to the Kansas City Kings for forward Ollie Johnson and a pair of draft choices.

For Allen, those trips down court had just become a lot tougher without Abdul-Jabbar waiting at the other end.

Almond tree ▶ Laker Coach Paul Westhead, a Shakespearean scholar and professor, was fond of using literary quotes and sayings. On the night in Utah in November of 1981 when Magic Johnson asked to be traded because of his frustration with Westhead's new offense, Westhead was asked about his controversial game plan. It was outside the Laker locker room minutes after the team had beaten the Jazz and only minutes before Johnson would publicly express his desire to be traded, a request that resulted in Westhead's firing soon thereafter.

Said Westhead, in typical fashion, of his critics: "The almond tree bears its fruit in silence."

The silence was soon broken by Johnson, and the quote was one of the last uttered by Westhead as Laker coach.

Anderson, Clifford V. "Cliff" (1944-) ▶ Anderson came out of St. Joseph's as a fourth-round draft choice of the Lakers in 1967.

That was the high point of his Laker career.

He was a 6-foot-4 center in college, which obviously, wasn't going to work at the professional level. So he was asked to switch to guard. With the position already occupied by Jerry West and Gail Goodrich, it was unlikely that Anderson would get much playing time.

Anderson's problems were compounded by knee surgery just before his rookie season.

The Anderson experiment ended after 53 games over two seasons.

Balance of Energy ➤ Sounds like a theory of physics, doesn't it? Actually, the term came to be regarded as the first indication that Coach Paul Westhead was starting to upset the chemistry of his team.

Westhead had taken over for the injured Jack McKinney early in the 1979-80 season and had gone on to win an NBA title.

But after the Lakers had lost Magic Johnson to a knee injury and lost three consecutive games early in the 1980-81 season, Westhead made a controversial move by taking forward Jim Chones and guard Michael Cooper out of the starting lineup and replacing them with forward Jim Brewer and rookie guard Butch Carter.

Westhead said he did it to provide "a better balance of energy," when Chones and Cooper came in off the bench.

But Westhead had neglected to tell neither Chones nor Cooper, insecure players in the best of times, that their roles had changed, even though their actual number of minutes played would remain about the same.

Chones found out when he asked Westhead during pregame introductions whom he was guarding.

Uh, nobody, Westhead told him, you're on the bench.

"Maybe the move was necessary," Chones said, "but he shouldn't have done it the way he did. I was pissed off… With the sacrifices I was making, the least they could do was tell me about it, but maybe I was being naive."

Westhead junked the "balance of energy" in a month, but the players used the term, or simply B.O.E., to make fun of their coach behind his back for the rest of the season.

SEE ALSO • *Carter, Butch; Chones, Jim; Cooper, Michael; Johnson, Magic; McKinney, Jack; Westhead, Paul.*

Balloons ➤ On May 5, 1969, the Lakers were preparing to play the Boston Celtics in Game 7 of the NBA finals at the Forum. The two teams had met in six previous finals, the Celtics having won all six. But the Lakers were confident that this time was going to be different. They had Wilt Chamberlain, Elgin Baylor and Jerry West. And they had home-court advantage for the first time.

Laker owner Jack Kent Cooke was so confident about his team's chances that he ordered balloons to be bought and placed in the rafters, set to be released at the final buzzer as part of the celebration Cooke was sure he'd be watching.

Cooke also had the USC marching band on hand, poised to play "Happy Days Are Here Again."

Red Auerbach, then the Celtics' general manager, spotted the balloons when he walked into the Forum. An angry Auerbach told a Laker publicist, "Those things are going to stay up there a hell of a long time."

Secretly, Auerbach later said, he was delighted that Cooke had inadvertently given the Celtics emotional ammunition.

The balloons stayed in the rafters at game's end as Boston defeated the Lakers, 108-106, to win another NBA title.

And what happened to the balloons?

"I sent them all to a children's hospital," Cooke said, "where the kids had a great time with them. Certainly a better time than I did."

Barnes, V. James "Jim," "Bad News" (1941-) ➤ It looked like bad news for the rest of the NBA when Barnes was selected by the New York Knicks as the first overall pick of the 1964 draft.

He had earned that nickname while playing college

ball at Cameron and Texas Western (which later became Texas El Paso).

The nickname was still applicable when Barnes played on the 1964 U.S. Olympic team for Hank Iba.

"Mr. Iba didn't want me practicing with the team because he was afraid I might hurt someone," Barnes said. "I was kind of rough and tough."

And so he was with the Knicks in his first season, averaging 15.5 points and 9.7 rebounds. But after his second season, Barnes' totals dropped considerably.

In his season and a half with the Lakers, he averaged 6.7 points and 5.4 rebounds.

Barnes lasted three more seasons in the league after splitting 1967-68 between the Lakers and the Chicago Bulls.

Barnett, Richard "Dick," "Fall Back Baby" (1936-) ➤

A great shooter and defender, Barnett had a flair for showmanship. He would kick up his heels as he shot, or fall back once he saw the ball he had just shot was on target. That's how he got the "Fall Back" nickname given to him by Laker announcer Chick Hearn.

Once, Barnett was dribbling down the court when he was hit by another player and knocked against the scorer's table.

The impact knocked a phone over and opened a cut on Barnett's elbow. He saw blood running down his arm, then spotted the dangling phone. He picked it up and spoke into the receiver, "Get me a doc." He hung up and raced back onto the court to catch up with his teammates.

But Barnett was much more than a showman.

"He took the game very seriously," teammate Rudy LaRusso said. "He was always working on his moves in practice. If he was on the court alone, he would go one on one with himself. That's why he became a complete player."

Barnett lasted 14 years in the league. After spending two seasons with the Syracuse Nationals, he was a Laker for three seasons and a New York Knick for nine. Over that period, he made it to the NBA finals five times and was on two championship teams, with the Knicks of 1969-70 and 1972-73, both times beating the Lakers for the title.

Barry, Jon Alan (1969-) ➤ It hasn't been easy for Barry to wear an NBA uniform. Not with that name on the back. Because no matter what he does, he can't avoid comparisons to his father, Rick, a Hall of Famer and a man voted one of the 50 greatest players in NBA history.

Jon's three basketball-playing brothers are also all too familiar with the great expectations.

Jon's career took a big dip when he put on the Laker uniform for 1997-98. Stuck as the fifth guard, Barry had the fewest minutes and smallest offensive production of his professional career which began with the Milwaukee Bucks in 1992

But he did uphold one family tradition. He shot a team-leading 93.1% from free-throw line, showing that he has his father's accurate eye from that distance.

But that only meant yet another comparison to you-know-who.

The Brothers Barry in 1997. The two were an alll-L.A. duo: Brent was with the Clippers and Jon with the Lakers.

Bates, Billy Ray (1956-) ➤ He once scored 40 points in a game for the Portland Trail Blazers. He averaged 26.7 points for them in three years of postseason play.

But that wasn't the Billy Ray Bates who appeared in four games for the Lakers at the end of the 1982-83 season. Same person, different player.

Bates, who joined the Lakers in April of 1983, trying to win a roster spot for the playoffs, had spent Christmas 1982 at a drug and alcohol rehabilitation clinic in Phoenix.

He suffered from extreme depression over the death of his mother.

And he was 10 pounds overweight and out of shape when he reported to the Lakers.

The Trail Blazers had let Bates go at the end of the 1981-82 season. The Washington Bullets had let him go after he played 15 games for them in 1982-83. Bates got his shot with the Lakers, but lasted only four games, the final four of his career.

Baylor, Elgin Gay (1934-) ➤ Before the basketball world wanted to be like Mike, it wanted to be like Elgin. Before Doctor J started practicing, Elgin was treating the fans to an aerial show unlike anything they had ever seen.

Back in the dark ages of the NBA, when the set shot was still king, Baylor took the game to new heights. He would leave defenders frozen on the floor with his explosive leaping ability, incredible hang time and dazzling moves, the kind of spectacular material that can be seen nightly on highlight shows today. But it was rare in the late 1950s when Baylor came out of the University of Seattle as the first pick of the Minneapolis Lakers in the 1958 draft.

Laker announcer Chick Hearn, then employed by CBS Radio, remembers being in Seattle to do a UCLA football game and being invited to the school to meet Baylor, word of Baylor's basketball talent beginning to spread beyond of the northwest.

"I took a cab and went to this old, dilapidated building on the Seattle campus," Hearn said. "I walk in a little door and here, sitting with his legs sprawled out, about 20 feet it seemed, was Elgin Baylor.

"He looked up [at a coach] and said, 'I can't practice today. I got back problems.' 'That's too bad,' Baylor was

Elgin Baylor makes a fast break against the San Francisco Warriors in a 1965 game.

told. 'I want to you to meet Chick Hearn, CBS Radio, Los Angeles.' "

"Baylor jumped to his feet," Hearn added, "grabbed a uniform and put on a show for me that was unbelievable."

It was a show the entire NBA was soon seeing thanks to Laker owner Bob Short, who convinced Baylor to sign with the Lakers after Baylor's junior year. Short knew what the flashy Baylor could mean both to his team and the league at a time when both hung by a financial thread.

"If he had turned me down then," Short said, "I would have been out of business. The club would have gone bankrupt."

Short's vision of Baylor's value was reinforced almost every time Baylor stepped onto the court.

On Nov. 15, 1960, he scored the most points ever in a NBA game up to that point, 71, against the Knicks in New York.

Wilt Chamberlain, the most dominating offensive

As head of basketball operations for the Los Angeles Clippers, Baylor, second from left, poses with team executive Gene Shue, center, and their 1987 draft picks, from left: Reggie Williams, Ken Norman and Joe Wolf.

force the game has ever known, later eclipsed that mark five times, including his incredible 100-point game in 1962. But even in an era when high-flying superstars seem to break offensive marks all the time, only one other man, David Thompson of the Denver Nuggets, has ever surpassed Baylor's total. Thompson scored 73 points in a 1978 game against the Detroit Pistons. David Robinson of the San Antonio Spurs tied Baylor's mark with 71 points in 1994 against the Los Angeles Clippers.

Baylor also set the NBA playoff scoring mark with 61 points against the Boston Celtics in the NBA finals at Boston Garden in 1962. Since then, there has been only one better scoring performance in the postseason, Michael Jordan's 63 points against the Celtics, also at Boston Garden, in 1986.

But Baylor, an 11-time all-star, could do more than score. He is the Lakers' all-time career leader in rebounds with 11,463, this from a man who stood only 6 feet 5.

Baylor played 14 seasons for the Lakers, the first two in Minneapolis. And he never seemed to slow down until the end.

After facing Baylor, who was then 35, Knick forward Dave DeBusschere said, "I thought I've seen all of the old man's moves, but he showed me a few tonight I have never seen. He's a marvel of the ages."

Along with his consummate talent was a spirit that kept Baylor going through all the disappointing Laker seasons that ended in defeat at the hands of the Celtics in the NBA finals.

That competitive spirit came out during a game in Detroit in the 1962-63 season. Baylor scored the 10,000th point of his career. The game was stopped so that Piston captain Bailey Howell could present Baylor with the ball. As the photographers snapped away, Howell, seeing a frown on Baylor's face, said, "Smile, Elg."

"What for?" replied Baylor. "We're losing, aren't we?"

In 1962, Baylor came as close as he ever would to an NBA title. If teammate Frank Selvy had made an open 15-foot jumper in the closing seconds of the seventh game of the finals against the Celtics at Boston Garden, the Lakers would have won. Instead, Selvy missed and the Lakers lost in overtime.

What Baylor remembers most about that moment is that he was standing under the basket with a clear shot at the rebound of Selvy's miss and time to stuff the ball back into the hoop. Instead, he was pushed out of bounds, but no referee's whistle blew.

Baylor didn't know who had pushed him until 16 years later when Celtic forward Sam Jones finally confessed.

As he told the story to a reporter recently, Baylor's old frustration at not getting the opportunity for the rebound and subsequent shot resurfaced. He was still angry 36 years later.

Along with talent and spirit, Baylor also contributed plenty of laughs to the Lakers. He was the emotional leader of the team. He ran the locker room and the almost nonstop poker games and made sure all the new arrivals got proper nicknames. It was he who gave Jerry West the nickname he hated, Zeke From Cabin Creek. Still for all his accomplishments, Baylor suffered through eight losing trips to the NBA Finals without knowing the feeling of holding up that championship trophy. Ironically, the Lakers finally won the title in his final season, but Baylor, limping around with knee problems and trying to recover from a severed Achilles' tendon, retired nine games into that 1971-72 season at the age of 37.

"I've always wanted to perform on the court up to the level and up to the standards I have established throughout my career," he said. "I do not want to prolong my career to the time when I can't maintain those standards."

On the day Baylor retired, the club began a 33-game winning streak, longest in the history of professional sports, and finished the season by beating the Knicks in five games in the NBA finals for their first title in Los Angeles.

Baylor returned to the game as an assistant coach and then a head coach with the New Orleans Jazz. He has been head of basketball operations for the Los Angeles Clippers' since 1985.

When Baylor signs players now, they are aware to varying degrees that he played the game, but none of them are old enough to have seen him in action.

That's their loss.

SEE ALSO • *Chamberlain, Wilt; Hearn, Chick; Selvy, Frank; Short, Bob; West, Jerry.*

Beaty, Zelmo Jr. "Big Z"
(1939-) ➤ Los Angeles was the last stop on a long and impressive journey through two basketball leagues by the 6-foot-9, 235-pounder who had played at Prairie View A&M in Texas.

Beaty was a prized pawn in the war between the two leagues–the NBA and the American Basketball Assn.–at the start of the 1970s. Made a first-round pick in the 1962 draft by the St. Louis Hawks, Beaty spent seven seasons with that club, including its first in Atlanta, before he was sent to the San Francisco Warriors in exchange for Clyde Lee.

With that choice, the Hawks got Pete Maravich. The Warriors got nothing.

Beaty, eager to play for Los Angeles, chose to sit out the option year of his NBA contract. Beaty had his eyes on Los Angeles Stars of the ABA, rather than the Lakers.

By the time Beaty joined the Stars for the 1970-71 season, they had moved to Utah. For the Stars, Beaty was worth the wait. With Bill Sharman coaching and Beaty on the court, Utah won the ABA title.

The Warriors had to wait five years, but they finally got Beaty before the 1974-75 season when he returned to the NBA.

But Beaty never played for them. Instead, the Warriors turned right around and gave Beaty the same thing he had been seeking when they first obtained his rights–a spot on an L.A. team coached by Sharman.

This time, it was the Lakers, who gave up a second-round draft choice and cash for what turned out to be the last season of Beaty's career.

Benjamin, Lenard Benoit
(1964-) ➤ All you need to know about Benjamin is that, in his days with the Clippers, he once showed up to play with two left shoes. Despite that, despite his inconsistent play and a perception that he didn't try as hard as he could, the Lakers took a chance on him.

In February 1993, Laker General Manager Jerry West sent center/forward Sam Perkins to the Seattle SuperSonics for Benjamin and the rights to swingman Doug Christie.

Christie was the key to the deal, though the Lakers

thought Benjamin, despite underachieving with the Clippers and then the SuperSonics, was not yet a lost cause. But Benjamin showed that nothing had changed. He got into only 28 games for the Lakers and averaged 4.5 points and 3.4 rebounds.

He was sent to the New Jersey Nets one day short of four months after his return to L.A. for center Sam Bowie and a second-round draft choice.

Despite spending five full seasons with the Clippers and parts of two others with the Clippers and Lakers, Benjamin's lasting legacy to L.A. sports fans remains a sound bite that was played repeatedly on the Jim Healy radio sports show. On the tape, Benjamin, reacting to the frequent boos directed at him by L.A. crowds who didn't appreciate his play, says gruffly, "I don't give a shit about the fans."

The feeling was largely mutual.

Bennett, Mario (1973-) ➤ Bennett could identify with Byron Scott. Like the former Laker guard, Bennett grew up near the Forum, dreaming about wearing the purple and gold.

But there, the similarity seemed to end.

Scott had fulfilled his dream by coming to the Lakers in a major trade after being a high-profile first-round draft choice; Bennett arrived as a second-year player without impressive credentials, without much to show for his rookie season with the Phoenix Suns, without a guaranteed contract and with a history of knee problems.

Hardly the building blocks for success.

But Bennett held a roster spot for the 1997-98 season and carved out a role as a backup power forward.

He gave the Lakers a glimpse of what he might be like in a starting role, averaging 15.8 points, 10.8 rebounds and a 65.9% shooting from the field in the four games he started.

But Coach Del Harris barely gave Bennett a glance in the playoffs, giving him a total of only 10 postseason minutes, the fewest of anybody on the squad.

Bertka, Bill (1927-) ➤ Every Laker head coach since Pat Riley took the job in 1981 has had the same familiar face sitting with him on the bench.

Bill Bertka, over more than 40 years in basketball, has

been a head coach, general manager, player personnel director, scout and an assistant coach.

He got the Laker job when Paul Westhead's career as head coach crashed in November of 1981 in Salt Lake City, as his tumultuous relationship with many of the players ended following a fiery confrontation with Magic Johnson

Riley, then Westhead's assistant, knew that Westhead and Johnson had had an angry showdown in an equipment room after a game against the Utah Jazz. Riley knew that Johnson had then told reporters he wanted to be traded.

Riley also knew Westhead, far more expendable than Johnson, was probably about to be fired. Riley figured he was probably gone as well.

Sitting in a hotel bar in Salt Lake City, bemoaning the expected end of his coaching career after a little less than two seasons, he felt the arm of a friend on his shoulder. Bertka, then a Jazz assistant, was there to tell Riley not to worry, that you never know how things will work out.

Bertka was right. Riley's coaching career wasn't ending; it was just beginning. Riley became head coach and Bertka was asked to come along for the ride.

The 1997-98 season was Bertka's 17th as a Laker assistant and his 26th overall in the league as an assistant coach.

Bertka played basketball at Kent State and in the now-defunct National Industrial Basketball League.

He soon realized his future in the game was in coaching. In 1954, he became head coach of Hancock, a junior college in Santa Maria, Calif., where he won 97 of 110 games, including 42 in a row. Bertka's team won a junior college state championship in 1957.

He was head coach at Kent State for four years.

Bertka left the game in 1961 to become director of the city of Santa Barbara's recreation department.

But he missed basketball. So he and his wife, Solveig, founded Bertka Views, one of the most successful college scouting services in the country.

In 1968, Bertka also began scouting for the Lakers. His workload with the team increased until, in 1972, he was named the team's director of player personnel.

Two years later, Bertka left to join the New Orleans Jazz in its first year of existence. Ultimately, he served the Jazz in various capacities including general manager, player personnel director and assistant coach.

But it is with the Lakers that Bertka has had the most impact. Coaches, players, statisticians and videotape specialists have benefited from his presence.

When Abdul-Jabbar's sky hook would occasionally misfire over a stretch of several games, Bertka would work with the center to regain his touch. When Riley decided that a certain statistical category might provide a coaching edge, Bertka researched it. And when Riley was looking for a good assistant, Bertka suggested a young member of his own staff at Bertka Views, Randy Pfund, who went on to become the Lakers' head coach himself.

Bertka was so dedicated to his job that, rather than drive to his Santa Barbara home from the Forum every night, he got a room across from the Forum at the Airport Park hotel, and wound up living there for seven years during the season until the place was finally demolished.

Bertka outlasted the hotel, he has outlasted three head coaches, and he will apparently outlast the Forum, which won't be the Lakers' home beyond the 1998-1999 season.

SEE ALSO • *Pfund, Randy; Riley, Pat; Sky hook; Westhead, Paul.*

Bicycle ➤ It was the kind of day to pull the covers over one's head and sleep late. The kind of day to grab a racket and whack a tennis ball around with a best friend. It was the kind of day Jack McKinney nearly forgot existed. His life had been a whirlwind of activity since Laker owner Jerry Buss had hired him to be the team's head coach for the 1979-80 season.

McKinney had brought Paul Westhead along as his assistant and the two former college coaches had worked around the clock to be successful at the professional level.

But not on Nov. 8, 1979. It was the first day off that season for the two men, who lived close to each other on the Palos Verdes Peninsula.

When McKinney's phone rang at 9:30 in the morning, he knew he couldn't stay in bed all day.

It was Westhead. Did McKinney want to play a little tennis?

McKinney agreed to meet at the courts at Westhead's condominium complex. But when he got to his garage, McKinney realized his wife, Claire, had taken the car to get to a class she was taking with Cassie Westhead, Paul's wife.

McKinney spotted a bicycle that belonged to his son, John, leaning against a wall. He grabbed his racket, hopped on the bike and took off for the courts about a mile and a half away.

As McKinney glided down a steep hill, something went terribly wrong.

"My impression was that he put his brakes on and something happened then," said Robert Clark, who watched from his car nearby.

The bike stopped suddenly, but McKinney, not wearing a helmet, flew over the handlebars. He crashed on the asphalt headfirst, bounced once and rolled 18 feet down the incline before stopping.

He was motionless as a pool of blood formed under his head.

McKinney would live, but he would not live his dream. He had suffered a major head injury that would cost him his job with the Lakers.

SEE ALSO • *McKinney, Jack; Westhead, Paul.*

Blackwell, Robert Alexander "Alex" (1970-) ➤ After playing his collegiate ball at Monmouth, Blackwell was convinced he was good enough for the NBA.

Even if the Lakers weren't.

When printing up the media guide, public relations director John Black and his staff routinely left out marginal players who were unlikely to make the club. Blackwell, before the 1992-93 season, was such a player.

On the first day of training camp, Blackwell approached Black, media guide in hand.

"Where am I?" Blackwell asked. Hearing the response nearly brought Blackwell to tears. He did, however, prove the Lakers wrong, if only for 27 games.

But in March, Blackwell was put on the injured list because of medical problems with his prostate.

He was not re-signed at season's end and never made it into the Laker media guide.

Block, John William Jr. (1944-) ➤

Block was the local kid who didn't make good.

At least not locally.

Taken as a third-round draft choice by the Lakers from USC in 1966, the 6-foot-9, 210-pounder averaged 2.9 points and 2.0 rebounds in 22 games for the Lakers in the 1966-67 season.

Somehow, that convinced the San Diego Rockets to select Block in the expansion draft of 1967.

And it turned out to be a wise choice.

Block averaged 20.2 points and 11 rebounds in the team's first year of existence, great numbers for an expansion team.

Block had two more solid seasons in San Diego, but after that he averaged double figures in scoring only once and never in rebounding in his final six seasons in the league.

Blount, Corie Kasoun (1969-) ➤ Perhaps it was fitting

that Blount's biggest regular-season game of 1997-98 came against the Chicago Bulls. Because for the 6-foot-10, 242-pounder, Chicago is where it all began.

The Bulls made Blount, who played at Monrovia High, then at the University of Cincinnati with Nick Van Exel, a first-round draft choice in 1993. Chicago traded Blount to the Lakers before the 1995-96 season.

His numbers were unimpressive in his first two seasons with the Lakers, and he was limited in 1997-98 by ankle injuries that slowed him for much of the first half of the season.

But on Feb. 1, in the spotlight of a national telecast, Blount, an adrenaline flow temporarily wiping away the

pain and frustration of the season's first half, showed what he could do with some minutes.

"It was just like signing another contract," he said of the moment Coach Del Harris told him he'd be starting. "As soon as he told me, I just talked to myself and said this is the chance I was waiting for, against the team I'd been traded from.... Revenge is sweet."

Blount responded with 13 rebounds, seven points and seven assists in 30 minutes.

Blount was just as impressive coming off the bench against the Utah Jazz in the conference finals. In Game 1, Blount had a team-high nine rebounds in only 17 minutes. In Game 2, he again led the team with 10 rebounds in 29 minutes. In the four-game series, Blount had 26 rebounds, a total second only to that of Shaquille O'Neal. Certainly not a big offensive threat (he averaged only 3.6 points in 1997-98), Blount has, nevertheless, shown enough on the boards to keep his job.

Boone, Ronald Bruce "Ron"
(1946-) ➤ Remember how major league baseball celebrated Cal Ripken Jr.'s all-time record consecutive-game streak? Imagine if baseball had chosen instead to ignore the accomplishment. Or even worse, discount it.

That would give you some idea of how Ron Boone feels.

Boone played in 1,041 consecutive pro basketball games, still the all-time record. But because 662 of those games were in the now-defunct American Basketball Assn., the NBA doesn't recognize those games.

What's amazing about Boone's streak is that he never missed a game in his career, which stretched over 13 seasons.

"Ron didn't take any games off," said Larry Brown, whose 229 coaching victories in the ABA are also discounted by the NBA. "He played every game. For that not to be counted.... That's bogus."

No argument from Boone, whose Laker career consisted of 88 games in the 1978-79 season and part of 1979-80.

"The ABA players felt the NBA considered themselves as superior," Boone said. "You know, 'We're in the NBA. You're in this minor league.' What other way can you look at it?"

Boozer, Robert Lewis "Bob," "Bullet Bob" (1937-) ➤ The Lakers gave up Dick Barnett for Boozer, figuring Boozer could fill in adequately for Elgin Baylor, who was suffering from knee problems at the time.

That's exactly what Boozer did, averaging 12.2 points and 7.0 rebounds in 78 games in the 1965-66 season.

But simply filling in wasn't what Boozer had in mind. In his only season as a Laker, he played a total of 1,847 minutes, ending a streak of four years in which he had played at least 2,100 minutes.

So when Boozer was taken in the 1966 expansion draft by a newly formed team, to be known as the Chicago Bulls, he at least knew he'd be getting his minutes back. That made him a lot happier than Laker Coach Fred Schaus, who insisted that the Lakers had suffered more than any other club in that 1966 expansion draft by losing Boozer and guard Jim King.

That might have been debatable, but there can be no debate over the value of the switch for Boozer. His minutes were back over 2,000 per season, and his scoring average reached a personal high in each of the three following seasons, peaking at 21.7 in 1968-69.

Bowie, Samuel Paul "Sam" (1961-) ➤ The career of the 7-1, 240-pound Bowie was a disappointment because of a seemingly never-ending series of injuries that forced him to spend almost as much time on the injured list as on the court. In his two seasons as a Laker, 1993-94 and 1994-95, Bowie appeared in 92 games, averaging 5.8 points and 4.6 rebounds.

But it was inevitable that Bowie's career, regardless of injuries, would be regarded as a disappointment unless he became a superstar. Why? He was drafted ahead of Michael Jordan.

In 1984, the Houston Rockets and Portland Trail Blazers had the first two picks in the draft with the Chicago Bulls going third.

The Rockets, needing a big man, took Hakeem Olajuwon, then known as Akeem Olajuwon. Fair enough.

Portland then had a choice between Jordan and Bowie. While Jordan had been a star at North Carolina, it wasn't clear at that time that he would become one of the best to play the game.

So the Trail Blazers, feeling fortunate there was another big man in the draft in addition to Olajuwon, took Bowie and left Jordan to the Bulls.

Branch, Adrian Francis (1963-) ➤ When it comes to assessing talent, Jerry West has the last word on the Lakers.

And when it came to Branch, West's word was that Branch was worthy of a spot on the Laker roster.

No one else in the NBA seemed excited about Branch when he came out of the University of Maryland.

At Maryland, Branch was a roommate of Len Bias, who was drafted second overall by the Boston Celtics, then died from a drug overdose before he put on the Boston uniform.

Branch, a year ahead of Bias, had spent a season in the Continental Basketball Assn., averaging 25 points. Then, he came to Los Angeles to play in the summer league, hoping to get an NBA offer.

Branch was in Los Angeles when his father called with the news of Bias' death. Branch was emotionally crushed, but he was determined to fulfill his dream and did well enough to draw West's attention.

The Laker executive went to Pauley Pavilion to watch Branch, saw a 6-8 player who could shoot from the outside and decided to grab him.

Branch didn't exactly live up to West's expectations. He lasted only one year with the Lakers, but it was 1986-87, a big season for the club. Although he averaged only 4.3 points, Branch shot 50% from the field and made modest contributions to a team that won an NBA title.

Brewer, James Turner "Jim" (1951-) ➤ By the time Jim Brewer got to the Lakers in 1980-81, he was an eight-year veteran playing for his fourth team.

He had been star for his first club, the Cleveland Cavaliers, who made him a first-round draft choice from Minnesota. Brewer was one of the Cavaliers' all-time rebounding leaders and an exceptional defender.

But when he came to the talent-laden Lakers, Brewer had to learn to function in a supporting role.

"I've had to develop a new attitude," he said then. "I realize that my job is to...provide a spark."

Actually, Laker Coach Pat Riley wanted Brewer to put out the sparks. He often used the power forward as a defensive specialist to cool off the opposing team's hot-scoring big man.

"He's a revelation," Riley said of Brewer. "I think he's one of the best defensive big men in the league. Here you've got a guy who weighs 220 pounds, and yet has the quickness to go along with it."

Brewer never won a full-time job with the Lakers. But in his two seasons in Los Angeles, Brewer did win one NBA title, one more than he would have gotten in Cleveland.

Brickowski, Francis Anthony "Frank," "Brick" (1959-) ➤

Brickowski spent 13 seasons in the league, playing for eight teams.

His best scoring season was 1992-93 when he averaged 16.9 points for the Milwaukee Bucks. His best rebounding season was 1987-88 when he averaged 6.9 for the San Antonio Spurs.

Brickowski was with the Lakers for only half of the 1986-87 season, appearing in 37 games before he was traded, along with Petur Gudmundsson, two draft choices and cash to the Spurs for Mychal Thompson.

But from the beginning, at one practice, Brickowski learned things were a little different on the Lakers than on other teams.

"[Coach] Pat Riley," Brickowski said, "was in the middle [of a huddle] and Pat said, 'All right, we're going to do this, this, this and this, and in two hours, we'll be out of here.'

"And everybody put their hands in and Magic [Johnson] said, 'All right, we'll do this, this, this and this, and in an hour and 15 minutes, we'll be out of here.' Riley insisted that the practice would take two hours."

Continued Brickowski: "And Magic said, 'Oh, I thought you said ... because we're tired from flying last night and playing back-to-back games ... we'd be out of here in an hour and 15 minutes.'

"And I'm just like, whoa. I look at Pat like, 'What are you going to say?' There's like dead silence and everybody's waiting. We have everybody's hand in the middle and Pat goes, 'All right, if we do this, this and this, and we're sharp, we'll get out of here in an hour, 15 minutes.'

"And Magic looked over at me and winked."

Bridges, William C. "Bill" (1939-) ➤

Look at Bridges' career total in rebounds: 11,054, an average of 11.9 over 13 seasons.

Then look at his height: 6 feet 5 inches. Is there a typographical error in there somewhere?

Nope, merely a tough 230-pounder who was built like a tight end and started playing in the early 1960s when the average height of the league's players was shorter than it is today.

After spending nearly 10 seasons with the Hawks, in St. Louis and Atlanta, Bridges was briefly in Philadelphia before coming to the Lakers early in the 1972-73 season with Mel Counts for LeRoy Ellis and John Trapp.

Although he was 33 by the time he got to Los Angeles, Bridges averaged 8.0 rebounds for the Lakers in 171 regular-season games before being waived early in the 1974-75 season to make room for guard Stu Lantz.

Brown, Anthony William "Tony" (1960-) ➤

One could understand if Brown was a little disillusioned with the NBA. In seven years in the league, the 6-6 swingman from Arkansas played with nine teams, making him one of the most traveled men in league history.

Included in there were seven games with the Lakers at the start of the 1990-91 season.

But there was no disillusionment evident in Brown.

When he made the roster of the L.A. Clippers, his eighth team, the next season, he said, "I'm very happy. A lot of guys out there would kill to be in my position."

A precarious position at best. Brown lasted only 22 games with the Clippers before moving on to Seattle for the rest of the season, his last in the NBA.

Brown, Clarence "Chucky" "Wild Thing" (1968-) ➤

A second-round draft pick of the Cleveland Cavaliers in 1989, Brown was considered a wild thing in a wide-open offense, but his effectiveness was considerably lessened in a set system.

Early in his third season, he was ineffective enough for the Cavaliers to waive him.

The Lakers took a chance, signing Brown in December 1991, but he averaged only 3.8 points and 2.1 rebounds in 36 games.

There was one bright spot for him in March of the 1991-92 season when he scored 10 points against the Knicks in New York and then came back with 15 points and six rebounds the next night in Atlanta. But he was gone at season's end.

Brown played the next season for New Jersey and one game for Dallas in 1993-94. He signed with the Houston Rockets for the 1994-95, playing 41 games for them for the season which ended in the Rockets winning the NBA championship. After the 1995-96 season, the Rockets traded him and Brown landed in Phoenix where he payed for part of the seaon before being traded again to Milwaukee. In the 1997-98 season, Brown signed as a free agent with Atlanta, where he played in 77 games.

Brown, W. Roger (1950-) ➤ He played at Kansas University, then for seven teams in seven years of professional basketball in the NBA and American Basketball Assn. Brown's Laker career consisted of five minutes in one game in the 1972-73 season in which he sank one of three free throws and committed a foul.

The Lakers released Brown on Oct. 20, 1972.

Bryant, Kobe (1978-) ➤ Sam Perkins simply shrugged at the reporter's question. "Kobe?" the Seattle SuperSonic forward said. "Oh, him. They don't even miss him. It seems like they are more at ease without him."

That wouldn't be Kobe Bryant he was talking about, would it?

Not the Kobe Bryant who was drafted as a 17-year-old out of high school by the Charlotte Hornets in 1996, then was acquired by the Lakers for center Vlade Divac? Not the Kobe Bryant who drew comparisons to Magic Johnson

as a child prodigy ready to jump in and lead his Laker elders to glory?

Not the Kobe Bryant who was being pictured in publicity for the 1998 All-Star game as the heir apparent to Michael Jordan, yet another gravity-defying, human video game in the making?

Not the Kobe Bryant who was described in a scouting report before he even put on a Laker uniform as "Grant Hill with a jump shot"?

Yes, that was the same Bryant who was being portrayed as a liability by Perkins and some of his Seattle teammates when Bryant sat out most of the 1998 second-round playoff series between the Lakers and SuperSonics because of flu. The Lakers had lost the first game with Bryant in the lineup, then swept the SuperSonics essentially without him.

Of course, much of what the SuperSonics were saying was off-the-court trash talk, the kind of remarks that are designed to drive wedges among opposing teammates.

But some of what Perkins and Co. said was also being asked among reporters and fans.

Anyone who has seen Bryant dribble a basketball knows that he has the skills to someday be among the best in the game. The only question is, when will he blend those skills into a team concept and play at a superstar level on a consistent basis? At times, he seems to have done that. At others, he has looked as if he's still on the playground, his game spectacular, but removed from his four teammates.

"There are times he still likes to go one on five," former teammate Nick Van Exel said.

"The sky is the limit," Jordan Cohn, who runs an NBA scouting service, said of Bryant, "but it will be a while."

However long it takes, Bryant certainly doesn't seem discouraged. He learns from his mistakes and moves on. At the end of the 1996-97 season, Bryant's rookie year, he shot an airball in the closing seconds of regulation and three more in overtime as the Lakers were eliminated by the Utah Jazz in a second-round playoff series.

But that didn't seem to put a dent in Bryant's confidence.

In the 1997 Southern California summer league, Laker assistant coach Larry Drew was trying to teach Bryant to balance his natural talent with the needs of the team.

Bryant would smile and nod and, like any teenager, sometimes ignore the advice of those who know better.

Kobe Bryant is all smiles after winning the slam dunk contest during the 1997 All-Star Weekend. Brian Bahr/Allsport

An exasperated Drew wound up getting in Bryant's face to get the message across.

Bryant, who had a shoe contract and a Screen Actors Guild card before playing a minute in the NBA, knew early he had much to learn.

"It's crazy," Bryant said. "If you sit back and start thinking about it, maybe you could be overwhelmed by the situation. You've just got to keep going slowly and keep working hard on your basketball skills. Then, I don't think your head will swell because you won't have time to think about it."

Bryant made those remarks before his rookie season, and he has tried to live up to them. He hasn't gotten in any off-the-court trouble, he hasn't had problems with teammates and he hasn't fought over his role on the team.

His only struggles have been on the court, and those might have been avoided if only he'd gone the conventional route and played in college.

Some contend that Bryant is the perfect example of why a basketball player needs at least a few seasons of college ball as an intermediate step between high school and the pros.

Johnson had two years at Michigan State, and his maturity and increased knowledge of the game showed when he first stepped onto an NBA court.

Johnson was ready to start in the NBA; Bryant has had to do most of his learning off the bench.

Still, Bryant averaged 15.4 points in 1997-98, his second pro season. That was the highest average in the NBA for someone with fewer than 10 starts, and the highest for anyone coming off the bench in Laker history. He averaged 26 minutes a game.

Bryant got an earlier look at the NBA's inside workings than any of his peers got. He is the son of Joe "Jellybean" Bryant, who spent eight seasons in the NBA, playing for three teams, before his retirement in 1983.

Kobe was named for a type of steak his parents, Joe and wife Pam, had seen on a restaurant menu.

Playing for Lower Merion High School in Ardmore, Pa., Kobe led the school to a 77-13 record in his final three seasons there and finished as the all-time leading scorer in Southeastern Pennsylvania history with 2,883 points, an impressive mark considering he surpassed the total of 2,359 points, scored by Wilt Chamberlain.

Will Bryant ever break any of Chamberlain's numerous NBA marks?

That, of course, is asking a lot. Which is what people have been asking of Bryant ever since he soared out of high school, flew past college without a second look and landed directly in the pros.

Buck ➤ For media and fans, Earvin Johnson's nickname has been Magic since he was in high school. But players are particular about the nicknames they give their teammates. Given names are rarely used, and Laker players wanted something special for this special young player. So, fellow guard Norm Nixon came up with "Buck" because Johnson was the strong leader of the herd.

And to his teammates, Buck he would always be.

SEE ALSO • *E.J. the DeeJay; Johnson, Earvin; Johnson, June Bug; Johnson, Magic.*

Bucknall, Steven Lee "Steve" (1966 -) ➤ Born in London of Jamaican parents, Bucknall grew up in England playing soccer.

But when he grew to 6-5 at 14, he decided to become a basketball player. After a year of basketball, Bucknall realized that the only way he could continue to grow as a player was to come to the United States.

He played high school basketball in Boston, then at the University of North Carolina. He signed with the Lakers for the 1989-90 season, becoming the first from his country to reach the NBA.

Bucknall appeared in only 18 Laker games, averaging 1.3 points, before he was cut and returned to England to play.

"Hell, I had a terrible time," Bucknall said. "I didn't train, didn't care for my body, didn't care if we lost. I didn't know what to do, didn't even know if I wanted to play ball anymore... .From the NBA to there, it was ridiculous. I think I felt I was too good to play [in England]. I thought it was an insult, degrading."

Bucknall played a season in Germany and two in France before finally going back to become a dominating player in Britain.

But playing with the Lakers was special.

"Being in the NBA," he said, "was like being in a dream."

Bulkhead seat ➤ Kareem Abdul-Jabbar was the unquestioned leader of the Lakers in 1980. That meant his accustomed seat on Laker flights–the first aisle seat on the left-hand side–was, in effect, the seat of power.

That bulkhead seat was empty on the morning of May 15, 1980 as the Lakers boarded a flight to Philadelphia. Abdul-Jabbar had scored 14 points in the fourth quarter the night before despite a badly sprained ankle to lead his teammates to a victory that moved them into a 3-2 lead over the Philadelphia 76ers in the NBA finals.

But Abdul-Jabbar's effort had taken its toll.

By the time the game ended, his ankle had swollen so much it was decided to leave the team captain home while Game 6 was played in Philadelphia. Even if the Lakers lost, as most expected them to do, they would still have Game 7 at the Forum.

And they hoped to have Abdul-Jabbar back by then.

Coach Paul Westhead had decided to go with a 6-9 player at center, 20-year-old Magic Johnson.

Most 20-year-olds would be stunned by such a burden. Not Johnson.

"I'd love to," he told Westhead, flashing his trademark smile. "I played some center in high school."

And then, to emphasize that he was not only taking over Abdul-Jabbar's position, but the leadership of the team as well, Johnson sat in that bulkhead seat favored by Abdul-Jabbar, smiled at his coach and told his teammates, "Never fear, E.J. is here."

Johnson played all five positions in his most memorable game, scoring 42 points, pulling down 15 rebounds and handing out seven assists as the Lakers beat the 76ers, 123-107, to win the NBA title.

The next year, Abdul-Jabbar got his seat back, but he would never again have the unquestioned leadership of the team. Instead, he would have to share it.

Buss, Dr. Jerry Hatten (1933-) ➤ As a Depression-era child, Jerry Buss' concerns were far more basic than owning the Lakers or the Forum or the Pickfair mansion. At 4, standing in a long line during a bitter Wyoming winter, his immediate need was the free can of food at the end of that line.

Abandoned by his father, Lydus, around his first birthday, Buss was raised by his mother, Jesse, in poverty.

Life was a struggle. To keep the modest home he shared with his mother warm, Buss, at about the age of 6, would search town for old telephone books that could be used in the fireplace.

When his mother remarried and the family settled in Kemmerer, Wyo., financial conditions improved. But life was still difficult for young Buss. His stepfather, Cecil Orville Brown, expected Buss to get up at 4:30 and dig ditches, sometimes through partially frozen Wyoming soil, for Brown's plumbing business before heading off to school.

Buss was determined to find ways to earn his own money, and thus, his independence. He worked on the railroad, shined shoes and even sold stamps through the mail.

Eventually, Buss figured out the best way to financial independence: education. He qualified for a science scholarship loan from the University of Wyoming. From there, he went on to USC in pursuit of a Ph.D. in physical chemistry.

That is how Jerry Buss became Dr. Jerry Buss.

How he became a multimillionaire is far more unconventional.

After college, Buss got a job at the Douglas Aircraft Co.,

Laker owner Dr. Jerry Buss talks with Kareem Abdul-Jabbar in the Laker locker room following a 1983 game.

working on the development of rocket fuel and in other classified areas. Becoming friendly with Frank Mariani, a fellow worker who also had a passion for poker and self-improvement, Buss began working on the development of a personal fortune.

He and Mariani decided that the quickest path to wealth in Southern California in the late 1950s was real estate.

It wasn't going to be easy. Buss and his wife at the time, Joanne, had an expanding family that would soon include four children. He was a long way from the food lines of his youth, but with a salary of a little more than $700 a month, he also wasn't exactly in a position to become an entrepreneur.

To make an initial real-estate investment, Buss and Mariani, who was making a little more than $500 a month, decided they needed $1,000 each. So, they put aside $83.33 a month.

It took them a year to get their grubstake. They added four partners, at $1,000 each, and, in 1959, made the down payment on a 14-unit apartment building in West Los Angeles that cost $105,000.

Buss later admitted that he and his partners were "scared" at being involved in such high finance.

They cut costs by buying paint, brushes, nails and hammers, and becoming jacks of all the building trades. By day, Buss and Mariani worked on propulsion systems. By night, they patched holes in walls and moved refrigerators.

In terms of a financial empire, Buss was still on the ground floor, but he was determined to get to the penthouse.

Buss and Mariani had their financial ups and downs, but, when the real-estate wave crested in Southern California in the 1970s, they rode it to untold wealth.

By the time he was 40, Buss was worth several million dollars, as was Mariani. By 1979, when Buss began negotiating with Jack Kent Cooke for the Forum, the Lakers and the Kings, the Mariani-Buss real-estate holdings stretched across three states and were valued at $350 million.

The complex negotiations that resulted in Buss obtaining Cooke's sports holdings involved nine pieces of property in all, including the Chrysler Building in New York, 12 escrows in three states and a total of 50 lawyers and advisors.

The deal was made so complicated by the desire of both parties to pull off real-estate trades, rather than simple buying and selling, to lighten what could have been a debilitating tax crunch.

When all the wheeling and dealing was over, a forest's worth of papers had been signed, Buss had spent $33.5 million for the Forum, $16 million for the Lakers, $8 million for the Kings and another $10 million for a 13,000-acre California ranch owned by Cooke, a total of $67.5 million.

Mariani, shunning the spotlight, became a part owner of the Forum, while Buss, who was by then divorced from Joanne, reveled in the public eye, created a glitzy, glamorous basketball team that played off its Hollywood image. From the stars at courtside to the Showtime flair of the players on the court to the performance of the Laker Girls during timeouts, the team reflected the image of Buss, its playboy owner.

He certainly didn't dress or act like Cooke, his predecessor. Cooke fired employees for the slightest slip-up; Buss was extremely loyal. Cooke dressed impeccably in tailored suits and abhorred the slightest appearance of scandal; Buss stuck with the Wyoming look– jeans, boots and a belt with a big shiny buckle–and dated starlets young enough to be his daughter.

But Buss was like Cooke in that he knew the success of the operation depended on what happened on the court. And while Buss knew that he knew a lot about business, he also knew that he didn't know a lot about basketball. So he turned the day-to-day operation of the team over to Bill Sharman and Jerry West early on, offered his opinion only on rare occasions, and watched his team grow into a dynasty worth well over $100 million.

Not bad for an investment of $83.33 a month.

SEE ALSO • *Cooke, Jack Kent; Mariani, Frank.*

Buzzards ➤ That was Coach Pat Riley's name for the media.

During a championship series against the Philadelphia 76ers, Riley banned the media from practice after claiming that a Los Angeles writer, whom Riley refused to identify, had come to him with a new play he had seen Philadelphia run in practice.

Most reporters said they didn't believe Riley. Rooting for their own teams was frowned upon, and many said such a breach of professional ethics would be inconceivable. In addition, most reporters from L.A., who saw the 76ers only a few times a season, wouldn't be able to recognize a new play anyway.

Those reporters covering the team agreed that Riley, who was sticking with his story, had merely made it up as an excuse to close practice.

When Riley took over the Lakers in November of 1981, amid reports about Laker dissension in the final, tumultuous days of Paul Westhead's reign as coach, Riley told his players he never again wanted to see their complaints in print or hear them on the air.

"Don't embarrass me, and I won't embarrass you," Riley said. "When problems come up, we'll keep them to ourselves and solve them together."

For the most part, that worked. And Riley, with seven trips to the finals and four championships in his nine years as Laker coach, didn't give his players a lot to complain about.

Still, Riley would occasionally greet reporters with, "Here come the buzzards."

So on one long, winter trip, with the Lakers stuck for several days in snowy Indianapolis, a group of reporters went to a store, bought baseball caps and had the word Buzzard inscribed across the front along with a patch showing a buzzard in flight.

The next day, the reporters took their seats at courtside during practice and donned their caps.

When Riley saw them, he broke into a big smile.

Byrnes, Martin William "Marty" (1956-) ➤ In the spring of 1980, officials of a new entry in the NBA, the Dallas Mavericks, were looking over the list of players available to them in the expansion draft.

From the Lakers, who had won the NBA title two weeks earlier, the Mavericks had a choice at forward of Spencer Haywood, who had been one of the premier players in the game only a few years earlier, or the seldom-used Byrnes.

Hesitant to deal with the controversial Haywood, who had been suspended by the Lakers during the 1980 NBA Finals for erratic behavior, and eager to build for the future, the Mavericks took the 24-year-old Byrnes.

A 6-foot-7, 218-pounder from Syracuse, Byrnes had played for the Phoenix Suns and the New Orleans Saints

in his rookie season before signing with the Lakers for 1979-80.

Buried on a team with superlative talent, Byrnes played in only 32 games for the Lakers, averaging 2.0 points and 0.8 rebounds.

On the day of the expansion draft, he went from the world champions to a team just coming into existence. But he also went from a team that didn't need him to one that needed all the help it could get. With the Mavericks, Byrnes got his chance, but had only moderate success. He played in 72 games, averaging 7.8 points and 2.5 rebounds.

After a year in Indiana, Byrnes' brief NBA career was over. But at least he had a championship ring from the Lakers to show for it.

C

Calhoun, David L. "Corky" (1950-) ➤ Calhoun's job was to stop the best shooting forward on the opposing team, and he was good at it.

The Phoenix Suns had made him a first-round draft choice in 1972, based on his performance at Pennsylvania, where he was an All-American.

He wasn't all-anything in the NBA because of knee problems that severely limited him with the Suns.

The Lakers purchased Calhoun from Phoenix early in the 1974-75 season, confident that his physical problems were behind him.

Laker Coach Bill Sharman put Calhoun on such players as Rick Barry, Spencer Haywood and Sidney Wicks, and the 6-foot-7, 210-pound Calhoun was able to slow down those offensive machines.

Calhoun was an adequate shooter; he made 46.7% from the field in his only full season with the Lakers, 1975-76.

But at the start of the next season, Calhoun was waived.

Calip, Demetrius (1969-) ➤ After playing at Michigan, the 6-foot-1, 165-pound Calip was realistic. He knew his size would probably keep him out of the NBA. But that didn't keep him from knocking on the door.

The Lakers signed him as a free agent in 1991, then cut him before the season began.

"I just went home to Flint [Mich.] to my grandmother's house," Calip said. "I did a little soul-searching, a little praying, got ready for my next task, whatever it was to be, [the Continental Basketball Assn.] or Europe.

"I was about to catch my flight to Columbus, Ohio, to play in the CBA. My plane left at 3:15. I received a call about 2:30 on my way out of the door. They said, 'Hold on.' "

"They" were the Lakers. They needed a guard to fill in because Magic Johnson had gotten ill.

The illness turned out to be HIV.

Calip played in only seven games for the Lakers before they again sent him on his way.

And this time, they didn't call back.

Calvin, Mack (1947-) ➤ Calvin had played for nearly everybody in Los Angeles except the Lakers by the time he joined the club.

He had played at Long Beach City College, USC and for the Los Angeles Stars of the American Basketball Assn. Calvin was a star for the Stars, helping lead the club into the 1970 ABA championship series against the Indiana Pacers. With the Stars facing elimination in Game 5 of the best-of-seven series, Calvin scored 33 points in an overtime victory, though the Stars lost the title in Game 6.

From there, Calvin went on to Miami, Carolina, Denver and Virginia in six more seasons in the ABA.

The Lakers spent two years trying to get him, but Calvin lasted only 12 games with them once he finally arrived. In the ABA, Calvin was able to penetrate the lanes to pass the ball or score. He had never been below double figures in scoring in the ABA.

In the NBA with the Lakers, Calvin, who was 6 feet and 170 pounds, found the lanes clogged and his effectiveness stifled. In his brief Laker career, Calvin averaged 7.9 points and 1.8 assists per game.

He was traded to the San Antonio Spurs for a first-round draft choice and cash. The star of the Stars hadn't been given much of a chance to shine in his return to L.A.

Campbell, Anthony "Tony"

(1962-) ➤ In the final week of March 1988, Campbell was playing for the Albany Patroons of the Continental Basketball Assn.

By the final week in April, Campbell, who had played in the NBA in each of the three previous seasons with the Detroit Pistons, was a contributing member of the Lakers.

A first-round draft pick of the Pistons in 1984 from Ohio State, where he was his team's leading scorer in his junior and senior seasons, Campbell was signed by the Lakers as a backup small forward. The 6-foot-7, 215-pounder, who hadn't averaged double figures in scoring in the pros to that point, responded by averaging 11 points in 18.6 minutes over the final 13 regular-season games.

Building on that promising beginning, Campbell earned himself another full season with the team, concluding his Laker career with a 7.0 scoring average in 76 games and a 4.3 mark for 24 playoff games.

In 1989-90, after being signed by the Minnesota Timberwolves as a free agent, he was a full-time starter for the first time and averaged a career-best 23.2 points.

Campbell, Elden Jerome

(1968-) ➤ On July 18, 1996, Laker fans reacted with near unanimous praise when the team shelled out $120 million to pay center Shaquille O'Neal.

Twenty-four hours later, the team committed $49 million to re-sign Campbell, a forward/backup center, to a seven-year deal. And again, the fans reacted, but this time for some, it was with disbelief and derision.

Forty-nine million dollars for Elden Campbell?

Forty-nine million dollars for a guy who seems to disappear in some games, who appears to be almost disinterested on the court at times?

But a look at the numbers actually shows steady improvement for the 7-foot, 255-pounder. Campbell's

Elden Campbell goes to his left to slam home two points against the Dallas Mavericks in a 1997 game.

scoring average increased in each of the six seasons after his rookie year, going from 2.8 to 14.9, making him only the seventh player in league history to show such improvement over that long a stretch.

Campbell seems to play better as a starter than as a reserve. In the 50 games Campbell started in place of O'Neal, he averaged 18.1 points and 7.8 rebounds.

Campbell's negative image can be partly blamed on his demeanor on the court. No one will ever confuse him with Magic Johnson in terms of exhibiting emotion in a game.

The questions about Campbell's desire have followed him since he played at Clemson.

Watching him perform sluggishly in a game against Villanova, Cambell's college coach, Cliff Ellis, yanked him out. Put back in for Clemson's next game, against Niagara, Campbell, who apparently had found inspiration on the bench, scored 21 point and pulled down 11 rebounds.

"There have been times," Ellis said, "when I've felt I've needed to get his engines revved up."

It's a need the Lakers, who made Campbell a first-round draft choice in 1990, can certainly relate to. Time and again, they've hoped to see their investment result in a player who can supply some consistent enthusiasm and emotion.

"That's what the Laker Girls are for," Campbell said. "If you want to see cheering and hollering, look at them. I am who I am. This is how I was taught, never to show my feelings on the court."

But too often at critical times, Campbell doesn't show much production, either. When the Lakers really needed Campbell to come off the bench and make an impact in the 1998 Western Conference Finals against the Utah Jazz, he was largely ineffective.

Playing an average of 10.5 minutes per game against Utah, he shot 21.4% from the field.

Campbell averaged 2.8 points and 3.3 rebounds in that series, which ended with the Lakers being swept.

All of which brings back the original question: $49 million?

Carr, Kenneth Alan "Kenny"

(1955-) ➤ Carr, at 6 feet 7 and 220 pounds, was muscular and powerful, yet had a nice shooting touch. It was that combination that enabled him to attract NBA scouts in his sophomore season at North Carolina State, a season in which he averaged 26.6 points, fifth best in the nation.

The result was a spot in the first round of the 1977 draft, the Lakers taking Carr sixth overall.

Yet for all his physical prowess, it was Carr's body that ultimately let him down. He sat out the first 21 games of his rookie season with the Lakers after breaking a bone in his left foot in the final preseason game. And he broke a bone in his right foot in an August pickup game before his second and final season with the team. Carr averaged only 6.9 points for the Lakers.

Traded to the Cleveland Cavaliers at the start of the 1979-80 season for two second-round draft choices, Carr went on to play eight more years in the league, never again averaging less than double figures in scoring.

It might have been that way with the Lakers as well, if only Carr had been able to get off on the right foot with them.

Carr, M.L. ➤ Carr spent a lot of time on the bench on the Boston Celtic teams of the 1980s, a team with such players as Larry Bird, Kevin McHale, Robert Parish and Dennis Johnson. But in the 1984 and 1985 NBA Finals, Carr made his presence known as a cheerleader who would sometimes infuriate the Lakers and their fans by waving a white towel wildly over his head whenever the Celtics would get a rally going.

In L.A., Laker fans struck back. One threw a beer in Carr's face as he was coming off the court.

"Are you all right?" a concerned teammate asked as Carr tried to clear his vision. "Don't worry about me. Worry about him," said the cocky and loquacious Carr, pointing in the direction from which the beer had come. "I got a good look at that guy."

Before one game in the 1984 finals at the Forum, a fan ran to the court while the players were loosening up.

"Hey, M.L.," the fan yelled, "I was going to be you for Halloween. But I got a hernia carrying the bench around."

Carter, Clarence Eugene Jr. "Butch"

(1958-) ➤ His rookie season in 1980-81 was Carter's only year with the Lakers. He appeared in 54 games, averaging 5.6 points and 1 assist.

He was briefly in the starting lineup, in the midst of a controversy that nearly split the team apart.

Coach Paul Westhead, eager to create what he termed "a balance of energy," started Carter at guard in place of Michael Cooper and Jim Brewer at forward in place of Jim Chones.

Chones' and Cooper's unhappiness over the switch caused Westhead to reverse himself in a month.

Carter's brief moment in the Laker spotlight was over.

After the season, the Lakers traded Carter, who had been co-captain at Indiana University, to the Pacers for a third-round draft choice.

Carter, Ronald Jr. "Ron"

(1956-) ➤ As a senior at Virginia Military Institute, Carter averaged 26.3 points, making him the seventh-leading scorer in the nation, and made 53.2% of his shots from the field. The Lakers were also impressed enough to use their second-round section in the 1978 draft, their first pick overall, to select Carter and to cut Brad Davis, a first-round pick by the Lakers the year before.

But the Lakers found somebody who impressed them even more before Carter's second season.

In his first and only training camp as the Lakers' head coach in 1979, Jack McKinney faced a tough decision. Should he keep Carter, who became a close friend of owner Jerry Buss, or should he go with the unheralded but impressive swing man from New Mexico, Michael Cooper, who had been drafted after Carter in the third round the year before?

McKinney posed that question to his assistant coach, Paul Westhead. Westhead, impressed by Cooper's defensive skills, thought he was the better choice. McKinney listened, and the Lakers benefited from that advice for a decade.

Carter played the 1979-80 season for the Indiana Pacers, then went to work in Buss' real-estate business.

Carty, Jay (1941-) ➤ After being an honorable mention All-American at Oregon State, Carty took a circuitous route to the NBA.

He stayed at Oregon State and earned a masters degree in education. He got a masters in public health at UCLA. He played AAU basketball and was an assistant freshman basketball coach at UCLA.

Finally, 6½ years after finishing his collegiate playing career, Carty signed as a free agent with the Lakers. Never a swift player, he earned the nickname "Golden Wheels."

He played one season, appearing in 28 games in 1968-69. But if ever anyone had studied and prepared himself for life after basketball, it was Jay Carty.

Ceballos, Cedric Z. "Ice" (1969-) ➤ Ceballos once won a slam dunk contest on All-Star weekend by dunking a ball while supposedly blindfolded.

He averaged more than 20 points a game in each of his two full seasons with the Lakers and was again in double figures in January 1997 when he was traded.

He was the only Laker, other than Magic Johnson, Elgin Baylor, Wilt Chamberlain and Kareem Abdul-Jabbar,

Cedric Ceballos glances over to the sidelines during a 1994 game.

to average at least 20 points and eight rebounds in a season.

But no matter what Ceballos achieved in purple and gold, his name will probably always be linked to another sport: water skiing.

Yes, Ceballos said he took off for Arizona's Lake Havasu in the midst of the 1995-96 season without informing the club, missing four days and two games, to deal with family matters.

The Lakers had every reason to believe that the real matter on his mind was not water skiing, but decreased playing time.

But the thought of Ceballos hanging out at Lake Havasu while his teammates were playing short-handed created a lasting problem. When Ceballos returned, he was removed from his starting role, stripped of his team captaincy and temporarily given the silent treatment by his teammates.

Ceballos and Coach Del Harris hadn't seen things the same way for awhile.

Several months earlier, after Ceballos, bothered by a sore knee, had played lethargically against the Utah Jazz, Harris said of the forward, "I would like to think his lack of effort and energy is related to the sore knee. If it's a sore head, that's something else. That's something he'll have to deal with."

And the Lakers, though they insisted it was not

because of the Lake Havasu incident, dealt with Ceballos by getting rid of him in January 1997, trading Ceballos and Rumeal Robinson to the Phoenix Suns for Robert Horry and Joe Kleine.

Chamberlain, Wilton Norman "Wilt" "Wilt the Stilt" "The Big Dipper" (1936-) ➤ He always seemed larger than life. Larger even than his 7-foot-1, 275-pound frame. With Chamberlain, all the numbers seemed beyond reach of even extraordinary men. He once scored 100 points in an NBA game, a mark that will probably never be broken. He claimed in his autobiography to have gone to bed with 20,000 women, a number that will never be verified. He once averaged 50.4 points over an entire season.

When it comes to NBA points and rebounds, his name can be found in every meaningful category.

Chamberlain is the NBA's all-time leader in rebounds with 23,924 and is second to Kareem Abdul-Jabbar in points with 31,419.

Chamberlain led the league in scoring seven times and in rebounding 11 times. He was like Babe Ruth when it came to dominating a sport. Ruth not only hit 60 home runs, but had more than 50 a record four times.

Chamberlain not only scored 100 points, but has the top four single-game scoring totals, five of the top six and six of the top nine. Twenty times in NBA history, a player has scored 65 or more points in a game. Fifteen of those times, the scorer was Chamberlain.

It's the same story in rebounding. Chamberlain has the highest single-game total, 55, five of the top eight games and eight of the top 12, the Boston Celtics' Bill Russell accounting for the others.

Annoyed that he was not perceived as a team player, Chamberlain announced that he would lead the league in assists and then did so, averaging 8.6 in 1967-68. But the number that many associate with Chamberlain, and one that hangs heavily around his neck, is two. That's the number of championships he won in 14 years in the league.

Wilt Chamberlain shows off his signature shot, the finger roll, against Kareem Abdul-Jabbar, then of the Milwaukee Bucks during a 1972 game.

That pales in comparison to the success of two of his chief rivals–Russell and Kareem Abdul-Jabbar. Russell won an incredible 11 championships in 13 seasons with the Boston Celtics, Abdul-Jabbar six in 20 seasons with the Milwaukee Bucks and Lakers. Of course, Russell had Bill Sharman, Bob Cousy, John Havlicek and the rest of that magnificent supporting cast in Boston. And Abdul-Jabbar had Oscar Robertson with him when he won a title in Milwaukee and Magic Johnson for the rest of his titles, which came in Los Angeles.

Chamberlain won his first championship as a member of the Philadelphia 76ers in 1967, a team that won a then-record 68 regular-season games and beat the San Francisco Warriors in six games in the NBA Finals.

So imagine the Lakers' excitement a year later when, on July 9, 1968, they obtained Chamberlain from Philadelphia for Darrell Imhoff, Archie Clark and Jerry Chambers.

Finally, Chamberlain appeared to have, in Jerry West and Elgin Baylor, a "supporting cast" that could help him establish a dynasty. Only under Chamberlain, could stars such as West and Baylor be referred to as supporting players.

"I don't know if I would have wanted Wilt three or four years ago," said Butch Van Breda Kolff, the Laker coach when the deal was made. "Somebody said to me that, if we ever had Chamberlain, we'd have to have two or three basketballs so he could share with Elg and Jerry. That's not true. We should be an even better team with Wilt."

Chamberlain certainly thought so. He arrived in Los Angeles smarting at the accusation that he had only begun to acknowledge his

four teammates on the floor in his final seasons in Philadelphia.

"I don't like the title that I have become a team player recently," he told Los Angeles reporters on his arrival in L.A. "No one says that Bill Russell is selfish. If you pro-rated my shots when I was scoring 50 points a game [over the full game], they probably wouldn't be as many."

Chamberlain was asked if it galled him that people regarded him as a loser.

"It doesn't gall me," said Chamberlain, who had signed a contract for the then-astronomical sum of $1 million over five years. "But people who say that are stupid."

That tag was revived after Game 7 of the 1969 NBA Finals between the Lakers and the Boston Celtics.

Chamberlain took himself out because of a bad knee with a little more than five minutes to play and the Lakers trailing by seven points.

Chamberlain asked back in when his team got within a point. Van Breda Kolff, who was no longer enamored of his superstar center, told Chamberlain he could stay on the bench.

Stay he did, and the Lakers lost the game by two points and thus, the series. Chamberlain finally won a championship banner for the Lakers in 1971-72. Again, he was part of a team that set a then-record for regular-season wins of 69. The Lakers also won a record 33 straight games and beat the New York Knicks for the Lakers' first title in Los Angeles.

Gail Goodrich, a Laker guard on that team, said that he knew heading into Game 5 at the Forum that the Lakers would wrap up the series that night because Chamberlain, an avid volleyball player, had scheduled a match for the next night and was determined that he would

Wilt Chamberlain and the Celtics' Bill Russell in one of their classic dueling stances, this one from a 1969 match-up. (AP photo)

not be denied.

And, for only the second time in his career, Chamberlain, in pursuit of an NBA title, was not denied.

Was he the greatest player of all time? Many would argue that the lack of more championships takes him out of consideration.

Was he the greatest offensive force of all time? Of that, there can be no argument.

SEE ALSO • *Conquistadores, Hundred Points, Wilt's War of Words.*

Chambers, Jerome Purcell "Jerry" (1943-) ➤

It was the height of the Vietnam War and Chambers, who had been the Lakers' first-round draft pick in 1966, was on active duty in the U.S. Army. Chambers had played in 68 games in his rookie season before being inducted.

Then on July 9, 1968 while in his nation's uniform, Chambers learned he had been traded to Philadelphia.

Chambers, Darrell Imhoff and Archie Clark were shipped east for the most dominating offensive force the NBA has ever known, center Wilt Chamberlain.

By the time Chambers returned from the service, he had been traded again, to the Phoenix Suns. This time, for a far less glamorous player: George Wilson.

After two seasons away, Chambers went on to play three more in the NBA and two in the American Basketball Assn. His six professional seasons were played with six teams: the Lakers, Suns, Atlanta Hawks and Buffalo Braves in the NBA and San Diego Conquistadores and San Antonio Spurs in the American Basketball Assn.

Chaney, Don "Duck" (1946-) ➤

L.A. basketball fans were already familiar with Chaney by the time the Lakers signed him for the start of the 1976-77 season. But just because they knew him didn't mean they liked him. In fact, Chaney had become an L.A. nemesis.

As a senior at the University of Houston in 1968, Chaney helped his team defeat UCLA, 71-69, in the Houston Astrodome to end the Bruins' 47-game winning streak. A first-round pick of the Lakers' perennial archrivals, the Boston Celtics, he spent seven seasons in Celtic green, becoming known for his defensive skill and rebounding totals that were exceptional for a guard.

But he lasted barely a season with the Lakers before being traded.

To what team?

Back to Boston, meaning L.A. fans could go back to booing him. But that animosity eventually softened when Chaney returned to Los Angeles in the mid-1980s as coach of the Clippers.

He suffered through nearly 2½ seasons trying unsuccessfully, like so many before and after him, to turn that franchise around. The low point was 1986-87 when Chaney's Clippers finished 12-70.

That was cruel and unusual punishment, even for an L.A. nemesis.

Chones, James Bernett "Jim" (1949-) ➤

At the start of the 1980s, there seemed always to be a question mark over the Lakers' power forward position.

They thought they had found an answer just before the start of the 1979-80 season when they shipped Dave Robisch and a third-round draft choice to the Cleveland Cavaliers for Chones, a 6-foot-11, 220-pounder who had begun his career in the American Basketball Assn. with the New York Nets and had spent the previous five seasons in Cleveland.

In his first season with the Lakers, Chones averaged 10.6 points and 6.9 rebounds on a team that went on to win the NBA title.

Chones worked hard in the off-season, lost weight, was in the starting lineup and had gotten his rebounding average up to about 10 per game when Coach Paul Westhead benched him as part of a controversial move designed, in Westhead's words, to provide "a better balance of energy." Chones had his starting job back in a month after Westhead's strategy backfired, but Chones' desire was another matter.

Hurt by what he saw as the Lakers' failure to appreciate his hard work and preparation, Chones struggled mentally to get his attitude back to where it had been. "They don't set any plays for me anymore," he said. "Maybe that's my punishment for speaking out."

Chones wound up averaging 8.0 rebounds for the

season, but that didn't save his job.

The Lakers sent Chones, Brad Holland and several draft choices to the Washington Bullets for Mitch Kupchak in the summer of 1981.

Chones suffered a knee injury early the next season, his last in the NBA.

Christie, Douglas Dale "Doug" (1970-) ➤ Southern California basketball fans became familiar with Christie when he played at Pepperdine and was West Coast Conference player of the year after his junior and senior seasons.

Christie was drafted by his hometown team, the Seattle SuperSonics, in 1992, but never played for them. Unable to agree on a contract with the SuperSonics, he was traded to the Lakers in February 1993 with Benoit Benjamin for Sam Perkins. The Lakers quickly signed Christie and tried to figure out where he fit in. At 6 feet 6 and 205 pounds, he was versatile but did not produce enough to stick with the Lakers.

In October 1994, he was traded to the New York Knicks for two second-round draft choices.

Clark, Archie L. (1941-) ➤ Clark became the personal project of Laker owner Jack Kent Cooke, who rarely got involved in player development.

In the 1966-67 season, the first of two that the 6-foot-2, 175-pound guard spent with the Lakers, Clark made 45.2% of his shots from the field and averaged 10.5 points in 76 games.

But Cooke thought Clark could do better. So he gave the rookie a basketball hoop and strict orders.

"I want you to hang that up over your garage, my boy," Cooke said, "and practice shooting."

Cooke soon returned to the locker room to check on Clark's progress.

"Well, my boy, are you using my basket a lot?" Cooke asked.

"No, I'm not, Mr. Cooke," Clark replied sheepishly.

"Why not?" asked Cooke, his legendary temper beginning to flare.

"Because my landlord wouldn't let me put it up, Mr.

Cooke," Clark said.

"Your landlord! What do you mean, your landlord? Why not?"

"Because he thought it would ruin the garage, Mr. Cooke," Clark said.

"Well, I'll just buy that building from him. What is your landlord's name?"

At that moment, fellow Laker guard Walt Hazzard was coming out of the shower. He heard the end of the conversation and, when Cooke asked for the name of the landlord, Hazzard made a U-turn and quickly headed back to the shower.

His tenant, Archie Clark, was about to cause him some serious trouble.

Clark played one more season with the Lakers–he was traded for Wilt Chamberlain–but lasted a decade in the league, his best season being 1971-72. Playing for the Philadelphia 76ers and the Baltimore Bullets that season, Clark averaged 25.2 points and 8.0 assists, both career highs.

As for Hazzard, Cooke eventually learned he was Clark's landlord, and it's probably no more than a coincidence that several months later, the Lakers left him exposed in the expansion draft and he wound up going to the Seattle Supersonics.

Cleamons, James Mitchell "Jim," (1949-) ➤ He played only the first of his nine NBA seasons with the Lakers, and his numbers were nothing to brag about. Cleamons got into 38 games in the 1971-72 season for Los Angeles, averaging 5.3 minutes, 2.6 points, 1.0 rebounds and 0.9 assists.

His totals increased markedly as he moved on to play for the Cleveland Cavaliers, New York Knicks and Washington Bullets over the next eight seasons.

Cleamons was a part of two extraordinary seasons–one in his rookie year and the other after he had retired as a player. In his first season, he was a member of the winningest team in NBA history at the time, a Laker squad that won 69 games, including a record 33 in a row.

And nearly a quarter-century later, Cleamons was an assistant coach on the Chicago team that won 72 regular-season games in 1995-96 to break the Laker record.

Cleamons was asked to speak to the Bulls early in that

record season by Coach Phil Jackson, who wanted his assistant to warn his players of the pressures ahead.

"I was just very fortunate to have been part of both teams," Cleamons said.

Coin Flip That Changed Laker History ➤ After the 1975-76 season, Laker guard Gail Goodrich became a free agent and signed with the Jazz, then located in New Orleans.

In those days, under league rules requiring compensation for the signing of free agents, the Jazz had to give the Lakers something in return–players, cash or draft picks. It didn't matter what it was as long as both clubs were satisfied. If they couldn't come to terms, Lawrence O'Brien, then the NBA commissioner, would decide on compensation, never a comfortable situation for the teams involved.

Attorney Allan Rothenberg, representing Jack Kent Cooke, then the owner of the Lakers, told Barry Mendelsohn, the Jazz general manager, that the Lakers wanted New Orleans' first pick in the 1977 and 1979 drafts and the club's second-round selection in 1980.

All this for Goodrich, a 33-year-old who was only 6 feet 1 and depended on his ebbing quickness to be effective.

Mendelsohn's first reaction to the Laker offer? No way. But Rothenberg remained firm.

Mendelsohn and the Jazz knew that NBA officials frowned on free-agent movement in those days because they considered it a threat to league stability. Jazz officials worried they might be made sacrificial lambs to discourage other teams from dipping into the free-agent pool, that O'Brien might not only agree that the Laker offer was fair, but might make it even stiffer. Grudgingly, Mendelsohn agreed to the Laker request.

But Cooke had another idea. The Jazz had just worked out a conditional trade to obtain forward Sidney Wicks, a former star in Los Angeles at Hamilton High and UCLA, from the Portland Trail Blazers.

Cooke, seeing a chance to land a hometown player with the potential to beef up his team's frontcourt, offered the Jazz the option of keeping their draft picks and handing Wicks over to the Lakers.

In effect, Cooke would have traded the aging Goodrich for the young and powerful Wicks. But the Jazz said no. Sam Battistone, owner of the Jazz, had promised

the Trail Blazers that he would never trade Wicks to a rival team in Portland's Pacific Division, a division in which the Lakers were usually strong contenders.

Wicks eventually wound up going to Boston, where he struggled, hardly performing like the player Cooke had envisioned.

So Cooke settled for the Jazz draft choices–including their top selection in 1979. At the time of the agreement, Magic Johnson was still a senior at Everett High in Lansing, Mich., hardly anyone who figured in the Lakers' immediate plans. But the 1979 draft choice became truly valuable when the Jazz finished the 1978-79 season with a 26-56 record, worst in the league.

At that time, before the draft lottery, the worst team in the Western Conference simply flipped a coin with the worst team in the Eastern Conference for the right to make the top selection.

In this case, it would be the Lakers, with the Jazz's pick, against the Chicago Bulls, who had finished 31-51 in the East–five years before the arrival of Michael Jordan.

The coin flip was made by O'Brien in his New York office with the Lakers and Bulls listening in on a conference call.

O'Brien asked the Bulls if they wanted to make the call. Chicago General Manager Rod Thorn called heads.

O'Brien made the toss and announced it was tails. In the Laker office, there was dancing and shrieking. The Lakers would use the pick on Johnson, who had just finished his sophomore season by leading Michigan State to the NCAA championship.

There would be another day for the Bulls, who settled for UCLA's David Greenwood in 1979. Picking third in the 1984 draft, Chicago would find Jordan still there, Hakeem Olajuwon and Sam Bowie having gone first and second to Houston and Portland.

But for the Lakers, their moment had arrived. A magical era was about to begin.

Coin Flip That Could Have Changed Laker History ➤ This is the flip Laker owner Jerry Buss is thankful he didn't make.

One night early in 1982 at Pickfair, the former home of movie star Mary Pickford that was owned by Buss through much of the 1980s, Buss was entertaining Donald Sterling, a friendly rival and owner of the Clippers, then located in San Diego. The Lakers and Clippers had the first two picks in the NBA draft, coming up later that spring.

Which team would draft first was a matter yet to be resolved by a league-authorized flip of a coin.

The consensus throughout the league that year was that the No. 1 pick, if he was available, was Ralph Sampson, the 7-foot-4 center at Virginia, generally considered the heir apparent to Kareem Abdul-Jabbar as the NBA's next dominating center. But Sampson, a junior, had another year of college eligibility.

Sampson had let it be known he wouldn't leave school a year early if it meant becoming a Clipper. Even in those days, joining the Clippers was considered the NBA's version of being sent to Siberia.

But joining the Lakers? That was another story. Yes, Sampson said, he would come out to join the Lakers.

There was one major problem.

Sampson's NCAA-mandated deadline for renouncing his college eligibility and thus making himself available for the draft would come well before the coin flip. And without some assurance that he would be headed for the Lakers, Sampson was willing to wait another year before going into the draft.

So that night at Pickfair, Buss made Sterling a proposition.

Buss suggested they flip a coin that night. If he won, he could guarantee Sampson a spot with the Lakers; if Sterling won, he could draft North Carolina's James Worthy, considered by some to be second-best choice that year.

"If we flip now," Buss said, "you can't lose. You get Worthy no matter what. If we don't flip now, you only have a 50% chance of getting Worthy."

Sterling turned Buss down, Sampson stayed in school, the Lakers won the official coin toss and, of course, took Worthy. Sterling, with the No. 2 pick, selected DePaul's Terry Cummings, who, while a solid player, remained with the Clippers only two seasons.

If Sterling flipped the coin, and the league allowed the private agreement between Buss and Sterling, the Clippers would have gotten Worthy either way. He might have made them a decent club, if still not a great one, and perhaps they could have gained enough support to have remained in San Diego rather than move to L.A.

Had the Lakers wound up with Sampson, they would soon learn, as the Houston Rockets eventually did, that he

Worthy stuffs the ball during the 1982 NCAA championship game , showing the form that made him the Lakers' top draft pick. (AP photo)

was injury-prone and was not a dominating player in the professional level around whom a franchise could be built.

Buss walked away the big winner without doing a thing on that night in 1982. And, as usual, the Clippers came out losers.

Conner, Lester Allen (1959-) ➤ Conner got to play with Magic Johnson. But that didn't mean Conner was a star with the Lakers. By the time Conner and Johnson hooked up, it was as a member of Johnson's touring team after the Laker superstar had retired for the first time.

Conner's Laker career consisted of two games in the 1994-95 season as part of a 10-day contract he signed with the team.

He was brought in strictly as an emergency backup after guard Sedale Threatt suffered a stress fracture of the right foot.

"It's just insurance," Laker Coach Del Harris said. "I don't want to take any playing time away from the guys we already have."

Conner had major playing time earlier in a career that was in its 12th year by the time he joined the Lakers. Primarily known for his defensive skills, Conner's best season was 1983-84 when he appeared in all 82 games for the Golden State Warriors, averaging 11.1 points and 4.9 assists.

By the time Conner joined the Lakers, nobody wanted him on a full-time basis, with the exception of Magic Johnson.

Cooke, Jack Kent (1912-1997) ➤ The day the Forum opened in 1967, before the crowd arrived, Cooke was conducting a last-minute tour of the facility.

Accompanied by an aide, Cooke, obsessed with detail as always, stopped at a vending machine and dropped in a quarter, just to make sure the machine was working.

It was working all right. When Cooke pressed a button, down came his soft drink–and through the coin return slot came $10 or so in change.

Cooke stuffed the coins into his pocket and said, with a big smile, "Story of my life."

That it was. It was a life he once described as being "better than any F. Scott Fitzgerald novel."

Born in Toronto, Cooke went from selling encyclopedias and soap to being a billionaire with holdings in sports, the media and real estate.

He owned the Lakers, Kings and Washington Redskins, built the Forum and was overseeing the finishing touches on a new stadium for the Redskins when he died of heart failure at 84.

Also a buyer and seller of various newspapers and radio stations, Cooke owned the Daily News of Los Angeles at the time of his death.

Cooke was as comfortable playing in a band, at a card table with serious bridge players or being at the controls of a yacht during a furious race as he was in the business world.

He was called cheap, arrogant, heartless and impossible to work for, but he was too busy showing up

Jack Kent Cooke, here in 1997, owned the Lakers for 14 years, buying the team in 1965 for $5.175 million and selling it in 1979 for $16 million.

his critics to respond to them.

He was also called determined, brilliant, visionary and charming.

Like the day in 1934 when he found himself at the end of the road. Literally.

Stuck in the mud on a lonely road in Saskatchewan in the middle of a rainstorm with his wife and a load of encyclopedias, but no money for food, Cooke walked to the nearest town when the storm let up and convinced the local high school principal to give him a $5 deposit on a set of encyclopedias so he and his wife could buy their next meal.

Throughout his life, where others saw questions marks, Cooke saw dollar signs. In 1965, after the Boston Celtics, who had won every NBA title since 1959, had just been sold for $3 million, Cooke paid Bob Short $5,175,000 for the Lakers. Short had bought the club for $150,000 in 1957.

A ridiculous move on Cooke's part?

Fourteen years later, Cooke would sell the team to Jerry Buss for $16 million as part of a $67.5-million package that included the Forum and the Kings.

When Cooke got into a dispute with the Coliseum Commission while his Lakers were playing in the Los Angeles Sports Arena, which was run by the commission, he threatened to build his own arena.

They laughed at him

When commissioners learned the arena would be built outside L.A., in Inglewood, they laughed again.

But there weren't too many chuckles heard from the commissioners' corner once the Forum turned into a Southern California showplace, home of the Lakers and Kings along with concerts, ice shows and even the 1984 Olympic basketball competition, while the Sports Arena remained dark far too often.

Cooke again drew some raised eyebrows when he got into boxing. He co-promoted the closed-circuit television showing of the first Muhammad Ali-Joe Frazier fight and wound up making more than the combined purses of the two fighters, which totaled a then-astronomical $5 million.

In 1979, Cooke, embroiled in a divorce with Barbara Jean, his wife of 45 years, needed to get rid of his holdings. But Cooke was already looking at a $41-million divorce settlement, then thought to be a record amount. He didn't need to add to his financial obligations by paying a huge chunk of money from the sale of his sports empire to the government in taxes.

So instead, Cooke and Buss put together a deal that involved the swapping of property to avoid a tax crunch, property that included the Chrysler Building in New York.

When it was done, the huge transaction included nine pieces of property and a dozen escrows in three states.

Cooke was off to the nation's capital to set up a new base of operations, but he had left behind a Laker tradition that would outlive him. He put up the Forum, enticed many of the stars of Hollywood through his doors, spent the money to bring in a basketball star such as Wilt Chamberlain and put up the first championship banner on the Forum wall.

He changed the uniforms from blue and white to purple and gold. But Cooke hated the word purple, so he insisted that it be called Forum blue.

Cooke knew what he wanted when he was planning the Forum. He didn't need blueprints. He told his architect he wanted "Something about 2,000 years ago

and about 6,000 miles to the east of here."

When the Forum went up, Cooke had just what he wanted.

Story of his life.

SEE ALSO • *Buss, Jerry; Coin Flip That Changed Laker History, Short, Bob; Sports Arena.*

Coop-a-loop ➤ Alley-oop plays, in which one player breaks to the basket and another lobs a pass above the rim for him to dunk or lay in, are commonplace in the NBA today.

But when Michael Cooper began playing for the Lakers, he and Norm Nixon, as well as Magic Johnson on occasion, teamed up on alley-oop plays that were so spectacular they were given a name of their own: Coop-a-loops. The smooth touch of a Nixon or Johnson pass, combined with the extraordinary leaping ability of the 6-foot-7 Cooper, made the Coop-a-loop almost a guaranteed two points.

During one game in Seattle, Cooper was moving so fast that, he insisted, time seemed to stand still for him. He remembered soaring above the rim. It seemed as if all the noise in the gym had faded, everybody below him was moving in slow motion, and the ball came to him at such a reduced speed that he could read the lettering on it as he shoved it through the basket.

Cooper said he was even able, in a flash of the eye, to look down and see the players below him. As his hang time ran out and he returned to the floor an instant later, Cooper said, everything speeded up and returned to normal. The players were back moving at full speed and the sound of the crowd returned.

The phenomenon Cooper experienced is not unique to the Laker forward. Other great athletes have described moments, when they are on their game, that everybody else seems to be moving in slow motion.

SEE ALSO • *Cooper, Michael.*

Cooper, Joseph, Edward "Joe"

(1957-) ➤ Cooper made it onto the Laker roster by putting up some solid numbers. In the Continental Basketball Assn. in the 1981-82 season, he was second in the league in blocked shots at 1.9 per game. Then playing for the Lakers in the Southern California summer league, he averaged 7.5 points and 7.8 rebounds.

That earned the 6-foot-11, 230-pounder a spot with the Lakers for the 1982-83 season, but he lasted only two games before being released.

Cooper, Michael Jerome, "Coop"

(1956-) ➤ As a child, Cooper had more critical concerns than whether he might someday play in the NBA–such as whether he would walk.

At the age of 2, Cooper slashed one of his knees so badly on a coffee can that it required 100 stitches. He wore a brace for nearly eight years.

Cooper, of course, did recover. He became a basketball star at Pasadena High, Pasadena City College and the University of New Mexico.

But Cooper's chances at excelling in the NBA were again threatened by injury, this time by a torn knee ligament suffered in a summer league game after the Lakers had made him the 60th pick in the 1978 draft. Cooper played only seven minutes in his rookie season.

Cooper returned for the 1979-80 season at full strength, but as a lower-round draft pick coming off a serious injury, there was some question whether he would win a job in the Laker backcourt. Along with Norm Nixon, the Lakers had a rookie by the name of Magic Johnson.

It came down to Cooper and Ron Carter. Coach Jack McKinney kept Cooper. Cooper never did win a full-time starting job. But in his 12 seasons with the Lakers, he became one of the best sixth men in the league. Frontcourt or backcourt, running the offense or shooting three-pointers, Cooper became adept at whatever he was asked to do.

But his greatest strength was defense. The 6-foot-7, 170-pounder had the quickness to shut down the best guards in the league and the temperament to battle the

Michael Cooper, socks high and short strings dangling, demonstrates the correct form to use when executing the Coop-a-loop in a 1982 game.

bigger forwards. Cooper took pride in never stepping back from a confrontation–and in never letting the opponent have the last word when it came to trash talk. Cooper had some extraordinary battles against the Boston Celtics' Larry Bird, who called Cooper the toughest defender he had to face.

Cooper, who barely hung on to his roster spot, who came off the bench for most of his career, thus stood out on a roster loaded with such superstars as Johnson and Kareem Abdul-Jabbar. His high-flying, Coop-a-loop slam dunks, his trademark over-the-calf socks and the strings dangling outside his shorts, and that finger pointed upward toward the Forum seats in acknowledgment to his wife, Wanda, when he scored at the north end of the building where she sat, were lasting images to fans.

But despite his success, Cooper had an insecure streak. He would sulk if Coach Pat Riley put another player off the bench in ahead of him. Whenever Cooper put a towel over his head on the bench, Riley knew that Cooper's inner demons were getting to him.

"I had to get him in fast," Riley said of those moments, "or I would lose him."

Even a brilliant defensive performance by Cooper wouldn't necessarily bring peace of mind. He might shut Bird down, only to go home and tell Wanda, "I scored only four points."

Cooper frequently worried about being traded or cut, and that insecurity drove him.

"If you leave, you may not come back," Cooper once said when Riley told him to go home from a trip and rest a sprained ankle. "They don't have time to wait on stragglers."

But Cooper knew his concern was occasionally irrational. He once gave reporters a screw he had found on the floor, told them it had come out of his head and asked them to hang onto it because, he assured them, "I'm going to get a lot crazier."

He was right. At one news conference, Cooper sat at a table in the back, against a wall.

"This is so that none of you reporters can stab me in the back," he explained.

On another occasion, when a reporter wrote something Cooper didn't like, he put the reporter on three games' probation. He said if the reporter wrote something else Cooper didn't like during the three games, Cooper would never speak to the reporter again.

The reporter need not have worried. Although he claimed to never read a sports section, Cooper, who became an assistant coach with the Lakers after his playing days and a brief stint in European basketball were over, actually read everything written about himself and his team with great relish.

At one point, Riley believed Cooper had overcome his insecurity.

"He has cleaned out the skeletons from his closet," Riley said, "and he found some self-esteem."

In reality, Cooper never did find that self-esteem. Which was a good thing for Riley and the Lakers. It was those skeletons and demons that drove Cooper to become the great player he was.

SEE ALSO • *Coop-a-loop; Curran, Jack.*

Conquistadors ➤ Wilt Chamberlain wasn't nearly as successful as a coach as he was as a player. But then, he didn't give it much of a try.

Chamberlain coached the San Diego Conquistadors of the American Basketball Assn. for one season, 1973-74.

Chamberlain's team wound up 37-47. That was good enough to make the ABA playoffs, but the Conquistadors didn't do much better there, losing four of six games to the Utah Stars.

Cooper, Samuel Duane (1969-) ➤ Duane Cooper loved to tell those who towered over him, that "the world is built for a 6-foot 2-inch man."

On an outing to Disney World, Cooper grinned while 7-1 Vlade Divac labored to squeeze into one of the rides.

"See, I told you," Cooper said to Divac, "the world's made for the 6-2 man." Unfortunately for Cooper, the NBA was not made for him.

He lasted only two seasons in the league, 1992-93 with the Lakers and 1993-94 with the Phoenix Suns.

The 6-2 theory? Maybe it would have been different if he had actually been 6-2. The former USC Trojan was listed at 6-1 and may have been shorter.

SEE ALSO • *Chamberlain, Wilt.*

Counts, Mel Grant "Goose" (1941-) ▶ It might be
understandable if Counts had never
unpacked his suitcase in the years he
spent in the NBA—and jumped every
time the phone rang.

After all, when the Lakers traded
Counts to the New Orleans Jazz before the 1974-75
season, it was the sixth time since being drafted from
Oregon State by the Boston Celtics in 1964 that the 7-
foot, 230-pounder had been traded.

The Lakers traded him twice.

The first time Counts came to Los Angeles, in January
of 1967, it was, in effect, for popular, long-time star
forward Rudy LaRusso. LaRusso was traded to the Detroit
Pistons, who sent Ray Scott to the Baltimore Bullets, who,
in turn, sent Counts to the Lakers.

Counts had three pretty good seasons in Los Angeles,
averaging double figures in points in all three and never
fewer than 7.8 rebounds.

The Lakers traded Counts to the Phoenix Suns in
1970 for Gail Goodrich, a future Hall of Famer.

Counts, who had moved from Phoenix to
Philadelphia, was traded back to Los Angeles in 1973 with
Bill Bridges for LeRoy Ellis and John Trapp.

But by then, Counts was 31 and slowing down. In his
last full season with the Lakers, he averaged 3.2 points
and 3.2 rebounds.

And then, the phone rang again.

Crawford, Frederick Russell Jr. "Freddie" (1940-) ▶ Getting to the
NBA was not Crawford's primary goal
early in his college career. He was
more concerned with simply regaining
his health and getting back on the
court.

Any court.

Because after his sophomore season at St.
Bonaventure, Crawford learned that he had tuberculosis.

Crawford not only recovered but became an All-
American, then signed with the New York Knicks for the
1966-67 season.

The Lakers, in need of someone to fill in for injured
Jerry West, acquired Crawford after he was waived
midway during the next season.

Crawford averaged 10.3 points in 38 games and
played one more season with the Lakers in a five-year
NBA career.

Critic ▶ Announcer Chick Hearn has hardly ever been
speechless.

But even he was too scared to talk when he was called
in to see owner Jack Kent Cooke at the Forum one
morning while preparing to go on a trip.

Cooke made Hearn sit down and listen to a tape of the
previous night's game between the Lakers and the
Cincinnati Royals at the Forum while Cooke made notes
on a legal pad.

Hearn had no idea what Cooke was doing.

When the first quarter ended, Cooke shut off the
machine and told Hearn, "You said 15 times–15, Mr.
Hearn–how great Cincinnati was. Twice you mentioned
that the Lakers played well."

By that point, Hearn had regained his composure and
said, "That's right."

"How do you account for that?" Cooke asked.

"What was the score at the end of the quarter?" Hearn
said.

"I don't know what the score was," an irritated Cooke
replied.

"Well," Hearn said, "I'll tell you. The score was 43-10
in favor of Cincinnati. Did you want me to make a fool of
myself? And of you?"

"No," Cooke barked. "Get out of here and go on your
trip."

SEE ALSO • *Cooke, Jack Kent, Hearn, Chick.*

Crowd-O-Meter ▶ It was a curiosity item during the
Lakers' first seasons in the Los Angeles Sports Arena.

The turnstiles in the Sports Arena were electronically
attached to a device above the court so that, as people
arrived, their entry was recorded. Those already sitting in
their seats, munching popcorn or watching the players
warm up, could look toward the ceiling and watch the
attendance figure grow from 100 to 1,000 to 8,130, or
9,873, or 10,198 or whatever it would reach.

The crowd-o-meter eventually went the way of short
trunks and the set shot. Perhaps it was the victim of
pregame laser light shows and high-tech video displays.
Perhaps arena organizers, in some cases, preferred using
the "official" attendance figure, which represents tickets

sold, not a turnstile count, which almost always made for a bigger total.

But the crowd-o-meter is a lasting image to those who watched it, some remembering it as clearly as they do the dazzling moves of Elgin Baylor and the clutch shots of Jerry West.

SEE ALSO • *Sports Arena.*

 **Curran, Jack** ➤ He was the third Laker trainer in Los Angeles, serving from the 1978-79 season through 1984-85

Curran had also worked in hockey, baseball and soccer and had been the Seattle SuperSonics' trainer for eight seasons before joining the Lakers. Curran could be gruff at times, but he was always willing to help others, whether it was a player who needed a favor or any member of the traveling party with lost luggage. And he knew his players.

When Michael Cooper injured his ankle on a Midwestern trip, Coach Pat Riley told his star sixth man before a game in Detroit to go home and rest the ankle. After all, Riley said, "You're not playing anyway."

Even though he was one of the league's premier defenders, Cooper became convinced it was a ploy to get rid of him.

"That is it," Cooper said at halftime of the Detroit game. "This could be the end. If I go home, I just might wind up off the team. They might use this opportunity to cut me.

"Well, the hell with them. Let them get rid of me. I'll come back and burn all of them."

After the game, Cooper was asked if he meant what he had said at halftime. "Nah," Cooper replied, "I'm just ... just ... what's that word, Jack?"

"You're paranoid," Curran said.

"Yeah," said Cooper with a smile, "I'm paranoid." While on the road, Curran often got an extra hotel room to use as a training room. Some players liked their wrists and ankles taped before a game even if they were not injured, and Curran preferred to do that, when possible, at the hotel in order to save time once he got to the arena.

On one trip to New York, Curran asked a clerk at the front desk for an extra room. As he walked away, Curran nodded at a sportswriter, making it obvious that the two knew each other. When the trainer left, the clerk asked the sportswriter if he indeed knew Curran and if Curran was indeed the Laker trainer.

The writer answered yes to both questions.

"OK," said the clerk, "because I was thinking of calling the police." "Why," asked the puzzled sportswriter.

"Because," said the clerk, "that man came over here and asked if he could have a room because he wanted to tape up people's ankles and wrists in there. I thought he had hostages."

SEE ALSO • *Cooper, Michael, Trainers.*

D

Dancing Barry ➤ With the Lakers, he was Dancing Barry. Now with the Charlotte Hornets, he has become Magic Barry.

He doesn't have quite as much hair now, but the same amount of rhythm.

Barry, whose real name is Barry Richards, was part of the fun of the Showtime '80s, his heyday. He was a performer who would emerge from the crowd during a timeout and join the Laker Girls in firing up the crowd.

But his parting was not sweet. When the Lakers advised him that his flashy feet were no longer needed, Richards said, "I don't think Laker management really ever appreciated me. They treated me like the Rams did Eric Dickerson."

Not quite. At least the Rams got something for Eric Dickerson.

Daniels, Lloyd (1967-) ➤ Daniels went from the playgrounds of New York, where he was a legend of sorts, to other playgrounds: from Mt. San Antonio College to the Continental Basketball Assn., from the U.S. Basketball League to the Global Basketball Assn., to a team in New Zealand.

By the time he signed with the Lakers in February 1995, Daniels had already played for and been waived by San Antonio and Philadelphia in the NBA.

A 6-foot-7, 205-pounder, Daniels was signed to back up George Lynch at small forward.

"If you play hard, you're going to get an opportunity," Daniels said. "That's all I ever wanted, an opportunity."

Daniels didn't get much of an opportunity with the Lakers. He appeared in 25 games, averaging 7.4 points and 2.2 rebounds.

Less than two months later, Daniels was gone, waived when Lynch and Tony Smith returned from injuries.

Dantley, Adrian Delano (1956-) ➤ Dantley's only full season with the Lakers was 1978-79, but it's nothing Dantley would want to draw attention to.

It was the only season of his first 12 in the league that Dantley averaged fewer than 20 points, the only year in that span he shot as low as 51% from the field. Before the start of the next season, with Magic Johnson having just joined a team that already had Kareem Abdul-Jabbar, the Lakers were gearing up for a run at an NBA title. They had talent at forward in

Dantley and Jamaal Wilkes. The problem was, they both were small forwards with similar styles. They could score, but neither was a force on the boards.

The Lakers thought Dantley was too one-dimensional, even though that dimension was an ability to score with a vast array of shots. So in August 1979, the Lakers traded Dantley to the Utah Jazz for Spencer Haywood, more in the mold of a power forward.

In the long run, the trade was one of the Lakers' worst. Haywood self-destructed, was suspended during the NBA Finals in 1980 and was subsequently released. Dantley averaged 28 points in the 1979-80 season for the Jazz and averaged more than 30 in each of the next four seasons.

Nonetheless, even without Dantley, and with Haywood gone for the final four games of the finals, the Lakers won an NBA title. And Wilkes was a productive forward for them into the mid-'1980s.

Davis, Bradley Ernest "Brad" (1955-) ➤ Davis had some impressive numbers at Maryland, where he became one of the best ballhandling guards in that school's history.

That earned Davis a first-round slot in the 1977 NBA draft. The Lakers had three first-round picks that season. They used their first on Kenny Carr and their second on Davis.

Unfortunately for Davis, the Lakers used the third of those first-round selections on another guard, Norm Nixon, whose speed, ballhandling ability and shooting earned him the starting job Davis had sought.

Davis was released by the Lakers at the beginning of his second season. That turned out to be a blessing for him. Davis would play 13 more seasons in the league, the last 12 with the Dallas Mavericks.

Davis never could have had such a career with the Lakers. If battling Nixon for a job had been tough, what would Davis' chances have been two years later when they drafted a guard named Magic Johnson?

Day, Doris ➤ The actress was considered the First Fan of the Lakers in the early 1960s when Bob Short owned the team.

He gave her free courtside seats, figuring the publicity

would help a team still trying to gain a foothold in its new city. Day was among the first of the show-business crowd that would eventually flock to the courtside seats. But, after Jack Kent Cooke bought the team from Short in 1965, he took back the free seats from Day. Why? For money.

Attendance was way up and Cooke knew he would have no trouble finding someone to buy those seats.

Dead Body ➤ It was in the 1960s when Elgin Baylor and Jerry West were superstars in the NBA and the irreplaceable core of the Lakers.

On a trip, a member of the Laker traveling party passed out in his hotel room from excessive drinking. When a hotel employee discovered the unconscious guest, he thought at first that he had discovered a dead body.

Coach Fred Schaus was informed by phone that someone in the Laker party had been found dead, and Schaus, without a pause, replied, "Yeah, well I sure as hell hope it isn't Baylor or West."

DiGregorio, Ernest "Ernie," "Ernie D" (1951-) ➤ Detractors used to say the best nickname for the 6-foot, 180-pounder was Ernie No-D because of his lack of height and limited defensive ability.

But DiGregorio sometimes compensated for his shortcomings by excelling in two categories–ballhandling and free-throw shooting.

After winning the Joe Lapchick Memorial Trophy as college player of the year his senior season at Providence College, DiGregorio joined the Buffalo Braves and won another honor, NBA rookie of the year.

He led the league in assists (8.2) and free-throw percentage (90.2) along with a 15.2-point scoring average. That 90.2% mark still stands as the highest free-throw percentage by a first-year player.

DiGregorio had 25 assists in one game, also still a league record for a rookie. His brief Laker career, however, was unspectacular. DiGregorio played in only 25 games for Los Angeles in 1977-78, averaging 3.9 points, 2.8 assists and shot 80% from the free-throw line.

Divac, Vlade (1968-) ➤ Divac was a project when he joined the NBA, and his mentor and source of inspiration in his early years was not Pat Riley, his first Laker coach, or those who followed–Mike Dunleavy, Randy Pfund and Del Harris. It was a teammate, Magic Johnson.

Johnson made Divac, born in Yugoslavia, his personal project. A player who prided himself on being smart on the court, on being aware of every move by the opposition and coming up with the right adjustment to those moves, Johnson demanded the same of Divac.

When Divac failed to box out an opponent or hustle on defense, he didn't have to wait for his coach to tell him. By the time Divac would turn around, Johnson would already be in his face.

But Divac took the verbal abuse well, learned from it and grew as a player from year to year.

His scoring average went up each season in L.A. but his last, from 8.5 points in 1989-90 to 16.0 in 1994-95.

In that same span, Divac's rebounding average grew from 6.2 to 10.4.

In 1993-94, he became the first Laker to lead the team in points and rebounds since Kareem Abdul-Jabbar in 1984-85.

Divac's Laker years ended abruptly. And bitterly, at first.

He was traded in the summer of 1996 to the Charlotte Hornets for Kobe Bryant. A significant benefit for the Lakers in cutting Divac loose was to remove his $4-million salary from the payroll to clear enough room under the salary cap for a serious run at center Shaquille O'Neal, who was about to become a free agent.

Hurt that the Lakers would ship him out, angry because his wife, Ana, was trying to start an acting career in Los Angeles and despondent because he had come to love the city, Divac threatened to retire rather than go to Charlotte.

That threat lasted only a few days, however, and he was soon the Hornets' starting center.

Dodgers ➤ Long before the idea of the Forum had made it onto a blueprint, Walter O'Malley, the man who brought the Dodgers to L.A. from Brooklyn, was trying to put the finishing touches on a deal that would have had the

Vlade Divac rejects a Jalen Rose shot attempt in the paint during a 1995 game against the Denver Nuggets.

Lakers playing alongside the Dodgers.

A blockbuster deal involving the two teams in 1965 would have included an arena for basketball adjacent to Dodger Stadium in Chavez Ravine.

Bob Short, then the struggling Laker owner, nearly consummated an agreement that would have given him and his partner, Frank Ryan, 20% of the Dodgers and Lakers and the facilities in which they would play, with O'Malley owning the rest. At the last minute, the deal was stalled because of some questions over a television contract.

While O'Malley tried to clear up the problem, Jack Kent Cooke moved in and tried to buy the Lakers.

Short didn't want to sell, so he set the outrageous price of $5 million. (Remember, the Boston Celtics had recently sold for only $3 million.)

Cooke agreed.

What was O'Malley's reaction?

"Hell, you gotta sell," he told Short. "That's a tremendous amount of money for 10 pairs of tennis shoes, as long as you get it in cash."

But Short wasn't quite satisfied. He had already sold $350,000 worth of season tickets for the upcoming season. He wanted at least half of that back. So he asked for an additional $175,000.

"I wanted the team so damn badly," Cooke later said, "had he asked for $575,000 extra, I would have paid him."

Short got his money, Cooke got the Lakers and Walter O'Malley, for one of the few times in his fortune-filled career, got left out.

Drew, Larry Donnell (1958-) ➤ After his retirement as a player in 1991, Drew worked toward becoming a head coach. He had a respectable NBA career, having averaged 11.4 points and 5.2 assists with five clubs, including the Lakers, where he was a backup guard in the 1989-90 and 90-91 seasons.

While with the Kansas City Kings, Drew once scored 33 points in a game and handed out 17 assists on another occasion.

But that kind of playing career doesn't automatically open head coaching doors. Drew went to work as a speaker, fund raiser and administrator for the Magic Johnson Foundation after retiring, then joined the Lakers as an assistant coach in 1992 with duties that included less-than-glamorous advance scouting, meaning he had to spend long, lonely weeks on the road, analyzing future opponents.

But Drew stuck with it and, after two years, he made it to the bench, where he has been ever since as an assistant coach preparing himself for the No. 1 job he he hopes will be his in college or the pros.

Dunleavy, Michael Joseph "Mike" (1954-) ➤ In 1990, at the age of 36, Dunleavy got the break most coaches never get. He was handed the reins of a dynasty, the Lakers. All he had to do as the new head coach was to follow Pat Riley and keep putting up those championship banners.

But, there were a few hitches.

Kreem Abdul-Jabbar, the game's all-time leading scorer, wasn't there any longer.

And before long, Magic Johnson would be gone, too. Just one season after Dunleavy had taken the Lakers into the NBA Finals as a rookie coach, Johnson announced that he was retiring because he had tested HIV-positive.

The dream was slowly turning into a nightmare.

But Dunleavy had encountered difficult problems before. He was the Philadelphia 76ers' sixth-round draft choice from South Carolina. At 6 feet 2½ and 180 pounds, he had to be scrappy and determined to compete against much larger players.It worked; he survived in the league for 11 seasons with four teams.

Dunleavy even spent part of one season as the player/coach of the Carolina Lightning in the All-America Basketball Alliance.

After playing for the San Antonio Spurs in the 1982-83 season, Dunleavy, at 29, put down his basketball, picked up a briefcase and went to work for Merrill Lynch on Wall Street.

But he still had plenty of basketball left in him. At least, the Milwaukee Bucks thought so. When injuries shredded their roster, they called Dunleavy at the end of the 1983-84 season. In 17 regular-season games, Dunleavy averaged 11.2 points, the best of his career. In 15 playoff games, he averaged 11.3 points, a postseason career high. The Bucks signed him for the next season, but Dunleavy's playing career appeared to come to a bizarre end when, after he had appeared in 19 games in 1984-85, he injured his back as an airplane in which he was a passenger came to an unexpected stop on a runway.

Milwaukee brought Dunleavy back as an assistant coach for the 1986-87 season. He held that position for four years and even made it back onto the court for seven games spread over two seasons when the Bucks again came up short-handed in the backcourt.

Dunleavy would become all too familiar with personnel problems of his own as the Laker coach.

Short-handed without Johnson and unable to adjust,

Mike Dunleavy used to yell out instructions to the Lakers, but here in 1998 he hollers out a play to his Portland Trailblazers.

the Lakers went 43-39 in 1991-92, leaving them 15 wins short of the total they had reached in Dunleavy's first season. They were then knocked out of the playoffs in the opening round, losing three of four to the Portland Trail Blazers.

The Lakers weren't about to give up on Dunleavy. But then, neither was Milwaukee.

Buck owner Herb Kohl, regretful that he had let Dunleavy get away in the first place, began negotiating with him and, in 48 hours, concluded an 8-year, $8-million deal to bring Dunleavy back to Milwaukee as coach.

"It came totally out of the blue," Dunleavy said. "It was a fastball that just happened."

Edwards, James Franklin (1955-) ➤
Edwards was a Laker at the beginning
and at the end of his career.

In between, he had quite
an impact.

The Lakers drafted the 7-foot,
255-pound center from the University
of Washington on the third round with the 64th pick
in 1977.

It didn't take Edwards long to move into the spotlight.
When starting center Kareem Abdul-Jabbar broke his
hand in a fight with Kent Benson in the 1977-78 season
opener, Edwards became the starter. He played 25 games
for the Lakers, averaging 14.8 points and 7.2 rebounds.

But when Abdul-Jabbar returned two months after
Edwards' debut, Edwards was traded with Earl Tatum to
the Indiana Pacers for Adrian Dantley and Dave Robisch.
After playing for five other clubs in all, including the
Detroit Pistons, with whom he earned two NBA
championship rings, and the Los Angeles Clippers,
Edwards returned to the Lakers as a free agent at the
age of 36.

This time, he lasted two seasons (1992-93 and 1993-94)
as a reserve before moving on to Portland, and finally,
Chicago, where he became a member of a championship
team for the third time in the 1995-96 season.

Edwards played 19 seasons in the league, which puts
him in a tie for third on the all-time list with Moses
Malone behind Robert Parish (21), and Abdul-Jabbar (20).

**Egan, John Francis "Johnny"
(1939-)** ➤ Although he was listed at
6-feet, Egan was actually a bit shorter.
As a matter of fact, he was known for a
time as the shortest man in the NBA.

But one area in which Egan didn't
come up short upon joining the Lakers
for the 1968-69 season was games played.

Already a seven-year veteran when the Lakers
purchased him from the Milwaukee Bucks, Egan was the
only Laker to play in all 82 regular-season and 18 playoff
games in his first year with the club.

Egan got better as that season progressed. He averaged
8.5 points and shot 85% from the free-throw line in the
regular season. He averaged 13.9 points in the postseason.
And in the NBA Finals that season against the Boston
Celtics, Egan's scoring average was up to 15.1.

Egan played one more season for the Lakers and then
caught the eye of the Cleveland Cavaliers. They obviously
weren't scared off by his height either, selecting him in the
1970 expansion draft.

E.J. the DeeJay ➤ Another of the many nicknames of
Earvin Johnson.

This one started in 1977 while Johnson was a student
at Michigan State. An ardent music fan, Johnson got a job
at Bonnie & Clydes, a student disco just off campus, to
play music, control the lights and inspire students to party
away the night. He called himself E.J. the DeeJay.

Even after he joined the Lakers, on team bus rides,
Johnson would plant himself in the back of the bus, turn
on his portable stereo and entertain, introducing the
music by saying somthing like, "This is E.J. the DeeJay
from the back of the Laker bus, as we leave beautiful,

downtown Cleveland."

Johnson could also be found in nightclubs at many NBA stops, microphone in hand, reliving those nights at Bonnie & Clydes.

Ellis, LeRoy (1940-) ➤ The timing of the 6-foot-11, 210-pounder on rebounds was excellent, but the same could not be said for his timing in joining the Lakers. On either tour of duty.

He first came on board in 1962 as a first-round draft choice, the sixth pick overall, from St. John's.

But Ellis found himself on a team with two superstars, Elgin Baylor and Jerry West, Baylor being not only one of the greatest scorers in league history, but also the greatest rebounder in Laker history.

Ellis also had the misfortune to play when the Lakers perennially reached the finals only to go up against the greatest defensive force the league has ever known, Boston Celtic center Bill Russell.

But one thing Ellis had going for him in his matchups against the towering centers was great speed for a big man. In a Laker press guide from the early 1960s, it was said that Wilt Chamberlain, then a member of the San Francisco Warriors, "had yet to see [Ellis'] face, except during timeouts."

Ellis was traded in 1966, but returned after a five-year absence only to find the Laker middle was now patrolled by Chamberlain and Happy Hairston.

His two best seasons were with other teams than the Lakers. In 1966-67, Ellis averaged 14.9 points and 12.0 rebounds for the Baltimore Bullets. In 1970-71, he averaged 15.9 points and 12.3 rebounds for the Portland Trail Blazers.

He might have done the same for the Lakers if only fate had placed him on the roster at a different time.

Erickson, Keith Raymond (1944-) ➤ Those following the Lakers in the 1980s know Erickson as the voice who backed up Chick Hearn in the Laker broadcast booth.

But Erickson, who played forward for the Lakers for five seasons, was more than a voice and more than a basketball player. He was one of the most skilled athletes to put on a Laker uniform.

The 6-foot-5, 195-pounder played at UCLA and was a member of the first two of Coach John Wooden's 10 championship teams.

Erickson also played volleyball well enough to make the 1964 U.S. Olympic team. It didn't seem to matter what the sport was. Give him a tennis racket and he could compete with the better players. Put a Ping-Pong paddle in his hands and stand back. But the Laker career of the mild-mannered, soft-spoken Erickson, a deeply religious father of five, came to end in a bitter public contract dispute with owner Jack Kent Cooke.

An eight-year veteran at the end of the 1972-73 season, Erickson wanted a raise for the first time in three years.

Cooke's response?

"Go take a jump."

Cooke didn't leave it up to Erickson, either. He supplied the push, sending his forward out the door to the Phoenix Suns in a trade for Connie Hawkins.

Fairchild, John Russell (1943-) ➤ No one can question the Lakers wisdom in making their first choice in the 1965 draft. They took Gail Goodrich and he went on to have a Hall of Fame career.

At the time, the Lakers' second-round pick, Fairchild, seemed just as logical. A 6-foot-7½, 205-pounder from Encinitas, Fairchild had gone from Palomar Junior College to a record-shattering career at Brigham Young. He broke six school records in his two years there.

In Fairchild's senior year, BYU was 21-7, losing to Goodrich's UCLA Bruins in the NCAA tournament.

The next time their paths crossed, the two players were headed in opposite directions.

Goodrich played nine seasons for the Lakers, separated by a stint with the Phoenix Suns; Fairchild got into a total of 30 games for the Lakers in the 1965-66 season, averaging 2.0 points and 1.5 rebounds. That was the end of his NBA career. He joined the Anaheim Amigos in 1967 in the American Basketball Assn. and played for four teams over three seasons in the ABA.

Felix, Raymond Darlington "Ray," "Baby Ray" (1930-1991) ➤ This original Laker was 6 feet 11 in the days when that height stood out in the NBA. Felix began his career with the Baltimore Bullets in 1953 and lasted nine years in the league, playing his final two seasons with the Lakers.

His numbers weren't eye-catching. He averaged only 6.6 and 5.4 points in his two seasons with the Lakers. His rebounding averages were only 6.9 and 5.9.

Felix played in an era when there were only eight teams and merely surviving was a challenge for a center, because two of those teams had centers named Wilt Chamberlain and Bill Russell.

Felix might be remembered more for the things he said than the things he did on the court.

In one game against Russell, listed as 6-9½, Felix put up four shots that were blocked by the Boston center.

A fifth time, Felix went up with the ball, tried a fake and then shot. The ball soared over Russell. Also over the basket, over the backboard and into the crowd. That drew a grin from Felix, who told Russell, "You didn't get that one, baby."

On another occasion, Felix was angered when a sportswriter referred to him as "gangling."

After ordering the writer to get out of the locker room, Felix asked a teammate, "What does gangling mean?"

But Felix's most memorable line occurred in the hush of the Laker locker room after they had lost Game 7 of the 1962 NBA finals to the Boston Celtics in overtime.

While his teammates sat agonizing over the disappointing end to their season, Felix yelled out, "Don't worry. We'll get 'em tomorrow."

Finkel, Henry J. "Hank" (1942-) ➤ The Lakers took a gamble on Finkel, who played college ball at St. Peters and Dayton, making him their second-round draft choice in 1966.

The attraction? Finkel's height.

He was a 7-footer at a time when they were far less common than today.

But the gamble failed to pay off. Finkel averaged 1.5 points and 2.4 rebounds over 27 games.

Still, somebody else was willing to take the gamble. When the Lakers left Finkel unprotected in the 1967 expansion draft, the new San Diego Rockets took him.

And it looked like a pretty good move. For a year.

Finkel averaged 11.6 points and 7.1 rebounds in his first season with San Diego. But he struggled the next year and wound up in Boston for the 1969-70 season. Again, Finkel started off impressively, averaging 9.7 points and 7.7 rebounds in his first season with the Celtics.

That again turned out to be the high point. He played five more years in Boston, but his statistics declined nearly every season.

Fire ➤ It was the early morning hours before dawn in Philadelphia on a late spring day in 1983.

For many Lakers, it had been a restless night. Their hopes of winning their second consecutive NBA title seemed to have died a few hours earlier with a loss to the Philadelphia 76ers in Game 2 of the NBA finals, putting the Lakers into an 0-2 hole in the best-of-seven series.

But all that was temporarily forgotten when a fire alarm went off in their Philadelphia hotel, the Bellevue Stratford, at 5:33 a.m.

Several halls quickly became filled with smoke after drapes in a stairwell between the third and fourth floors of the 19-story, 79-year-old building caught fire.

And several players showed they could be heroes off the court as well as on it.

Michael Cooper went door to door to alert guests that this was not a false alarm. Kurt Rambis helped team physician Robert Kerlan, who suffered from debilitating arthritis, down the stairs.

But perhaps the strangest sight was that of Magic Johnson leading a group of guests down a hallway. Johnson was then 23. Most of the other guests were far older. Some may have had more experience in truly harrowing situations.

On this night, however, they all believed in Magic.

He made his way along the eighth floor, found a stairway and went down two flights, his followers in line behind him.

They stuck close together even after encountering heavy smoke on the sixth floor. Johnson led the group onto the fire escape outside. They made it to the third floor, where the fire escape's steps were replaced by a metal ladder that could be lowered to the street–but only if somebody gave it the necessary weight by standing on it. Johnson hesitated.

"Go ahead, you can do it," a voice behind him said.

Johnson glanced back. It was Kareem Abdul-Jabbar.

Johnson stepped tentatively onto the ladder and down he went, smoothly, to the street, all those behind him following quickly.

By then, fire trucks were arriving. When fire fighters spotted Johnson, a couple of them rushed over to get his autograph. First things first.

But they soon had put out the fire, which had not spread.

The danger had passed. All the Lakers had to worry about was Philadelphia. Worrying didn't help. The 76ers swept the Lakers in four.

Fisher, Derek Lamar (1974-) ➤ When the Lakers selected the 6-foot-1, 200-pounder from Arkansas Little Rock with a first-round pick in the 1996 draft, they saw him as a backup point guard.

But they knew that the word backup might disappear at any time. Because Fisher was playing behind the always unpredictable Nick Van Exel, whose explosive temperament and fragile knees left his starting role in a perpetual state of uncertainty.

Sure enough, Van Exel hurt his right knee midway through the 1997-98 season. And when he returned from arthroscopic surgery, Van Exel told Coach Del Harris that he would prefer to remain out of the starting lineup to try providing a spark off the bench.

So that left the ball in Fisher's hands for the rest of the season.

He had shown what he could do at lower levels of competition. He had led Parkview High in Little Rock to a 35-1 record and the No. 4 ranking in the country in his senior season. He had concluded his career at Arkansas Little Rock with the second-highest career totals in school history in points, assists and steals.

But the NBA is a long way from the courts of Arkansas. The Lakers finished the year 29-7 in the games Fisher started, but, while keeping the mistakes and turnovers down, Fisher showed a troubling inability to effectively run the offense at crucial times.

Considering his limited background and the role into which he was thrust, that's understandable. But whether that's acceptable over the long haul is another matter.

Derek Fisher drives past the Suns' Sam Cassell in the Lakers' home opener of the 1996-97 season.

Florence, Mal ➤ A sportswriter for the Los Angeles Times for nearly half a century, Florence was assigned to travel with the Lakers during the record 33-game winning streak in the 1971-72 season.

In those days, the Lakers were not the major attraction in Los Angeles that they have become, so the coverage of road games by the paper was determined by budgetary constraints and the fortunes of the club.

On Jan. 10, 1972, the morning after the Lakers' streak had been broken in Milwaukee by the Bucks, led by Kareem Abdul-Jabbar, Florence received a phone call in his hotel room. It was Times sports editor Bill Shirley telling Florence to come home.

As Florence, bags packed, passed Laker Coach Bill Sharman in the lobby, Sharman asked, "Mal, where are you going?"

Florence, a look of mock seriousness on his face, replied:

"We don't cover losers."

Ford, Donald J., "Don" (1952-) ➤ Although he was UC Santa Barbara's leading scorer and rebounder and most accurate shooter as a junior, that's still a long way from the NBA. So when Ford passed up his senior season with the Gauchos to sign with the Lakers, after they had made him a sixth-round draft choice in 1975, many doubted whether Ford would last.

He lasted long enough to make believers out of the doubters, playing $4\frac{1}{2}$ seasons with the Lakers, averaging 7.6 points and 3.8 rebounds.

Ford was sent to Cleveland midway through the 1979-80 season for guard Butch Lee in a trade that involved a swap of the teams' first-round draft choices.

That deal indirectly might have been Ford's biggest contribution to the Lakers. Using what was the Cavaliers' first-round pick in 1982, the first overall, the Lakers selected James Worthy.

Forum ➤ It has been known as the Fabulous Forum. It has been known as the Great Western Forum.

But, most important, it has been known as the site of some of the most memorable sporting and entertainment events held in Southern California since it opened at the end of 1967.

The Forum was the brainchild of Jack Kent Cooke. But when he first proposed it, some wondered whether he had simply lost his mind.

After all, his Lakers were comfortably settled in the Sports Arena, then a relatively new structure next to the Coliseum, within view of the heavily traveled Harbor Freeway and only a few miles from downtown Los Angeles.

But Cooke, determined to land an NHL franchise and faced with Coliseum Commission officials who refused to renegotiate his contract, threatened to build his own arena.

That drew a laugh from the Coliseum Commission.

After failing to obtain a site in the San Fernando Valley, Cooke announced he would build his arena in Inglewood, a long drive away for most Angelenos.

Cooke's idea was to build an arena next to Hollywood Park racetrack that would resemble the Colosseum in ancient Rome.

He described his proposed building as "something

about 2,000 years ago and about 6,000 miles to the east of here."

Cooke's building would be oval shaped, framed by 80 white concrete columns. The Roman theme extended all the way to the original ushers, who dressed in togas. Cooke's dream didn't come cheaply. It cost $12.5 million to put up the Forum, a building that would hold 17,505 for basketball. It was finished 5 years after the completion of Dodger Stadium, which, with a capacity of just over 56,000, had cost $18 million.

Groundbreaking for the Forum was held July 1, 1966. On Dec. 30, 1967, the L.A. Kings and the Philadelphia Flyers played to a 2-2 tie in the first event held at the Forum.

There was some hockey excitement in the building. There was the Miracle on Manchester comeback playoff game against the Edmonton Oilers in 1982, the successful playoff run that ended in a berth in the Stanley Cup finals in 1993, and there was Wayne Gretzky, who played for the Kings for eight seasons.

But mostly, there was frustration for a team whose seasons ended in defeat. Even in 1993, the Kings lost four in a row to the Montreal Canadiens in the finals, including both games played at the Forum, after winning the first game in Montreal. The Lakers were another matter. Championship banners from their six NBA titles decorate the Forum walls.

The Forum was also the site of the men's and women's basketball competition in the 1984 Olympic Games, the floor on which the U.S. won gold medals in both competitions.

It was the site of a heavyweight fight in which Muhammad Ali beat Ken Norton on Sept. 10, 1973, producing a live gate of $475,640, largest ever on the West Coast.

Over the years, the Forum has also attracted the biggest names in the music business–from Elvis Presley to Duke Ellington, Tony Bennett to Neil Diamond, Elton John to Tom Petty.

Cooke more than got his money back on an investment that seemed to some in 1966 like folly. In 1979, Jerry Buss paid Cooke $67.5 million for the Forum, the Lakers and the Kings in a highly complicated deal that also involved the swapping of several large pieces of property.

For the 1999-2000 season, the Lakers and Kings were set to return to Los Angeles to play in the new Staples Center.

But for more than three decades, the premier arena in the area was the Forum, with the Sports Arena, home of the Clippers and USC basketball, in its shadow.

SEE ALSO • *Buss, Jerry; Cooke, Jack Kent; Sports Arena.*

Four-point play ➤ The most productive play in basketball, and among the rarest, it occurs when a player makes a three-point shot, is fouled while shooting and then makes the free throw. Cedric Ceballos, was the first Laker to make a four-point play; he did it on April 20, 1995 against the Portland Trail Blazers. Others who have made one are: Anthony Peeler against the Clippers on Nov. 19, 1995; Nick Van Exel against Minnesota on Dec. 21, 1996; Derek Fisher against Boston on Dec. 27, 1996; and Eddie Jones, the first time against San Antonio on Nov. 13, 1997 and again against Minnesota six days later.

The Lakers have given up 12 four-point plays. The first was by John Douglas of the then-San Diego Clippers on Dec. 27, 1981. The most recent was by Detlef Schrempf of the Seattle Supersonics on April 29, 1995 in a playoff game, the third time the Lakers have given up a four-pointer in postseason play.

Fox, Ulrich Alexander "Rick" (1969-) ➤ After becoming the only Laker to start all 82 regular-season games in 1997-98, playing despite a sore foot and back spasms in the second half of the season, showing that he could muscle underneath and make shots from outside, after taking the reins of leadership on the court, helping his team fight its way to the conference finals only to be swept by the Utah Jazz, Fox lost it on the day after his team's elimination.

Returning to the Forum to clean out his locker stall, he couldn't hold back the tears. Some of the reaction came from Fox's disappointment at falling short of the top, some at his uncertainty over his future with the Lakers.

"I'm just sad, that's all," he told a reporter. "I just hope somewhere, some day, to win a championship."

Fox did all he could, happily serving as a role player on a team loaded with individual stars.

Fox, who was born in Canada and grew up in the Bahamas, was a star himself at the University of North Carolina.

He was the eighth player under Coach Dean Smith to be given a spot in the starting lineup in his first game as a Tar Heel, and Fox went on to play in every game of his four-year career, appearing in 140 games to tie a school record.

A first-round draft choice by the Boston Celtics in 1991 (24th overall), Fox was the first Celtic rookie to start on opening night since Larry Bird in 1979.

After six seasons in Boston, Fox was signed as a free agent by the Lakers in August 1997. Putting on the purple and gold to play for a team with a chance to win a championship meant so much to Fox that he turned down a four-year deal from the Cleveland Cavaliers worth about $20 million, and a three-year offer from the Celtics worth $5.4 million to sign with the Lakers for one year at $1 million, the most they could pay because of the salary cap.

"When you walk away from the game," Fox said, "you still have to look back and say, 'Yeah, I maximized my earning potential at the same time I got the most out of my career on the court.' "

The Lakers wanted Fox for his versatility and they got it. He finished second on the team in assists and fourth in points, rebounds and steals.

Freeman, Donald E. "Donnie" (1944-) ➤ Freeman, like the Lakers, began playing basketball in Minnesota. But Freeman began with the Minnesota Muskies of the American Basketball Assn., a team that became the Miami Floridians.

Freeman went with the Muskies to Florida for two seasons, then moved on to three other ABA teams before finally coming to the NBA and the Lakers for the final season of his career, 1975-76.

Freeman had some big years in the ABA, averaging more than 20 points in four consecutive seasons, his best being 1969-70 when he averaged 27.4 for Miami. But, as good as he was, Freeman never seemed to realize his potential.

"He had quick moves and he was a good shooter," said Bill Sharman, who coached Freeman with the Utah Stars of the ABA and with the Lakers. "But he didn't bear down enough. He wasn't dedicated, serious. It seemed like the game was not that important to him."

G

Garrett, Calvin Eugene (1956-) ➤

Garrett was ready to give up his NBA career before it had even begun.

A third-round draft choice of the Chicago Bulls after being a high-scoring star at Oral Roberts, Garrett's draft rights were traded to the Houston Rockets in June 1980.

But because he was limping on a sprained ankle, Garrett figured he wouldn't make the club. So he decided to take a shot at European basketball without taking a shot in the NBA.

Rocket officials, however, wouldn't accept that. They convinced Garrett he had a genuine chance to make the team.

And it almost paid huge dividends. In Game 6 of the NBA Finals in Garrett's rookie year, 1980-81, the 6-foot-7, 195-pounder nearly helped his club pull off an incredible comeback against the Boston Celtics.

With Houston trailing by 17 points in the fourth quarter, Garrett scored eight points and had a crucial steal to help bring his club to within three. But the rally fizzled and Boston won the title, four games to two.

After three years with Houston, Garrett had another shot at a championship in 1984 with the Lakers. A part-time player who averaged 4.6 points that season, he again reached the NBA Finals against the Celtics. But again Boston won, this time in seven games.

Garrett, Eldo "Dick" (1947-) ➤

A second-round Laker draft choice from Southern Illinois, Garrett had not only made the Laker roster for the 1969-70 season, but had made an impact. He had averaged 11.6 points and 2.5 assists in the regular season and had become a starter by the playoffs.

A long career in purple and gold seemed ahead.

But three days after the Lakers were beaten by the New York Knicks for the NBA title, they left Garrett exposed in the expansion draft. He was taken by the Buffalo Braves.

"It was a blow to my pride," Garrett said at the time. "But it may turn out to be a blessing in disguise. Now I don't have to play in anybody's shadow. Maybe my talents will be more appreciated."

They were. The next season, his numbers were up to 12.9 points and 3.5 assists from 11.6 and 3.2 with the Lakers.

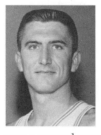

Gibson, Melvin L. "Mel" "The Cordova Comet" (1940-) ➤

This Mel Gibson had a much shorter run in Los Angeles than did the movie star of the same name.

Gibson, who came from Cordova, N.C., and played at Western Carolina, was a second-round draft choice of the Lakers in 1963. He didn't exactly live up to the billing he received from Lou Mohs, then the Lakers' chief scout, who said of Gibson, "This kid has all the characteristics to be a sort of junior-grade Jerry West."

Not quite.

Gibson had received his rave reviews after shooting 57% from the field and 80% from the free-throw line in his senior year of college, and following that with an impressive performance for the U.S. in the 1963 Pan-Am Games.

With the Lakers, he appeared in only nine games, the sum total of his NBA career, scoring 13 points and getting six assists.

Like a true Comet, the Cordova variety flamed out quickly.

SEE ALSO • *Mohs, Lou.*

Goodrich, Gail Jr. (1943-) ►

Goodrich was only 6 feet 1 and 170 pounds but overcame his size with long arms, big hands, constant move-ment, brilliant court sense and a jump shot that the left-hander could launch from all around the court. As a result, he played 14 years in the NBA, nine with the Lakers in two segments. He scored 19,181 points, 30th on the all-time list. He averaged 18.6 points in the regular season and 18.1 in the postseason. And in 1996, he was inducted into the Basketball Hall of Fame.

He also played two seasons with the Phoenix Suns and his last three with the New Orleans Jazz, but Goodrich has a special place in Laker lore.

His uniform was retired and hung in the Forum and his name appears in many categories in the team's record book. Goodrich is sixth in club history in points (13,044), seventh in assists (2,863) and free throws made (2,830), and ninth in games played (687). He led the Lakers in scoring four seasons in a row. Only two others in the Los Angeles era–Kareem Abdul-Jabbar and Jerry West–have matched that feat.

Nobody in club history has matched Goodrich's 40 consecutive free throws. And he did that twice.

Goodrich's size was a factor in his career from the start. At Poly High School in the San Fernando Valley, he thought he could make the basketball team as a sophomore.

He was greeted with less than great enthusiasm. He stood all of 5 feet 2 and weighed 99 pounds.

"Looking back, I think that was the turning point of my life," Goodrich said. "The encouragement I got from my high school coach [Nelson Burton] meant everything.

That, and the early instruction I got from my own dad [Gail Goodrich Sr., an All-Southern Division guard at USC].

"My high school coach let me play on the JV team as a 10th grader. I didn't have enough size to play on the B team. I wasn't even a D. But here I was at 99 pounds playing with varsity-size guys."

By the time Goodrich left Poly, he was a towering figure, though still not literally. Goodrich was named player of the year for leading the school to a city championship.

Next he went to UCLA, where he was an All-American and helped the team win NCAA championships in 1964 and 1965.

And then he completed the Los Angeles hat trick by joining the Lakers, who used the third pick in the 1965 draft to select him.

Goodrich found more doubters when he stepped into the land of the NBA's giants. There were questions about whether he could effectively handle the ball or play adequate defense.

But there was never any question about his ability to score.

After averaging 13.8 points and shooting 48.6% from the field in the 1967-68 season, his third with the Lakers,

Gail Goodrich as starting guard for UCLA in 1963.

In 1973 Goodrich was in his second stint with the Lakers.

Goodrich was left unprotected in the 1968 expansion draft.

The Suns grabbed him.

"I had asked to be put on the expansion list," said Goodrich, unhappy over his playing time on a Laker team rich with guards.

No longer forced to share the ball with Jerry West, Goodrich averaged 23.8 points in his first season with Phoenix and 20.0 his second.

Then in 1970, the Lakers brought him back to L.A., trading center Mel Counts for Goodrich, whose greatest years in purple and gold were ahead of him. It was a different team now. Wilt Chamberlain had been brought in to play center. And Goodrich turned out to be the missing link to the championship that had remained just out of the grasp of the Lakers since their arrival in L.A.

In the 1971-72 season, even with Chamberlain and West on the team, Coach Bill Sharman wanted Goodrich shooting the ball.

"When you come down on the break," Sharman told Goodrich, "if you have an open shot, take it. If the other guys complain, we'll just tell them to get down faster." Nobody complained as Goodrich averaged a career-high 25.9 points and made 48.7% of his shots.

With Goodrich standing tall next to Chamberlain and West, the Lakers won 33 consecutive games in the regular season, still an all-time record for any professional team, and then their first NBA title in Los Angeles.

Even after he left the team in 1976, Goodrich made one final, momentous contribution to the Lakers, although this one was not by design.

A free agent at the age of 33, Goodrich signed with New Orleans. Under the rules at that time, the Jazz had to compensate the Lakers. It gave up three draft choices, including a first-round pick in 1979.

With that pick, the Lakers selected another guard, one named Magic Johnson. And Johnson and Goodrich would be linked forever, because, when their careers were over, their jerseys would hang together on a Forum wall.

Grant, Travis "Machine Gun" (1950-) ➤ Grant was a high-flying star at Kentucky State. He became college basketball's all-time leading scorer with 4,045 points in three years at the school. Grant shot 64% from the field and led Kentucky State to a National Assn. of Intercollegiate Athletics championship in each of the years he was there.

Then he landed in the NBA.

With a thud.

A first-round draft choice of the Lakers in 1972, Grant played sporadically over two seasons with the team, averaging 3.6 points while shooting 43.3% from the field.

"They find out what you can't do," he said of life in the NBA. "When I came out of college, I liked to shoot from 20 feet away all the time. So they put a guy up on me out there."

Grant played in only 36 games with the Lakers.

"I should have been playing," he said. "In preseason training, I was as good as any forward. But I don't think the Lakers wanted me to score. They had Gail Goodrich and Jerry West to do the scoring.

"Also, there are a lot of politics involved. Certain guys have to play. If they make a trade and spend a lot of money, that guy has to be in there."

But others saw it differently. Grant was criticized for his failure to play tough defense and rebound effectively.

He finished his career in the American Basketball Assn.

Green, A.C. Jr. (1963-) ➤ It was fitting that Cal Ripken Jr. was present for Green's greatest moment as a pro, because no one illustrates better what Green is all about.

Green played on some of the great Laker teams of the19'80s, though he was sometimes overlooked because he couldn't shoot like Kareem Abdul-Jabbar, pass like Magic Johnson or run like James Worthy.

All he could do was play. And play.

Solid and dependable, he received a memorable tribute for those attributes Nov. 20, 1997 in Dallas when Green played in his 907th consecutive game, breaking the NBA record set by Randy Smith.

Smith was there. So was Ripken, who had received the accolades of the nation when he broke Lou Gehrig's consecutive-game streak in major league baseball in 1995.

Green had played in every game since Nov. 19, 1986 to break Smith's record, which had stood for 14 years.

It was the Lakers who first took advantage of Green's talent and durability. They drafted him on the first round from Oregon State in 1985.

Many rookies would be intimidated going to a team loaded with stars, a team that had finally defeated their archrivals, the Boston Celtics, to win the 1985 NBA title.

Not Green.

"I don't think it will be that hard," he said when asked if he thought he could make the squad. "It just depends how hard I want to work."

Green brought a solid work ethic and fundamentals he had learned under Coach Ralph Miller at Oregon State.

Laker Coach Pat Riley took one look at Green and said, "That's it. He's gonna play."

And, of course, he did. He played every game as a rookie before missing three his second year, then played six consecutive seasons with the Lakers without missing a game. Green averaged double figure in scoring in five of those six seasons and six of his eight with the Lakers. Green averaged 11.3 points and 8.5 rebounds as a Laker and was on two NBA championship teams.

In 1993, Green, a free agent, signed a five-year, $15-million contract with the Phoenix Suns.

The uniform might have changed, but one thing

A solid and dependable player, Green, No. 45, broke the NBA's consecutive-games-played record in 1997. But as a Laker, Green was often overshadowed by the Showtime superstars, such as Magic Johnson, right.

didn't. Through a bout with dehydration, through dental problems, through the normal wear and tear of the NBA, Green continued to play, in every city in every game as he went from the Lakers to the Suns to the Mavericks.

"I know," Ripken said, "that, in the 11 years during which this streak has existed, there had to be many nights where the body said, 'No,' but somewhere down deep inside, he had to go down there and dig it out and say, 'I'm going to do it. I'm going to go out and play.' That's spirit. That's heart."

Grims, Boris ➤ Anyone who sees Laker center Shaquille O'Neal as nothing more than a self-centered superstar should talk to Grims before passing judgment.

In 1995, Grims, then a 14-year-old living in Mississippi, went through a growth spurt in which his feet grew five sizes in one month. O'Neal, then a member of the Orlando Magic, heard about the teenager's difficulties and shipped him a pair of packages filled with O'Neal's size-20 footwear, from dress shoes to gym shoes to casual shoes.

The 7-foot-1 O'Neal also a included a uniform and left a message on Grims' answering machine that said, "This is your lucky day. Shaq's been cleaning out his closet and wants to send some stuff to the young man."

SEE ALSO • *O'Neal, Shaquille.*

Grote, Jerry C. (1940-) ➤
Grote failed in his first attempt to reach the NBA, and it's not hard to figure out why.

The 6-foot-4 guard was drafted by the St. Louis Hawks from Loyola Marymount. The only problem was that Grote weighed 242 pounds, great for a guard in football, but horrible for a relatively short basketball player trying to keep up in the backcourt.

So Grote went on a strict diet while playing in the American Basketball League and on AAU teams.

It was while playing for the AAU that Grote was spotted by Lou Mohs, then the Laker general manager, who remembered Grote from the guard's collegiate days in Los Angeles.

"I noticed this fella throwing accurate passes," Mohs said, "and keeping his team running. But at first, I didn't even know it was Grote. That's how much weight he had lost."

Grote signed with the Lakers for the 1964-65 season. But it was a short-lived dream. He got into only 11 games, scoring a total of 14 points and getting four assists.

That's all he had to show for his NBA career. That and a trim body.

Gudmundsson, Karl (1958-) ➤
At the start of the 1986-87 season, Laker Coach Pat Riley had big plans for this big man.

Those plans lasted one day.

The Lakers had signed Gudmundsson for the 1985-86 season after Mitch Kupchak had gone on the injured-reserve list, and the 7-foot-2, 260-pound Gudmundsson showed enough in eight games to get an invitation to return.

Gudmundsson, who came from Greenland, had already played for the Portland Trail Blazers. The Lakers got him from the Kansas City Sizzlers of the Continental Basketball Assn.

But Riley didn't care about Gudmundsson's past, only his future. He saw Gudmundsson as a backup to center Kareem Abdul-Jabbar.

But on the first day of practice for the 1986-87 season at the team's Palm Desert training site, Gudmundsson stopped after two hours.

"That's all I can do," he said.

The Lakers soon learned that Gudmundsson had torn a disk in his back.

Two hours into the 1986-87 season, his season–along with his Laker career–was over. He was traded to San Antonio in February of 1987 as part of the package to get Mychal Thompson.

Haircut ► Fans in Madison Square Garden could be merciless. Some seemed to consider it their duty to insult every visiting player, no matter how far they had to stretch to find a fault.

Sometimes it was easy. When Laker Coach Paul Westhead was fired after Magic Johnson demanded to be traded, the fans called Johnson a spoiled brat. They would be all over Kareem Abdul-Jabbar, a native New Yorker, for deserting his hometown. But on one night at the Garden, while the Lakers were being introduced, the fans seemed stumped when reserve forward Mark Landsberger came out.

Landsberger wasn't playing much, so there wasn't much to say.

But somebody had to say something. The fans' reputation was at stake.

Finally, as Landsberger started to trot back to the bench, a fan yelled, "Hey, Mark, way to go on the haircut."

It wasn't much, but at least no one could say a Laker had gotten a free ride in the Garden.

Hairston, Harold "Happy" (1942-) ► Some used to joke that Hairston valued his rebounding statistics so much he would hang around the basket at the end of each quarter, hoping that a player would throw up a desperation shot at the buzzer, enabling him to grab the ball and pad his rebounding total.

But Hairston didn't need to pad that total. He averaged 10.3 rebounds in an 11-year career spent with three clubs. Hairston also averaged 12.4 rebounds in 395 games as a Laker. What makes that even more impressive is that in most of those games, he played alongside Wilt Chamberlain, the greatest rebounder in league history. Hairston was the power forward on the 1971-72 Lakers team that won 69 regular-season games, 33 in a row and the first NBA title for the Lakers in Los Angeles. He averaged 13.1 rebounds.

Hairston also averaged double figures in scoring in every season but his first, when he averaged only 12.1 minutes for the Cincinnati Royals.

Haley, Jack Kevin (1964-) ► Haley was never a starter in the NBA and even at times had trouble keeping his spot on the bench. In the year they won a record 72 regular-season games, the Chicago Bulls kept Haley on the injured list most of the season, activated him for the final home game but didn't put him on the playoff roster.

So what kept the 6-foot-10, 240-pounder in the game?

In part, his friendship with Dennis Rodman.

With the San Antonio Spurs and the Bulls, Haley served as a buffer between the unpredictable, off-the-wall superstar, Rodman, and the rest of the world. Rodman would talk to Haley, and maybe even listen to him on occasion.

When Haley was activated at the end of the record-setting 1995-96 season, his Bull teammates had a good time putting cobwebs on his dressing stall, dust on his uniform and drawing up a welcoming sign.

"For me, it means a lot," Haley said in an interview. "I've felt it's important to be a part of the greatest team in history, and to get out and show people I'm not Dennis' baby-sitter. I never have been. I've been a basketball player from Day 1."

However, Haley's days with the Lakers weren't much to write about. He appeared in 49 games for them in the 1991-92 season, averaging 1.6 points and 1.9 rebounds.

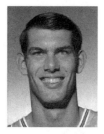

Hamilton, Dennis Eugene (1944-) ➤ Hamilton, 6 feet 8 and 210 pounds, had an unusually good shooting touch for a big man.

The Lakers wanted to use the former Arizona State player in the frontcourt to defend and rebound against other big men, but Hamilton wasn't particularly effective at that. Shooting was another matter.

In three seasons of professional basketball, two in the NBA and one in the American Basketball Assn. (a second ABA season consisted of only three games), Hamilton never made fewer than 50% of his shots from the field.

In 1967-68, his only season with the Lakers, Hamilton made 54 of his 108 shots. Failing to make the Lakers the year before, Hamilton had spent a season playing for a team sponsored by Gulf Oil that went on an 80-game tour of Europe.

That earned Hamilton a season on the Laker roster, but even his sharp shooting wasn't enough to enable him to keep it. He was left exposed and taken by Phoenix in the expansion draft.

Hardy, Alan Timothy (1957-) ➤ Playing for the University of Michigan, Hardy watched from a distance as Magic Johnson led Michigan State to the NCAA championship in 1979.

Signing with the Lakers after leading the 1980 Southern California summer league with a 33.5-point scoring average, Hardy watched from the bench as Johnson led the Lakers.

When a knee injury knocked Johnson out of action for 45 games in the 1980-81 season, Hardy got some playing time at guard even though he was a natural forward.

But once Johnson was ready to return, Hardy was cut, having played 22 games for the Lakers. His NBA career ended after playing in 38 games for the Detroit Pistons the next season.

Del Harris waves to his players from the sidelines during a 1995 game.

Harris, Delmer W. "Del" (1937-) ➤ When he arrived in Los Angeles to coach the Lakers for the 1994-95 season, Harris was still occasionally hit with the distasteful nickname, Dull, a leftover from his days as head coach of the Houston Rockets and the Milwaukee Bucks.

In L.A., however, Harris shook that nickname in a hurry.

He has not won an NBA title, but he can't be accused of running a dull operation. His four years were successful, but they were also seasons with controversy.

Harris was NBA coach of the year his first season with the Lakers, when they improved from 33-49 to 48-34, and went from a team that failed to reach the playoffs to one that got to the second round.

From there, it kept getting better, the Lakers improving for four straight years under Harris, the first time that has happened under one coach in franchise history. And in 1997-98, Harris climbed over the 60-win plateau for the first time.

But despite that success, Harris has heard his critics, from the Forum seats to talk-show studios to the newspaper columns.

The bottom line was that Harris had not put any new championship banners up on the Forum wall in a city spoiled by the Lakers' success of the 1980s. Once the team obtained center Shaquille O'Neal before the 1996-97 season, nothing short of a title would do.

Along with the high expectations came a lot of trouble.

In the 1995-96 season, Harris had to deal with the controversy caused by forward Cedric Ceballos, who took off for Lake Havasu in the middle of the season, claiming it was because of a family matter. Most suspected it was because of unhappiness over the way Harris was using him.

In the same season, Harris had to deal with the controversy caused by the return of Magic Johnson and the questions over where to play him.

And through much of his time on the Laker sidelines, Harris had to deal with the controversy generated by guard Nick Van Exel, with whom Harris repeatedly clashed over the guard's role

Then there was March 4, 1998, the day the players supposedly voted, 12-0, to ask Laker executive Jerry West to fire Harris.

That never happened, of course.

"You couldn't get 12 NBA players to agree on anything," said Bill Fitch, then the coach of the Clippers. No, it was just a bad rumor spread across the country to the delight of some of Harris' strongest critics.

"I've been doing this for 20 years," Harris said, "so I can handle most anything you can throw at me."

Actually, Harris has 34 years of coaching experience in high school, college, Europe, South America, Puerto Rico, the American Basketball Assn. and the NBA.

After having graduated cum laude from Milligan College in Tennessee with a degree in religion, followed by a master's degree from Indiana in history in 1965, Harris started coaching Earlham College in Indiana in the 1965-66 season.

His NBA head coaching experience before the Lakers consisted of four seasons with the Rockets and five with the Bucks.

It was a Harris team that handed the Lakers their first major setback in the Magic Johnson era, which, in turn, led to Harris' greatest coaching triumph in the NBA. His Rockets pulled off a huge upset by knocking the Lakers

out in the first round of the 1981 playoffs. Harris reached the NBA Finals that season for the only time in his coaching career, his Rockets losing in six games to a Boston Celtic team led by Larry Bird.

Harris has been trying to get back ever since.

There were high hopes that he would do so in 1995-96 when Johnson returned for the second half of the season. But instead, the Lakers were bumped off in their first postseason series, by the Rockets again, with Harris forced to serve as referee as much as coach.

Van Exel was talking about Eddie Jones getting the ball more and Johnson was talking about Van Exel playing instead of talking and Harris was left running his hands through his white hair and saying in exasperation, "We've got a lot of coaches on this team, don't we?"

The next season ended with a real question whether Harris and Van Exel could coexist.

That is no longer a question. Van Exel was traded after the 1997-98 season, which will stem one source of criticism for Harris, whose NBA record is 550-451. But he knows that all his victories and all his trips to the playoffs won't silence the rest of his detractors. Only a title will do that.

"It is frustrating sometimes," Harris said, "when you look at my record against the other recognized great coaches and find out that my record is better than their [record] head to head. Sometimes, I find myself having to answer questions that are obviously rather condescending types of questions. Other than winning a championship, I've done about everything that any coach ... in the history of the league has done."

They don't call him Dull anymore, but until they call him a champion, Harris, like his critics, won't be satisfied.

Harvey, Antonio (1970-) ► Harvey went straight from Pfeiffer College, a National Assn. of Intercollegiate Athletics school, to the Southern California summer league, escaping notice by NBA scouts and mention in the NBA draft.

Big surprise.

NAIA players, even players like Harvey, who is 6 feet 11 and weighs 225 pounds, don't get much consideration in the draft.

But the Lakers noticed Harvey in the summer league

and signed him in 1993.

Impressed with Harvey's leaping ability, quickness and defensive skills, Coach Del Harris loved having him around.

"He keeps our other big people honest," Harris said. "Our other big people, as good Laker fans know, have a tendency to relax. When I see that happen, I figure a good place to relax is on the bench. I feel Antonio can give us some zip."

But eventually, reality caught up with Harvey. Left unexposed by the Lakers in the 1995 expansion draft, Harvey was selected by the Vancouver Grizzlies.

Hawkins, Cornelius L. "Connie" (1942-) ➤ Those who saw Hawkins operate in the air space above the baskets on the playgrounds of Bedford Stuyvesant in New York say he was one of the best to ever stuff a basketball, the precursor to Dr. J and Michael Jordan.

By the time he came to the Lakers, the young Hawk who soared with eagles had become the old Hawk who was often grounded by his own shortcomings.

The body remained superb, but the mind was less well conditioned. He sometimes forgot team meetings and failed to remember to get to games on time. "I've had trouble sustaining concentration for really long periods of time," Hawkins conceded when he joined the Lakers from the Phoenix Suns in a 1973 trade for Keith Erickson.

Hawkins averaged 11 points and 6.3 rebounds in 114 games with the Lakers. Not bad for many players.

For the Hawk, who had averaged more than 20 points each of his first four seasons in professional basketball, it was nowhere near the potential.

Hawkins, Thomas Jerome "Tommy," "Hawk" (1936-) ➤ Some know Tommy Hawkins as a Dodger executive, a position he has held since 1987. Others remember him as a radio and television sportscaster.

But before that, he was a basketball player, good enough to have been a two-time All- American at Notre Dame and a forward in the NBA for 10 years, six with the

Lakers and four with Cincinnati Royals. Hawkins started with the Lakers in their last season in Minneapolis, was on the first Laker team to play in Los Angeles in the 1960-61 season and then played with them one more year before going on to Cincinnati. He returned to close out his career in Los Angeles.

Of the teams Hawkins has been with, none have left the emotional attachment he still feels for the Lakers.

How else can you explain his behavior on June 9, 1985?

In Boston Garden, the Lakers were within reach of defeating their bitter rivals, the Boston Celtics, in the NBA Finals, something they had failed to do in eight previous finals against the Celtics. And they were about to do so on the Garden's parquet floor, where the Lakers had left so many other times in dejection.

Hawkins, long retired, was nervously watching the game on television in his Los Angeles home and felt the need to do something to help his old team. So he found his old Laker uniform and put it on–jersey, shorts and socks.

And there Hawkins sat, on his living room couch, dressed as if he were back on the Laker bench, counting off the final seconds of the Lakers' 111-100 victory in the sixth and final game.

"There was a monkey on my back," Hawkins said, "just as there was with everyone else who ever played on the Lakers in that losing tradition. You know, it reminds me of that talk Martin Luther King made where he said he had a dream. This was my dream. When the Lakers walked out of Boston Garden with a victory, we were free at last, free at last. It felt like two tons of weight had been lifted off my chest."

Hawthorne, Nate (1950-) ➤ Hawthorne had such little impact in his 33 games with the Lakers that, years later, when his coach, Bill Sharman, and others were asked about Hawthorne, they could barely remember the 6-foot-4, 190-pounder from Southern Illinois.

It was a only a little different in Phoenix, where Hawthorne wound up after being picked up from the Lakers in the 1974 expansion draft by the New Orleans Jazz and then traded to the Suns before he had played a minute for New Orleans.

Hawthorne had one moment that stood out, and anyone who saw the Suns' 1974-75 highlight film remembered it, an electrifying shot of Hawthorne soaring across the court to block a Golden State Warrior shot.

Unfortunately for Hawthorne, such moments were as fleeting as his time in the air.

Hawthorne lasted two seasons with the Suns before ending his NBA career, his season scoring average never soaring above 6.1.

Haywood, Spencer (1949-) ►

Many players came to the Lakers and found fame and fortune. Haywood was already a star when he came to play what turned out to be his only season in Los Angeles, 1979-80.

An All-American at Detroit University and the center on the gold-medal U.S. team at the 1968 Olympics in Mexico City, Haywood began his pro basketball career in 1969-70 with the Denver Nuggets of the American Basketball Assn.

After only a year, Haywood jumped to the NBA, signing with the Seattle SuperSonics. After five seasons there, three-plus seasons in New York and a brief stop in New Orleans where he played 34 games for the Jazz, Haywood came to the Lakers in a big trade for Adrian Dantley just before the start of the 1979-80 season. The Lakers had high hopes for the 6-foot-9, 225-pound Haywood, even though he was 30 years old and playing for his fifth club. He had career averages of 22 points and 10.7 rebounds. It was thought that he would be the perfect complement in the frontcourt to Kareem Abdul-Jabbar.

But Haywood never seemed to fit in with the Lakers. His skills were diminishing, and he was seen as flaky by some.

This is a man who would take a shower before games to wash the pollen off his body. As it became evident he wasn't the piece to the Lakers' championship puzzle, his playing time decreased.

And as his playing time decreased, his agitation increased.

He became the Dennis Rodman of the day, a distraction on the bench who would wave his fist or towels, inciting the crowd to chant for him to be put into the game. During the 1980 NBA Finals against the Philadelphia 76ers, Haywood's behavior became even more eccentric. Three incidents stood out:

• While the Lakers were in a room watching tape of the 76ers, Haywood dozed off.

• Before one practice, the team was going through its customary stretching exercises. When the players were done, they stood up to await the start of a full-court practice session.

Haywood didn't get up. He remained in a hurdler's position as if frozen in mid-leap.

Haywood was sound asleep. He later claimed exhaustion.

• In the Forum locker room after Game 2, guard Brad Holland was using a pair of tape cutters. Haywood demanded them in what Holland thought was a rude manner. He asked Haywood to use the word please.

Haywood, the volume of his voice increasing as he spoke, said, "If I have to say please, I don't want to use them."

Holland, getting angry himself, snapped back and the two were suddenly in each other's faces, eye to eye.

Before contact could be made, forward Jim Chones got between them and shoved Haywood away.

"You crazy, Wood?" Chones said. "Man, you're lettin' us down."

Not for long.

Coach Paul Westhead had long been feuding with Haywood over his playing time. During the playoffs, Haywood told a Seattle newspaper, "If it were talent, I'd be out there."

Westhead ended Haywood's brief Laker career by suspending him the night of the tape-cutter incident.

The Lakers, after they had won the championship, voted Haywood only a quarter share of their postseason pot.

"It's more than he deserved," Abdul-Jabbar said.

Haywood played two more years in the NBA with the Washington Bullets, but he was never again the player he had been in his glory years.

"I never felt I did anything wrong," he said of his season with the Lakers. "I just didn't get a chance to ride my float."

Tommy Hawkins, left, then of the Cincinnati Royals blocks Walt Hazzard's drive to the key during a 1964 game at the Sports Arena. Hawkins and Hazzard were Laker teammates during the 1966-67 season.

Hazzard, Walter Raphael, Jr., (formerly Mahdi Abdul-Rahman "Walt" (1942-) ➤ Hazzard was a star in L.A., but not with the Lakers.

His biggest days came at UCLA, where, in the 1963-64 season, he led the Bruins to a 30-0 record and their first NCAA basketball championship, and was named college player of the year. Two years earlier, in his first season at UCLA, Hazzard had helped lead the Bruins to the Final Four for the first time.

Those credentials were enough to make him the No. 1 pick in the 1964 NBA draft. And it was all the sweeter because the Lakers selected Hazzard, allowing him to remain in Los Angeles.

But the sweet soon became sour. In three seasons with the Lakers, Hazzard's best scoring average was 13.7. His highest assist average was 4.9.

And in 1967, he was gone, taken by the Seattle SuperSonics in the expansion draft.

Hazzard had the ball in his hands at UCLA. With the Lakers, he had to share it with others who were used to having the ball in their hands, such players as future Hall of Famers Elgin Baylor, Jerry West and Gail Goodrich.

"Going to Seattle," Hazzard said, "gives me an opportunity I haven't had in my three years with the Lakers ... . To be effective, I need to play more than I could with the Lakers, who had too many good guards. There was a conflict between my style and the Lakers."

In Seattle, Hazzard, who went on to play for Atlanta, Buffalo and Golden State before returning to Seattle, showed what he could do playing his style. He averaged 24 points, nearly double his Laker high.

Hazzard played 10 years in the league, then returned

to Los Angeles, where he became head coach at his alma mater, UCLA, for four seasons and was eventually hired by the Lakers to serve in an administrative capacity and to do some scouting.

Hearn, Francis Dayle "Chick" ➤ He has never scored a basket, pulled down a rebound or handed out an assist in the NBA. But he has been as integral a part of the Lakers in L.A. as anyone.

He first sat down behind the Laker microphone in 1961, a time when the NBA was still largely bush league, but he has managed to sell the team and the league to three generations of fans ever since, currently operating on a consecutive-game streak longer than Cal Ripken Jr.'s, even before Ripken sat out a game. In January of 1998, Hearn broadcast his 3,000th consecutive Laker game, and he's still going strong.

A member of the basketball Hall of Fame and the American Sportscasters Hall of Fame, Hearn has held the interest of the fans in the few lean years the Lakers have experienced, punctuated the glory years, cheered during the great moments, scolded during the not-so-great moments, informed and forever left his mark on the game by creating catch phrases that have become part of the Laker lexicon.

Hearnisms include:
• He faked him into the popcorn machine.
• The mustard is off the hot dog.
• Yo-yoing the ball up and down.
• And, of course: The game is in the refrigerator, the door is closed, the light is out, the eggs are cooling, the butter is getting hard and the Jell-o is jiggling.

It was Hearn who first talked about offering "a word's eye view" of the game, and Hearn who has made an art out of the simulcast, his word for doing radio and television at the same time.

The Lakers left Minneapolis to avoid financial ruin, but they didn't exactly land in a pile of riches in Los Angeles.

When the Lakers arrived in 1960, the Rams had long been packing the fans into the Coliseum, and the Dodgers, having just concluded their third season on the West Coast, were doing the same.

So who needed the Lakers, members of a league that usually couldn't draw as much attention or as many fans as the Harlem Globetrotters, a comedy act in shorts? Bob

Short, the Laker owner, was concerned. His team was in the playoffs at the end of its first season in its new city and few seemed to care.

He needed a spark, and so he hired Hearn, a transplant from Illinois who was a jack-of-all- sports broadcaster in Los Angeles.

Hearn seemed to pop up everywhere in L.A. after arriving in 1956. He did USC football and basketball. He did an Emmy Award-winning nightly sportscast.

He has also done NFL football, PGA golf tournaments, tennis and was the voice of Nevada Las Vegas basketball. He hosted a game show called "Bowling for Dollars," has made numerous cameo appearances on television and hundreds of commercials. Hearn has a star on the Hollywood Walk of Fame. Few faces have been seen and few voices heard as often as his in Hollywood and the surrounding areas over the last four decades.

But above all else, Hearn has been the voice of the Lakers. From Elgin Baylor and Jerry West to Magic Johnson and Kareem Abdul-Jabbar to Shaquille O'Neal and Kobe Bryant, Hearn has been there. His colorful language is matched by an opinionated style that keeps listeners involved and either elated or infuriated most of the time. If he thinks an official has blown a call, Hearn says so. If he thinks a player has blown an opportunity, he says so. He is almost like a coach without the title. At one time, he was listed as assistant general manager.

Under Jack Kent Cooke's regime, Hearn had real influence. When Pat Riley was a player and wanted to come back to L.A., he appealed to Hearn. When Cooke was contemplating a trade, he would consult with Hearn.

Hearn regards the Lakers as part of his extended family, as his kids. He is proud when they do well, angry when they do poorly.

Hearn's nickname came about in his younger days when he was playing for an AAU team. Given a box that he thought contained a pair of sneakers, Hearn opened it only to see a chicken pop out.

And he has been Chick ever since.

His wit is not limited to broadcasts. The Chick Show goes on all the time, with sportswriters, bus drivers, hotel personnel and anyone else crossing his path serving as foils for his unceasing humor. With Hearn, it's always Showtime.

One night, Hearn was in an elevator when the door opened on the second floor and a man in a Superman outfit got on. The elevator went up one floor, stopped and "Superman" got out.

As the door closed, Hearn remarked, "You would think that silly son of a gun could have jumped that high."

On a Laker bus trip, Hearn was annoyed by a sportswriter talking in the seat behind him.

The bus pulled up to a corner where jackhammer smashing into the concrete could clearly be heard.

"Hey, you want to make some extra money?" asked Hearn, turning around to the sportswriter.

The sportswriter nodded in amusement and anticipation.

"Then get out there," Hearn said, pointing to the construction area, "put your chin on the sidewalk and start talking."

Hearn loved to do crossword puzzles and always had one at the start of every trip. So did Elgin Baylor. After a while, the two got into fierce competition over who could finish first.

One day, Baylor decided to cheat a bit. He finished his puzzle before even getting on the Laker plane, then produced the finished product as the plane's landing gear went up.

Hearn just grinned, then pulled out his crossword puzzle, which was also finished.

How long can Hearn go on broadcasting Laker games?

Although he guards his age as fiercely as any of the league's best defenders guard their men, it is known that

Chick Hearn takes a brief break from his broadcasting duties during a December, 1994 game.

Hearn was in his early 80s in when his broadcasting streak reached its 3,000th game in early 1998. To be sure, he's a medical marvel who is able to maintain an incredible pace that would break men half his age. Yet he's not ready to put his career in the refrigerator just yet. And no one is about to tell him to do so. Because it's difficult to imagine the Lakers without Chick Hearn.

Heathcote, Jud ➤ Heathcote was Magic Johnson's coach at Michigan State, the coach when Johnson led the Spartans to a 75-64 victory over Indiana State in the 1979 NCAA title game.

But it almost didn't happen, because Johnson hesitated before attending Michigan State. And one of the main reasons was Heathcote.

Growing up in Lansing, Mich., playing at Jenison Field House on the Michigan State campus while still in high school and often attending Spartan games, Johnson had had plenty of opportunities to watch Heathcote.

What he often saw was a short-tempered man who yelled at his players.

That bothered Johnson, who figured he was serious enough about the game and knowledgeable enough to be treated with respect.

Johnson narrowed his choice to Michigan and Michigan State.

With the decision at hand, Heathcote visited Johnson.

"With your height, they'll probably have you playing center," the coach told the high school star about Michigan. "You're not a center, Earvin. I've seen you play and you're definitely a point guard. I want you to run our offense."

That sounded tempting to Johnson, who wound up running that offense all the way to the top.

Yes, Heathcote continued to yell at the players. Johnson lost track of the number of times he heard the coach scream, "Be a guard, not a garbage."

But Johnson said he didn't mind as long as he continued to improve as a player and his team continued to win.

Heathcote provided the national platform from which Johnson jumped to the NBA, making himself eligible for the NBA draft after the national championship in his sophomore year.

And even after he wound up with the Lakers, picked first overall in the 1979 draft, Johnson kept in close contact with Heathcote.

During his first few seasons with the Lakers, when Johnson struggled at times, he often called his former coach, the man he at one time didn't even want to play for, for advice.

SEE ALSO • *Johnson, Magic.*

Henderson, Jerome D. (1959-) ➤ Henderson had high hopes of playing professional basketball when he left the University of New Mexico after his junior year. And those hopes were realized. Sort of.

He played for all sorts of pro teams, though nearly all of them were far removed from the NBA.

He played for Detroit and Rochester in the Continental Basketball Assn. and for teams in the Philippines, Mexico and Turkey.

Henderson got his chance in the NBA in the spring of 1986 when the Lakers signed him to a 10-day contract.

But eight days after he signed, Henderson, who had appeared in only one game for the Lakers, was cut loose so that the team could sign Petur Gudmundsson, another CBA product.

Henderson got one more shot at the NBA the next season with the Milwaukee Bucks, but he got into only six games.

Hetzel, Fred W. (1942-) ➤ Although Hetzel and fellow Laker John Wetzel never played in purple and gold at the same time, Laker announcer Chick Hearn liked to pretend they did in later years in order to use his classic line, "Hetzel to Wetzel made my tongue a pretzel."

By the time Hetzel came to the Lakers, he couldn't do much more than inspire funny lines.

It hadn't always been that way.

An All-American at Davidson, Hetzel improved in each of his first three seasons in the NBA, peaking in 1967-68 with the San Francisco Warriors when he averaged 19 points and 7.1 rebounds.

After that, the biggest numbers Hetzel racked up were in the mileage department. In the two years before he joined the Lakers, Hetzel went to Milwaukee, Cincinnati, Philadelphia and Portland.

The Lakers got him on waivers from the Trail Blazers, but, in 59 games of the 1970-71 season, Hetzel averaged only 4.8 points and 2.5 rebounds. Hetzel lasted only one season with the Lakers. Just like Wetzel.

Hewitt, William Severlyn "Bill"

(1944-) ➤ While Hewitt was a star forward at USC, averaging 19.1 points and earning All-Coast honors in his two seasons, Rudy LaRusso was a star forward in the NBA, for the Lakers in Hewitt's first season as a Trojan and for the San Francisco Warriors in Hewitt's second, 1967-68.

A year later, they came face to face in the NBA playoffs, LaRusso still a Warrior and Hewitt in LaRusso's old spot in the Laker frontcourt.

Part of the reason the Lakers had made Hewitt their first pick in the 1968 draft, the 11th selection overall, was because of his defensive skills.

After LaRusso had led the Warriors to victories by scoring 61 points in the first two games of the 1969 first-round playoff series in L.A., the Lakers put Hewitt on LaRusso.

The result: LaRusso scored only 48 points in the remaining four games, and the Lakers won all four to eliminate the Warriors.

Did that performance guarantee Hewitt he'd be staying in the city where he had played his college ball?

Hardly. Seven months later, he was traded to the Detroit Pistons for Happy Hairston, another forward who would make an even greater impact than had Hewitt.

Higgins, Michael "Mike"

(1967-) ➤ Like several others who have briefly won a spot on the Laker roster, Higgins earned his shot by doing well.

He set 23 school records at Northern Colorado, a Division II university. And playing for the Laker team in the Southern California summer league, he averaged 12.3 points and 6.3 rebounds.

Then, reality kicked in. Signed for the 1989-90 season, Higgins quickly found out why so few have been able to leap from Division II collegiate ball to the NBA.

Higgins got into six games for the Lakers, scoring one point and pulling down one rebound. He played five more games with Denver that season, then seven with Sacramento the next season before his fling with fantasy ended.

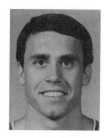

Holland, John Bradley "Brad"

(1956-) ➤ Players like Brad Holland normally would be only a footnote in Laker history. After all, the reserve guard played sparingly for the Lakers for two seasons, averaging 3.0 points and 6.2 minutes per game as a Laker.

But Holland earned a special place by coming up with several big shots in the biggest game of his life–and one of the biggest games in Laker history.

It was at the Spectrum in Philadelphia, the sixth game of the 1980 NBA Finals, with the Lakers leading the 76ers, 3-2, in the best-of-seven series. It was the game in which Magic Johnson played all five positions in the absence of injured Kareem Abdul-Jabbar.

Late in the second quarter, the Lakers trailed by six and needed a boost when Holland went into the game. Shaking off the rust of inactivity and any lingering nervousness, he scored six points in rapid fashion, the Lakers wound up tied at the half, 60-60, and they went on to win, 123-107.

Afterward in the Laker locker room, Julius Erving, one of the reigning superstars of that era, came up to Holland, who had finished with eight points in nine minutes, shook his hand and congratulated him.

Dr. J himself! Holland couldn't even answer.

"This isn't really me sitting here," he later said he was thinking. "This isn't really happening. I'll come to my senses soon."

Holland was an All-Pacific 10 player at UCLA who set school shooting-percentage records for a guard, but in the summer of 1981 he was traded to the Washington Bullets, along with Jim Chones and two draft choices, for Mitch Kupchak.

Holy Providence School ➤ An all-black boarding school in Cornwall Heights outside Philadelphia, it is the birthplace of one of the most recognizable and effective shots in basketball history.

In 1956, 9-year-old Lew Alcindor was a 5-foot-8 fourth grader in his first year at the school. Selected to play basketball because of his height, although he was awkward and unsure of himself, Alcindor one day had the ball in his hands and a defender at his back, between him and the basket.

Looking over his shoulder, Alcindor threw up a hook

shot. It missed. A few minutes later, he tried it again. Another miss. But, because the shot felt natural to him, and his height made it so easy to get it over defenders, he tried it again. And again. Eventually, the shot became known as the sky hook, the primary shot Alcindor used at UCLA to score 2,325 points and, after he became known as Kareem Abdul-Jabbar, to score an NBA-record 38,387 points in his 20-year NBA career.

SEE ALSO • *Sky Hook.*

Horn, Ronald Leroy "Ron" (1938-) ➤ Horn played college ball at Indiana before becoming a pro basketball nomad. He signed with the St. Louis Hawks of the NBA as a rookie, but appeared in only three games for them.

Then, it was on to the Long Beach Chiefs of the American Basketball League, but that league folded halfway through the season.

Then, it was up the freeway to Los Angeles. The Lakers needed help in the frontcourt because Howie Jolliff was out with a knee injury. Horn appeared in 28 games for them in 1962-63, but his numbers were hardly the kind that would keep him in the NBA. He averaged 2.6 points and 2.5 rebounds.

After five years away from the game, Horn signed with the Denver Nuggets, then in the American Basketball Assn., for the 1967-68 season.

In three undistinguished seasons, he played in four leagues. When the Nuggets used him in only one game, he sued them for $100,000 to get out of his contract and move on.

But, as it turned out, Horn had no place to go. He didn't play pro basketball again.

Horry, Robert Keith (1970-) ➤ Horry loved the giant leap he took on Jan. 10, 1997.

What's not to love?

When the Phoenix Suns traded him and Joe Kleine to the Lakers on that date for Cedric Ceballos and Rumeal Robinson, Horry went from last place to first in the Pacific Division.

"People are gunning for you now," he said. "Whereas in Phoenix, people were laughing at you."

The Lakers were pretty happy too. They had gotten rid of Ceballos, whose skills had been counterbalanced by his problems with Coach Del Harris over Ceballos' place in the Lakers' scheme of things. In the minds of many, Ceballos would always be the Laker who took off for four days in the middle of the season without permission to go to Arizona's Lake Havasu after his playing time had diminished, though he claimed there was no connection between the two.

Horry arrived in L.A. with some baggage of his own. He had just completed a two-game suspension for throwing a towel in the face of his coach, Danny Ainge, after the two had exchanged angry words.

But the Lakers preferred to look at the plus side. They had obtained a player who had been a starter for the Houston Rockets when they had won back-to-back NBA championships. They saw a solid 6-foot-10 defensive player who could perform at either forward position (though he seemed more comfortable at small forward), could connect from three-point range and was comfortable fitting into a supporting role among superstars. There were no towels flying in Harris' direction after Horry's arrival. But there were plenty of compliments flying in Horry's direction.

Robert Horry swings from the rim after slamming in two points during a 1997 game.

asked Horry to concentrate on power forward. The result was that he went from 237 rebounds in 54 games in 1996-97 to 542 rebounds in 72 games in 1997-98, increasing his average from 4.4 per game to 7.5, the third best increase in the league in 1997-98.

After proving to be solid in rebounding, blocked shots and steals, Horry stepped up his offense in the postseason, shooting 55.7% from the field.

With all the other things Horry does, the Lakers regard his offense as a bonus. They know he's not Ceballos in terms of scoring. But then again, they can be confident he'll show up to play every game during the season.

Hot Seat ➤ It was a clear November morning in Salt Lake City. What was clear to the Laker traveling party gathering at the airport for a flight to Los Angeles was that Coach Paul Westhead was about to be fired.

It was clear to nearly everyone except Westhead.

The coach had gotten into an argument the night before with Magic Johnson after a Laker-Utah Jazz game. The argument was the explosion resulting from weeks of tension between Westhead and his players over the direction of the team.

Mitch Chortkoff, a beat writer who covered the Lakers for more than 20 years, broke the tension when he approached the Laker party, out of earshot of Westhead, with a look of mock horror on his face.

"They just made a horrible mistake," Chortkoff said. What's that? he was asked.

"They just gave Westhead a boarding pass that says coach."

Hudson, Louis Clyde "Lou" "Sweet Lou" (1944-) ➤ Hudson was wearing a Laker uniform on Oct. 28, 1977 when he had one of the most emotional moments of his 13-year NBA career.

But what got Hudson so emotional that day was a Hawk uniform bearing the No. 23 he had worn with the team. The jersey was being retired at the Omni in Atlanta. Hudson spent only the final two years of his career with the Lakers, but it was during his years with the Hawks, in St. Louis and Atlanta, that he had his greatest success.

Hudson was a first-round pick of the St. Louis Hawks

Lou Hudson crashes around Paul Westphal of the Phoenix Suns in a 1977 game.

in 1966, the fourth player taken overall. He became a six-time all-star and once scored 57 points in a 1969 game against the Chicago Bulls.

With a dependable jump shot, Hudson scored 17,940 points in his career.

He was only 6 feet 4 but had explosive jumping ability. In college at Minnesota, he gave himself a scalp wound when he banged his head on the underside of the backboard in the first half of a game against Purdue.

It was Hudson's first Big Ten game and he wasn't about to let a little blood stop him. After intermission, he came back and scored 24 points to finish with 36 and lead the Gophers to victory.

The Lakers got Hudson from Atlanta for Ollie Johnson before the 1977-78 season, and Hudson, 33 when he became a Laker, went on to average 11.8 points for them over two seasons. That wasn't bad, but it was far from his career mark of 20.2.

Had Hudson come along 15 years later, after NBA salaries skyrocketed, he could have been a very wealthy man, but he insisted he didn't care.

"I stayed away from the fast track," Hudson said. "I don't need millions to live. Oscar Robertson came up to me at a golf tournament and said, "I envy you, Hudson. You have a nice, low-key life. You do the things you want to do.' "

Hundley, Rodney Clark "Hot Rod" (1934-) ►

It was only logical that Hundley would become a basketball broadcaster after his playing days ended. Hundley played to the crowd throughout his career, which spanned the Lakers' Minneapolis and Los Angeles years.

A guard who preceded Jerry West at West Virginia, Hundley was a master ballhandler on the court and a master carouser off it.

Owner Bob Short once warned Hundley to tone down his lifestyle after finding him flagging down a cab in St. Louis late at night to set off on yet another wild evening. Finally, an exasperated Short fined Hundley and Slick Leonard, Hundley's running mate during working hours and after hours, $1,000 each.

Small change?

Not in those days. Hundley was making only $10,000, Leonard $9,000.

Compare that to Laker center Shaquille O'Neal, who made $12,850,000 in 1997-98. One-tenth of his salary would be a fine of $1.29 million for missing curfews. But Short couldn't complain about Hundley's actions on the court. In 1960, in the first game the Lakers played in Los Angeles, the account in the Los Angeles Times mentioned that "the audience cheered the Lakers' Hot Rod Hundley when he pulled his behind-the-back dribbling routines."

Hundley could also entertain with his wit.

On the night in 1960 when Elgin Baylor scored a then-NBA record 71 points against the Knicks in New York, Hundley scored two points. After the game, he and Baylor hailed a cab and took off down the canyons of Manhattan.

"Be careful," Hundley told the driver, "you've got 73 points in this cab."

But behind all the fun and games was a player who carved his own niche on a team with superstars like Baylor and Jerry West.

Hundley's best seasons were the Lakers' last one in Minneapolis and first one in Los Angeles, when he averaged 12.8 and 11.0 points, respectively. He also averaged 4.4 assists in 1960-61, the first season the Lakers called Los Angeles home.

Hundred points ►

Mention Hershey, Pa., and most people think of candy bars.

But mention Hershey to a pro basketball fan and what comes to mind is an event one night in 1962 that pushed a little-noticed sport to the top of many of the nation's sports sections.

In those days, the NBA was eager to expand its small fan base. That's why the Philadelphia Warriors played about once a month in Hershey. And that's why they were there on the night of March 2, 1962, hosting the New York Knicks at the Hershey Sports Arena.

The unquestioned star of the Warriors, and one of the two biggest stars in the league along with the Boston Celtics' Bill Russell, was Wilt Chamberlain.

That season, the 7-foot-1 Chamberlain was having an extraordinary year, even by his own oversized standards. Without much talent around him, he had been expected to carry the Warrior offense. And he did. He averaged an incredible 50.4 points per game, almost 13 more than any other player has ever averaged over a season.

But riding into Hershey on the team bus that day, Chamberlain had planned to do something besides score.

"Pass a little more, do something," he told himself. "Because next year, they are going to be asking for 60 points a game."

Only three months earlier, Chamberlain had set the NBA record with 78 points in a triple-overtime game against the Lakers, the team he would lead to an NBA title in Los Angeles a decade later.

But that Friday night in Hershey, Chamberlain's shot was working.

By halftime, Chamberlain had 41 points. He added 28 more in the third quarter, and suddenly, this was more than a basketball game.

With victory out of reach, the Knicks had a new mission: Keep Chamberlain out of triple figures.

In 1975, Willie Nauls, a New York forward and a friend of Chamberlain's, said in a published interview that Knick Coach Eddie Donovan had told his players that night to hold the ball for as long as they could, right up to

After setting it, Wilt displays the number that may become the longest-standing record in pro sports: 100 points in a single game. (AP photo)

the last few ticks of the 24-second clock, to keep it out of Chamberlain's hands.

Although Naulls wouldn't confirm that report later, he did concede that "there was a certain amount of pride involved."

There were all sorts of little games going on. The Knicks claimed the Warriors were fouling them in order to get the ball back for Chamberlain. The Warriors claimed the Knicks were fouling players other than Chamberlain to keep him from shooting.

"I wasn't going to be part of that fooling around," Naulls said. "That fouling, playing keep-away, that wasn't basketball."

In the closing minutes, the fans started chanting, "We want a hundred." With a little more than a minute to play, Chamberlain had 98 points.

He missed two straight shots, but teammate Tom Luckenbill got the second rebound and passed it to Joe Ruklick, who passed it back Chamberlain, and the 100-point mark was reached with thunderous dunk.

With 46 seconds left in the game, fans stormed the court. Chamberlain clutched the ball firmly and raced into the locker room.

He had taken 63 shots from the field and had made

36. And at the free-throw line, where his career mark was an abysmal 51.1%, he sank 28 of 32. Only 4,124 spectators in an arena that seated 9,000 saw the game, though in ensuing years, the number who would talk about the accomplishment they witnessed that night might lead one to believe 100,000 had been on hand.

Chamberlain avoided the subject of his 100 points for a long time and downplayed his scoring prowess when others brought it up. He was more willing to talk about the season he led the league in assists, or his impressive rebound totals. On the night he scored 100 points, Chamberlain had 25 rebounds.

"I just had done so many more things in basketball that had more meaning to me," he said in explaining why he had not liked talking about the 100-point game for so long. "You get downgraded all the time because you're a scorer. Hey, somebody's got to put the ball in the damn basket."

As the years passed, Chamberlain put aside the negative thoughts.

"Now sometimes, I look back at it in amazement," he said recently. "I just say, like, 'Wow.' "

SEE ALSO • *Chamberlain, Wilt, Imhoff, Darrell.*

Imhoff, Darrell Tucker "Ax"
(1938-) ➤ He got the nickname because, according to teammate Rudy LaRusso, "he used to chop on guys in practice."

Imhoff used the rough techniques to make up for the lack of a shooting touch. Although he was a 6-foot-10, 220-pounder who could play inside, Imhoff didn't shoot more than 40% from the field until his fourth season in the NBA and shot above 50% only once, in 1969-70. He averaged 7.2 points and 7.6 rebounds in 12 NBA seasons, 7.6 points and 9.4 rebounds in four seasons with the Lakers.

Imhoff was widely respected for the hard work he put in on the court, but no amount of hard work could stop what happened on March 2, 1962.

Imhoff, then a member of the New York Knicks, was in Hershey, Pa., that evening to play Wilt Chamberlain's Philadelphia Warriors.

With Phil Jordan, the Knicks' regular center, unable to play because of the flu, it fell to Imhoff to guard Chamberlain–or least be the main defender on the double- and triple-teams Chamberlain usually faced. Imhoff got into early foul trouble and wound up playing only 20 minutes.

No one else had any more success than Imhoff. Chamberlain scored an NBA-record 100 points that night.

Imhoff later said that the Hershey Sports Arena rims were very soft, thus making it easier for the ball to roll into the basket.

Jim Heffernan, who covered the game that night for the Philadelphia Bulletin, later pointed out: "Wilt must have played on soft rims more than once in his career."

Two days later, the teams met again in New York's Madison Square Garden. Once again Imhoff had to guard

Darrall Imhoff lays up a shot against the high-jumping Bill Russell in a 1965 game.

Chamberlain. "He was trying to get another 100," Imhoff said. "I fouled out with a minute to go and got a standing ovation because I held him to [58]."

Whenever it was brought up that Imhoff had guarded Chamberlain in the 100-point game, Imhoff was quick to say that he played only 20 minutes on that unforgettable night.

No matter. Imhoff couldn't avoid the tag of being the man who gave up 100 points in a single game.

After a while, he simply shrugged his shoulders when the name Chamberlain came up.

"It was a privilege," Imhoff said, "to have spent 12 years in his armpits."

The two were linked again on July 9, 1968, when the Lakers traded Imhoff, Archie Clark and Jerry Chambers to the Philadelphia 76ers for Chamberlain, who eventually helped lead Los Angeles to the 1971-72 title.

J

Jackson, Anthony Eugene "Tony"

(1958-) ➤ There seemed to be no question Tony Jackson could run an offense. He had proved that at Florida State, where he had 550 assists, including 15 in one game, and again in the 1980 Southern California summer league, where he averaged 7.3 assists.

The real question was, could Jackson, a 1980 fourth-round draft choice, find a spot on the roster of the NBA-champion Lakers, who already had guards Magic Johnson, Norm Nixon, Michael Cooper, Brad Holland, Eddie Jordan and Butch Carter? The answer was a disappointing 'no' for Jackson. He got into only two games for the Lakers in the 1980-81 season, scoring two points and getting two assists.

Johnson, Clayton H. "Clay"

(1956-) ➤ It wasn't easy being the other Johnson on the Lakers in the early 1980s.

But Clay Johnson was happy simply to be on the team, considering the leap he had made to get there.

One minute in the spring of 1982, he was in Lancaster, Pa., a member of a team from Billings, Mont., preparing to play Lancaster in a Continental Basketball Assn. playoff game.

The next minute, he was a member of a Laker team headed for an NBA title, called up to replace injured guard Eddie Jordan.

Johnson appeared in seven regular-season games with the Lakers in the 1981-82 season and 48 the next. Despite limited playing time, Johnson used his quick hands to lead the team in steals in six games and in offensive rebounds in three during the 1982-83 season. He shot 56.3% in 14 postseason games with the Lakers, who reached the NBA finals both seasons he was with the team.

Johnson, Earvin Jr., "Magic"

(1959-) ➤ Early in his career, in a game at Madison Square Garden, Johnson went up for a rebound and pulled the ball down firmly. Teammate Norm Nixon took off down one sideline at the instant Johnson's powerful hands grabbed the ball.

Without turning his head for as much as a peek downcourt, Johnson threw the ball straight over his head on a huge arc. Nixon didn't break stride, caught the ball like a receiver catching a perfect pass from John Elway and took it in for a layup.

Asked later how he had known Nixon was there, Johnson said he had turned around and looked.

No, Johnson was told, you never looked. The replay clearly shows your eyes staring straight ahead until the ball was already on its way downcourt behind you.

Johnson shrugged his shoulders. He thought he had seen Nixon. Or maybe he simply knew the guard was there.

If Johnson couldn't explain his magic, how could anyone else?

How can anyone explain a 6-foot-9 player who could run with the game's small speedsters, rebound with its giants, score with its sharpshooters and pass like nobody else the game had ever seen.

In this age of big guards, it is easy to forget that Johnson was one of the first, a big backcourt player

Magic Johnson blocks the path of Seattle's Nate McMillan during a 1990 game against the SuperSonics.

without the weaknesses generally associated with big men. Only a decade earlier, the Boston Celtics' Bill Russell had been the most successful center in the game, a master shot-blocker, overall defender and rebounder. He was 6-9$\frac{1}{2}$.

But at the dawn of the 1980s, there was Johnson, roughly the same height, but doing things formerly reserved for the little men of the game–ballhandling, passing and directing the offense.

Add to that Johnson's height and you had a new breed of guard.

The game would never be the same.

No one could regularly stop Johnson, and the Philadelphia 76ers certainly couldn't figure him out in spring of 1980. Not Magic Johnson the center, Magic Johnson the forward or Magic Johnson the guard.

They saw all three on May 16, 1980, at the end of Johnson's rookie season, still the most amazing night in Johnson's career despite all the accomplishments that would follow.

It could be argued that it was the most stunning single-game performance in NBA history. After all, when Wilt Chamberlain scored his 100 points, when Michael Jordan came up with all his clutch, game-winning shots, they were excelling at the one thing they did best.

What Johnson did as a 20-year-old was to excel in every aspect of the game while filling in for one of the all-time greats and lead his team to an NBA title. The Lakers were in Philadelphia, leading the 76ers, three games to two, in the best-of-seven NBA Finals. Center Kareem Abdul-Jabbar was at home because of a severely sprained left ankle.

Asked by Coach Paul Westhead if he could play center on offense for part of the game, Johnson replied, "No problem."

Said Westhead: "If anyone can pull it off, it is Houdini."

Even Houdini never pulled off a magic act like the one Johnson unveiled that Friday night.

Playing all three positions at various times in the game, Johnson scored 42 points, including a 14-for-14 night from the free-throw line, pulled down 15 rebounds and handed out seven assists–and led his team to the NBA championship. It was the real opening act of a magic show that would continue throughout the 1980s.

Having already won an NCAA title at Michigan State in his sophomore season before joining the Lakers, and having already been given credit, along with longtime rival

Magic fakes a drive to the basket and passes the ball off in a 1988 game.

Larry Bird, for beginning the revitalization of the NBA, which was at the time staggering under the weight of financial difficulties and public apathy, Johnson had accomplished more before the age of 21 than many players did in their entire careers.

But the world of sports, the business community and the entertainment field would all learn that Johnson was never satisfied with his last achievement. The Lakers, with Johnson in the backcourt, Abdul-Jabbar at center and a powerful supporting cast, would win five NBA titles in the 1980s and reach the NBA Finals on three other occasions.

Johnson's highlights could fill a book. He never averaged fewer than 14.6 points a season. For five seasons in a row (1982-83 through 1986-87) he led the league in assists per game. He was the NBA MVP in 1987, 1989 and 1990. He is the Laker career leader in assists and steals. He was the NBA Finals MVP in 1980, 1982 and 1987. And he was on the All-Star team 12-times.

Some of his most extraordinary moments, in addition to the stunning championship game in 1980, include:

–Beating the Celtics for the first time in the NBA

An intent and intense Magic Johnson drives upcourt during a 1991 preseason game.

Finals in 1985– and doing it at Boston Garden.

–Making his famous junior sky hook in the 1987 finals to clinch a key victory over Boston, also at the Garden. Johnson would later call it "the biggest basket of my life."

–Beating the team from his home state, the Detroit Pistons, in the 1988 NBA Finals.

–Coming back after having announced his retirement because he was HIV-positive to become the most valuable player of the 1992 All-Star game.

–Being a member of the 1992 U.S. Olympic gold medal-winning squad known as the "Dream Team."

–Returning to the Lakers to play early in 1996 after a $4\frac{1}{2}$-year absence from the game.

But over the years, the wide smile that was one of

Johnson's trademarks was occasionally missing, and that was never more the case than in November of 1991 when he told a shocked world that he had contracted HIV.

He did not play that season or in the next three, though rumors of his return were never far from the surface.

There were other incidents. In the spring of 1981, Johnson sat out 45 games because of a knee injury and came back in a swirl of controversy, whipped up by point guard Norm Nixon, who resented being forced to give the ball back to Johnson. When the Lakers were bumped out of the 1981 playoffs in the first round by the Houston Rockets, much of the blame was attributed to the Johnson-Nixon clash.

The next autumn, Coach Paul Westhead was fired the

day after Johnson said he wanted to be traded. Although owner Jerry Buss insisted he had already decided to get rid of Westhead, Johnson was criticized by fans as a spoiled player who had the owner wrapped around his finger. Even a teammate sympathetic to Johnson's view of Westhead stayed mum, noting later: "I can't say anything. He can say what he wants because he's Magic."

In the fall of 1992, Johnson tried a comeback only to retire again before the start of the regular season when several in the NBA questioned whether he ought to be competing while HIV- positive.

In the spring of 1994, Johnson coached the Lakers for the last 16 games of the season–going 5-11– then was ripped in the media for giving the job up even though he had taken it only on a temporary basis as a favor to Buss.

In the spring of 1996, Johnson's comeback ended badly, as the team was ousted in the first round of the playoffs, by Houston again, and Johnson criticized for his part in that failure.

But any controversies were minimal compared to his extraordinary accomplishments. He changed the game and left an indelible impression.

Johnson became a highly successful businessman who owned a small piece of the Lakers and invested heavily in Los Angeles. What will endure is the image of a man embracing basketball the way he embraced life, with a smile on his face and a magic touch in his fingers.

SEE ALSO • *Buck; E.J. the Deejay; Heathcote, Jud; June Bug; Westhead, Paul.*

Johnson, Ronald F. "Ron" (1938-) ➤ Johnson stood 6 feet 8 and weighed 215 pounds. In college at Minnesota, he used his size to his advantage and earned a spot on the 1960-61 Detroit Pistons.

But in the pros, Johnson couldn't compete with the league's big men. Some complained privately that it was because he wasn't tough enough.

Johnson certainly couldn't stop the new 1960s breed of high-flying small forwards who were carving out air space around NBA baskets, a breed led by Elgin Baylor.

Johnson became a teammate of Baylor's when the Lakers bought Johnson from Detroit before he had a chance to play for the Pistons.

But he didn't play much for the Lakers. Fourteen games was enough to convince the Lakers that Johnson, despite his height, didn't fit in.

Magic coached the Lakers for 16 games in 1994. It wasn't a winning time.

Jolesch, Bruce ➤ A Laker public relations director for two seasons beginning in 1980-81, Jolesch invented the term "triple-double."

He loved statistics and was one of the first to see the potential power of the computer to double and triple the volume of facts and figures previously available for sporting events. Jolesch would leave mountains of computer printouts on the hotel doorsteps of sportswriters on the road, giving them more information than they ever needed about the Lakers and the NBA.

Jolesch could supply everything from the Lakers' record on Halloween to their record on presidential election days.

Jolesch came along right after Magic Johnson arrived in the 1979-80 season, and he knew he needed some special way to describe those special moments when

Johnson would get 10 or more points, rebounds and assists in a single game.

So he named them "triple-doubles" for double figures in three categories–points, rebounds and assists.

He had to explain the term at first. But now, it is a common statistic around the NBA. Triple-doubles are counted on a per-game, per-season and per-career basis, no explanation necessary. Thanks to Jolesch.

Jolliff, Howard (1938-) ➤

Jolliff, a 6-foot-7, 220-pounder, never played more than 64 games in any of his three seasons with the Lakers and never averaged more than 3.9 points or 6.0 rebounds. He had a career shooting average of only 36.7% from 1960-61 through 1962-63.

To many of his teammates, he was the Norm Crosby of the team, the guy who had his own way of using the language.

On one occasion, Jolliff complained, "I can't sleep. I must have amnesia." Said a teammate in response, "Does that mean you forgot how to sleep?"

Jones, Dwight E. (1952-) ➤

Jones was an 11th-hour acquisition by the Lakers.

Almost literally.

Needing a center to back up Kareem Abdul-Jabbar in the 1982-83 season, the Lakers obtained the 6-foot-10, 210-pound Jones from the Chicago Bulls a few hours before the trading deadline.

It cost the Lakers $125,000 and a second-round draft choice for a 31-year-old, 10-year veteran of whom they didn't expect great things. The Lakers' first choice was Clemon Johnson of the Indiana Pacers, but he would have cost them $400,000. "We decided that instead of taking a star, from the business end, this may be the better deal for us," said Jerry West, the Lakers' general manager. "There are only so many good players you can have on a roster."

The Lakers got about what they had expected. Jones appeared in 32 games for them, averaging 4.9 points and 3.6 rebounds.

Howard Joliff shoots over the arms of Celtic Bob Cousy.

Jones, Earl (1961-) ➤
The Lakers gambled and lost with their first pick in the 1984 draft, the 23rd choice overall.

They selected Jones, a skinny center/forward from Division II University of the District of Columbia. Jones was 6 feet 11 but only 215 pounds, and his rebounding average in college had dropped every season, from 13.3 to 10.5 to 9.6 to 6.9. "We'll have to give him silicone shots and pump some air into him to get him up to 230," Coach Pat Riley joked.

But the Lakers weren't laughing after Jones wound up playing only seven minutes in two games that season, getting no points and no rebounds.

Jones went to Milwaukee the next season and played in a dozen games before his NBA career ended.

Jones, Eddie Charles "E.J." (1971-) ➤ So who is the real Eddie Jones, the player who slammed and jammed against the Seattle SuperSonics in the 1998 playoffs, or the player who stumbled and struggled against the Portland Trail Blazers and the Utah Jazz in the same postseason? Was it the Eddie Jones who shot 37.5% in the 1995 playoffs or the Eddie Jones who shot 55.1% in the 1996 postseason? When Jones is good, he can be spectacular. He can soar with the giants, he can slam with the legends, he can run with the rabbits.

When he's bad, he can disappear during crucial stretches.

The 1998 playoffs offer a good example of the peaks and valleys included in Jones' package.

He was matched against the Trail Blazers' Isaiah Rider in the first round.

"Eddie Jones is a good player, but I can post Eddie Jones up all day," Rider boasted.

And in the opening game of the series, Rider did outplay Jones.

But in the second game, Jones, whose focus on the team concept sometimes causes him to slip into a passive role, was fired up enough by Rider's remarks to ask for the ball.

"I've got a lot of pride," Jones said. "My whole life, everybody has always said, 'Eddie can't do this. Eddie can't do that. I'm better than you.' I've always been proving them wrong... .Sometimes in this game, it's important for me to be the aggressor, to be even a little selfish. That is hard because I'm not a selfish player, but sometimes you have to do it."

Jones scored a playoff career-high 21 points in that second game against the Trail Blazers. He then tailed off in that series and scored only four points in Game 4, when the Lakers won and moved on to the second round.

But against the SuperSonics, Jones scored 23 points in Game 2, 29 points in Game 3 and 32 points in Game 4.

"You'd have to look at some Hall of Fame guys to put together three better games than that," said Jones' coach, Del Harris, getting carried away a bit by the moment.

But don't reserve that spot at the Hall of Fame just yet for Jones.

After bringing his shooting up from 37.9% against

Eddie Jones drives around a pick from Elden Campbell in a 1997 game.

Portland to 54.4% against Seattle, Jones dropped back to 41.2% against Utah in the Western Conference Finals.

Still, Jones can do a lot more than score. He's an excellent defender, is highly effective on the fastbreak and has made the steal his specialty. Jones was the first rookie to lead the NBA in steal-to-turnover ratio and finished among the top 10 in the league in steals in each of his four seasons.

But to fulfill his superstar potential, most agree that Jones needs to remain aggressive, play more consistently and assume more of a leadership role.

Or maybe he simply needs to spend more time listening to Rider pop off.

Jordan, Edward Montgomery "Fast Eddie" (1955-) ➤ In his seven-year pro career, Eddie Jordan averaged 8.1 points, 3.8 assists and 1.8 steals.

But during almost three full seasons with the Lakers in the early 1980s, he was a guard waiting for the few precious minutes of playing time still left after Magic Johnson, Norm Nixon, Michael Cooper and, on occasion, Mike McGee, had gotten their share.

Jordan's scoring average, which was in double figures in his two full seasons with the New Jersey Nets, dropped to single figures when he came to Los Angeles. His combined minutes for his two full seasons with the Lakers–941–were less than his minutes for any previous single season.

But occasionally, Jordan got enough playing time to show what he could do. In one game against the Clippers in San Diego, he scored 17 points, 13 in the final quarter, and added seven assists and four steals. He also was seven for seven from the field in one game at Kansas City.

But Jordan knew those moments would be few, that he simply didn't have the talent to crack the best starting lineup in the league.

Jordan, Reginald "Reggie" (1968-) ➤

The biggest pro basketball accomplishment of Jordan's life was making the Continental Basketball Assn. All-Star team– until early February 1994. For one 25-minute stretch, the rookie free agent struggling simply to remain on an NBA roster looked like Michael Jordan.

Reggie Jordan had been signed to a 10-day contract with the Lakers and was put in a game against the Utah Jazz at the Forum after guard Nick Van Exel got two fouls in the first three minutes.

Jordan electrified his teammates and the crowd of 11,777 by scoring 28 points in those 25 minutes after having previously played a total of 11 minutes for the Lakers.

"Yeah," he later acknowledged, "I surprised myself."

Of his new surroundings, Jordan said, "It is a real big change from the CBA. This is where you want to be all your life, since I was a kid. Then, it was like, 'I'm here, so I've got to fulfill my dream.' "

Jordan got a contract for the rest of the season and appeared in 23 games, averaging 5.4 points.

His NBA dream ended after that season, but he'll always have those 25 minutes.

June Bug ➤

Before he was Magic, before he was Buck, Earvin Johnson's nickname was June Bug. That was back when he was growing up in Lansing, Mich., a basketball nut who would dribble a ball almost all the time, whether he was on the way to the store to pick up something for his mother or on the way to the Main Street courts where he first developed some of the moves that would later dazzle the basketball world.

"There goes that crazy June Bug, hoopin' all day," people in Lansing would say. Johnson has said he's so glad the name didn't stick. It would be pretty tough to gain respect from opposing players after they heard the introduction of the point guard for the world champion Los Angeles Lakers, June Bug Johnson.

SEE ALSO • *E.J. the DeeJay; Johnson, Buck; Johnson, Earvin; Johnson, Magic; Stabley, Fred, Jr.*

Kerlan, Robert (1922-1996) ➤

Surgeon to the stars of the sports world, Kerlan was co-founder of the Kerlan-Jobe Orthopaedic Clinic. He and his staff took care of the medical needs of nearly all of Los Angeles-area teams, from the Lakers and Dodgers to the Kings and Angels. He even found time to work on the jockeys at Hollywood Park. Kerlan's patients ranged from the Dodgers' Sandy Koufax to the Rams' Merlin Olsen, from jockey Bill Shoemaker to Lakers Wilt Chamberlain, Elgin Baylor, Jerry West and Kareem Abdul-Jabbar.

Rheumatoid arthritis made it difficult for Kerlan to get around, especially in the latter stages of his life. He walked with great difficulty.

But that didn't keep him from attending sporting events. He was a fixture at Laker games and often traveled with the team in the playoffs. And he was nearly as competitive as the athletes he treated.

One night in Phoenix in the 1980 playoffs, he was at dinner with a group of Laker officials. As the evening was winding down, Kerlan looked at Bill Sharman, then the team's general manager, and said, "See you when you get back to the hotel." Sharman, a former member of the Brooklyn Dodgers and the Boston Celtics, a former Laker coach and a terrific competitor himself, said something to indicate that he'd already be at the hotel by the time Kerlan got there.

The gauntlet had been thrown.

And soon the two distinguished men, in their 50s, were racing their rental cars on the streets of Phoenix toward the hotel.

There was some debate as to who won that race, but there was no question that the competitiveness Kerlan often demonstrated also drove him as he established a medical practice that continues to serve the Lakers and many other Los Angeles teams. The Kerlan-Jobe Clinic is considered among the top sports medicine centers in the country.

Steve Lombardo, a Kerlan associate, became the Lakers' primary physician after Kerlan cut back on his practice.

When Magic Johnson learned in 1991 that he was HIV-positive, the diagnosis and subsequent care was handled by Michael Mellman, another Kerlan associate.

SEE ALSO • *Lombardo, Steve, Mellman, Michael*

Kersey, Jerome (1962-) ➤

When they signed the 6-foot-7, 222-pound Kersey for the 1996-97 season, the Lakers got a player with impressive numbers. In 11 seasons with the Portland Trail Blazers, he had become the second man in that franchise's history with more than 10,000 points and 5,000 rebounds, following Clyde Drexler. Unfortunately for the Lakers, they got Kersey when he was 34 and the days of the big numbers were behind him.

It also didn't help that he got off on the wrong foot. Literally.

Kersey fractured his left foot in the Lakers' season opener and missed nine games.

He was also involved in another mishap in mid-February. Kersey and teammate Robert Horry collided, causing Horry to sprain his right knee. That cost Horry 21 games.It wasn't all injuries and mishaps for Kersey. He got into 70 regular-season games for the Lakers, averaging 6.8 points and 5.2 rebounds.

The Lakers elected not to re-sign Kersey after acquiring Rick Fox in the off-season and Kersey returned to the Pacific Northwest, with the Seattle SuperSonics.

Keys, Randolph "Rudy" (1966-) ➤ When forward George Lynch suffered a stress fracture of the right foot at the end of February 1995, the Lakers, looking for help, came up with a first-round draft choice.

Unfortunately for them, it was Keys, who had been a first-round pick from Southern Mississippi by the Cleveland Cavaliers in 1988, but hadn't played like one. By the time the Lakers got Keys, he had spent the previous two seasons with Quad Cities in the Continental Basketball Assn.

Keys appeared in six games for the Lakers, getting 20 points and 17 rebounds over that span.

Killum, Earnest "Ernie" (1948-) ➤ Killum was a small-town kid who had some big moments in college but couldn't quite make it in the NBA.

A native of Clarksdale, Miss., the 6-foot-3, 185-pound Killum averaged 25.6 points for Stetson College in Deland, Fla., to lead his team to a 22-7 record in the 1969-70 season. His best game came in the NCAA college division playoffs when he scored 43 points against Georgia Southern.

Killum was picked by the Lakers in the second round of the 1970 draft, but he played in only four regular-season and two postseason games.

If he could have held on a little longer, Killum would have had a championship ring.

He was waived just before the 1971-72 season, when the Lakers won their first NBA title in Los Angeles.

King, Frankie Alexander (1972-) ➤ The pressure was on King's shoulders before he even put on a Laker uniform.

For one thing, he was the only player the Lakers took in the 1995 draft. For another, they had to give up two second-round draft choices to get that pick from the Washington Bullets.

And, with local favorite Tyus Edney available, the Lakers passed up the UCLA guard to take the 6-foot-2, 185-pound King, a guard from Western Carolina. Playing at a school with an enrollment of only 6,300, King finished second in the nation in scoring as a senior.

He was described by Duke assistant coach Tommy Amaker as "an explosive backcourt player who has an uncanny ability to score."

After selecting King with the 37th pick, Laker Vice President Jerry West said, "He's the player we want to take a chance on."

King didn't get much of a chance. After appearing in only six games for the Lakers, King was a casualty of the Shaquille O'Neal acquisition, another body cleared off the roster to make room for the giant center and his giant salary.

King, James Leonard "Jimmy," "Country" (1941-) ➤ Dick Klein, president of the newly formed Chicago Bulls in 1966, did a double-take when he looked over the list of players available to his team in the expansion draft.

There, from the Lakers, was guard Jimmy King.

"King is a better guard than some of the other fellows the Lakers have," Klein said. "He's definitely a front-line guard."

King's Laker numbers didn't reinforce that view. He had not averaged more than 7.5 points or 2.9 assists in his three years with the club. But Coach Fred Schaus, impressed by King's steady progress and a little thin at the guard position, had started him in the last five games of the 1966 NBA finals against the Boston Celtics.

Still, the Lakers weren't about to part with Jerry West, Gail Goodrich or Walt Hazzard in the backcourt. So they left King exposed, and the Bulls grabbed him. But before playing a game for Chicago, he was traded to the San Francisco Warriors where he averaged double figures in scoring in his first two seasons, fulfilling the potential Schaus had seen in him. He finally wound up in Chicago for his last three seasons, as a reserve guard averaging about five points a game.

Kleine, Joseph William "Joe" (1962-) ➤ When the Boston Celtics obtained Kleine in the 1988-89 season, a Boston columnist wrote that the theory about great players making everyone around them better was about to be tested. If Larry Bird could make Kleine a better player, the columnist said, then Bird was truly a superstar.

Despite such unflattering sentiments, in 1997 the Lakers were eager to be rid of Cedric Ceballos and anxious to obtain Robert Horry from the Phoenix Suns. So they took Kleine and gave up Rumeal Robinson, as well.

Kleine had attended Notre Dame and Arkansas, was a member of the gold medal-winning U.S. team in the 1984 Olympics and had been a first-round draft choice by the Sacramento Kings in 1985.

But by the time the Lakers got Kleine, whatever chance he had had to star in the NBA was past. He was 35 and part of the deal only for salary-cap maneuvering.

Kleine stayed with the team for a little more than a month, appeared in eight games and got a total of nine rebounds and six points before being traded to New Jersey for George McCloud.

Knight, Travis James (1974-) ➤ Choice? What choice?

In the summer of 1997, Knight could either sign a seven-year deal with the Boston Celtics for $22 million or remain with the Lakers and receive $326,000 for the 1997-98 season, the maximum the Lakers could pay under salary-cap restrictions.

Knight took the Boston offer, but it wasn't a slam dunk that he'd go that way.

"I really have mixed emotions," Knight said after making the decision. "I should be elated right now, but I'm not. I feel so much loyalty [to the Lakers]... . But you work at something as hard as you can, and then it's there. The security. That's the rest of my life right there. I think, without a question, this has been the hardest decision I've made in my life. It was much harder than choosing a college."

It wasn't so easy on the Lakers, either, although they did get something out of it. After securing Knight, the Celtics cut loose forward Rick Fox, who became a Laker.

The Lakers got Knight, a first-round pick of the Chicago Bulls in the 1996 draft, for the 1996-97 season for the rookie minimum of $220,000 after the Bulls renounced draft rights to him.

Knight soon proved to be a bargain for the Lakers, going from being the 12th man to being used as a starter in 14 games and in 71 overall. In one game, Knight, 7 feet and 235 pounds, pulled down 11 offensive rebounds, two short of the club record since its move to Los Angeles.

Knight averaged 16.3 minutes, 4.8 points and 4.5 rebounds while shooting 50.9% from the field.

And then, he chose to leave.

"My heart said one thing," Knight explained, "but my head said another."

Krebs, James "Jim" (1935-1965) ➤ Krebs spent his entire career with the Laker organization, playing in the team's final three seasons in Minneapolis and its first four in Los Angeles. A 6-foot-8, 230-pounder, Krebs had a modest career, averaging 8.0 points and 6.2 rebounds.

He retired at 28 as the Lakers underwent a rebuilding process that resulted in more playing time for younger players and less for him.

"I guess you could say I was a little bitter about that," he remarked at the time his career ended.

Less than 13 months later, on May 6, 1965, helping a neighbor cut down a tree near his Woodland Hills home, Krebs was killed when the tree fell on him.

He was 29.

Jim Krebs works on form during a practice session in the early 1960s.

Krystkowiak, Larry Brett "Special K" (1964-) ➤

It was Laker Coach Del Harris who saw something special in Krystkowiak.

After playing college ball at Montana, Krystkowiak blossomed under Harris at Milwaukee, enjoying his finest NBA season there in 1988-89 when he averaged 12.7 points and 7.6 rebounds.

Harris and Krystkowiak were reunited on the Lakers in the 1996-97 season. By then, Krystkowiak's career appeared over. He was 32, he hadn't been in the NBA in two years, having played in France in 1995-96, and he hadn't played at all in 1996-97.

But down to 11 players in February, Harris called Krystkowiak, and the 6-foot-9, 240-pound forward agreed to come on board.

Krystkowiak was nothing special this time, but he did provide an extra body in practice and appeared in three games for the Lakers.

Kupchak, Mitchell "Mitch" (1954-) ➤ Since the 1986-87 season, Kupchak has been in the Laker front office, working his way from assistant general manager to general manager. But he originally came to Los Angeles on a different mission: to get rebounds.

In 1981, after a three-year search for an effective power forward to replace Kermit Washington, the Lakers believed they had finally found one in Kupchak. Kupchak had learned the game under Dean Smith at North Carolina, then had gone to the Washington Bullets, where he could be depended on to score in double figures and get more than six rebounds a game.

In the summer of 1981, eager to give Kareem Abdul-Jabbar some help in the frontcourt, the Lakers traded Jim Chones, Brad Holland and first- and second-round draft choices to Washington for Kupchak.

Unfamiliar with the Showtime offense and gingerly trying to fit in on a roster loaded with big stars carrying big egos, Kupchak started slowly.

But he soon found his touch. On Nov. 20, 1981, against the San Antonio Spurs, Kupchak made 11 of 11 shots from the field.

On Dec. 19, he and his teammates were in San Diego to play the Clippers, who hadn't yet moved to L.A.

At breakfast the day of the game, Kupchak said, "I feel great. I slept well last night for the first time in weeks. I'm really relaxed with things now."

Kupchak wouldn't know another day of peace for a long time.

That night, he took a pass from Magic Johnson in the opening minutes of the second quarter, spotted a crack in the Clipper defense and took off for the basket. He never made it.

Instead, Kupchak tumbled to the floor. Without any contact, Kupchak's knee had simply given out like a balloon popping. Kupchak crashed into San Diego's Joe Bryant (father of future Laker Kobe Bryant) and rolled out of bounds, clutching the knee in agony.

Kupchak had a broken bone in his knee, a torn ligament and cartilage damage, the kind of injuries one might expect from a car accident, one doctor said. Kupchak was never the same player.

He limped back for three more seasons but never averaged more than six points or 3.5 rebounds.

His loss would eventually result in the emergence of Kurt Rambis.

And Kupchak would, of course, find a new life as an executive.

Kupec, Charles J. "C.J." (1953-) ➤ A severely sprained ankle limited Kupec to 16 games in his first Laker season. His ability limited him in his second.

Moving from forward to center, Kupec, considered an exceptional ballhandler and outside shooter for a big man, appeared in all 82 regular-season games of the 1976-77 season, but averaged only 4.7 points and 2.4 rebounds.

What the Lakers were hoping to see was the player who had led Michigan in scoring and rebounding on the way to a 19-8 record as a senior. In an NCAA tournament game, Kupec nearly derailed UCLA Coach John Wooden, who was on his way to his 10th and final NCAA championship. Kupec scored 28 points against UCLA in a regional game and nearly sank the game-winner in the closing seconds of regulation time. The Bruins won in overtime.

Kupec, a fourth-round draft pick, couldn't come close to his collegiate numbers at the pro level. He was cut after his second year with the team.

Lamar, Dwight "Bo" (1951-) ▶

Those who argued in the late 1970s that the American Basketball Assn. wasn't close to being the equal of the established NBA could point to Lamar as Exhibit A.

He had led the nation in scoring as a junior at Southwest Louisiana, averaging 36.3 points and was a bona-fide star in the ABA with the San Diego Conquistadors (later the Sails) and the Indiana Pacers. Lamar averaged 20.4 and 20.9 points in his first two seasons with San Diego. He once scored 55 points in a game, 28 in one quarter.

Then, before the 1976-77 season, the Lakers obtained Lamar from the Detroit Pistons. He appeared in 71 games for Los Angeles, averaging 7.1 points. In the playoffs, that average dropped to 3.3.

And then, Lamar dropped out altogether, his pro career over after a single season in the NBA.

Lamp, Jeffrey Alan "Jeff"

(1959-) ▶ Lamp's first season with the Lakers, his fifth in the league, was over almost before it began.

Having logged only seven minutes in three games, Lamp went up to try to block a shot by Benoit Benjamin, then the Clippers' 7-foot, 250-pound center, only to end up grabbing his own left shoulder.

Lamp was injured so badly that he required season-ending surgery.

In 37 games the next season, Lamp averaged only 1.6 points. The Lakers renounced their rights to Lamp before the start of the 1989-90 season.

Landsberger, Mark Walter

(1955-) ▶ One Laker coach says that when Landsberger joined the team in February 1980, he patiently listened while he was given a crash course on the team's offense.

When the session was done, Landsberger was asked if he had any questions. "Yeah," he replied, according to the coach, "do you have any plays where I can get rebounds?"

It was the first Landsberger story for the Lakers, but not the last.

After a shootaround on the road one morning, he decided to go to lunch, still wearing his uniform.

"Better not do that," trainer Jack Curran warned him. "I didn't bring any other uniforms along."

No problem, insisted Landsberger.

But at lunch, Landsberger spilled a chocolate shake on himself. He played that night with a brown streak running down the side of his uniform.

Asked for his autograph on one occasion by a young fan, Landsberger obligingly jotted it down.

The fan asked him to put his number beside it.

Landsberger wrote down his phone number.

But Landsberger's rebounding was no laughing matter.

In a seven-year career, during which he spent most of his time as a reserve, he averaged 6.1 rebounds per game. One season, he averaged a rebound every 2.98 minutes, the best total in the NBA that season among non-starting forwards.

But when the Lakers' power forward job opened up early in the 1981-82 season because of an injury to Mitch Kupchak, Landsberger failed to get the call because of his lack of offense. He never averaged more than 5.7 points in a full season as a Laker and had a disturbing habit of turning offensive rebounds into ill-advised shots that were often blocked.

But Landsberger remains the only Laker to add a dash of chocolate to the Laker purple and gold.

Lantz, Stuart Burrell "Stu"

(1946-) ➤ He came out of Nebraska to play eight seasons in the NBA, including 109 games with the Lakers in the final two seasons of his career.

But he is better known by many for the years after a back injury forced him to retire after the 1975-76 season. Lantz was a 6-foot-3, 180-pound guard, but the assists he handed out on the court were eventually overshadowed by the assistance he has given behind the microphone to his broadcasting partner, Chick Hearn.

In Lantz's first game as a Laker, after being obtained from the New Orleans Jazz for a second-round draft choice and cash on Dec. 6, 1974, he scored 26 points.

That proved to be an aberration. Lantz averaged 7.1 points in his brief time with the Lakers. But he did wind up third on the team's career list for free-throw percentage with an 84.9% mark.

Lantz's best season was 1970-71, when, as a member of the San Diego Rockets, he averaged 20.6 points and 5.0 rebounds.

Stu Lantz as a Lakers broadcaster in 1991.

He became Hearn's sidekick before the 1987-88 season and has been Hearn's partner longer than any of his six predecessors in that role.

Lantz found his own voice as an analyst and has made himself heard, no easy task next to a broadcasting giant.

LaRusso, Rudolph "Rudy"

(1937-) ➤ LaRusso looked like a power forward. Or an NHL defenseman. He had the tough face, and the body and mind to match.

He made his living underneath the basket, banging his way to rebound after rebound at a time when NBA referees seemed willing to let the games turn into battles of the fittest.

LaRusso, 6 feet 8 and 220 pounds, was right at home mixing it up with the toughest players in the league, though it occasionally had its drawbacks. In one exhibition game, LaRusso took a punch in the face from Woody Sauldsberry of the then-Philadelphia Warriors merely for guarding Sauldsberry too closely.

LaRusso averaged 9.4 rebounds over a 10-year career, and was a solid scorer. He was with the Lakers in their last season in Minneapolis and their first seven in Los Angeles, playing along side of both Elgin Baylor and Jerry West for all but one of those years.

Despite the competition for the ball, LaRusso averaged at least 12.3 points in each of his seasons with the Lakers and had a high of 17.2 points in 1961-62.

What would LaRusso have done without Baylor and West? LaRusso played for the San Francisco Warriors in his final two seasons. Although he was 30 by then, LaRusso averaged 21.8 points in his first year with San Francisco and 20.7 the next season.

Off the court, LaRusso's teammates saw a different, more playful face. Any Laker who ever walked through the airport in Detroit with LaRusso knew about that face.

There was a large, stuffed lion on display in that airport. And when the Lakers came through, LaRusso, who had gone to Dartmouth, would grab the lion and wrestle with it, rolling on the floor to the amazement and delight of his teammates.

LaRusso also once stuck a tie clasp with a silver ball on the end into an order of clams and stifled his laughter while some of his teammates believed they had discovered a pearl.

Lee, Alfred "Butch" (1956-) ➤ At first glance, it might appear the 1980 trade in which the Lakers acquired Lee was inconsequential. They traded forward Don Ford and a No. 1 pick to the Cleveland Cavaliers for Lee and Cleveland's top choice in 1982.

The most valuable player in the 1977 NCAA tournament with national champion Marquette, the 6-foot, 185-pound guard was a first-round draft pick of the Atlanta Hawks in 1978. After averaging 9.2 points in his first season, Lee had knee surgery and was never the same.

He played only 11 regular-season games for the Lakers, who released him after the season. But for the Lakers, the trade for Lee couldn't have worked out better. The Cavaliers finished last in the Eastern Conference in 1982, and with that No. 1 pick, the Lakers selected James Worthy.

Leonard, William Robert "Slick" (1932-) ➤ He was a perfect match for Hot Rod Hundley, his close companion both in the backcourt and off the court.

They played together on the Minneapolis and L.A. Laker teams, they ran together, they broke curfew together and they got fined together.

In six pro seasons, Hundley averaged 8.4 points, shot 34.7% from the field and averaged 3.4 assists. In seven seasons, Leonard averaged 9.9 points, shot 34.9% from the field and averaged 3.3 assists.

And between them, Leonard and Hundley had enough late-night adventures to turn the most easy-going coach into an insomniac.

One of the stories Leonard's former teammates tell about him—of those they are willing to tell—has to do with a night on the road when he couldn't be awakened. Leonard was in such a deep sleep his snoring was not only driving Hundley, his roommate, crazy, but also Elgin Baylor in the next room.

Finally, Baylor and Hundley wheeled Leonard's bed into the hallway, without disturbing Leonard.

Still Leonard slept.

The Lakers got up in the morning, packed and prepared to board the bus for the airport.

Still Leonard slept.

Baylor and Hundley, giggling, tiptoed around their teammate as they headed down the hallway.

But when the Laker bus pulled up at the airport, there was Leonard, pulling up at the same time. He had awakened just in time, made a fastbreak from the hotel, found a cab and got to the airport in time to catch the flight and avoid a fine.

If he could have moved that fast on the court, he would have been a superstar.

Lester, Ronnie (1959-) ➤ Lester came out of the University of Iowa as a big name with big promise. An All-American, he left the school as its all-time leading scorer. But the promise was never realized in an injury-plagued professional career.

Lester was selected by the Portland Trail Blazers with the 10th selection of the 1980 NBA draft, then was traded on draft day to his hometown team, the Chicago Bulls. He enjoyed his best pro year with Chicago in 1981-82, averaging 11.6 points and 4.8 assists.

He spent the final two seasons of his career with the Lakers. He played in only 59 games for them in that two-year span, but he got to be part of one of the great moments in team history, the first championship-round victory over the Lakers' longtime tormentors, the Boston Celtics, in the 1985 NBA Finals.

Lester's career ended after the 1985-86 season, but his connection with the Lakers was only beginning. He went on to become a team scout, focusing on the Midwest, and he has remained in that position.

Liebich, Mary Lou ➤ She has never scored a basket, grabbed a rebound or blocked a shot.

Yet without her, the Lakers might have struggled a lot more than they have over the last quarter-century.

Not on the court, but everywhere else.

Whether it's getting an airline reservation, obtaining housing for a rookie, jotting down an important call from an opposing general manager or checking on the details of running a summer-league team, Liebich, the team's administrative assistant, is there to do whatever is necessary.

Lombardo, Dr. Steve ➤ A Laker physician since the mid-1970s, Lombardo has been about as up close and personal to the team's great stars as one can get.

He has operated on Magic Johnson's knee and has assured Shaquille O'Neal that a long needle required to deaden the pain of a cut around the center's eye would not pierce his eyeball.

Known for his surgical skills and cool demeanor, Lombardo is usually a voice of reason, but even he has his moments.

During one NBA Finals game between the Lakers and Celtics in Boston Garden, Lombardo and fellow doctor Robert Kerlan were incensed about a call made against the Lakers by referee Earl Strom.

As both men voiced their displeasure about the call, Kerlan, who required crutches for an arthritic condition, accidentally let one of the crutches slip out of his hand. It sailed through the air and, landing on its rubber tip, bounced to the free-throw line.

Now it was Strom's turn to be angry. He came over to the two physicians and said to Kerlan, "I can't believe you did that."

To which Kerlan replied, "I can't believe you made that call."

So what was it like operating on Johnson's knee, knowing that a mistake could have ruined one of the great careers in NBA history?

"That thought goes into it," Lombardo said. "The stature of the person may be different and so there are a lot of eyes on you. But you're trained to do your job and so all that other stuff doesn't impact you that much."

Love, Stanley S. "Stan" (1949-) ➤ After playing at Morningside High down the street from the Forum, Love took a circuitous route to get back to Inglewood.

First, he went to the University of Oregon, where, after three seasons, he was the school's all-time leading scorer. Then, he went to the Baltimore Bullets, who made him a first-round draft choice in 1971.

Finally, Love returned to Inglewood when the Lakers obtained him from Baltimore before the 1973-74 season for a second-round draft choice and cash.

He lasted only a season and a half with the Lakers,

but, if nothing else, he had his own personal all-star weekend in November of his first year with the club.

If appeared as if it was going to be a rough weekend for the Lakers. They had three games in three nights, Chicago and Cleveland at home with a road game against Phoenix in between, and they had to play them without Jerry West and Bill Bridges, who were injured.

Enter Love, who:

• Scored eight points in 16 minutes against the Bulls.

• Scored 18 points, 16 in the fourth quarter, against the Suns while playing center and forward after center Elmore Smith was kicked out nine minutes into the game.

• Scored 12 more points against the Cavaliers as the Lakers completed a weekend sweep.

For the three games, Love averaged 12.7 points (he never averaged double figures in scoring for a season) and shot 55.2% from the field (he never finished a season over 50%).

Unfortunately for Love, rather than a glimpse of things to come, the weekend turned out to be an aberration, a glimpse of what would never be.

Lowest Score ➤ With such players as Wilt Chamberlain, Kareem Abdul-Jabbar, Elgin Baylor and Jerry West having worn the purple and gold, it's no surprise the Lakers have had some of the great offensive clubs in league history.

But on Nov. 22, 1950, the Minneapolis Lakers and Fort Wayne Pistons produced the lowest-scoring game in NBA history.

The Pistons, outscoring the Lakers, 3-1, in the fourth quarter, won the game at Minneapolis, 19-18. Laker center George Mikan, a three-time league scoring champion, had 15 of the Lakers' 18 points.

Guard John Oldham was the Pistons' top scorer with five points. Among the players for Fort Wayne that night was forward Fred Schaus, who would become the Lakers' first coach in Los Angeles.

The NBA-recognized record for lowest-scoring game was the 119 points in Boston's 62-57 victory over Milwaukee on Feb. 27, 1955.

Records for "fewest" and "lowest" do not include games before the 1954-55 season, when the NBA began using the 24-second shot clock.

Lucas, Maurice "Luke" (1952-) ➤

The scowl helped keep Lucas in professional basketball for 14 seasons.

Beyond the points and the rebounds, the scowl helped him to be an intimidator.

Away from the game, many were surprised to find him very pleasant. But Lucas put that scowl on his face as sure as he put on his uniform before every game. He was not to be trifled with.

His first two professional seasons were spent in the American Basketball Assn., with the St. Louis Spirits and the Kentucky Colonels. He spent 12 years in the NBA with six teams, including the Lakers in 1985-86.

Lucas posted double-digit scoring averages in all but his final two seasons and averaged 9.1 rebounds for his career.

But some of his best work was as a force who could handle opposing rebounders, high scorers and troublemakers with his physical presence, his sometimes underrated skills and, when necessary, his strong-arm tactics.

Lynch, George DeWitt III (1970-) ➤

Lynch and Anthony Peeler were the first two casualties of the Shaquille O'Neal era. Both were jettisoned by the Lakers on July 16, 1996 to free up money for O'Neal, the dominating center who was signed two days later.

The Lakers parted with Lynch and Peeler for next to nothing, sending them to the Vancouver Grizzlies for the right to exchange second-round draft picks in 1998 and '99.

Never mind Peeler. That's not much simply for Lynch, who was the Lakers' first-round draft pick, 12th overall, in 1993.

But Lynch, who had played at North Carolina, never lived up to the accomplishments of previous Laker Tar Heels such as James Worthy, Mitch Kupchak and Bob McAdoo.

Such expectations were not realistic. Lynch is a defensive specialist. The 9.6 points and 5.8 rebounds he averaged in his first season with the Lakers were the best of his three-year stay.

The problem was Lynch wasn't a natural power forward. And he didn't have the quickness to defend other small forwards in the league.

So he and his $2.09-million contract wound up as an offering to appease O'Neal, the looming giant on the horizon.

Lynn, Michael Edward "Mike" (1945-) ➤

Lynn made a name for himself in the Los Angeles area, but it was in Westwood rather than Inglewood.

An All-Southern Section player at Covina High, the 6-foot-7, 215-pounder arrived at UCLA just in time for the start of Coach John Wooden's incredible run of 10 NCAA championships.

Freshmen couldn't play varsity ball in those days, but Lynn made the Bruins' starting lineup as a sophomore on a team that went 28-2 and won the 1965 NCAA championship. As a senior, he was a starter on a UCLA team that won 29 of 30 and another NCAA title.

Lynn spent a season playing in Italy, then returned to Southern California when the Lakers bought his contract from the Chicago Bulls before the 1969-70 season. It was, however, a less than spectacular return. Lynn appeared in 44 games in his only season as a Laker, averaging 2.7 points and 1.5 rebounds.

The Buffalo Braves took Lynn in the 1970 expansion draft, but he played in only five games with the Braves before his NBA career ended.

M

Mack, Oliver "O" (1957-) ➤ His Laker career consisted of 27 games in the 1979-80 season, over which he averaged 1.9 points.

Although he was gone three months before the Lakers won the NBA championship in six games from the Philadelphia 76ers, Mack still contributed indirectly to that title. It was his trade to the Chicago Bulls on Feb. 14, 1980 that brought Mark Landsberger, a man who proved to be a clutch rebounder in big games for the Lakers. From Chicago, Mack went on to Dallas, where his NBA career ended after three seasons.

Mack's greatest moments on the court were as a junior at East Carolina in 1977-78, when he was the fourth-leading scorer in the nation with a 28-point average. Mack, the first player ever selected from his school in the NBA draft, was picked in the second round by the Lakers.

SEE ALSO • *Landsberger, Mark.*

Mariani, Frank (1934-) ➤ Few people know who Mariani is, and that's the way he likes it.

A partner of Jerry Buss' in the real-estate business, Mariani played a key, behind-the-scenes role in putting together the complex deal that enabled Buss to buy Jack Kent Cooke's sports empire, which included the Lakers.

Mariani wants to be as far from the spotlight as he can get. His genius is his marketing ability which keeps the Lakers and the Forum in the spotlight.

Mariani was there from the beginning. He and Buss worked together as aerospace engineers at the Douglas Aircraft Co. where they dreamed of saving part of their paychecks and using that money to build a fortune.

Mariani and Buss decided that their path to riches lay in real estate. They formed a partnership with several others and bought apartment buildings.

And to save money in the early days, Buss and Mariani even did the repairs on the buildings by themselves, although being handymen was hardly their forte.

On one occasion, stuck in the middle of the night trying to repair a hole in the wall of one of those buildings, Buss and Mariani were stumped. What would they fill the hole with?

They were tired and were facing a long day ahead at Douglas.

What to do?

Buss took off his dirty T-shirt, wadded it into a ball, put it in the hole and the two plastered over it.

Needless to say, their future didn't lie in construction. They stuck with buying buildings and real estate and were successful enough at it to build a financial empire.

But when the chance for fame came along with the fortune, Mariani chose a more private role.

SEE ALSO • *Buss, Jerry.*

Matthews, Wes Joel (1959-) ➤ Matthews excelled at one of the most difficult jobs in the NBA.

As a reserve with the Lakers, he knew it would take an injury to one of the starters to put him in the opening lineup. But Matthews learned to make his contributions either from the bench or during practice, where he worked hard against the starters to help keep them sharp.

During his eight-season career, Matthews averaged 20 minutes a game, but only 12.3 minutes in his two seasons with the Lakers.

"A lot of guys who don't play are not into it," Laker trainer Gary Vitti said. "But Wes was totally focused. He might not play for five games, but he could tell you, without looking at the stat sheet, exactly how many points, rebounds and assists everybody on the team had, what plays we were running, and what plays the other team was running."

Matthews earned two championship rings with the Lakers, in 1986-87 and 1987-88.

SEE ALSO • *Vitti, Gary.*

McAdoo, Robert Allen, Jr. "Doo" (1951-) ➤ Bob McAdoo once lost a game of table tennis to a sportswriter on a Laker trip.

McAdoo then bought a ping-pong table and practiced for a year. When the team returned to the hotel where McAdoo had lost the year before, he got a rematch with the sportswriter and avenged his defeat.

That probably says more about McAdoo than a page of statistics. He led the league in scoring three consecutive seasons, from 1973-1974 to 1975-76. He was the NBA's most valuable player in 1974-75 with the Buffalo Braves, the team that eventually became the Los Angeles Clippers, and was rookie of the year in 1972-73. McAdoo was so competitive there was no such thing as a casual defeat for him.

On Laker flights, he would boast to his teammates about how he could beat them in everything from baseball to tennis.

When he was once asked how good a bowler he was, and McAdoo replied that this was a sport he didn't participate in, his teammates yelled in chorus, "Doo don't bowl?"

To which he quickly responded, "But give me a week and I'll bowl 300."

It was that competitive spirit that intrigued Laker Coach Pat Riley in December 1981 when he was looking for another frontcourt player after a knee injury prematurely ended Mitch Kupchak's season.

But by the time he arrived in Los Angeles, McAdoo was 30, had been with five teams in eight seasons and some were questioning his attitude. He had been a big disappointment in Boston at the end of the 1978-79 season.

But as it turned out, what McAdoo needed was a team with a winning attitude to boost his own.

He became a valuable reserve for the Lakers in the four seasons he was with them. The team reached the NBA finals in each of those seasons and won two titles. And McAdoo was a big part of those.

He didn't score as he had in his first seven seasons, but he didn't need to on the Lakers. He gave them the kind of depth they needed to be one of the NBA's premier teams.

McAdoo was successful at everything the Lakers asked him to do, even if he never was challenged to bowl.

McCarter, Willie J. (1946-) ➤ McCarter led Drake to an unexpected third-place finish in the 1969 NCAA tournament, then was taken in the first round, 12th overall, by the Lakers in the NBA draft.

The 6-foot-3, 175-pound guard scored 16 and 28 points in two summer rookie games against the San Diego Rockets, but the promise of his first NBA season was put on hold when he suffered torn ligaments in his right ankle.

He played in only 40 games in the 1969-70 season, shooting a dismal 37.8% from the field and averaging 7.7 points and 2.3 assists.

His second season wasn't any better, averaging 7.1 points and 1.7 assists. The Lakers waived McCarter, who played one more season with the Portland Trail Blazers.

McCloud, George Aaron (1967-) ➤ McCloud went from a lottery pick, chosen No. 7 in the 1989 draft by the Indiana Pacers, to Italy to Rapid City of the Continental Basketball Assn.

Most players who suffer such a fall don't get up.

But McCloud not only made it back to the NBA, he became a starter as well.

Signed to a 10-day contract by the Dallas Mavericks in February 1995 after two seasons out of the NBA, he worked his way into their lineup after Jamal Mashburn suffered a knee injury.

Then in 1995-96, McCloud averaged 18.9 points in

79 games for the Mavericks.

At 6 feet 8 and 215 pounds, he was big enough to play in the frontcourt, but a good enough shooter, especially from three-point range, and ballhandler to operate from the backcourt.

The Lakers got McCloud cheaply enough in February 1997, trading 12th man Joe Kleine and a couple of draft picks to New Jersey for him shortly after the Mavericks had dealt him to the Nets. The Lakers hoped he could provide some needed outside shooting.

"To be put in this situation is really a blessing," McCloud said.

But it was a situation McCloud failed to take advantage of. In 23 games with the Lakers, he made only 35.4% of his shots and averaged 4.1 points.

When Shaquille O'Neal returned from a knee injury in April, McCloud was put on the injured list to make room for the center. He signed with the Phoenix Suns as a free agent the following fall.

McDaniels, James Ronald "Jim" (1948-) ▶ Although he was 6 feet 11 and weighed 230 pounds, McDaniels had problems with two areas of the game: defense and rebounding.

He couldn't use lack of coaching as an excuse. While he was a member of the Seattle SuperSonics, McDaniels was coached by Bill Russell, the Hall of Famer and longtime Boston Celtic who knew a thing or two about defense and rebounding. After wearing out his welcome with Russell, McDaniels played in Italy and for the Kentucky Colonels of the American Basketball Assn., before asking the Lakers for a tryout.

With both Kermit Washington and Stu Lantz injured and Gail Goodrich a holdout, the Lakers gave McDaniels a chance in the 1975-76 season. He didn't make much of it, averaging 2.6 points and 2.1 rebounds in 35 games. On Feb. 3, 1976, the Lakers waived him.

McGee, Michael Ray "Geeter" (1959-) ▶ McGee was the Lakers' top draft choice in 1981 after leaving Michigan as the Big Ten's all-time scoring leader.

But professional basketball was another matter.

In five years with the Lakers, McGee averaged double figures in scoring only once, averaging 10.2 points in 76 games in 1984-85.

McGee joined the Lakers at a time when breaking into the starting lineup at guard meant beating out Magic Johnson and Norm Nixon.

After Nixon left, there was Byron Scott to deal with.

And there was Michael Cooper, a swingman who also didn't start, but was the first man off the bench.

McGee, a shooting guard, never seemed to blend into the fast-moving Showtime offense, one that required an intimate knowledge of the offense and the players who ran it.

On one occasion in the 1982-83 season, Coach Pat Riley, frustrated that McGee was struggling to learn the offense, walked off the court after a practice, saying, "I keep calling, 'Mike McGee! Mike McGee!' But there's never anybody home."

McGee, turning around in surprise, said, "I was home all day, Coach. What time did you call?"

McGill, Bill "the Hill" (1939-) ▶ McGill was a star at Los Angeles' Jefferson High School, a two-time All-American at Utah, credited with being one of the first to use a jump hook shot and a first-round draft choice of the Chicago Zephyrs. But he had only one year in the NBA in which he averaged in double figures.

McGill, who had single-game highs of 60 points and 24 rebounds at Utah and once averaged 29.8 points over four games of an NCAA tournament, averaged 15.1 points in 1963-64, a season he split between the Baltimore Bullets and the New York Knicks.

A knee injury limited McGill's mobility in the pros.

The Lakers bought him from Grand Rapids of the North American League, but McGill lasted only eight games with them in the 1964-65 season, getting a total of 15 points and a dozen rebounds.

He finished his career in the American Basketball Assn., then experienced some hard times. Looking for work, he was homeless for a while before taking a job in the aerospace industry. After a 23-year career in that field, in 1995, he was laid off and again faced difficult financial times, particularly because he had played only three seasons in the NBA, one short of qualifying for a pension.

McKenna, Kevin Robert
(1959-) ➤ McKenna, a 6-foot-5, 195-pounder from Creighton, spent only one of his six seasons in the NBA with the Lakers.

Picked by the Lakers with the 88th choice in the 1981 draft, he played in only 36 games his first year and averaged 1.9 points, but he contributed to an NBA championship for the Lakers.

In a home game early in the 1981-82 season, with the Lakers struggling under Coach Paul Westhead's new offense, the team trailed the Indiana Pacers by two points with 33 seconds to play in the second overtime.

McKenna was in the game, but he wasn't the first option to take a shot. Or the second.

But with everyone else covered, he got the ball and put up a shot from 18 feet. It banked in for the tying basket, and the Lakers won, 124-123, on a free throw by Kareem Abdul-Jabbar.

McKinney, Jack (1935-) ➤ For McKinney, it was the job of a lifetime. For the Lakers, he seemed to be the ideal coach for Showtime.

And indeed, it was the system installed by Jack McKinney during his few months in command that served the Lakers so well through the glory years in the 1980s. Yes, Paul Westhead tinkered with it. And Pat Riley changed it to meet the needs of new players and new responses by the opposition.

But it was basically the same system designed by McKinney, a system that stressed a running game triggered by an aggressive defense and superlative rebounding, and propelled by sharp passing and quick ball movement.

McKinney learned basketball in Pennsylvania, where he played high school and college ball. He became a head coach first in high school, then at Philadelphia Textile and St. Joseph's.

But, most of all, he learned his basketball from his mentor, Jack Ramsay. McKinney played under Ramsay at St. Joseph's, then coached for him as an assistant at St. Joseph's and later in the NBA with the Portland Trail Blazers. McKinney also spent two seasons as an assistant with the Milwaukee Bucks, which gave him an opportunity to get to know their center–Kareem Abdul-

Jack McKinney intently watches the action during a 1981 game.

Jabbar.

That relationship gave McKinney a boost when Laker owner Jerry Buss and his chief lieutenants, Bill Sharman and Jerry West, were looking for a coach to replace West, who had grown disenchanted with the day-to-day demands of the job.

No coach during the Abdul-Jabbar era could succeed without the backing of the Laker center. All systems, all game plans started with Abdul-Jabbar. If he wasn't on board, the ship wasn't sailing.

Hired by the Lakers for the 1979-80 season, McKinney knew he had the ignition switch for his running machine in the team's top draft choice, Magic Johnson. But, if the Lakers were going to base their offense around a running game led by Johnson, everybody was going to have to run. Including Abdul-Jabbar.

"I'll run," he told McKinney.

The Lakers were off and running early in that season,

winning nine of their first 13 games.

But just as McKinney seemed to be turning his dream job into a dream season, it was all taken away from him.

Riding a bicycle to meet Westhead, his assistant coach and longtime friend, for a game of tennis, McKinney was thrown off the bike as he went down a steep hill. He suffered a severe concussion, a broken cheekbone and elbow, and numerous cuts and bruises.

Westhead took over, temporarily, it was thought at first. "I'm a substitute teacher," he said. "Once you go into the classroom, you have to teach. Sometimes it's just for a day and sometimes it's for a whole year."

It turned out to be for a whole year. Westhead led the Lakers to the 1980 NBA title. In the meantime, McKinney struggled to regain his health. But his mind was slow to recover from the damage caused by his fall on the asphalt.

At one game that season, while trying to convince Buss he was ready to take his job back, McKinney walked past the Laker owner without acknowledging him.

It turned out that McKinney hadn't recognized the man who had hired him. When the season was over, Buss, forced to choose between a man who had just won him a title and a man he feared might never again be the same coach he had been, offered Westhead the job on a full-time basis.

Westhead hesitated. McKinney was one of his best friends, the man who had always watched out for him, who had gotten him several great coaching assignments, who had brought him along to Los Angeles.

"Jack will not be the coach of this team," Buss told Westhead. "Do you want the job now that we know Jack isn't going to be the coach ... or do we get somebody else?"

Westhead decided to take the job. He signed a four-year deal worth about a million dollars.

McKinney was bitter, and that caused friction between the McKinneys and the Westheads, two families that had once been so close.

"They can't share our joys," said Cassie Westhead, Paul's wife, "and we can't share their sorrows."

McKinney recovered sufficiently to go on and coach the Indiana Pacers for four seasons and Kansas City Kings for nine games.

Those teams, lacking the talent of the Lakers, never won more than 44 games.

SEE ALSO • *Bicycle; Buss, Jerry; Carter, Ron; Westhead, Paul.*

McMillian, James M. "Jim" (1948-) ➤ Not many players in Laker history have faced a bigger challenge. McMillian was a 6-foot-5, 225-pound forward from Columbia who was content to be the understudy of Elgin Baylor, learning his trade in the shadows of such great players as Wilt Chamberlain, Jerry West and, of course, Baylor.

But he discovered he had a much bigger role his first year with the Lakers, 1970-71. Baylor played only two games that season because of injury, and McMillian played in 81, averaging 8.4 points and 4.1 rebounds in 21.6 minutes a game. Then nine games into the 1971-72 season, Baylor, aware that at 37 he was unable to perform at anywhere near the superstar level he had, retired. McMillian was now being counted on to replace one of the greatest players in Laker history.

"I knew what Elgin Baylor meant to the game," McMillian said. "And I knew that wasn't me. But it wasn't like they depended on me."

They did depend on him for his defense, which was an area in which he excelled. But they got some offense too.

Jim McMillian in mid-shot during a 1972 game.

With his minutes increased to 38.1 per game in the 1971-72 season, McMillian averaged 18.8 points and 6.5 rebounds, a significant contributor on one of the greatest teams in NBA history. That team won a record 33 games in a row, finished 69-13 and beat the New York Knicks in five games to win the first Laker title since the team had moved to Los Angeles.

McMillian wound up playing three seasons in Los Angeles before being traded to Buffalo for Elmore Smith. He played nine seasons in the NBA, finishing up with the Portland Trail Blazers in 1978-79.

McNamara, Mark Robert

(1959-) ➤ It takes more than talent and a sense of timing to sit on an NBA bench. It takes the proper frame of mind.

Some sit there with great anticipation, convinced that all they need is a few minutes on the court to show that they belong in the starting lineup.

Some sit there in despair, knowing in their hearts that they will never be a starter.

And there are some who accept their limited role and take pride in it.

In the 1987-88 season, the 6-foot-11, 235-pound McNamara had started 18 straight games for the Philadelphia 76ers. But after signing with the Lakers for the 1988-89 season, he knew he wouldn't even be the first or second man off the bench. Never having averaged more than 5.5 points or 4.5 rebounds in five years in the league, he realized his limitations.

"People say to you, it's got to be hard to be in that position," McNamara said of the role as 11th or 12th man, "but that's what I do. I realize I'm not going to go in there and rock the house, but I might grab a few rebounds and, more important, not make a mistake and break our momentum.

"You have to prepare to play at all times, but you can't be obsessed about it. The key for me is if the coaches think I'm contributing. I'm still here, so ... "

He stayed with the Lakers one more season before being traded to San Antonio for future considerations.

McNeill, Robert J. "Bob" (1938-) ➤ McNeill played only 50 games for the Lakers in the 1961-62 season. He

averaged only 2.9 points.

But he got a chance to realize his dreams in basketball. He got a chance to be an All-Big Five point guard at St. Joseph's under Coach Jack Ramsay. He got a chance to play in the NBA for two seasons, under Fred Schaus during his time with the Lakers. And he got that chance because of his high school coach at Philadelphia's Northeast Catholic High School.

McNeill was a star on Edward P. Scullin's 1956 team, which won a city championship.

But McNeill was so eager to play basketball that he was also competing in a recreation league under an phony name.

"You're throwing away a college education by playing in this [rec] league, and you ought to think about it," Scullin told McNeill.

McNeill realized if he was caught playing on that second team, he would be thrown off the Northeast squad.

So he quit his rec league.

"Ed Scullin built the foundation that helped me be a success in college," McNeill said. "Without Ed Scullin, I might not have gotten there."

Or to the Lakers.

Meely, Cliff (1947-) ➤ Meely went from the University of Colorado to the Houston Rockets to the Lakers.

He went from being one of the greatest to play at his college to being a first-round draft pick of the Rockets to being a seldom-used reserve with the Lakers.

After spending $4\frac{1}{2}$ seasons with the Rockets, Meely, a free agent, signed with the Lakers in January 1976, appearing in 20 games. After averaging 3.2 points and 2.3 rebounds, he was waived and played a couple of seasons in Europe.

But Meely had trouble adapting after his basketball career. He became a guard at a jail, developed a cocaine addiction and at 37 was arrested for possession of cocaine and selling the drug to an undercover officer in Boulder, Colo.

He was sentenced to three months in jail and three years' probation.

Menmotum ➤ This was a phrase made up by Laker coach Pat Riley to describe a downhill slide by a team. Playing off the word momentum, Riley would tell his club when it was struggling that it was suffering from menmotum.

That got a laugh. It got his team's attention. And once Riley had that, he could go to work at trying to solve the problems.

SEE ALSO • *Riley, Pat.*

Michaels, Al (1946-) ➤ He is one of the most recognizable and talented sportscasters in the nation, known for everything from "Monday Night Football" to his "Do you believe in miracles?" call in the 1980 Winter Olympics.

Less well known is one of Michaels' early broadcasting jobs. In 1964-65, he was the first analyst assigned to work on Laker broadcasts with Chick Hearn.

But Michaels soon moved out of Hearn's shadow to become a star in his own right.

SEE ALSO • *Hearn, Chick.*

Mikkelsen, Arild Verner "Vern" (1928-) ➤ There are no surprises among the first four names on the Lakers' all-time rebounding list: No. 1 is Elgin Baylor with 11,463, followed by Kareem Abdul-Jabbar with 10,279, Magic Johnson with 6,559 and Wilt Chamberlain with 6,524. But the No. 5 player on the list is one fans never even saw play in Los Angeles.

In a 10-year career, from the 1949-50 season through 1958-59, Vern Mikkelsen was credited with 5,940 rebounds, ahead of such players as James Worthy and Happy Hairston. And that total did not include rebounds from the 1949-50 season, one season before the statistic was officially kept.

Mikkelsen, an especially physical player who averaged 14.4 points and about 8.5 rebounds a game in his career, holds an NBA record of less distinction. He fouled out of games a record 127 times, more than any other player. It's a record that hasn't been broken in the four decades since he retired the year before the Lakers moved from Minneapolis to Los Angeles. And Mikkelsen's disqualification total does not include any from his first season, a year before the NBA began compiling the statistic.

A 6-foot-7, 230-pound forward/center, he twice led the Lakers in scoring, averaging 18.7 points in 1954-55, and 17.3 in 1957-58.

Miller, Anthony "Pig" (1971-) ➤ Miller said he didn't mind being called Pig. What he minded was the reason behind the name—his eating habits.

He was given the unflattering tag by a cousin when he was a youngster because of a weight problem, and, like the nickname, the problem carried over into adulthood. The extra pounds didn't stop Miller from playing at Michigan State or being picked in the second round of the 1994 NBA draft by the Golden State Warriors.

Twenty-four hours after they had selected Miller, all 6 feet 9 and 275 pounds of him, the Warriors sent him to the Lakers.

He played two seasons for the Lakers, appearing in 73 games, averaging 3.1 points and 2.4 rebounds.

Miller was one of the players cleared off the Laker roster in July 1996 to make room for the arrival of Shaquille O'Neal.

Miller became determined to shed the weight and the pig image

"I feel I let myself down," he said. "I've got to come back and work harder and show I'm capable of playing at this level."

So, while playing in Italy in the 1996-97 season, Miller lost 20 pounds and earned himself a trip back to the NBA, where he played for the Atlanta Hawks in 1997-98.

Milwaukee Bucks' winning streak ➤ The Lakers won 33 consecutive games in 1971-72, the longest team winning streak in professional sports history.

Who has the second-longest winning streak in NBA history? The Milwaukee Bucks, who won 20 in a row during the 1970-71 season. Their center? Kareem Abdul-Jabbar.

It was Abdul-Jabbar's Bucks who ended the Laker streak, 120-104, Jan. 9, 1972 at Milwaukee.

Mix, Steven Charles "Steve" (1947-) ➤

Mix offered a blend of outside shooting and inside muscle.

But toward the end of his 14th year in professional basketball, one season in the American Basketball Assn. and the rest in the NBA, Mix was running out of offers. He had spent nine seasons with the Philadelphia 76ers, but, in his final season there, he had been used in only seven of Philadelphia's 21 postseason games.

So, at the start of the 1982-83 season, he went to Milwaukee. But there he clashed with management over his role in a threatened players' strike and was unhappy with his playing time.

When the Bucks wanted to activate center Dave Cowens, Mix was waived and the Lakers picked him up.

"I think I can still play," he said. "I can help somebody ... . I had 13 good years [in the NBA]. If I get a 14th, fine. If I retire after 13, that's also fine."

Mix retired after getting into only one game for the Lakers.

Not much could be said for his timing. When the Lakers beat Philadelphia in the 1982 finals, Mix was on the losing side. When Philadelphia won the rematch in 1983, Mix was again on the losing side.

Mohs, Louis R. (1897-1967) ➤

There was Bob Short and there was Fred Schaus and there were Elgin Baylor and Jerry West.

But without Mohs, the Lakers might not have been able to keep their foothold in Southern California.

Mohs, who had previously worked in the newspaper business in promotion, advertising and circulation, was picked by Short to be the Lakers' first general manager in Los Angeles. Mohs served in the post from 1960 to 1967, building a supporting cast around Baylor and West that enabled the Lakers to reach the NBA finals four times in those seven years.

Mohs might not have received the credit he deserved, but that was nothing new to him.

Mohs bragged to his players that he had received letters in seven sports in college and drew nothing but laughter until he finally brought in documentation. He talked about how he had played football at the University of Minnesota with Bronko Nagurski, earning raised

eyebrows and skepticism until he brought in newspaper clippings as proof.

"He was a funny, entertaining guy," Baylor said. "One time, he told me that, as a young man, he had been hired to work in a rock quarry. He said, 'I did so much work, they got rid of two of their mules.' "

As part of the old-time sports establishment, Mohs had only contempt for the sports agent, still a radical concept when Mohs went to work for the Lakers.

When one player brought in his agent to talk about his contract, Mohs left the room and returned with the team's attorney.

"You two talk together," Mohs told the attorney and the agent, "and when you're done, let me know and I'll get this finished. Because neither one of you knows a thing about basketball."

Most, Johnny ➤

The Boston Celtics' play-by-play announcer for more than a quarter of a century, Most never made much of an effort to hide his love for the Celtics. Which meant, of course, that he had no fondness for the Lakers. In fact he openly rooted against the Lakers.

In one game during the 1985 finals between the Lakers and Celtics, Most thought Magic Johnson was complaining too much about a referee's call.

So Most started calling him "Crybaby Johnson." Then he dropped the Johnson part.

And for the rest of of that broadcast, Most referred to the star guard only as "Crybaby."

As in "Crybaby dribbles to the top of the key," or "Crybaby dishes out a no-look pass."

When it came to the Celtics, Most saw it only one way, and made no apologies about it.

Most regrettable news conference ➤

It was a rare news conference in which members of the media were deeply moved, trying to see their notes and focus their cameras through tears.

It was a moment of shock and dismay at the Forum. Magic Johnson, seemingly the epitome of health and exuberance, was standing before them and a stunned world on the afternoon of November 7, 1991, announcing his retirement from basketball because he had tested positive for the HIV virus.

It was a time when most people, many reporters included, had only a vague knowledge of AIDS. Many

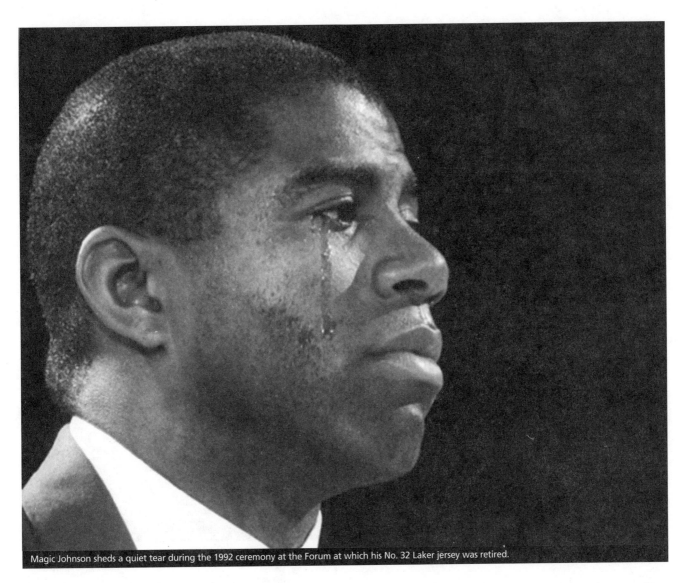

Magic Johnson sheds a quiet tear during the 1992 ceremony at the Forum at which his No. 32 Laker jersey was retired.

didn't understand the difference between being HIV positive and having full-blown AIDS.

To many that day, it seemed as if Johnson was announcing that he had been handed a death sentence because of his reckless approach to sexual activity. Soon, it was thought, Johnson would be suffering through a public deterioration.

There had been no warning. He had been preparing for his 13th season with the Lakers as if nothing were wrong.

As far as Johnson knew, nothing was wrong. But on Oct. 25, while he was in Salt Lake City preparing for an exhibition game against the Utah Jazz, Johnson was told by his agent, Lon Rosen, that his doctor, Michael Mellman, wanted him to fly home. Immediately.

Upon arriving, Johnson learned that a routine physical

for a life-insurance policy had revealed HIV, the virus that causes AIDS.

The Lakers put out a story that Johnson was suffering from flu while additional tests were run.

The initial diagnosis was correct. Doctors, uncertain about the long-term effects of extensive traveling and the physical demands of basketball on a body infected with HIV, recommended Johnson's retirement.

For Johnson, learning he couldn't play basketball was nearly as bad as learning he had the virus. He followed the advice and announced his retirement before a stunned world.

Johnson did come back to play in the 1992 NBA All-Star game and the 1992 Olympics. He had tried a full-scale comeback to the Lakers in 1992 but backed off when fears were expressed by some in the NBA over the possibility, remote as it was, that he could transmit the disease on the court.

Johnson joined the National Commission on AIDS for a while, but quit after disagreeing with President Bush's policy on the disease.

Johnson was put under the care of AIDS specialist Dr. David Ho. The virus was controlled, Johnson's activity level remained high and he eventually made that long-anticipated comeback, playing the second half of the 1995-96 season.

Then Johnson quit again, this time not because of the disease but because he was 36 and unable to play with the old magic.

So he threw himself into his business ventures and a short-lived stint as a television talk-show host.

SEE ALSO • *Johnson, Magic.*

Mueller, Erwin, L. (1944-) ➤ The Lakers got Mueller because they needed muscle. They got rid of him partly because they needed speed.

In January 1968, the Lakers traded Jim "Bad News" Barnes and a draft choice to the Chicago Bulls for Mueller, a 6-foot-8, 230-pounder who was expected to help Elgin Baylor and Tommy Hawkins in the frontcourt. Mueller struggled in his first game, a 115-101 loss to the New York Knicks. It was the Lakers' fifth defeat in a row.

"I'm not in shape because I haven't been playing much," said Mueller, who had been struggling with a knee injury. "And I made some mistakes out there. But I'll get better."

Mueller averaged 8.3 points and 5.7 rebounds for the Lakers.

But eight months after his arrival, Mueller was traded back to Chicago for quick, slick Keith Erickson.

What about all the help Mueller was going to supply up front? It turned out the Lakers didn't need as much help up there because, in the interim, they had picked up a guy named Wilt Chamberlain.

Mullaney, Joseph "Joe" (1925-) ➤ Mullaney was fired as Laker coach after the 1970-71 season.

But he didn't go quietly.

The firing of Mullaney was a surprise. In the two years he was at the helm, the Lakers went to the seventh game of the NBA finals before losing to the New York Knicks, then the next year reached the second round of the

Joe Mullaney along the sidelines during a practice session before the 1969-70 season.

playoffs before falling to the Milwaukee Bucks, the club that would win the league title.

Mullaney accomplished all of this despite a series of injuries that left him without at least one of his three superstars–Wilt Chamberlain, Elgin Baylor and Jerry West–in all but 13 of the 164 regular-season games he coached.

West missed all of the 1971 postseason because of a knee injury.

So Mullaney and his supporters felt that his dismissal was hardly justified.

"I am shocked," West said at the time. "I thought he did an outstanding job. I don't want to say anything else."

Mullaney, however, got his say.

When owner Jack Kent Cooke offered Mullaney, who still had a year left on a three-year contract, a job as an administrative vice president with the team, Mullaney rejected it.

"Coaching has been and remains my first love. I'll stand on my record," Mullaney said defiantly.

It was a record worth standing on. Even as a player, Mullaney had been impressive. He was captain of the 1947 Holy Cross team that won the NCAA championship. Mullaney shared the backcourt that season with a guard named Bob Cousy.

In 14 years as head coach at Providence, Mullaney took the Friars to the National Invitation Tournament—in the days when that tournament meant something—nine consecutive times, winning it twice.

But none of that mattered to Cooke and his general manager, Fred Schaus, who felt that Mullaney was not enough of a disciplinarian or communicator.

So they got rid of him and brought in Bill Sharman, who, in turn, would bring Cooke his first and only NBA title.

Murphy, Allen (1952-) ➤ Murphy was one of those marginal players who might have found a home in the American Basketball Assn.

If there still was an American Basketball Assn.

But a year after he had come out of the University of Louisville and spent a season with the Kentucky Colonels, the 6-foot-5, 190-pound Murphy was a man without a league when the ABA folded.

Murphy's rights wound up with the Chicago Bulls, who traded him to the Lakers for future considerations

He didn't get much consideration from the Lakers, getting into only two games before his NBA career ended.

Nash, Charles Francis "Cotton" (1942-) ➤ The Lakers figured they had hit a double jackpot in the 1964 draft.

The nation's college basketball writers had named UCLA's Walt Hazzard player of the year and Nash of Kentucky as the runner-up.

The Lakers, who had the first pick in the draft, took Hazzard. Nash was still available in the second round, so they got him too.

At 6 feet 5 and 225 pounds, Nash played every position at Kentucky and became the school's all-time leading scorer.

"Beyond his scoring and rebounding," said Laker Coach Fred Schaus, "Nash could become a defensive standout. We know that any boy turned out by [Coach] Adolph Rupp has to be sound defensively."

It sounded good.

But Nash appeared in only 25 games with the Lakers that season, averaging 2.1 points and 1.4 rebounds, and was released in the off-season.

SEE ALSO: *Hazzard, Walt.*

Nater, Swen Eric (1950-) ➤ By the time Nater came to the Lakers in 1983-84, he was 33 and in his 11th season of professional basketball. It turned out to be his last in a career that had begun in the 1973-74 season with the Virginia Squires of the American Basketball Assn.

Nater averaged only 4.5 points and 3.8 rebounds with the Lakers, well below the 13.4 points and 12.0 rebounds he had averaged in his previous NBA seasons, most of which were spent with the Clippers, and the 13 points and 13.1 rebounds he averaged in the ABA.

Many seemed to expect more out of Nater than he produced. He had been a member of two NCAA championship teams at UCLA. And at 6-feet-11 and 250 pounds, he had the physique of a bodybuilder, the scowl of a boxer and, on occasion, the manner of a bouncer who had just been informed there was a drunk at the bar who refused to leave.

Occasionally, all those attributes came together for Nater. There was the night in 1979 when, as a member of the Clippers, he was facing the Lakers at the Forum. In the final minute of the first quarter, Nater had a shot blocked by Kareem Abdul-Jabbar.

Nater stormed around the court with a clenched fist, occasionally smacking it into his other hand. His face was red, his eyes narrowed, his lips clenched. At the time, he had only four points.

But he dominated Abdul-Jabbar the rest of the game–something he rarely did in their frequent meetings.

Nater led the Clippers to a 116-108 victory by scoring 28 points and pulling down 27 rebounds.

If Nater had found something to set off his fuse every night, he could have been a superstar.

SEE ALSO: *Abdul-Jabbar, Kareem.*

NBA logo ➤ Everyone who has ever watched a league game, worn a league jacket, seen a league program or read a league book is familiar with the NBA's logo, a silhouette of a player, all in white, dribbling with his left hand against a blue and red background.

But few know that the figure in that logo is Jerry West, one of the league's all-time great guards as a Laker, who became the team's coach and later general manager.

SEE ALSO: *West, Jerry; Zeke From Cabin Creek.*

Nelson, Donald Arvid "Don" (1940-) ➤

The mention of Nelson's name elicits memories of a long NBA career that began in 1962 as a player and continued as a coach and general manager. He played for 14 seasons, two of them–1963-64 and 1964-65–were spent with the Lakers.

But that's not what many Laker fans remember when the name Don Nelson comes up. They don't even dwell on the 11 seasons he played for the hated Boston Celtics. No, Nelson's name brings up the memory of one agonizing shot.

It was the seventh game of the 1969 NBA Finals between the Lakers and Celtics, a series the Lakers had led, two games to none.

With slightly more than a minute to play and Boston leading, 103-102, at the Forum, Nelson put up a shot from the free-throw line that was short.

Barely short.

It hit the front of the rim, bounced four feet in the air and then, to the elation of the Celtics and the horror of the Lakers, the ball came back down through the hoop.

It was a bad break from which the Lakers could not recover.

They lost the game, 108-106, and thus yet another series to Boston. Since the Lakers had moved to Los Angeles, they had met the Celtics six times in the finals and lost each time.

And for years afterward, Laker announcer Chick Hearn would describe a basket resulting from a similar lucky bounce as a "Don Nelson shot."

And every Laker fan knew just what he meant.

Neumann, Johnny (1951-) ➤

Neumann played seven seasons of pro basketball, starting in 1971-72 with the Memphis Sounds of the American Basketball Assn. He finished with the Indiana Pacers in 1977-78.

Neumann played for five other teams, including the Lakers in 1976-77. In 59 games, he averaged 5.9 points, 1.1 rebounds and 2.3 assists.

But the lasting image announcer Chick Hearn has of Neumann's short Laker career is a moment Neumann might not include in his personal highlight film.

The 6-foot-6, 200-pounder, sitting on the bench during one game, got the call to go in. He jumped up and whipped off his sweatpants only to discover that he'd neglected to put on his basketball shorts.

"He got the biggest ovation of his career," Hearn said.

Nevitt, Charles Goodrich "Chuck" (1959-) ➤

He played on arguably the greatest Laker team, the 1984-85 squad that finally made up for the many heartbreaking, championship-round defeats to Boston by finally beating the Celtics in Boston Garden for the NBA title.

He was on a team loaded with stars, from Kareem Abdul-Jabbar to Magic Johnson to James Worthy.

He rarely played, and, when he did, he was largely ineffective.

But he was the darling of the Forum fans. He could draw more cheers by simply standing up and removing his warmup jersey than others could get by scoring.

He was easy to spot, at 7 feet 5 and 250 pounds. And he was easy to like because he was sincere and a hard worker who simply didn't have the skill to compete for a starting job.

Maybe that's why the crowd loved him, because he was one of them. Except a little taller.

Nevitt, who was waived early in his second season with the club, played 15 regular-season games for the Lakers, averaging 1.5 points and 1.8 rebounds.

His numbers on the applause meter, however, were a different matter.

Newell, Peter ➤

Newell's greatest moments came as a coach in amateur basketball. He won the triple crown at the amateur level with championships in the NCAA tournament and National Invitation Tournament with California and a gold medal in the Olympics.

He was coach of the 1960 U.S. Olympic team, the original Dream Team with Jerry West and Oscar Robertson in the backcourt.

Newell coached at Cal for 14 seasons and had a winning percentage of .657.

For more than 20 years, he has run a basketball camp designed for big men. They've all come to him for advice, if not actual camp time, from Kareem Abdul-Jabbar to Shaquille O'Neal.

Newell's official connection with the Lakers was brief. He served as the team's general manager for four years (1972-73 through 1975-76), succeeding Fred Schaus, whose West Virginia team Newell had beaten for the 1959 NCAA title.

Yet, despite his short tenure with the Lakers, Newell made one move that put his stamp on the organization and launched the team's most spectacular and successful era since it was in Minneapolis.

On June 16, 1975, Newell traded Elmore Smith, Brian Winters, Dave Meyers and Junior Bridgeman to the Milwaukee Bucks for Abdul-Jabbar and Walt Wesley.

SEE ALSO: *Bridgeman, Junior; Meyers, Dave; O'Neal, Shaquille; Robertson, Oscar; Smith, Elmore; Wesley, Walt; Warner, Cornell; Winter, Brian.*

Nicholson, Jack ➤ He has long been known as the Lakers' "First Fan." He attended Laker games long before they were fashionable, long before the concept of Showtime had even entered Jerry Buss' mind.

One of Hollywood's biggest stars, a winner of three Academy Awards, a nominee 11 times, Nicholson is a regular in his familiar court-side seat at the Forum, parked next to the visiting bench.

That has created some interesting moments. Like the one in a game in 1980 between the Lakers and the Washington Bullets.

In a matchup they would win, 111-107, the Lakers put on a 22-2 run in the second quarter. During it, Washington's Kevin Grevey took a shot from the corner with Michael Cooper in his face.

Grevey hit the floor after Cooper hit him, but there was no call from the referee, which led Washington Coach Dick Motta to protest loudly. That drew Motta a technical foul.

Enraged, the coach charged the scorer's table. That's when Nicholson went from being a fan to being a participant.

"He grabbed my leg and I don't need that," said Motta after the game.

Jack Nicholson watches the a 1996 game from his regular seat next to the visitors' bench.

At halftime, the two came face to face again, but this time, the confrontation was more civil.

"I asked him if he really needed the publicity that bad," Motta said. "I told him that I invested in one of his films once and lost a lot of money. I asked him if he wanted to be one of my assistant coaches, and he said he'd like that."

Nicholson, who has been known to have Laker games taped and sent to him on location while he's filming a movie, once gave the choke sign to fans in Boston Garden during a Laker-Celtic game in the 1984 NBA Finals.

He drew boos and threats from the Boston crowd, but the act again made him the toast of Hollywood.

Nixon, Norman Ellard (1955-) ➤ At first, they shared the backcourt, shared the workload and shared in the glory of an NBA title.

But for a while, the sharing turned into sniping. The Laker backcourt was not big enough for Norm Nixon and Magic Johnson.

When Johnson arrived, most of the Lakers saw a young phenom who could take them to the top. Nixon saw a rival for his job as the team's point guard.

Nixon gave up some of his ballhandling responsibilities grudgingly to the hot rookie. Sure, Johnson was quickly evolving into the best point guard in the league. But Nixon was an extremely proud player and had struggled to get where he was. Nixon was listed in the

Norm Nixon takes the ball downcourt during a 1978 game.

program as 6 feet 2. But when a friend, who stood an even six feet, asked Nixon to explain how, if he was really 6-2, they could be standing eye to eye, Nixon told the friend that obviously he didn't know how tall he was.

But the Laker guard made up for his lack of height with impressive quickness, tenacious defense and a strong, dependable jump shot. He used his skills and a strong will to jump from Duquesne into one of the plum starting spots in the league.

He had survived a bad relationship with Jerry West, who was the coach when Nixon was drafted. West, one of the game's all-time great guards, was determined to see that Nixon reached his potential. Nixon thought West was merely picking on him because the coach was afraid to antagonize the veterans.

When West stepped down, Nixon figured his troubles were over. Then, along came Johnson.

In 1979-80, the first season he and Johnson played together, Nixon's numbers actually went up. He played more minutes (3,226) than he had the previous year (3,145) and his scoring average went up too, from 17.1 to 17.6. His assists went down from a team-leading 9.0 in 1978-79 to 7.8, still good enough to lead the team. And considering the end result was an NBA title, what was there to complain about? The next season was a different story.

Johnson sat out 45 games because of a knee surgery, games in which Nixon again got comfortable at the point.

Johnson's return to the Forum became a wild celebration, with fans wearing "Magic Is Back" buttons.

Not Nixon. For him, the frustration was back.

"I thought Magic would come in and have to adjust to our game," Nixon said, "but we had to adjust to his."

The tension exploded in the first round of the playoffs in the 1980-81 season. Johnson accused some teammates of jealousy. Nixon was clearly one of the teammates he was pointing at.

"If Norm Nixon feels that strongly about having the ball," Johnson said, "we'll get him a ball, put his name on it and he can keep it under his arm during the game. It'll be his ball. I just want to win. If it takes him having the ball, fine. If that makes him more secure, fine."

The Lakers were eliminated in the first round by the Houston Rockets.

Owner Jerry Buss sat down with Johnson and Nixon in Las Vegas after the season had ended and asked them if they could co-exist.

If not, Buss said, Nixon would have to go.

Nixon was not one to back down when he thought he was right. When Coach Paul Westhead once suggested that Nixon play in the summer league to work his way back into shape after suffering an injury, Nixon said, "Sure, just have Kareem [Abdul-Jabbar] pick me up on his way out there."

But this time, Nixon stifled his pride, and forged a bond with Johnson that was stronger than ever. Nixon and Johnson became the consummate backcourt as the Lakers went on to win the NBA title the next season and reached the championship round the year after that.

And despite all of Nixon's concerns about losing his ballhandling responsibilities, it was he, not Johnson, who led the team in assists in each of the first three seasons of the Magic era.

On most other teams, Nixon would have been an all-pro fixture for years. It took one of the greatest guards in history to move him aside.

Nixon's Laker career ended on Oct. 16, 1983, when he and Eddie Jordan were traded to the San Diego Clippers for Byron Scott and Swen Nater.

SEE ALSO: *Buss, Jerry; Johnson, Magic; West, Jerry.*

Oceaneers ➤ Had Bob Short, owner of the Lakers at the time, gone along with one suggestion when he moved his Lakers from Minneapolis to Los Angeles in 1960, the team's longtime public address announcer, Lawrence Tanter, might have spent years telling the fans, "Welcome to the Fabulous Forum, home of the your Los Angeles Oceaneers."

That's the name Short considered when it was suggested that a change might be in order for the club when it relocated.

A team playing in Minnesota, the land of a thousand lakes, would logically be called the Lakers.

But Los Angeles? McCarthur Lake was hardly worthy of having a sports franchise named after it.

Ultimately, Short stuck with the name he had.

"We have a lot of trophies," he explained.

The team had won five NBA championships before leaving Minneapolis.

Oldham, Jawann (1957-) ➤ For a couple of years in the mid 1980s, Oldham was a force in the middle for the Chicago Bulls.

After blocking 101 shots in 106 games during his first four seasons in the league, Oldham blocked 127 shots in 63 games in 1984-85. The next season, he was even better, blocking 134 in 52 games. His average of 2.6 was sixth best in the league.

But by the time the Lakers obtained Oldham, he had sat out one season and been largely grounded by reconstructive surgery on his left knee.

Oldham had been cut by the Sacramento Kings before the 1989-90 season, had played 15 games for the Santa Barbara Islanders of the Continental Basketball Assn. and three games with the Orlando Magic.

In three games for the Lakers, he scored five points and blocked one shot. He played four more games with Indiana the next season before his NBA career ended.

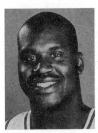

O'Neal, Shaquille Rashaun "Shaq" (1972-) ➤ His first and middle names mean "Little Warrior."

But there is nothing little about him. Standing 7 feet 1, weighing 315 pounds and dominating a basketball court like no other center in the game, O'Neal seems larger than life.

That's why he seemed so perfect in the genie's role that he played in the movie "Kazaam."

But despite all his basketball talent, despite secondary careers in movies and music, despite a seven-year Laker contract that pays him $120 million, there is also frustration because he has not yet been able to bring the Lakers another NBA title. That's the reason owner Jerry Buss signed O'Neal to a deal that pays him about $17 million a year, a million more than Buss paid for the entire Laker club in 1979.

But O'Neal is no stranger to frustration.

He put up big numbers in college at Louisiana State, averaging 21.6 points, 13.5 rebounds and 4.6 blocked shots in 90 games. As a sophomore, O'Neal was named college basketball player of the year by Associated Press, United Press International and Sports Illustrated after averaging 27.6 points and 14.7 rebounds, the latter figure good enough to lead the NCAA.

But O'Neal didn't have a championship.

That was supposed to change in the NBA.

Shaq roars approval for his own slam dunk during a 1997 playoff game.

Shaq slams in another dunk during a 1998 playoff game.

That's what Orlando Magic officials thought when they made him the No. 1 pick in the 1992 NBA draft.

The Magic improved dramatically with O'Neal in the middle. He led Orlando to the playoffs in his second season and to the NBA Finals in his third season, a season in which O'Neal led the league in scoring. Orlando was swept in the those finals, however, by the Houston Rockets.

Then things started to turn ugly. Orlando no longer seemed like a magic kingdom to O'Neal. And he no longer seemed like a jolly giant to Magic management.

When his grandmother died in the middle of the 1995-96 season, O'Neal felt that Magic officials weren't understanding about the length of his absence. They were reacting to reports that he was seen in a nightclub, reports he denied.

Said O'Neal: "They should have just said, 'Shaq's grandma died. Whenever he wants to come back, he can come back.' "

He also felt his teammates were too sensitive to criticism about their play and were not supportive of him.

"They never stood up for me," O'Neal said. "I got fouled a lot and they never said anything."

Also, O'Neal and his coach, Brian Hill, didn't always see eye to eye.

So it should not have come as a shock to anyone in Orlando that, when he became a free agent, O'Neal took the money and ran all the way to L.A., where he was not only in an organization with a winning tradition, but in a city known as the entertainment capital of the world.

There was still plenty of anger and hurt when the big man made his big move. Anger in Orlando, where Magic officials said they were trying to confirm their suspicions of tampering by the Lakers, that the O'Neal signing was a done deal before the free-agent signing period had begun.

The hurt was felt by Laker Executive Vice President Jerry West, a proud man who said his honor had been so besmirched, he considered quitting. The whole process,

West said, was "very, very distasteful" and had taken "a horrible toll" on him.

But once the papers were signed, optimism took over in L.A., easing West's emotional pain. Finally, the Lakers had another big man to follow in the tradition of George Mikan, Wilt Chamberlain and Kareem Abdul-Jabbar.

But as those big men had learned in their time, it takes a great supporting cast and someone to get them the ball for the big centers to realize their potential. Mikan had Slater Martin, Chamberlain had West and Gail Goodrich and Abdul-Jabbar had Magic Johnson.

Nick Van Exel didn't quite fit into that company.

And so, although O'Neal's numbers remained constant in Los Angeles, although his 28.3 scoring average in 1997-98 was within a point of his career high, although he kept his rebounding average in double figures, although he even got his woefully weak free-throw shooting back above 50% in 1997-98, O'Neal's second season as a Laker ended in frustration as had the season before. Both were far short of the glory that had been envisioned when he signed.

In O'Neal's first season, the Lakers were knocked out in the second round of the playoffs by the Utah Jazz in five games. In his second season, the Lakers reached the Western Conference Finals, only to be ousted again by the Jazz, this time in a four-game sweep.

O'Neal's second year in Los Angles was especially tough. He led the league in shooting percentage from the field, finishing second in scoring, was eighth in blocked shots and would have been fourth in rebounds had he not been out 21 games because of an abdominal strain. In the postseason, O'Neal averaged 30.5 points, shot 61.2% from the field and had 10.2 rebounds and 2.6 blocks.

But none of that put a ring on his finger. The Laker weaknesses showed in the Western Conference Finals. They didn't have an effective backup for O'Neal, and they had other problems as well, from inconsistency in the backcourt to defensive lapses. O'Neal didn't help himself with his sometimes horrible free-throw shooting, the one major weakness in his game.

O'Neal can accept the criticism. What he can't accept is any hint that he doesn't care, that he feels no emotion on the court, that he's content to take his $120 million and concentrate on his entertainment career.

Ask Greg Ostertag, whom O'Neal slapped to the court between shoot-arounds at the Forum before the 1997-98

season opener. O'Neal was still fuming over remarks the Jazz center had made about him after the previous season's playoffs.

Ask O'Neal if he cares, but then stand back.

"I like to do rap and I like to do movies," O'Neal said when he first put on a Laker uniform. "Hey, I know how to win. I've been winning all my life, from Little League [on]. I've never, ever played on a losing team. I might not have won the championship all the time, but I know what it takes to win."

He has yet to prove that in Los Angeles. And ultimately, all the big numbers in his world, from his shoe size to his contract to his statistics, won't mean as much as one particular figure: the number of championship banners he adds to the Laker collection.

O'Neill, Frank ➤ He was the first Laker trainer after the team's arrival in Los Angeles, lasting 15 years.

But his most valuable contribution, beyond all the wrists and ankles he taped and the care he gave the players, was the advice he gave owner Bob Short and General Manager Lou Mohs in 1961 when they were looking for a play-by-play announcer.

It was O'Neill who recommended Chick Hearn.

Owens, Keith Kensel (1969-) ➤ Owens played on the 1991-92 Lakers, which is a pretty amazing accomplishment.

Never mind that it was the only year he played in the NBA or that he appeared in only 20 games and averaged 1.3 points.

What's amazing is that he made it at all. This is a guy who had to convince the UCLA Bruins he was good enough to play for them, making the team as a walk-on. He had to convince the Lakers to put him on their summer league team after they initially told him there was no room on the roster.

"When I think about [his rise from walk-on to the Lakers], I've got to wonder about the experts," the 6-foot-7, 225-pound Owens said. "Either they aren't experts or I've just been able to overcome incredible odds."

Ultimately, the experts were right. Owens wasn't good enough to play in the NBA. But Owens was right as well. He did overcome incredible odds, at least for a while.

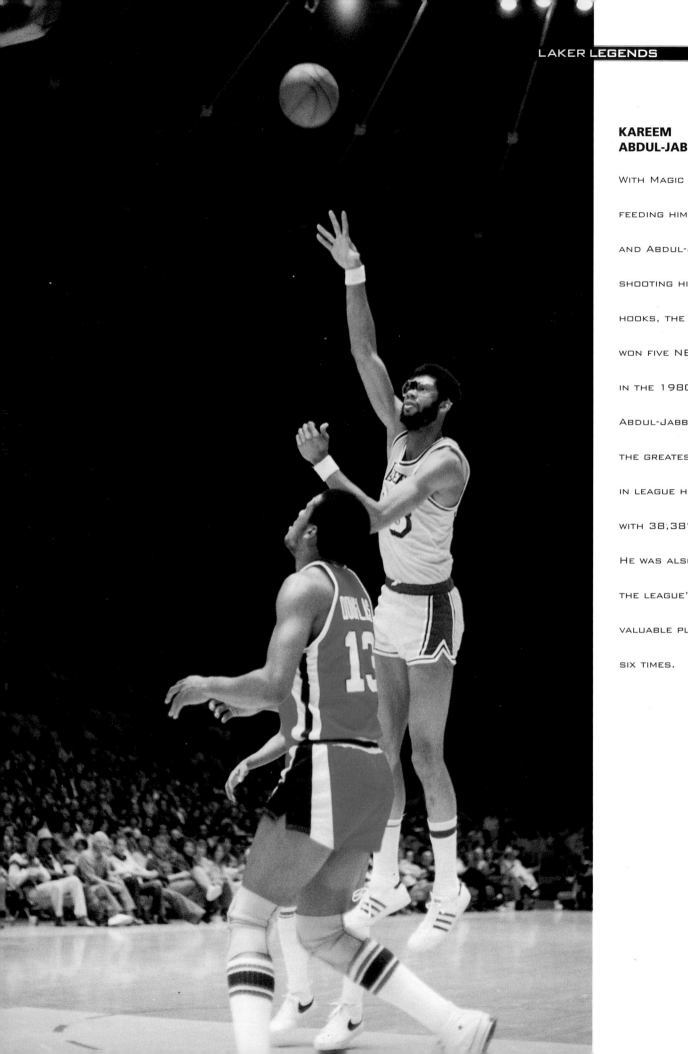

KAREEM ABDUL-JABBAR

WITH MAGIC JOHNSON FEEDING HIM THE BALL AND ABDUL-JABBAR SHOOTING HIS SKY HOOKS, THE LAKERS WON FIVE NBA TITLES IN THE 1980s, AND ABDUL-JABBAR BECAME THE GREATEST SCORER IN LEAGUE HISTORY WITH 38,387 POINTS. HE WAS ALSO NAMED THE LEAGUE'S MOST VALUABLE PLAYER SIX TIMES.

ELGIN BAYLOR

BEFORE THE BASKETBALL WORLD WANTED TO BE LIKE MIKE, IT WANTED TO BE LIKE ELGIN. BACK IN THE DARK AGES OF THE NBA, WHEN THE SET SHOT WAS STILL KING, BAYLOR WOULD LEAVE DEFENDERS FROZEN ON THE FLOOR WITH HIS EXPLOSIVE LEAPING ABILITY, INCREDIBLE HANG TIME AND DAZZLING MOVES. ALTHOUGH IT'S ORDINARY STUFF TODAY, IT WAS RARE THEATRICS IN BAYLOR'S TIME AND MADE HIM THE FIRST PICK OF THE MINNEAPOLIS LAKERS IN THE 1958 DRAFT.

WILT CHAMBERLAIN

WHEN IT COMES TO CHAMBERLAIN, ALL THE NUMBERS SEEM BEYOND THE REACH OF EVEN EXTRAORDINARY MEN. HE ONCE SCORED 100 POINTS IN AN NBA GAME, A MARK THAT WILL PROBABLY NEVER BE BROKEN. HE CLAIMED IN HIS AUTOBIOGRAPHY TO HAVE GONE TO BED WITH 20,000 WOMEN, A NUMBER THAT WILL NEVER BE VERIFIED. HE ONCE AVERAGED AN ASTONISHING 50.4 POINTS OVER AN ENTIRE SEASON.

GAIL GOODRICH

WITH GOODRICH
STANDING TALL NEXT
TO WILT CHAMBERLAIN
AND JERRY WEST,
THE LAKERS WON
33 CONSECUTIVE GAMES
IN THE REGULAR SEASON,
AN ALL-TIME RECORD
FOR ANY PROFESSIONAL
TEAM, AND THEN
THE TEAM WENT ON
TO CLAIM ITS
FIRST NBA TITLE
IN LOS ANGELES.

EARVIN "MAGIC" JOHNSON

HOW CAN ANYONE

EXPLAIN A 6-FOOT-9

PLAYER WHO

COULD RUN WITH

THE GAME'S

SMALL SPEEDSTERS,

REBOUND WITH ITS

GIANTS, SCORE WITH

ITS SHARPSHOOTERS

AND PASS LIKE

NO ONE ELSE

THE GAME HAD

EVER SEEN?

IT HAD TO BE,

AS THEY SAID,

SIMPLY "MAGIC."

SHAQUILLE O'NEAL

LEADING THE
LAKERS TO ANOTHER
NBA TITLE IS THE
SOLE REASON
TEAM OWNER
JERRY BUSS SIGNED
O'NEAL TO A DEAL
THAT PAYS HIM ABOUT
$17 MILLION A YEAR,
A MILLION MORE
THAN BUSS PAID
FOR THE ENTIRE
LAKER CLUB IN 1979.
SO FAR, BUSS' BET
HASN'T PAID OFF.

JERRY WEST

HE BECAME A LAKER THE YEAR THE TEAM BECAME THE LOS ANGELES LAKERS. AND HE HAS BEEN A LAKER EVER SINCE, MOVING UP THE LADDER FROM PLAYER TO COACH TO CONSULTANT TO GENERAL MANAGER TO EXECUTIVE VICE PRESIDENT, AND IN THE PROCESS HE HAS MATURED FROM ONE OF THE GAME'S GREATEST GUARDS TO ONE OF ITS BEST GENERAL MANAGERS.

JAMES WORTHY

SAVING HIS BEST PERFORMANCES FOR THE BIGGEST GAMES WAS A PATTERN WORTHY FOLLOWED THROUGHOUT HIS CAREER. HE PLAYED WITH CONFIDENCE AND MATURITY, TRAITS HE DISPLAYED EARLY IN LIFE AND AGAIN AS A ROOKIE ON A LAKER TEAM OF HARDENED VETERANS, AND FINALLY AS ONE OF THE TEAM'S SEASONED PLAYERS HIMSELF.

Patrick, Myles (1954-) ➤ Patrick didn't miss a game at Auburn in his four seasons there, winding up with 869 points and 683 rebounds.

But his luck ran out at the worst possible time.

After playing for the Maine Lumberjacks of the Continental Basketball Assn. and the Montana Sky of the Western League, and then averaging 15 points and six rebounds in the 1980 summer league in Southern California, Patrick finally caught the attention of the Lakers.

But with two weeks to go in the summer season, he suffered a broken jaw. Patrick finally signed with the Lakers for the 1980-81 season, but his NBA career lasted only three games, in which he got five points and two rebounds.

Peeler, Anthony Eugene (1969-) ➤ It was understandable that Laker Vice President Jerry West raised some eyebrows when he used a 1992 first-round draft choice to get Peeler.

After all, Peeler had pleaded guilty the week before the draft to a felony weapons charge and two related misdemeanors after he allegedly attacked a woman and put a gun to her head. Peeler was given five years' probation, though a civil suit from that incident eventually resulted in a $2.4-million judgment against him. Then three days before the draft, he was arrested for assault, though charges were subsequently dropped.

Three years earlier, after his freshman year at Missouri, he had entered a rehabilitation program because of a

Anthony Peeler slashes to the basket against Seattle in 1995.

drinking problem.

"A lot of people think we're probably crazy," West said after selecting 6-foot-4, 215-pound Peeler. "Obviously all those things concern you when you hear them ... . We're going to view him as a player whose future is ahead of him and whose past is behind him."

Peeler had averaged 23.4 points as a senior at Missouri and was the school's all-time leader in assists (479) and steals (196).

After being selected by the Lakers, Peeler said he had learned from his troubles. "I feel I've made some mistakes, but that's just a part of growing up," he said. "I think that matured me a lot ... . You've just got to think before you do things ... . It's time for me to move on. The only way you can do good is look up and try to reach the stars."

Peeler validated West's faith in him, lasting four largely productive seasons with the team.

And the only reason Peeler was gone after those four years was because West had set his sights on a bigger target–center Shaquille O'Neal.

To free up salary-cap money, West traded Peeler and George Lynch in the summer of 1996 to the Vancouver Grizzlies for next to nothing. All West got out of the deal was the right to exchange second-round draft positions with Vancouver in 1998 and 1999.

But West also got Peeler's $1.54-million salary off the books.

And having freed up that money, West signed O'Neal two days later.

Peripheral opponents ▶ That was Coach Pat Riley's name for all the outside forces that he saw as threats to his team's focus and intensity.

It could be the media–as it often was in Riley's eyes–or it could be the fans, or it could even be a cleaning crew.

During a practice at Boston Garden one year, Riley suspiciously eyed the crew that was cleaning up the arena.

When the Lakers found a container of drinking water awaiting them on their arrival in Boston Garden on one occasion, Riley even viewed the container with suspicion. He had trainer Gary Vitti dump it out and refill it.

Never underestimate, Riley often preached, the power of the peripheral opponents.

Or the cleverness of a coach who turned "us against them" into an art form.

SEE ALSO • *Buzzards; Riley Pat.*

Peripheral opponents (Fire alarm department) ▶ During the 1984 NBA Finals, the Lakers seemed to be followed by false fire alarms going off in the middle of the night when they were staying in Boston.

Laker Coach Pat Riley suspected that the Celtics, or Celtic fans, were responsible.

Riley, always eager to catch any opponent off guard, stayed in three hotels during that series, finally escaping the false alarms in the third hotel.

The moves didn't make a difference. The Lakers still lost the series in seven games.

SEE ALSO • *Peripheral opponents; Riley, Pat.*

Perkins, Samuel Bruce "Sam" (1961-) ▶ Jerry West has had many brilliant days with the Lakers, on the court and in the front office.

February 22, 1993 was not one of them.

That day, West faced skepticism and second-guessing when he traded center/forward Perkins to the Seattle SuperSonics for center Benoit Benjamin and the rights to swingman Doug Christie.

The Times' sports section the day after the trade summed up the feelings of many. One headline read "This Deal Will Take Its Toll." Another read "Lakers Left Comfort Level to Take a Chance on the Future."

Perkins had been a star with the Dallas Mavericks for six seasons before coming to Los Angeles before the 1990-91 season, never averaging below double figures in scoring or fewer than seven rebounds a game.

He maintained his high standards with the Lakers, averaging 14.6 points and 8.0 rebounds in 2½ seasons

Sam Perkins drives to the basket as the Houston Rockets' Hakeen Olajuwon blocks his path in a 1991 game. (AP photo)

with them. Perkins, 6 feet 9 and 255 pounds, became a productive three-point shooter. He made 33 three-pointers in his two full seasons with the Lakers, with one of them helping to beat the Chicago Bulls in Game 1 of the 1991 NBA Finals.

No one was more surprised about the trade than Perkins.

"I'm in shock," he said.

Perkins said the deal might have been easier for him to accept if he had heard about it from West, rather than assistant general manager Mitch Kupchak.

"Just to talk to [him] would have been easier, but I have no resentment toward anyone. I really didn't know what they were trying to do until they emphasized they were going young," said Perkins, who was 31 at the time of the deal. Benjamin was 28, Christie 22.

"Our objective all along is to get a little bit younger, and a little more productive, and I think we've done that," West said. To me, sports is the ultimate gamble, and every once in a while, [owner] Jerry [Buss] likes to gamble a little bit."

West and Buss should have stuck with the hand they had. Benjamin was traded by the Lakers four months later, Christie a little more than a year and a half after he arrived.

Perkins was still with the SuperSonics five years later.

Pfund, Randy (1951-) ▶ Having watched his father, Lee, coach basketball and having played for him at Wheaton College in Illinois, where he was an honorable mention All-American, Pfund was determined to become a coach himself.

He started at the high school level in Illinois and went halfway across the country to be an unpaid assistant at Westmont College in Santa Barbara for two seasons.

He also found time to work for the scouting service of Bill Bertka, a Santa Barbara resident.

Bertka was a longtime Laker assistant and the man Laker Coach Pat Riley trusted most.

So when Laker assistant Dave Wohl left and Riley was looking for a replacement, he heeded Bertka's advice and hired Pfund in 1985.

For seven years, Pfund stayed as an assistant with the Lakers, resisting the temptation to leave with Riley when Riley became head coach of the New York Knicks. Pfund worked under Mike Dunleavy for two seasons, and when

Coach Randy Pfund on the sidelines during a 1993 game against the New York Knicks.

Dunleavy left after the 1991-92 season, Pfund, 40, was given Dunleavy's job.

These were no longer the Showtime Lakers. Kareem Abdul-Jabbar and Magic Johnson were gone and Shaquille O'Neal and Kobe Bryant hadn't arrived.

Pfund was rumored to be gone near the end of his first season, which he finished with a 39-43 record.

The Lakers took a 2-0 lead over the Phoenix Suns in a best-of-five, opening-round playoff series that season. The Suns came back to win three in a row but were taken into overtime of the final game.

Pfund's Lakers had shown enough to earn him a second chance.

But again the Lakers struggled. Finally, owner Jerry Buss appealed to a close friend to see if he could supply some of the magic that was missing.

The friend was Magic Johnson. Reluctantly, he agreed to take over the Lakers' head coaching job.

Pfund, who finished with a coaching record of 66-80, was fired on a Monday. But because Johnson wasn't ready to take over immediately, Pfund, the loyal employee, left on the Lakers' charter flight Tuesday to begin a trip in Texas, then came back on his own after the details of the transfer of power were worked out.

Pfund wound up as Riley's general manager in Miami after Riley went there from New York.

One of the reasons Pfund was fired from the Lakers was because of the Laker defense. One of the reasons Riley hired Pfund in the first place was because defense was one of his specialties.

Michael Cooper, a defensive specialist on the court when he played and the man tabbed by Johnson to be his assistant, labeled the Laker defense under Pfund "very, very lacking."

Others said the problem was that Pfund was too nice.

"Randy Pfund is one of the great people I've met," Laker General Manager Jerry West said. "I'll say that until my dying day."

Points prophet ➤ On Nov. 15, 1960, Laker forward Elgin Baylor, playing against the New York Knicks at Madison Square Garden, set an NBA single-game scoring record with 71 points, breaking the mark of 64 points he had set a year earlier. But this new mark wasn't any more durable.

One year and 23 days later, Wilt Chamberlain, playing with the the Philadelphia Warriors, scored 78 points against Baylor and the Lakers.

Baylor could have taken some comfort in that it took a triple-overtime game to erase his mark.

That's what Laker announcer Chick Hearn stressed to Baylor in the locker room after the game. But Baylor wasn't buying it.

"Don't worry about it," he told Hearn. "One day, the Big Fella will make a hundred."

Three months later, in Hershey, Pa., Chamberlain did exactly that, setting a record that could prove to be the

most durable in sports history.

SEE ALSO • *Baylor, Elgin; Chamberlain, Wilt; Hershey, Pa.; Hundred Points*

Price, James "Jim" (1949-) ➤ A second-round draft choice of the Lakers in 1972, a member of the all-rookie team in 1972-73 and a member of the league's all-defensive second team a year later, Price was crushed when the Lakers traded him early in his third pro season.

Price was only 25, had averaged 15.4 points and 4.5 assists the previous year, and scored 26 points on the night he was to learn he had been traded.

But the Lakers wanted a veteran to run the offense and handle the ball. So they sent Price to the Milwaukee Bucks for Lucious Allen.

Price averaged 16.1 points that season, but never again approached that figure in a career that took him to Buffalo, Denver and Detroit before he finished up his NBA experience back where he had started, with the Lakers, in the 1978-79 season.

Quadruple overtime ➤ It took 3 hours and 17 minutes. When it was over, eight players had scored 20 or more points and seven had fouled out.

On Jan. 29, 1980 in Richfield, Ohio, the Lakers and Cleveland Cavaliers played the longest game in Laker history.

Only three others in league history have gone longer. The record is held by a six-overtime game between the Indianapolis Olympians and the Rochester Royals in 1951. The Olympians won, 75-73, in an era before the installation of the 24-second clock.

Cleveland defeated the Lakers, 154-153, though the top two scorers were Lakers. Jamaal Wilkes had 43 points and Kareem Abdul-Jabbar had 42, along with 17 rebounds, eight blocked shots and seven assists.

"I'm spent," Cleveland Coach Stan Albeck said. "I'm just hollow-eyed." And he was on the winning side.

Rambis, Darrell Kurt (1958-) ➤ Some called him Superman because he looked like Clark Kent.

But Kurt Rambis certainly didn't look like a basketball player.

He appeared awkward without the benefit of either great speed or a great jump shot.

All he had was his size (6 feet 8 and 220 pounds), his spirit, his tenacity, his understanding of the game and the appreciation for his opportunity.

After attending Santa Clara University, he was picked in the third round of the 1980 draft by the New York Knicks. Rambis made it as far as training camp before being cut. He was signed to a 10-day contract by the Knicks in December of that year, but never played in a game. Rambis, without a lot of options in the NBA, took off for Greece.

For him, it was ideal.

"The Greeks let the Americans get beat up over there," Rambis said. "It's a rough game. I like a good, rough game."

And that's the game he might have stayed with had it not been for Laker assistant coach Mike Thibault. Thibault noticed Rambis in the Southern California summer league and he was signed to a contract for the 1981-82 season.

Rambis' Clark Kent image was taking shape. Here he was, a seemingly mild-mannered guy with thick, black-framed glasses that made him look more a college student than a NBA star. He was a hard-hat laborer whose work ethic drew little mention on a team loaded with high-flying, headline-grabbing superstars and a sloppy dresser lost among the fashion plates of the league's Hollywood team.

Magic Johnson said Rambis looked like "an aging hippie," claimed that Rambis wore the same shirt to every home game for five years and "came to practice looking like he'd just crawled out of bed."

Rambis also had a reputation among his teammates for being extremely cheap. Rambis would take home a bath mat from his hotel, he would take soft drinks home from the team locker room, and he would get his hair cut by one of the secretaries at the Forum in order to save money. Rambis didn't seem to fit in...until he stepped onto the court.

As the 1981-82 season began, the Lakers appeared set at power forward with Mitch Kupchak, who had been obtained from the Washington Bullets. But in December, a serious knee injury ended Kupchak's season.

The Lakers tried Jim Brewer and Mark Landsberger at power forward.

Finally, Coach Pat Riley went to Rambis on a January

night in Indianapolis when the Lakers had fallen behind the Pacers by 19 points early in the second quarter. Rambis pulled down 14 rebounds in 25 minutes as the Lakers came back to win by five.

Riley kept calling on Rambis, and he kept answering.

After Rambis had grabbed 16 rebounds in 35 minutes against the Detroit Pistons in his fourth start, Riley was asked if Rambis had become his starting power forward.

"I think," Riley said, "that Kurt has made that decision for himself."

Exit Clark Kent, enter Superman.

Rambis became one of the league's forces on the boards. He became an instant crowd favorite, and even got his own rooting section, Rambis Youth, a strange group in their own right who dressed like their hero.

Rambis played for the Lakers for the first seven seasons of his career, including four championship seasons. Cut loose by the Lakers after the 1987-88 season, Rambis went on to play for the Charlotte Hornets, Phoenix Suns and Sacramento Kings.

With his NBA career seemingly over, he toured with Magic Johnson's All-Stars. But when the Lakers found themselves short-handed in the frontcourt, they again turned to Rambis. He played briefly for two more seasons with the Lakers, 1993-94 and 1994-95, also beginning a second life with the team as an assistant coach. The 1997-98 season was his fourth as a Laker assistant under Coach Del Harris.

SEE ALSO • *Rambis Youth.*

Rambis Youth ➤ Has there ever been a more eccentric fan club in sports?

Those in the club wore the same type of horn-rimmed glasses, with the strap in the back, as did their hero, Laker forward Kurt Rambis, who had been known to be a bit eccentric himself. They wore their hair in the same shaggy style as did Rambis. Anyone who didn't know of Rambis might have thought Rambis Youth was actually a fan club for the Hansen brothers, those out-of-control hockey players in the movie "Slap Shot."

The Rambis Youth consisted of 18 fans from Arcadia, Monrovia and West Covina who regularly attended Laker games in full dress to cheer on their role model. They even had a poem, written by member Scott Casey:

"Don't close your eyes now, Kurt Rambis is here.
By the boards, he's always near.
Not an offensive threat? you say.

Block him out or you will pay.
He came quietly from a league in Greece.
Crashing the boards and playing good 'D.'
Then from Arcadia, the Rambis Youth came.
Giving Kurt his much-deserved fame."

And what was Rambis' opinion of Rambis Youth?

"It sounds like a political group ready to take over something," he said, "but I don't know what."

SEE ALSO • *Rambis, Kurt.*

Reed, Hubert F. "Hub" (1936-) ➤ When Laker Coach Fred Schaus saw that Reed had been put on waivers by the Cincinnati Royals just before the 1963-64 season, Schaus grabbed him. Reed's numbers had been less than overwhelming for Cincinnati, but Schaus figured there was a reason for that: Reed had been misused.

No longer would the 6-foot-9, 220-pounder be stationed at the hub of the action in the center of the court, where he gave away as much as 50 pounds to other centers such as Wilt Chamberlain.

Instead, Schaus would move Reed to the corner, where his soft shot would be more effective and he could concentrate his defensive efforts almost exclusively against other natural forwards.

It sounded good, but Reed played in only 46 games in his only season with the Lakers, and had career low totals in points (1.7), rebounds (2.3) and shooting percentage (36.3).

Rex the Peanut Man ➤ In a city known as the entertainment capital of the world, in a building whose courtside seats were filled with some of the world's best-known show-business personalities, on a court filled with some of the most celebrated cheerleaders in sports, Rex the Peanut Man was an unlikely addition to Showtime.

He was a regular "performer" at Laker games in the early 1980s.

A heavily wrinkled, frail-looking man who appeared to be about 80 and seemed to weigh no more than his age, Rex sold peanuts at the Forum. But on one occasion, Rex pranced down onto the floor and danced away a timeout.

From then on, either alone or with Laker cheerleaders in a truly strange scene, Rex could be counted on for one or two appearances at each home game. Laker management might not have been too excited about Rex's uninvited shows, but once he caught on with the fans, management dared not tell him to stick to the peanuts.

After two or three years, he was given a party at Jerry Buss' Pickfair home and retired.

SEE ALSO • *Dancing Barry; Laker cheerleaders.*

Riley, Lee ➤ Pat Riley had amassed a notebook full of motivational speeches in his nine seasons as Laker coach.

But he saved one of the best for one of the team's toughest moments.

It was after the smoke and fire had settled following the "Memorial Day Massacre."

That's what sportswriters were calling the Lakers' 148-114 loss in Game 1 of the 1985 NBA Finals at Boston Garden a year after the Lakers had lost in the finals to the Celtics in seven games.

Riley was fearful that another series was slipping away to the Celtics, a team the Lakers had never beaten in the finals.

The coach needed to fill the Laker locker room with emotion before Game 2. He needed to pull a Knute Rockne.

Kareem Abdul-Jabbar had asked for and received special permission from Riley to have his father, Ferdinand Lewis Alcindor, travel to Boston Garden on the team bus for the second game of the series.

That caused Riley to think about his own father, Lee, a former minor league manager. Riley remembered a poignant moment after his father had attended Riley's wedding in 1970.

As his father was driving away, he told Pat, "Just remember what I always taught you. Somewhere, someplace, some time, you're going to have to plant your feet, make a stand and kick some ass. And when that time comes, you do it."

Riley never saw his father again; Lee died of a heart attack soon thereafter. Riley never forgot that moment, and he shared it with his players. The Lakers went out, planted their feet, made a stand and won, 109-102, going on to beat the Celtics in the finals for the first time after eight unsuccessful tries.

Rockne would be impressed. So would Lee Riley.

SEE ALSO • *Riley, Pat.*

Riley, Patrick James "Pat"
(1945-) ➤ It was a dreary night in Portland before the 1970-71 season.

Dreary because rain was falling and dreary because the Portland Trail Blazers had just been blown out by the Lakers in an exhibition game.

Riley, a guard who had played his first three seasons with the San Diego Rockets, had just arrived in Portland, but he was already eager to leave, and the season hadn't even started.

So eager that he stood in the rain outside Memorial Coliseum to talk to Laker broadcaster Chick Hearn.

"You've got to get me out of here," Riley implored Hearn, who had considerable influence with Laker owner Jack Kent Cooke.

Word of Riley's desire got through and, after Portland put Riley on waivers, the Lakers picked him up Oct. 7, 1970.

Athletics were part of Riley's life from the time his hands were big enough to grasp a ball.

His father, Lee, was a catcher who briefly made it to the major leagues and became a minor league manager. Pat's brother, Lee, was a defensive back in the NFL. Riley's father was so determined to see Pat succeed that when Pat was 9, Lee had Pat's older brothers take him to Lincoln Heights, the rough section of their hometown of Schenectady, N.Y., to play basketball so that Pat could learn first-hand the tough side of the sport.

Pat played basketball and football at Schenectady's Linton High.

The highlight of his high school basketball career was a victory over Power Memorial, a team that had a towering sophomore center named Lew Alcindor.

Riley went on to play at Kentucky, where he learned under one of the sport's masters, Adolph Rupp. As a junior, Riley averaged 22 points and helped lead Kentucky into the NCAA finals, where his team lost to Texas Western.

The Rockets, in their first year of existence, picked Riley on the first round of the draft, seventh overall.

But the 6-foot-4, 205-pound Riley had caught the attention of more than the NBA. He hadn't played football since high school, but the Dallas Cowboys chose him in the 11th round of the 1967 NFL draft.

Riley chose the NBA, but had to struggle for everything he achieved on the court. He was never a star. In nine seasons, he averaged double figures in points only once, 11.0 in 46 games in the 1974-75 season, his last full season with the Lakers.

But Riley wanted to stick around, so early on he became a role player.

In the 1971-72 season, when the Lakers won their first NBA title, Coach Bill Sharman knew that if he needed some muscle underneath the boards, an opposing body banged, someone to protect superstars Wilt Chamberlain and Jerry West, he could always depend on Riley.

When Riley left basketball as a player after the 1975-76 season, limited by a knee injury, he found himself, at 31, cut off from the only world he had ever known. What now?

He hung out at the beach, remodeled his home and spewed out his frustrations on long legal pads.

But an incident at the Forum hardened Riley's resolve to get back into the NBA. Trying to enter the press lounge after a game, he was halted at the door by an usher even though he was wearing the championship ring he had won as a Laker.

"Sorry, no ex-players," the usher said.

Riley fumed and vowed he'd be back.

Again, it was Hearn who interceded.

Hearn helped Riley get the job as his broadcast partner. And when Laker Coach Jack McKinney was injured in a bicycle accident and assistant coach Paul Westhead took over early in the 1979-80 season, Westhead picked Riley as his assistant. Two years later, when Westhead was fired, Riley got the head job, despite the concerns of owner Jerry Buss.

Uncertain about putting Riley at the controls alone, Buss named West and Riley as co-coaches at a hastily called news conference. West, wanting no part of the head job, handed the microphone to Riley in front of the media, putting himself in an advisory role.

Could Riley do the job? Nobody knew.

Some saw him as merely a pretty boy with fancy clothes, a Hollywood type who would get chewed up by a tough game and huge superstars with egos to match.

How quickly they had forgotten that Riley was no more a Hollywood guy than Buss, who had grown up in hard times in Wyoming, or West, who had come from the courts of West Virginia.

Pat Riley lays one up against New York in an early 1970s game.

Riley was blue-collar Schenectady, he was a student of Rupp and he was a self-made survivor in the NBA.

And, as it turned out, he was just what the doctor, Buss, ordered.

The first thing Riley did was to loosen the controls that Westhead had put on his team, and the players responded like wild horses freed from a corral, running the court with the best fastbreak in the league.

Riley let them run for a while, but he soon put in his own controls. He was more subtle about it than had been Westhead, more respectful of his superstars, more determined to retain those elements that had resulted in an NBA championship only two years earlier.

The result was four more titles in the 1980s.

Riley, who coached the Lakers nine seasons, impressed his players and rival coaches with his willingness to roll up the sleeves on his expensive shirts and work as hard as he had as a player, designing his practices, which were

Riley, here in 1998, has been NBA Coach of the Year three times, once with each team he's coached: the Lakers, the Knicks and the Heat. (AP photo)

planned down to the last bounce of the ball, staying up most of the night studying videotapes, or preparing his next psychological gimmick to stir the emotions of his players.

Whether it was throwing scripted tantrums in the locker room or sending carefully crafted off-season letters to his players, Riley was a master of motivation.

Some also saw him as the prince of paranoia. He once ordered a cleaning crew out of Boston Garden because he thought they might have some sort of recording device in their brooms. He once accused a writer of relaying information from one team's practice to another.

Whatever his methods, they worked for a long time. When he guaranteed the Lakers would win a second consecutive title in 1988 while the Lakers were still celebrating the championship of 1987, his players initially reacted with dismay and some anger at the pressure placed on their shoulders.

But they did win that second title.

Finally, however, Riley's act grew old in Los Angeles. He was like a teacher who had taught the same students for nine years. The old motivational talks fell on deaf ears.

He was able to renew his act with the New York Knicks and the Miami Heat, though not with the same success.

But he had already made his point in Los Angeles. He was more than a pretty face. Much more.

SEE ALSO • *Riley, Lee; Peripheral opponents; Strangest press conference; Westhead, Paul.*

Rivers, David Lee (1965-) ➤ Rivers was in awe of the superstars he could suddenly refer to as teammates when the Lakers selected him with their first-round pick in the 1988 draft.

Rivers had known his share of big names while playing for Notre Dame. But when he found himself sitting next to Kareem Abdul-Jabbar on the team's flight to Hawaii for training camp, Rivers didn't say a word to the big center.

That didn't mean Abdul-Jabbar didn't notice the scrappy, 6-foot, 175-pound guard. Not when he saw Rivers go through his ballhandling drills, dribbling a ball in each hand simultaneously.

In his book "Kareem," Abdul-Jabbar says the only players he ever saw with Rivers' ability to see everybody on the court were Magic Johnson and Isiah Thomas.

One of Rivers' most memorable moments with the team didn't happen during a game. Johnson had made a 37-foot shot at the end of regulation to send a game into overtime. The next day, Coach Pat Riley said if any player could duplicate the shot, practice would be canceled.

Rivers alone swished it.

Unfortunately for him, he couldn't do the same very often when it really counted. He lasted only one season with the Lakers, averaging 2.9 points, before being taken by Minnesota in the expansion draft, being waived and signed as a free agent by the Clippers.

Roberson, Rick (1947-) ➤ Roberson was the University of Cincinnati's leading scorer and rebounder for three straight seasons and was a first-round draft choice of the Lakers, the 15th pick overall, in 1969. But the 6-foot-9, 235-pound Roberson figured he wasn't going to get a lot of playing time in a frontcourt of Wilt Chamberlain, Elgin Baylor and Happy Hairston.

Then nine games into Roberson's first season, all that

Check One: ☐ 1. Library   ☐ 2. Religious   ☐ 3. Legal   ☐ 4. Programs   ☐ 5. Other

Maricopa County Sheriff's Office
Joseph M. Arpaio, Sheriff
Inmate Request Form

Name (Nombre):	Jail (Carcel):
Booking No. (Numero Fichado):	House (Casa):
Date of Birth (Fecha De Nacimiento):	Cell (Celda):

1.   Inmate Library Request (Biblioteca)   ☐ English   ☐ Espanol

☐ Adventure/Western (Aventura)
☐ Education/Careers (Educacion/Carrera)
☐ Mystery/Horror (Misterio/Horror)
☐ Romance (Romantica)
☐ Spy/War (Espia/Guerra)

☐ Classics/Poetry (Clasico/Poesia)
☐ Large print/Easy Reading (Letra grande)
☐ Non-Fiction/Biography (Literatura de Novelesca/Biografia)
☐ Sci-Fi/Fantasy (Ciencia ficcion/Fantasia)
☐ Self-help/Inspiration (Esfuerza propio/Inspiracion)

2.   Inmate Religious Request (Solicitud Religiosa)

Religion: ☐ Catholic (Catolico)   ☐ Protestant (Protestante)   ☐ Muslim (Musulman)
☐ Other religion (Otra religion) _____

Request (Solicitud):   ☐ Bible (Biblia)   ☐ Bible Study (Estudio biblico)
☐ Inspirational Material (Material inspirante)   ☐ Religious Counseling (Consejo religioso)
☐ Religious Diet (Dieta religioso)

3.   Inmate Legal Requests (Solicitud Legales)
☐ Legal Research (Investigacion legal)   ☐ Legal Forms (Formulario legal)   ☐ Notary Service (Servicio notario)
☐ Court Filings (Archivar)   ☐ Legal Indigent Supplies (Legal articulos indigente)

4.   Inmate Programs (Programas)
☐ Self-help (Esfuerza propio)   ☐ GED   ☐ Juvenile Education (Educacion juvenil)
☐ Adult Special Education (Educacion especial de Adulto)
☐ Alpha Program (Programa Alpha) **(Substance Abuse Treatment – *for Sentenced Inmates ONLY*)**

5.   Other Inmate Information Request (Otra Informacion)
☐ Court date (Fecha de corte)   ☐ Release date (Fecha de liberar)   ☐ Property release (Liberar del propiedad)
☐ Legal call (Llamada legal)   ☐ Other _____

Please explain your request or question. Print clearly. (Por favor de explicar su solicitud o' pregunta. Escribir claramente.)

_____
_____
_____
_____
_____
_____

Inmate Signature: _____

Receiving Officer

Date: _____   Time: _____

Signature: _____

Response (if needed): _____
_____
_____

changed. Camberlain was gone because of a ruptured tendon in his right knee and Roberson became the Lakers' starting center.

Chamberlain sat out 70 games, and Roberson took advantage of the unexpected playing time. He averaged 8.7 points and 9.1 rebounds for the season and was honorable mention on the all- rookie team.

But with Chamberlain's return, Roberson's role diminished considerably. He was traded to the Cleveland Cavaliers at the start of the 1971-72 season and averaged double figures in points and rebounds the next three seasons for the Cavaliers and Portland Trail Blazers.

Had Roberson come along at a different time, he might have done that for the Lakers. But not in the Chamberlain era.

Roberts, Frederick Clark "Fred" (1960-) ▶ By the time Roberts joined the Lakers, he had learned to pack lightly. The Lakers were his sixth NBA club in 12 years, and that's not counting the Miami Heat, which took him in the 1988 expansion draft and immediately traded him to the Milwaukee Bucks. He also played parts of two seasons in Spain and the Continental Basketball Assn.

Of all his previous clubs, Roberts had a special feeling for the Boston Celtics, even though they failed to protect him at expansion time.

"I have nothing bad to say about Boston," Roberts told the Boston Globe. "I compare it to getting my master's degree in basketball, a great learning experience."

His experience with the Lakers was brief. Roberts got into 33 games and averaged 3.7 points before being part of the group that was cut loose to make room for the arrival of Shaquille O'Neal.

Roberts, Marvin James "Marv" (1950-) ▶ Stan Albeck was a big fan of Roberts.

When Roberts, who went from Utah State to the American Basketball Assn., was playing for the Carolina Cougars, Albeck, then an assistant with the Kentucky Colonels, was determined to get the 6-foot-8, 220-pounder.

Albeck got him, and the Colonels couldn't have been happier. Roberts averaged 10 points and shot 52% from the field in the 1975 ABA championship series, helping

Kentucky beat the Indiana Pacers.

Almost two years later, Albeck was an assistant with the Lakers, and Roberts had signed with the Phoenix Suns after five years in the ABA. After the Suns waived him, Albeck and the Lakers picked him up.

But this time, it wasn't worth the effort. Roberts appeared in 28 games for the Lakers in the 1976-77 season, shot 35.5% from the field while averaging 2.1 points and was waived after the season.

Robinson, Clifford Trent "Cliff" (1960-) ▶ By 1989, Robinson, who had played at USC, had been in the NBA for 10 years. He had played with five teams, none of them close to Los Angeles.

Then, he was involved in a serious automobile accident that made it questionable if he'd ever play anywhere again.

It took Robinson three years to return to the basketball court and, when he did, it was on a team in Naples, Italy. From there, Robinson went to Rapid City, Iowa, to play for the Thrillers of the Continental Basketball Assn.

And from there, he finally made it to the Lakers, signing with them in March 1992.

"I'm the comeback kid," Robinson said. "I had to go all 'round the world to come back home."

The first time Robinson touched the ball as a Laker, he sank a turnaround shot from 17 feet.

But he didn't make enough of those. He got into only nine regular-season games, averaging 3.2 points.

He was released at season's end, but the impressive thing was that, after the devastating accident and the three years away from the game, he could come back at all.

Robinson, Flynn James (1941-) ▶ A 6-foot-1, 190-pound guard, Robinson played with four teams in five seasons, including two tours with Cincinnati, before arriving in Los Angeles at the opportune time, the 1971-72 season that produced the league-record 33-game winning streak and the first NBA title won by the Lakers in Los Angeles.

Robinson, who was gone before the end of the next season, averaged 9.6 points per game as a Laker, shot 49%

from the field and averaged 2.1 assists. His nickname was "Instant Offense."

His best season was 1969-70, when he averaged 21.8 points and 5.5 assists for the Milwaukee Bucks.

But Robinson's most memorable moment as a Laker, at least in the mind of announcer Chick Hearn, had nothing to do with his basketball skills.

Few players at the time, if any, knew that Robinson wore a hairpiece. But after one attention-grabbing drive down the lane, everybody knew.

Just as Robinson had run past midcourt, the glue on that hairpiece apparently loosened. The front end of the wig blew back, but the rear end remained attached.

"It looked like the bill of a cap," Hearn said.

Robinson, never hesitating, continued down the floor and scored.

Robinson, Rumeal (1966-) ►
Many of the nation's basketball fans became aware of Robinson in 1989 when he was a member of the Michigan team that won the NCAA championship.

For Robinson, it was never quite that sweet again.

Drafted by the Atlanta Hawks, he also played for the New Jersey Nets, Charlotte Hornets and the Portland Trail Blazers before signing with the Lakers for the 1996-97 season.

Robinson got into 15 games for the Lakers, averaging 3.0 points, hardly the kind of numbers that would assure him longevity in a Laker uniform.

In the meantime, the Lakers were trying to get rid of forward Cedric Ceballos. They insisted it had nothing to do with his taking off in the middle of the previous season to go water skiing in Arizona. They were concerned about Ceballos' defensive liabilities and his inability to fit into a role.

So when the Lakers got the opportunity to trade Ceballos to the Phoenix Suns in January, they tossed Robinson into the deal and got forward Robert Horry and center Joe Kleine in return.

Robisch, David George "Robo" (1949-) ► Robisch arrived in December of 1977 from the Indianapolis Pacers as the second man in the deal that brought offensive punch to the Lakers in the form of Adrian Dantley.

And Robisch left a little less than two years later in the deal that brought a rebounding force in Jim Chones from the Cleveland Cavaliers.

Robisch started in pro basketball with the Denver Nuggets when they were in the American Basketball Assn., and nine seasons later, he was back with the Nuggets, who were by then in the NBA. Robisch played for eight teams in 13 seasons.

His ABA career numbers (14.6 points and 8.4 rebounds) were appreciably better than his NBA numbers (8.7 and 5.2). His Laker numbers (4.8 and 3.4) were the least impressive of all.

He had a few games that stand out. Starting at center against the Pacers in the 1978-79 season because of an injury to Kareem Abdul-Jabbar, Robisch pulled down 12 rebounds. In another game, he had 14.

But those kinds of games were the exception by the time he got to the Lakers because, by that point, his career had gone downhill.

Robisch's early promise was never realized. He had 804 rebounds in his first season of pro ball. He never had that many again.

Roche, John Michael (1949-) ►
A two-time All-American at South Carolina, Roche spent four years in the American Basketball Assn., scoring in double figures each season.

But early in the 1975-76 season, the 6-foot-3, 170-pound guard got a chance at the NBA when the Utah Stars folded after 16 games.

Roche's rights went to the Phoenix Suns, but the Lakers obtained him in January 1976 for future draft considerations.

Roche played only 15 games for the Lakers, averaging half a point a game. He was waived at the start of the next season.

But after sitting out three seasons, he returned with the Denver Nuggets and averaged 11.4 points in his first year with them, finally proving he wasn't out of his league in the NBA.

Rooks, Sean Lester (1969-) ➤

Rooks had one of the best seats at the Forum for Laker games in the 1997-98 season.

The problem for him was that he rarely left it.

Rooks was used to playing, not sitting, all the way back to his days as an All-Pacific 10 first-team center at Arizona as a senior.

From there, he went to Dallas, selected in the second round of the 1992 draft by the Mavericks. Rooks also played for the Minnesota Timberwolves and the Atlanta Hawks, appearing in a career-high 80 games with Minnesota in 1994-95.

But after joining the talent-laden Lakers as a free agent in the summer of 1996, Rooks gradually became more of a spectator than a participant.

He showed what he could do with some minutes in the final 10 regular-season games of 1996-97, averaging 12.6 points and 5.4 rebounds.

But he played in a career-low 41 regular-season games in 1997-98, averaging 10.4 minutes per game. He played at least 10 minutes in a game only twice after Jan. 6. And he played a total of only 11 minutes in the postseason.

Jack Nicholson may love his courtside seat, but, for Rooks, the appeal has long since faded.

Rosen, Lon ➤ He was a 19-year-old kid in the 1979-80 season with ideas about making it big in the NBA.

And fortunately for Rosen, he found another 19-year-old starting out with some big ideas of his own–Magic Johnson.

Rosen was a student at USC and a Laker intern that season. He ran the scoreboard clock, ran the 24-second clock and ran to get postgame quotes for the media. Although Rosen was there to serve the whole team, Johnson was his favorite.

The feeling was mutual.

On one occasion, Rosen was driving Johnson's new Rolls-Royce. The car broke down in the middle of a street and Rosen was forced to abandon it, but he worried what Johnson's reaction would be.

And what was his reaction?

"Did I leave anything in there?"

That's all Johnson wanted to know. Never mind the car.

Rosen became director of promotions for the Lakers, but, under Coach Pat Riley, his duties expanded into unexpected areas.

One day the Lakers arrived at McNichols Arena in Denver for practice, and Riley, always suspicious of opponents, noticed a closed-circuit camera pointed at the court, beaming its image back to an area where a security guard was stationed. Riley ordered Rosen to stand near the guard to make sure he wasn't spying on the team's practice.

Rosen left the Lakers in 1987, becoming Johnson's agent. He has been at Johnson's side since, through the sad times as well as the happy ones. Rosen was with his longtime friend when Johnson was informed by Dr. Michael Mellman in 1991 that he was HIV-positive.

Russell, Cazzie Lee Jr. (1944-) ➤

Russell averaged 15.1 points over a 12-year career that included three seasons with the Lakers. He averaged in the 20s twice. But Russell's game was ahead of its time. He played before the advent of the three-point shot, and he did some of his best work from three-point territory.

He loved to dribble into the corners and shoot from there. His range extended to 25 feet.

And he worked at making himself successful from that distance.

"He was the first one to practice," recalled one of his Laker coaches, Bill Sharman, "and the last one to leave."

But unfortunately for Russell, he couldn't last long enough to reap the benefits of the three-point bonus. The rule came into effect in 1979-80, two years after Russell's career had ended.

Saperstein, Abe ➤ Most remember him as the man who started the most famous team to never play in the NBA, the Harlem Globetrotters.

Some might even remember him as the man who started the short-lived American Basketball League.

But not many know that Saperstein was indirectly responsible for the Lakers coming to Los Angeles for the 1960-61 season.

The year was 1960.

The scene was New York's Roosevelt Hotel.

The issue was a proposed move to Los Angeles by Minneapolis Laker owner Bob Short at a league meeting.

The vote was 7-1. Against moving.

Although the NBA owners had viewed with interest and some envy the enormous fan support the Dodgers were enjoying after having moved to L.A. in 1958, they were reluctant to take such a leap.

The NBA was nowhere near the financial success it is today, and certainly not the equivalent of major league baseball at that time. NBA owners, many of them operating on the financial edge, couldn't see increasing their travel budget by putting a team on the West Coast. After all, Minneapolis was already the westernmost city in the league.

But after voting Short down in the morning, the owners decided to vote again in the afternoon.

This time, the tally was 8-0. In favor of the move.

What had changed? Saperstein had announced that day that he was forming the ABL in direct competition to the NBA. A newspaper heralding that move was on sale in the lobby of the Roosevelt, catching the eye of more than one owner.

Short couldn't have written a more persuasive headline. Suddenly, California looked appealing. And

valuable. The NBA owners couldn't allow Saperstein to establish a foothold on the West Coast.

There was one stipulation that tempered Short's joy over the final vote. He was going to be required to pay the difference in travel expenses between Minneapolis and Los Angeles for every team in the league.

But even under those circumstances, Short was better off in L.A.

Among the eight charter members of the ABL was a Los Angeles team, but the NBA's move to the West helped doom the upstart league, which folded after a season and a half.

Schad, Dick (1923-1996) ➤ Schad spent only one season as Chick Hearn's color commentator, Schad's 18th year in sportscasting.

But he gained a unique distinction that year. He was the last man to do the play-by-play of a Laker game before the start of Hearn's consecutive-game streak, which has surpassed 3,000 games.

On Nov. 20, 1965, Hearn was stuck in Arkansas, grounded by bad weather after broadcasting a USC football game.

The Lakers were playing in Las Vegas. When it became obvious Hearn could not get there in time, Schad was sent from Los Angeles to fill in behind the microphone. No one else has since.

Schad had a tough act to follow when he became Hearn's sidekick. Schad had been preceded by the popular Hot Rod Hundley, a lively storyteller who had been a longtime player.

The Lakers missed having a former player for Hearn to bounce his lines off and use for additional insight. After Schad's departure, Lynn Shackelford, who played at UCLA and in the American Basketball Assn., took over the microphone next to Hearn.

Schaus, Frederick Appleton "Fred" (1925-) ➤ It might have been natural to assume that Schaus was named the first head coach of the Los Angeles Lakers to placate Jerry West.

After all, West, a superstar at West Virginia, was the team's first draft pick of its Los Angeles era, the second selection overall in the 1960 draft. Going from the roads of West Virginia to the streets of Los Angeles could make someone a prime candidate for culture shock.

So why not bring along Schaus, his coach at West Virginia?

But any ideas that the 6-foot-5 Schaus was in over his head were quickly dispelled. He had the credentials. Schaus, who also played at West Virginia, played in the NBA as well, starting in 1949-50 with the Fort Wayne Pistons.

After five seasons, Schaus returned to his alma mater as head coach and led the school to six Southern Conference championships in as many years.

Success continued with the Lakers. In 1960-61, his first season, Schaus took a team that had gone 25-50 in its final season in Minneapolis, improved it to 36-43 and then took it into the second round of the playoffs before it was eliminated by the St. Louis Hawks in seven games.

Schaus was merely warming up.

In each of the next two seasons and four of the next five, Schaus reached the NBA Finals with the Lakers, losing each time to the Boston Celtics.

Red Auerbach was the Boston coach in those days and, when asked about his rivalry with Schaus 18 years after their last meeting, Auerbach couldn't resist sticking the needle in one more time.

"We out-psyched them many times," Auerbach boasted. "We used to psych Schaus pretty good. He became a little confused. It got to the point he started [Elgin] Baylor [a forward] in the backcourt."

As might be imagined, when those remarks were relayed to Schaus, some of the old fire reignited in him.

"He always had a gimmick, all right," Schaus said. "It was called Bill Russell. It was amazing how great a coach he became after he got Bill Russell. Russell made a hell of a coach out of him. Before that, with [Bob] Cousy and [Bill] Sharman, he couldn't even win his division."

Fred Schaus, here in 1965, coached the Lakers seven seasons, reaching the NBA Finals four times, before becoming its general manager.

After the 1966-67 season, Schaus turned the reins of the Lakers over to Butch van Breda Kolff and became general manager.

After the Lakers finally won an NBA title in 1971-72, Schaus returned to West Virginia to become the school's athletic director.

But the Laker ties remained strong. When the club was about to finally beat the Celtics for the NBA championship, in Boston no less, in 1985, Schaus was so nervous back home in West Virginia that he couldn't bear to watch the title-clinching game on television. He went outside to pull weeds in his backyard and told his wife to relay the score to him.

When it was finally over and his old team was triumphant, Schaus discounted any thought that the law of averages had finally caught up with his old, hated rivals. "I never believed in the law of averages in athletics," he said. "That is hogwash. If you execute, you get it done."

Oh yeah, and one other thing.

"I enjoyed watching Red walk out without that lit cigar," he said. "I enjoyed that."

Schayes, Daniel Leslie "Danny" (1959-) ➤

Schayes definitely had the right genes. His father, Dolph, was a 12-time All-Star in a 16-year pro basketball career.

The younger Schayes also had the size at 6 feet 11 and 260 pounds, and the Utah Jazz made him a first-round draft choice in 1981.

Thirteen seasons later, after having proved himself a competent, if not exceptional, big man, Schayes became a Laker, obtained from the Milwaukee Bucks in the middle of the 1993-94 season for a second-round draft choice.

The Lakers didn't expect a lot from Schayes. He was 34 and had done little for the Bucks. All they were looking for was a fourth center—behind Vlade Divac, Sam Bowie and James Edwards—who could supply a little muscle inside and give them a little more spending power when the season was over. Schayes' salary could be used by the Lakers to pursue other free agents while remaining under the salary cap.

Maybe he had the ability, but Schayes didn't have much of an opportunity. He appeared in 13 games for the Lakers, averaging 2.8 points and 2.6 rebounds, and was released at the end of the season.

Scott, Byron Antom (1961-) ➤

Few players have first put on a Laker uniform in a more hostile environment.

It wasn't the way Scott had dreamed it would be when he was growing up near the Forum and attending Inglewood's Morningside High.

While he was setting a school scoring record at Morningside, Scott was rooting for his favorite Laker, Jerry West, down the street and dreaming of the day he would wear the same uniform.

It was West who made it possible for Scott to become a Laker. In October 1983, West, who had become the general manager, traded Norm Nixon and Eddie Jordan to the San Diego Clippers for Scott and Swen Nater.

Scott had the credentials to be on a contender like the Lakers. A pure shooter, Scott had increased his scoring average every year at Arizona State.

Scott had been drafted by the Clippers in the first

Byron Scott, right, was regarded more as a shooting threat but he was also a solid defender, averaging better than a steal a game in 14 years.

round of the 1983 draft, the fourth player and first guard taken.

No, there was nothing suspect about Scott. The suspicion, and the resentment, focused on West. Nixon and West didn't get along.

With the Lakers having been swept by the Philadelphia 76ers in the NBA Finals the previous spring, and with Nixon having just had his 28th birthday, West saw a chance to give Magic Johnson a younger backcourt mate and an outside shooting threat to take some of the pressure off him.

Johnson's attitude was, thanks, but no thanks. He, Michael Cooper and Nixon, who called themselves the Three Amigos, had been inseparable on the road.

Now, West was breaking them up—perhaps, they thought, because of a personal vendetta. So when Scott reported to the Lakers, he found the practices almost harder than the games. Driving the middle against opposing teams was tough. Driving the middle against his own Lakers was tougher. They wouldn't give him a break, or a shot.

It might have been a difficult way to break in, but, as it turned out, it was the best thing that could have happened to Scott at that stage of his pro career.

By keeping his mouth shut and his enthusiasm up, he eventually earned the respect of his new teammates. And by keeping the pressure on their new teammate and a game-level defense in his face during practice, they might have speeded up his maturation process.

Scott was intimidated at first.

After 16 games, he was shooting only 36.4%. But he

began to find his game, and the Lakers found that he really was talented, that perhaps West knew what he was doing after all.

Scott moved into the starting lineup, just as West had envisioned. After Jan. 1, Scott made 50.9% of his shots from the field and wound up as the third-leading vote-getter on the all-rookie team. He started 49 games.

Johnson and Cooper had found themselves a new Amigo.

Scott went on to sink better than 50% of his shots from the field in three of the next four seasons, including a career-high 53.9% in 1984-85, a season in which he also led the NBA in three-point field-goal percentage at 43.3%.

Scott set the Laker record for highest three-point percentage in a season at 43.6% in 1986-87.

He made all 10 shots he tried during one game in the 1985-86 season.

But it wasn't merely Scott's shooting that made him an integral part of three NBA championship teams. He also became a good defensive player and wound up among the club's all-time top 10 in assists and steals, along with games, minutes and, of course, several shooting categories.

He was with the Lakers for 10 seasons, spent three with the Indiana Pacers, and then returned to the Lakers for the 1996-97 season.

Not bad for a guy who began his Laker career as an outcast.

Scott, Charles Thomas, "Charlie" (1948-) ➤ Charlie Scott didn't come cheaply to the Lakers. Acquired in December 1977 from the Boston Celtics, Scott cost the Lakers Don Chaney, Kermit Washington and a first-round draft choice.

Washington's Laker career had effectively ended a month earlier when he threw a punch that shattered the face of Rudy Tomjanovich. From that moment on, the Lakers were eager to move Washington out of town. The chance to pick up Scott seemed like an added bonus.

Scott had impressive credentials. In a career that began with the Virginia Squires in the American Basketball Assn., he averaged more than 25 points four times, his high a 34.6 average with Virginia in 1971-72.

But Scott didn't prove to be worth the price the Lakers had paid. He averaged 11.7 points for them in 48 games

of the 1977-78 season and was traded at the end of the season to the Denver Nuggets for Ron Boone and two second-round draft choices.

SEE ALSO • *Boone, Ron; Chaney, Don; Tomjanovich, Rudy; Washington, Kermit.*

Seals, Shea (1975-) ➤ Because Seals managed to come down with back spasms at the start of the 1997-98 season, he was carried all year long.

The Lakers liked what they saw in the preseason of the 6-foot-5, 210-pound guard from Tulsa. They liked his three-point shooting (three of seven in exhibitions). They didn't like Seals enough to put him on the active roster all season, but the injured list was a different matter. So Seals conveniently came down with back spasms.

When fellow guard Nick Van Exel underwent arthroscopic knee surgery in February, Seals conveniently recovered from his back problems and got into four games, playing a total of nine minutes.

Selvy, Franklin Delano "Frank," "Pops" (1932-) ➤ Of all the men to wear the Laker uniform, no one was the equal of Wilt Chamberlain–except Frank Selvy.

At least in one regard.

Because those two accomplished the most extraordinary feat on a basketball court: scoring 100 points in a game.

Chamberlain set his mark at the highest level, scoring 100 points as a member of the Philadelphia Warriors on March 2, 1962 against the New York Knicks at Hershey, Pa.

Selvy scored his 100 points while playing for Furman University against Newberry College on Feb. 13, 1954.

But while Chamberlain's big game in 1962 may be the most-remembered achievement of an extraordinary career, Selvy's incredible performance was overshadowed by the two points he didn't score in 1962.

Selvy played nine years in the NBA, the last four for the Lakers.

In the spring of 1962, in the second meeting against the Boston Celtics in the NBA Finals, Selvy had the chance to give Los Angeles its first league championship and stop a Laker losing streak to Boston in the finals that would eventually stretch to eight series.

All Selvy had to do was make a 15-foot jump shot.

His opportunity came with three seconds remaining in the seventh and deciding game and the score tied, 100-100, in Boston Garden.

Red Auerbach, then the Celtic coach, admitted that when he saw the ball in Selvy's hands that close to the basket, he was ready to throw up his own hands. "I thought it was all over," Auerbach said.

Boston's Tom "Satch" Sanders had a similar reaction when Laker guard Hot Rod Hundley fed the ball to Selvy.

"There was very little breathing in the Garden when the ball went to Selvy on the baseline," Sanders said. "I thought, 'Anybody but him.'"

Hundley recalled that he had looked first for guard Jerry West.

"I turned to face the basket," Hundley said. "West wasn't open. [Bob] Cousy was on Selvy. Cousy was a terrible defensive player. We used to fight over who would be guarded by him. He would steal the ball a lot because he just ran around, but he never guarded his man."

After getting the pass from Hundley, Selvy, protected by a screen, was open for an instant before Cousy moved in.

"The screen delayed him just a second," Selvy said. "I had to get it off fast. I sort of hurried ... but I thought it was going in."

Selvy's shot hit the front of the rim, went high in the air and came down in the hands of Boston center Bill Russell.

"I thought Cousy fouled him," Elgin Baylor said. "Something happened to the shot. I was in good position to get the rebound and Sam Jones just shoved me out of bounds. He didn't get called for it."

Baylor knew he had been shoved, but he didn't know it was Jones who had done the shoving. Not for 16 years.

And then one day, Jones simply admitted it to Baylor and kidded him about it for years afterward.

"I'm sure poor Frank still wakes up in the middle of the night and sees the ball hit the rim and go up," Cousy said. "I was so relieved. I don't think Frank had missed that shot since 1928."

It certainly seemed better to have Selvy, who shot 42% from the field that season, put the ball up than Hundley, who shot only 34%.

But considering the result, Laker Coach Fred Schaus was willing to reassess his thinking.

"Hot Rod told me he had had a dream that he made the winning shot," Schaus said. "Damn, he should have taken it."

Instead, time ran out in regulation and the Celtics went on to win in overtime, 110-107.

"I get the blame for missing that shot," Selvy said, "but I don't think that was the ballgame. We could have done better in overtime. I think a lot of people don't realize that I made the last two baskets to tie the game up."

Afterward in the Laker locker room, Hundley, the man who had passed Selvy the ball, came over to find his teammate with his head hanging down.

"It could happen to anybody," Hundley told Selvy, jokingly adding, "Don't worry, baby. You only cost us about $30,000."

SEE ALSO • *Biggest games.*

Shackelford, Lynn ➤ Shackelford was the first Laker analyst to survive long enough to carve out his own identity alongside Chick Hearn.

Shackelford worked the microphone next to Hearn from 1970 through 1977 and also served as the team's traveling secretary.

Shackelford was already well-known in Southern California basketball circles before sitting down in the broadcast booth, having been a standout at Burbank's Burroughs High School and at UCLA during the Lew Alcindor years.

After getting out of basketball and broadcasting, Shackelford began a successful career in golf course management.

Sharman, William Walton "Bill" (1926-) ➤ Early in his career, Sharman suffered through perhaps his most crushing defeat. His team, which had been well ahead of its closest pursuer, broke down, was caught at the end of the season and then beaten in the last minute of its last game by the Shot Heard Around the World.

It wasn't a jump shot or a slam dunk. It was a home run that landed in the seats of the Polo Grounds in New York.

Sharman's team was the Brooklyn Dodgers. He was sitting in the dugout disconsolately watching with many of his teammates as Bobby Thomson hit the home run that ended the Dodgers' 1951 season and won the pennant for the New York Giants.

Sharman was a good baseball player who spent five seasons as a minor league outfielder and was called up by the Dodgers late in 1951. He never played in a major league game. But he found greatness and handed out crushing defeats to others as a basketball player.

Sharman was successful at every level of the game and in every position he assumed.

He was a star in high school at Porterville, Calif., where he also won a state tennis championship. Sharman went to USC, where he was a two-time All-American in basketball and began to establish himself as one of the sport's all-time great free-throw shooters, making 80.3% from the line in college.

Selected by the Washington Capitols in the second round of the 1950 NBA draft, Sharman wound up with the Boston Celtics in his second year and went on to become a member of four championship teams while wearing the Celtic green.

A Hall of Famer and a member of the All-NBA team seven times, Sharman once made 55 free throws in a row, then an NBA record. He still holds the record for most seasons leading the league in free-throw percentage (seven) and most consecutive seasons as the leader (five).

A career 88.3% free-throw shooter in the NBA, Sharman was over 90% three times, with a high of 93.2% in 1958-59.

Sharman was so aware of the fine points of shooting a basketball that he once determined that the rim of a basket in St. Louis before a Hawk-Celtic game was a fraction of an inch too low. Sharman thus triggered a dispute that ended with Boston Coach Red Auerbach punching Hawk owner Ben Kerner.

But Sharman didn't need to stand at the free-throw line to be effective. He could shoot from long range as well. He once sank an 88-foot shot and then teased the man guarding him about lax defense.

Sharman himself never played lax defense.

In his book "Heinsohn, Don't You Ever Smile?" former Celtic Tommy Heinsohn wrote of his old teammate, "Sharman was like a treacherous bulldog that would suddenly bite and refuse to let go. You spelled his name T-E-N-A-C-I-O-U-S ... . They mention K.C. Jones as the perfect example of a defensive guard, but Sharman played defense as well and maybe even better. Bill didn't have the

Bill Sharman signals from the sidelines during a 1974 game.

quickness, but he intimidated his man. He played him in his socks. He picked him up and stayed with him all the way to his girlfriend's apartment."

Sharman's tenacity carried beyond the basketball court. He once found himself face to face with a shark off the coast of Acapulco and safely escaped by banging the shark with one of those stiletto-sharp elbows that left bruises on many an opposing rebounder.

Sharman retired after the 1960-61 season, but his days of basketball were far from over.

He became a coach, first at Cal State Los Angeles, then in three professional leagues, winning a championship in each, a feat unmatched in the history of professional basketball.

Sharman guided the Cleveland Pipers to the American Basketball League championship in 1962, led the Utah Stars to the American Basketball Assn., title in 1971 and then took the Lakers to the 1972 NBA title, the first championship won by the team after its move to Los Angeles.

Sharman was the coach who put together the longest winning streak in the history of professional sports, the 1971-72 Lakers' 33 consecutive victories.

But there was a downside to all his success as a coach. Unable to step on the court himself once his playing days were over, Sharman expressed his emotions on the sideline, and the years of screaming and cheerleading and protesting took their toll. Sharman's strong, vibrant, inspiring voice was reduced to a whisper because of permanent damage to his vocal cords.

After coaching the San Francisco Warriors for two years, then the Lakers for five, he moved to the Laker general manager's job in 1976. But when even talking on the phone proved difficult, Sharman moved up still further in the Laker hierarchy to become team president in 1982. He is now a special consultant to owner Jerry Buss.

But one thing Sharman never has to worry about is his accomplishments in basketball. They speak for themselves.

Shootaround ➤ It has become as much a part of the pregame routine in the NBA as a layup drill, as much a part of the players' preparation as stretching.

The morning before a night game, players regularly practice moves and shooting on the court. But it wasn't always that way.

Before the 1971-72 season, Bill Sharman, newly appointed Laker coach, wanted to introduce his players to shootarounds, an activity that he had used as a coach in the American Basketball League and the American Basketball Assn.

But there was one potential problem: center Wilt Chamberlain.

Sharman didn't know if Chamberlain would be opposed to a mandatory shootaround. But he did know that if Chamberlain, whose dominating game was matched by an equally dominating personality, didn't buy into the program, the shootaround would die without even getting a fair shot.

So Sharman took Chamberlain to lunch to present his plan, hoping that it wouldn't sound too disruptive to the players' routine–which often involved sleeping late after nights out, particularly on the road.

Sharman was about to suggest his plan when the bill came. Much to his chagrin, Sharman discovered he had misplaced his wallet.

"Great," he thought. "This will go over real big. I'm about to squander my goodwill. And I haven't even brought up the shootaround yet."

At that moment, the owner of the restaurant, spotting his famous customers, snatched the check. He wouldn't allow Sharman or Chamberlain to pay.

Sharman took the moment to present the proposal before something else went wrong.

"I don't sleep well at night," Chamberlain said, "so I like to sleep in the mornings. But let's try it and see what happens."

Chamberlain came to accept the new routine, the shootaround became a fixture and the Lakers' went on to win a then-record 69 regular-season games and their first NBA title since moving to Los Angeles.

SEE ALSO • *Chamberlain, Wilt, Sharman, Bill.*

Short, Robert Earl "Bob" (1917-1982) ➤ In 1997, Laker owner Jerry Buss was paying his center, Shaquille O'Neal, about $17 million a season.

Forty years earlier, such a figure would have been beyond Short's comprehension. He and a group of other Minnesota businessmen had bought the Lakers, then located in Minneapolis, for $150,000.

A bargain? Not in those days, when things looked bleak for the NBA in general and the Lakers in particular. The new owners added another $50,000 for operating expenses, and that was eaten up in two weeks.

It was discouraging even to Short, who had made a fortune in the trucking and hotel industries. Nevertheless when the club reached a financial precipice, needing $14,000 immediately to stay afloat, Short supplied the money.

As a result, the other owners awarded him with enough common stock at five cents a share to eventually give him one-third of the franchise.

But at the rate the team was losing money, that meant one-third of a debt growing at an alarming rate.

Short would sell a player to raise money, or sell a player to save money because that player was demanding a raise.

At one point, Short went into the Laker locker room and told his players, "Hey, guys, I like basketball as much as the next guy, but not when it's going to cost me $50,000 a week."

Short was considered a bold visionary for taking a gamble by moving the Lakers in 1960 to the West Coast, virgin territory for the NBA in those days.

"A gamble?" Short said. "Hell, we were broke in Minneapolis." Short sold the Lakers for to Jack Kent Cooke in 1965 for $5,175,000.

Originally, the two had agreed on $5 million. But Short, always looking for another angle, told Cooke that he had already sold $350,000 worth of season tickets for the upcoming season. Surely he should profit from that somehow. Half that amount would be fine, Short told Cooke.

At that point, with the team nearly in his grasp, Cooke would have agreed to nearly anything except giving up Elgin Baylor and Jerry West.

So Short got his extra $175,000.

Having cut his ties to basketball, Short plunged into baseball, buying the Washington Senators in 1968. Again, with mounting losses, this time totaling $3 million, he backed up the moving vans. The Senators relocated in Arlington, Texas, in 1971 as the Texas Rangers. Short later sold them as well.

Other than sports, Short's great love was politics. A close friend of former Sen. and Vice President Hubert Humphrey, Short was treasurer of the Democratic National Committee and unsuccessfully ran for governor and U.S.Senator in Minnesota. He lost $1 million of his own money in the Senate race.

SEE ALSO • *Cooke, Jack Kent; Minneapolis Lakers; Saperstein, Abe.*

Showtime ➤ In the early 1960s, before he even thought of owning the Lakers, Jerry Buss was a regular at the Horn, a nightclub on Wilshire Boulevard in Santa Monica.

The Horn's nightly show always began the same way: The lights went down and an entertainer, planted at one of the tables, would get up and start singing, "It's Showtime." Then a second singer would join in from another table. And then a third. Buss never forgot the excitement that little act created or the way it woke up the room.

And so, nearly two decades later, when he did buy the Lakers, he decided he was going to re-create that same anticipation and excitement in the Forum crowds by putting together a team that would not only win, but would be entertaining.

And, of course, he had no doubt what he would call that unique brand of basketball entertainment. He would call it Showtime.

SEE ALSO • *Buss, Jerry.*

Sims, Robert Antell Jr. "Bobby" (1955-) ➤ Sims was the first fully home-grown product to join the Lakers. He played at L.A. Jordan High and at Pepperdine.

After playing one year with the Seattle Buchan Bakers of the AAU National Industrial League, Sims attended a Laker tryout camp, staged after the team's first season in Los Angeles.

He was the first player signed from that camp.

Sims was an attractive player for several reasons. At 6 feet 5 and 220 pounds, he had the size and strength to play in the NBA. He also had leaping ability (6 feet 7½ inches in the high jump), speed (9.9 seconds in the 100-yard dash) and a nice shooting touch.

Despite all those gifts, Sims lasted only 18 games with the Lakers in the 1961-62 season before being sold to the St. Louis Hawks.

Sky Hook ➤ The favorite shot of Laker center Kareem Abdul-Jabbar.

Abdul-Jabbar, at 7 feet 2, made the shot look easy. He would glide to his right, plant his legs, leap high enough off his left foot to bring himself near eye level to the basket and then softly shoot a hook shot that carried well above the arms of the tallest defenders.

Largely because of the sky hook, Abdul-Jabbar scored 38,387 points, the most in NBA history, and also made 55.9% of his shots from the field.

But it wasn't an easy shot for others. No one since Abdul-Jabbar's retirement in 1989 has managed to use the shot with anywhere near his effectiveness.

Magic Johnson came close with what he

called the "baby sky hook." Vlade Divac had limited success copying Abdul-Jabbar's style.

"It was the the the most indefensible shot in basketball," Laker assistant coach Bill Bertka said. "But unfortunately, nobody teaches it anymore. It has been lost in the archives."

And why is that?

Said Bertka: "The players treat shots like they do clothing. If it's not in style, they don't want anything to do with it. The players don't want to try a shot if it's not something they see other players shoot.

"But it was a great, great shot."

Even Abdul-Jabbar sometimes had trouble with the sky hook. And when he did, he would go to Bertka to get back on track.

"Once in a while, the shot would get a flatter arc," Bertka said. "That's because Kareem wouldn't be getting enough spring in his legs. He would get stiff out there." So Abdul-Jabbar would go off in a corner during practice and shoot sky hook after sky hook until he got his form back. Then he would come back to Bertka and announce, "I'm all tuned up."

SEE ALSO • *Abdul-Jabbar, Kareem; Bertka, Bill; Holy Providence.*

Smith, Charles Anton "Tony" (1968-) ➤ At
Wauwatosa East High School in Wisconsin, Smith was a versatile athlete, running the 110-meter hurdles in 14.5 seconds, high-jumping 6 feet 6 and long-jumping 22-6. He was a two-time state triple-jump champion and played volleyball.

But he wasn't quite as versatile in basketball, the sport he devoted his professional life to.

Oh, he could run and jump on the court pretty well and was an excellent defender.

But as a shooter and ballhandler, the 6-4, 205-pound guard never made a huge impact with the Lakers. Smith's best season with the Lakers was in 1993-94, when he started 31 games and averaged 8.8 points and 2.0 assists. He had been drafted on the second round of the 1990 draft from Marquette, the 51st selection overall, at the urging of Laker Coach Mike Dunleavy, who became familiar with Smith when Dunleavy was coach of the Milwaukee Bucks. Following five seasons with the Lakers, Smith was not re-signed after the 1994-95 season.

Smith, Elmore (1949-) ➤ Who
blocked the most shots in an NBA game? Was it Wilt Chamberlain or Bill Russell, the most dominant centers of their day?

It might have been either, but blocked shots weren't tabulated in the league until the 1973-74 season, five years after Russell was gone and the year after Chamberlain retired.

The record belongs to Smith, who had an incredible 17 for the Lakers against the Portland Trail Blazers on Oct. 28, 1973. That was in the first month of the first season the statistic was kept.

Smith's total that night was no fluke; he blocked 14 shots on two occasions. All three of Smith's big shot-blocking games came in a nine-day span with the Lakers.

He blocked 393 shots that season, the third largest single-season amount in league history through 1997-98. In the five additional seasons he played, Smith never came close to that figure.

Smith's career with the Lakers ended on June 16, 1975, when he was one of four L.A. players traded to Milwaukee for Kareem Abdul-Jabbar.

SEE ALSO • *Chamberlain, Wilt; Russell, Bill.*

Smith, Robert Joseph "Bobby"
(1937-) ➤ Like Jerry West and Hot Rod Hundley, Smith went from West Virginia to the Lakers.

There, however, the resemblance ended.

Smith, a 6-foot-4, 190-pound guard, played 13 games over his two seasons with the Lakers, one in Minneapolis and one in Los Angeles.

To his teammates, he might be more remembered for his free spirit than his play. He would get his car up to 90 mph or so and scream, "James Dean, I love you!" He survived his road antics, but not in the NBA, never playing again after his 1961-62 season with the Lakers.

Smithsonian Institution ➤ Along with Charles
Lindbergh's Spirit of St. Louis and a capsule from the early days of the space program in the Washington, D.C., museum are James Worthy's protective goggles and his No. 42 jersey.

Worthy, although he never achieved the superstar

status of Magic Johnson or Kareem Abdul Jabbar, was also the first athlete to be taped for the Smithsonian's oral history project, his memories of the Lakers' glory years preserved for future generations.

SEE ALSO • *Worthy, James.*

Smrek, Michael Frank "Mike" (1962-) ➤ Ever see a 7-foot, 250-pound hockey player?

That's what the sports world would have seen if Smrek had stayed with his favorite childhood activity. Born in Welland, Canada, Smrek was mostly a hockey player until he starting growing. And growing.

Canisius College recruiters decided he was better with a basketball in his hands than a stick.

Smrek did so well at Canisius, a marginal Division I program, he was picked in the second round of the 1985 draft by the Portland Trail Blazers.

When the Lakers' Peter Gudmundsson was injured and declared out for the season in November of 1986, General Manager Jerry West decided to take a chance on Smrek, plucking him off the waiver wire.

A native-born Canadian had never been on an NBA championship team. Smrek was on two in his two seasons with the Lakers.

Smrek didn't have impressive numbers, but, as the strongest man on the team, he could be a force in the middle.

Just ask Robert Parish.

The Boston Celtic center, who effectively banged bodies with the best of them, tried to drive around Smrek one time in the key at Boston Garden. Parish crashed into Smrek's left side and was sent flying to the parquet floor. Smrek never moved. Maybe he should have played hockey after all.

Sparrow, Rory Darnell (1958-) ➤ Sparrow changed teams seven times in 12 seasons in the NBA.

After leaving Villanova, Sparrow played for New Jersey, Atlanta, New York, Chicago, Miami, Sacramento, Chicago again and then, at age 33, the Lakers.

"There are certain teams you always want to play for,"

Sparrow said, "the Celtics, the Lakers, the Bulls and the Knicks. I've been fortunate enough to play for three of them."

After averaging only 3.0 points for the Lakers in 42 games, Sparrow was cut loose before the 1991-92 season when Magic Johnson announced he was coming back, an announcement that proved to be premature by more than three years.

That didn't help Sparrow. His NBA career had been grounded.

Sports Arena ➤ John F. Kennedy was nominated for the presidency there in 1960 at the Democratic National Convention. Martin Luther King spoke there in 1961 against racial injustice. Cassius Clay won a big fight there in 1962 on his way to becoming Muhammad Ali and a three-time heavyweight champion. The Los Angeles Kings briefly played there in 1967, their first year of existence. UCLA won an NCAA basketball championship there in 1968 by beating North Carolina.

The Lakers played their first game in Los Angeles there. And many, many more.

While the Lakers were still in Minneapolis, and struggling financially, owner Bob Short scheduled two regular-season games on the West Coast, one in San Francisco and one in Los Angeles.

The Los Angeles game, pitting the Lakers against the Philadelphia Warriors, was played at the Sports Arena on Feb. 1, 1960, drawing a crowd of 10,202.

The Lakers played two more games later that season at the Sports Arena, and, a year later, it became their home.

They stayed there for seven seasons, and would have stayed longer if the Coliseum Commission had gone along with Jack Kent Cooke, who owned the Lakers and wanted to land an NHL franchise.

The commission was backing a rival group also trying to get an NHL team. Already locked into a power struggle over hockey, Cooke and the commission fought over his contract to play in the Sports Arena. He wanted a better deal. Commission officials told him he'd have to wait two years until his contract ran out—or look for a new site.

Those who knew Cooke, even casually, knew that waiving an ultimatum in his face was like waving a red cape in the face of a bull.

"I didn't know about the machinations of these guys," Cooke recalled, "Machiavellian kind of birds.

"So I said, 'You know, you're making this whole thing so difficult, I'm liable to build my own arena.' And this fella [a commission official whose name Cooke couldn't recall] looked at me and said, 'Ha, ha, ha.'

"Now if he'd only laughed, I would have laughed with him, you see? But he actually said, 'Ha, ha, ha.' I said, 'In that case, I am going to build my own arena.' "

Cooke told his attorney, Clyde Tritt, who was sitting next to him, "I've had enough of this balderdash."

When the commissioners learned it was Inglewood that Cooke was considering, a city then thought to be too far away from Los Angeles' population centers to draw decent crowds, they had another good laugh.

But, as was usually the case in his life, Cooke had the final chortle. Eighteen months after the July 1, 1966 groundbreaking in Inglewood, the Forum was open for business.

The Sports Arena had to wait 18 years until it landed another pro basketball client, the void finally filled by the arrival of the San Diego Clippers in Los Angeles in 1984.

SEE ALSO • *Cal State LA; Crowd-O-Meter; Cooke, Jack Kent; Forum; Shrine Auditorium.*

Spriggs, Larry Michael (1959-) ➤ Finding himself on the Lakers in the mid 1980s, battling for playing time against such players as Kurt Rambis and Jamaal Wilkes, Spriggs knew he'd be spending much of his time on the bench.

But that didn't mean Spriggs accepted his fate quietly. Not after the 1984-85 season.

Spriggs started 32 consecutive games after the Lakers got off to a 3-5 start that season, one in which they defeated the Boston Celtics in the NBA Finals for the first time. And his averages of 6.7 points and 3.0 rebounds were about twice what they had been the season before, his first in L.A.

So what was Spriggs' reward?

At the start of the next training camp, he again found himself battling for a job, this time against new arrival A.C. Green.

"There's no end to proving yourself if you're not a big name," Spriggs said. "There's nothing given to you. There isn't a bed of roses anywhere. I've always had to plant my own."

After three years with the Lakers, however, he ran out of roses. And hope. With a new crop of rookies for the Lakers to choose from, Spriggs took off for Europe, where he finally got his playing time.

While in Greece, Spriggs was an innocent bystander when he was shot in an incident outside a nightclub but was not seriously injured.

Stabley, Fred Jr. ➤ He was a sportswriter for the Lansing State Journal in the mid 1970s when Earvin Johnson started playing for Lansing Everett High.

In the seventh game of Johnson's first season at Everett, against Jackson Parkside, the 15- year-old had the kind of game he would become known for in his later years as a Laker. He scored 36 points, pulled down 18 rebounds and handed out 16 assists.

In the locker room afterward, Stabley approached Johnson.

"Listen, Earvin," the sportswriter said, "I think you should have a nickname. I was thinking of calling you Dr. J, but that's taken [by Julius Erving]. And so is Big E [Elvin Hayes]. How about if I call you Magic?"

Johnson, surrounded by his teammates and embarrassed at being singled out for such a splashy nickname, told Stabley to do whatever he wanted.

That's not what Stabley's editor told him. Stabley was warned that the kid's fast start wouldn't last and he probably wouldn't be able to live up to the name.

But when Johnson had another big game, Stabley referred to him as Earvin "Magic" Johnson. And soon, it was the Earvin, not the Magic, that was dropped from his name.

SEE ALSO • *E.J., the DeeJay; Johnson, Buck; Johnson, Earvin; Johnson, June Bug; Johnson, Magic.*

Steals off the court ➤ Where would you imagine the safest place at a basketball arena would be?

A team's locker room?

That seems a good guess. But on one night in 1982, it was wrong.

While the players are on the court, they feel confident that their valuables–money, jewelry and other personal belongings–are safe in the locker room with their clothes.

That confidence was shattered for the Lakers when someone, who was never caught, managed to steal all of the players' money from the Forum locker room during a game. While on a flight out of town the next morning, the Lakers were discussing what they had lost (few knew exactly how much).

The discussion amused Magic Johnson, who laughed about the losses suffered by his teammates until someone asked him how much had been stolen from him. Johnson's face froze. Stolen from him? He hadn't heard anything about the theft the night before and hadn't even considered that he might have been victimized too. Slowly, Johnson reached into his pocket and pulled out his money clip.

It was empty.

Laughter roared through the first-class cabin.

Everyone else's spirits had gotten a lift.

Donald Sterling is all smiles during the 1984 press conference held to announce his purchase of the then-San Diego Clippers basketball team.

Sterling, Donald (1933-) ➤ Sterling's Los Angeles Clippers have been in the shadow of the Lakers since he moved the team from San Diego to Los Angeles in 1984. He bought the San Diego Clippers in 1981 and brought them north to the Los Angeles Sports Arena three years later, hoping to emulate fellow owner Jerry Buss.

But if it hadn't been for Sterling, the Lakers might not have been worth emulating or cast such a big shadow.

In 1979, Buss and his partner, Frank Mariani, were trying to buy the Lakers, Forum and Kings from Jack Kent Cooke. But in the final hours of the tense, complicated

negotiations, Mariani and Buss found themselves $1 million short of the $67.5 million they would need to complete the deal.

Sterling, owner of a Southern California real-estate empire, was a friend of Mariani's. Mariani appealed to him and Sterling came up with a million-dollar loan. The deal went through, and Sterling's Clippers have been trying to catch up ever since.

SEE ALSO • *Buss, Jerry; Cooke, Jack Kent; Forum; Mariani, Frank.*

Strangest press conference ➤ It was one of the oddest news conferences in sports history–and turned out to be one of the most important in Laker history.

It was hastily called on Nov. 19, 1981 to announce the successor to Laker coach Paul Westhead.

The night before in Utah, Magic Johnson, expressing the players' frustrations over a new offense installed by Westhead, said he wanted to be traded. Many of the players said they felt alienated from the coach and the offense had stifled them. Owner Jerry Buss, also frustrated over the inability of his coach to communicate with his players, later he said he had already decided to fire Westhead. But Johnson's comments hastened that announcement, because the Lakers certainly weren't interested in trading Magic.

When the team returned the next day, Westhead was fired and a meeting was quickly called at Buss' Pickfair home involving the owner and his chief lieutenants: President Bill Sharman and General Manager Jerry West.

Buss figured West, who had coached the Lakers from 1976-77 through 1978-79, could again coach the team, at least until order and morale were restored. And that's what Buss thought had been agreed upon in the meeting.

But at the news conference, Buss announced that Westhead was out, West would be the "offensive coach" and assistant coach Pat Riley would "stay as coach."

Nobody seemed to know what Buss meant. Including West, who did not want to return to coaching.

In the five seconds or so it took West to make it from his seat at the table to the microphone, he decided the fate of the Lakers for the 1980s.

West looked at the confused reporters and said confidently and forcefully, "I'm going to be working for and with Pat Riley. I feel, in my heart, he is the head coach." Buss later said of West's announcement: "It was a total shock."

When Buss was asked by a reporter who would make out the starting lineup, he said, "Well, obviously that's the job of the coach. I'm sure they should be able to get together and decide on that sort of thing."

Later, when Los Angeles Times Sports Editor Bill Dwyre asked Laker official Bob Steiner what was going on, Steiner replied, "Bill, we proved one thing, that we don't know how to run a press conference."

And that is how Riley, who would become the winningest coach in Laker history, got his job.

SEE ALSO • *Johnson, Magic; Riley, Pat; Westhead, Paul.*

Stratton, Susan ➤ Whenever he needs something while on the air, announcer Chick Hearn inevitably yells, "Susan!"

Stratton has been the producer of Laker telecasts since 1976. If statistics were kept in the production truck, Stratton would have been credited with more assists than Magic Johnson for all the things she has done to keep Laker telecasts running smoothly.

She has a million Hearn stories. One of her favorites is the time Hearn's clock radio in his hotel room awakened him in the middle of the night.

"Chick is not the least bit mechanical," Stratton said. "The simplest devices confuse him.

"Now here he was with this radio blasting and he had no idea how to shut it off. So what did he do? Instead of finding the off switch or calling the front desk, he got a scissors or a knife and cut the power cord, left it dangling and went back to sleep. "That's Chick."

Strong, Derek (1968-) ➤ For Strong, who attended Palisades High School, Los Angeles is home, even if he played only one season with the Lakers.

Strong's road back to Los Angeles after high school was a long one. He played at Xavier in Cincinnati, then in Spain, with Miami of the United States Basketball League, the Philadelphia 76ers and Washington Bullets of the NBA, Quad Cities of the Continental Basketball Assn., the Milwaukee Bucks, Boston Celtics and, finally, with the Lakers. The Lakers signed him in October 1995.

Strong's playing time was reduced after Magic Johnson made his comeback early in 1996 and settled in at forward.

Strong was cut as part of the push to provide enough money to sign Shaquille O'Neal and to re-sign Elden Campbell.

Back on that road again, Strong wound up signing with the Orlando Magic.

Tatum, William Earl (1953-) ►

Tatum was another casualty of forward Kermit Washington's devastating punch.

When Washington was suspended by NBA Commissioner Larry O'Brien for the punch that knocked the Houston Rockets' Rudy Tomjanovich out of the 1977-78 season, the Lakers found themselves with a big hole in the frontcourt.

They filled it with high-scoring Adrian Dantley.

Tatum and center James Edwards were sent to the Indiana Pacers for Dantley and center Dave Robisch, a deal that Laker guard Ernie DiGregorio called "a steal for the Lakers."

But even if Washington hadn't been suspended, Tatum's chances of remaining a Laker weren't good.

Laker Coach Jerry West looked at Tatum, who was 6 feet 4½ inches, and saw a guard. And that's where he put Tatum in his second season after using Tatum as a part-time small forward in his rookie season. But, although the former Marquette forward was averaging 14 points and shooting 49% from the field, Tatum wasn't happy in the backcourt.

It wasn't a surprise when the deal was made. In his last game as a Laker, a game that went into overtime, Tatum had played only seven minutes.

The switch in uniforms didn't do Tatum much good. His career lasted only two more seasons and he didn't average double figures in scoring again.

Teagle, Terry Michael (1960-) ►

Laker General Manager Jerry West figured he had scored big at the start of the 1990-91 season by obtaining Teagle from the Golden State Warriors for a first-round draft pick.

But the assist had to go to Magic Johnson.

There was a hole to fill at guard with the departure of Michael Cooper, and Teagle was coming off his best season, having averaged 16.1 points for the Warriors. In order to free up money under the salary cap for Teagle, Johnson had agreed to give up $75,000 of his $2.5-million annual salary.

Teagle had already been up to the heights and down

Terry Teagle drives around Paul Graham of the Atlanta Hawks in a 1991 game.

to the depths in his NBA career. He had been a No. 1 draft choice of the Houston Rockets from Baylor, but had dropped all the way down to the Continental Basketball Assn. before resurrecting his career as a valuable contributor off the Golden State bench.

But with the Lakers, Teagle's scoring average dropped more than six points in his first season, going from 16.1 to 9.9. The Lakers renounced the rights to Teagle after the 1991-92 season.

Johnson didn't get a refund.

Thomas, Irving (1966-) ➤ Thomas was a player who was good enough to excel in college, overseas and in pro summer leagues but out of his league when he finally got a chance in the NBA.

As a senior at Florida State, Thomas averaged 16.7 points and 7.6 rebounds. In the Southern California summer league, he averaged 17.1 points and 8.8 rebounds. Those numbers got him a contract with a team in Greece, but Thomas wanted a shot with an NBA club.

He got that too, signed by the Lakers for 1990-91. But Thomas, a 6-foot-8 forward, got into only 26 games, averaging 1.8 points and 1.2 rebounds.

He was waived a year and two weeks after his arrival and never again played in the NBA.

Thompson Mychal George (1955-) ➤ Thompson had heard the rumors. He knew that the Lakers, Boston Celtics and Houston Rockets, top teams in 1986-87, all wanted to get him from the San Antonio Spurs. They saw the 6-foot-10, 226- pounder–who could score, rebound and light up a locker room with his personality– as a key element in a championship run.

But on the February day in 1987 when Thompson became a Laker in a trade for Frank Brickowski, Petur Gudmundsson, two draft choices and cash, Thompson was clueless.

He strolled into HemisFair Arena to prepare for that night's game against the Los Angeles Clippers and sat on the trainer's table for his normal pregame ritual of having his ankles taped.

That's when Thompson was told, "I don't tape the enemy."

He might have become the enemy in San Antonio, but he became an instant hero in Los Angeles.

Thompson arrived just in time to face the rival Boston Celtics at the Forum. Laker assistant coach Bill Bertka hurriedly went over the game plan with the new arrival.

"If you remember half of these plays," Bertka told Thompson, "you're a genius."

Three hours later, after the Lakers had won and Thompson had scored 10 points, pulled down four rebounds and played well with his new teammates, he told Bertka, "You're looking at a certified genius 'cause I remembered them all."

Thompson, whose scoring averaged double figures for nine consecutive seasons beginning with the Portland Trail Blazers in 1978-79, went on to do just what the Lakers' biggest rivals had feared. He became a key contributor to another NBA title for his new team in the 1986-87 season.

And he played three more years for them, producing on the court, entertaining his teammates with his sharp, biting wit off the court, while still finding time to serve as an unofficial ambassador for the Bahamas, his native land.

When Laker Coach Pat Riley and his wife, Chris, vacationed in the Bahamas after the 1986-87 season, Thompson saw to it that they were treated like royalty. Riley was impressed, but not as impressed as he was at 7 a.m. the morning after the Lakers had defeated the Celtics at the Forum for the 1987 NBA title. Thompson was in the weight room, beginning to prepare for the next season.

Thompson, William Stansbury "Billy," "B.T. Express" (1963-) ➤ He was a Laker for only two seasons, but Thompson couldn't have picked two better seasons to wear the uniform–the club's championship runs in 1986-87 and 1987-88.

Thompson's Laker years were actually his second and third consecutive seasons on a championship team. He came to the Lakers several months after helping Louisville win an NCAA title.

Thompson was a first-round draft pick of the Atlanta Hawks, but they immediately shipped him and Ron Kellogg to Los Angeles for Mike McGee and a first-round draft choice.

Thompson impressed his new team right away with his quickness, jumping and rebounding ability and skill

Sedale Threatt is fouled by Michael Williams of the Minnesota Timberwolves in a 1995 game.

around the basket.

But Coach Pat Riley couldn't abide Thompson's habitual lateness to practices and shootarounds, and it cost him money and playing time. On one occasion, Riley was pleased to see Thompson at practice on time, only to learn the talented but frustrating small forward had arrived with two left shoes.

Thompson averaged 5.1 points, 2.6 rebounds and 11.8 minutes in the 68 regular-season games he played for the Lakers.

The mention of Thompson's name to his former teammates sometimes brings a smile for moments like this one before a game in Cleveland during the 1986-87 season.

Thompson had promised a fan he met at Cleveland's airport two tickets, but he forgot the fan's name. So when a worker in the Cavalier box office asked for whom Thompson wanted to leave his tickets , Thompson said to reserve them under the name, "the guy from the airport."

Threatt, Sedale, Eugene

(1961-) ➤ Few players have reached such heights after such a low starting point.

Threatt was a sixth-round draft choice of the Philadelphia 76ers in 1983, the 139th player selected. But he had a solid career with five teams over 14 seasons, providing effective scoring from the backcourt.

The Lakers were Threatt's fourth team, acquired from the Seattle SuperSonics for future second-round draft choices. Threatt's years with the Lakers were his most productive.

He was brought in at age 30 in October 1991 as a reserve guard. But on Nov. 7, 1991, before playing his first regular-season game for the Lakers, his role expanded dramatically. On that date, the world learned that Magic Johnson was retiring after testing HIV positive.

Threatt was suddenly being asked to fill the hole

being created by the departure of one of the greatest players of all time.

Threatt played all 82 games that season, averaging career highs in points (15.1) and assists (7.2).

He wasn't Magic Johnson. But he was more than the Lakers could have hoped for, playing in 82 games in three of his five seasons in L.A.

Tolbert, Raymond Lee "Ray" (1958-) ►
Tolbert never averaged more than five points or four rebounds in a season. He survived five years in the league on his defense.

That was what the Lakers wanted from Tolbert when they signed the 6-foot-9 forward in December 1987. Jeff Lamp was gone because of arthroscopic shoulder surgery and James Worthy was hobbled by a sore knee.

"I didn't want to bring in just a proverbial body," Coach Pat Riley said. "We didn't get him just to help out in practice. He's an excellent defensive player."

But after averaging 3.0 points and 1.4 rebounds in 14 games with the Lakers, Tolbert, his defense notwithstanding, was waived.

Trapp, John Quincy "Q" (1945-) ►
To his teammates, he was simply "Q." To opponents, he was trouble coming off the bench, with or without the ball.

Trapp was a member of the Lakers' 1971-72 squad, winners of the club's first NBA title in Los Angeles. He shot 44.3% from the field and was a tough defender who had 140 personal fouls in his 63 games as a Laker.

The year before he arrived in Los Angeles, Trapp was called for 337 fouls in 82 games with the San Diego Rockets, not the worst record in the NBA, but certainly up there.

Early in the 1972-73 season, Trapp and LeRoy Ellis were traded to the Philadelphia 76ers for Mel Counts and Bill Bridges.

That 76er team would win a record-low nine games, 60 fewer than the title-winning Lakers of '71-72.

Tresvant, John B. (1939-) ►
It shouldn't have come as a shock that Tresvant joined the Lakers. After all, he had already played for four other teams in six seasons. But Mel Counts was surprised to see him. Pleasantly surprised.

Counts, a 7-foot center, had been told by former Laker coach Butch Van Breda Kolff that he was about to be traded to the Phoenix Suns for Jim Fox, a 6-10 center. Instead, the Lakers purchased the 6-7 Tresvant from the Seattle SuperSonics for cash in January of 1970.

Counts was thrilled because he got to stay.

But only temporarily. In May, he was traded to Phoenix for Gail Goodrich, a much better deal for the Lakers, who would get Counts back several years later.

Tresvant didn't last much longer than Counts. After averaging 5.7 points and 3.1 rebounds in 28 games, Tresvant was sent to the Baltimore Bullets for a future draft choice early in the 1970-71 season.

Tresvant stayed with the Bullets until his nine-year career ended in 1973.

Turner, William R. III "Bill" (1944-) ►
At 6 feet 7 and 220 pounds, Turner had the body to bang with the NBA's big boys. But he didn't seem to have the temperament. "He had a great attitude and was fun to coach," said Bill Sharman, who coached Turner with the San Francisco Warriors in the 1967-68 season and for the 21 games Turner played with the Lakers at the end of the 1972-73 season. "His biggest problem was a lack of aggression. He was just not very physical for his size and strength." Sharman added. "But he had a lot of talent. He could run, jump and shoot well."

In the 1968-69 season, in which he played a career-high 79 games for the Warriors, Turner averaged only 4.8 rebounds.

His stop in Los Angeles was his last. Turner was out of the game at age 29.

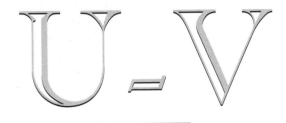

Unforgettable line No.1 ➤ Laker guard Sedale Threatt when asked if he had signed a multiyear contract: "No, it's for three years."

Unforgettable line No. 2 ➤ Guard Dexter Boney, who never appeared in a regular-season game with the Lakers, was asked, along with the other players, to fill out a biographical sheet. When it came to the category titled Music You Like, Boney wrote, "Songs."

Vagabonds ➤ It was Feb. 1, 1960, 13 years since Jackie Robinson had broken the color barrier in major league baseball. Wilt Chamberlain and Bill Russell were already stars in the NBA.

Yet racial equality was far from a reality. The Vagabonds, a traveling group of players, could still be seen as unique by being advertised as "an all-Negro basketball team."

On that night in 1960, the Vagabonds played a Los Alamitos Navy squad in the Los Angeles Sports Arena.

Their game was the warmup for the main attraction: the Minneapolis Lakers against the Philadelphia Warriors in a regular-season game that marked the Lakers' first appearance in Los Angeles.

It was a test by Laker owner Bob Short, who was suffering huge financial losses in Minneapolis. Licking his lips over the incredible crowds being drawn by the Dodgers, who had moved to the Memorial Coliseum, next door to the Sports Arena, in 1958, Short dreamed of a similar reception for his own team.

The Lakers and Warriors drew 10,202 that night.

Before the 1959-60 season was over, Short scheduled two more L.A. appearances for his club, both against the St. Louis Hawks.

Those games didn't do nearly as well, drawing a total of 8,300 for the two games.

It didn't matter. Short's mind was made up; he saw the Lakers' future was in Los Angeles, not Minneapolis, and they began to play full-time in L.A. the next season.

Van Breda Kolff, Willem H. "Bill" "Butch" (1922-) ➤ Any mention of Van Breda Kolff and the Lakers must include the words "what if."

What if he and his center, Wilt Chamberlain, had gotten along better?

What if he had put Chamberlain back into Game 7 of the 1969 NBA Finals.

Van Breda Kolff had an impressive career in professional basketball. He played for the New York Knicks for four years beginning with the 1946-47 season. He coached in the NBA and the American Basketball Assn. He took over as coach of the Lakers in 1967-68, following Fred Schaus. He led them to a 52-30 record, despite the absence of the injured Jerry West for 31 games, and then took the Lakers all the way to the NBA Finals, where they lost to the Boston Celtics in six games.

Things appeared even better a year later. The Lakers won 55 games in the regular season, again reached the NBA Finals, this time with home-court advantage, and won the first two games of the best-of-seven series against the Celtics.

The championship came down to a seventh game at the Forum.

Chamberlain, the dominating 7-foot-1 center, hurt his right knee coming down with a rebound with a little more than five minutes to play and the Lakers down by seven points.

He was replaced by Mel Counts. Back the Lakers

came. A 10-foot jumper by Counts pulled the Lakers within one.

Chamberlain told Van Breda Kolff he was ready to go back in. Van Breda Kolff, who had clashed with Chamberlain in the past, told the center, "We're doing well enough without you."

Chamberlain stayed on the bench and the Lakers lost the game by two points, 108-106.

Chamberlain was back the next year. Van Breda Kolff was not.

SEE ALSO • *Chamberlain, Wilt.*

Van Exel, Nickey Maxwell "Nick" (1971-) ➤ When he was selected by the Lakers in the second round of the 1993 draft, the 37th pick overall, there were questions about how good this 6-foot-1, 190-pounder from Cincinnati would become.

After he started playing, no one questioned Van Exel's talent.

Only his attitude.

The Lakers loved Van Exel's fiery, competitive spirit, which he demonstrated by shadowboxing his way down court after making a big play.

On the other hand, they hated it when he turned that combative spirit on a referee. Angry at being ejected from a game in the spring of 1996, Van Exel responded by giving referee Ron Garretson a shove with his forearm that was powerful enough to send Garretson onto the scorer's table.

The Lakers loved it when Van Exel offered to accept whatever role Coach Del Harris might have for him after Magic Johnson returned to the team in the second half of the 1995-96 season.

On the other hand, they hated it when Van Exel publicly questioned Harris' coaching in the 1996 playoffs. Van Exel wanted to know why Eddie Jones didn't get the ball in the fourth quarter and why Sedale Threatt had been taken out of a game in which he had the hot hand.

Van Exel and the Lakers, particularly Harris and Executive Vice President Jerry West, were developing a classic love-hate relationship.

Van Exel made great plays on the court, but offset them by making ill-timed, disruptive remarks off it.

In five years with the team, Van Exel averaged 14.9

Nick Van Exel brings the ball up court in a January, 1995 game.

points and 7.3 assists. In the postseason, his numbers were 14.7 points and 5.9 assists.

But he also seemed to average one morale-damaging incident per season toward the end of his Laker career.

By the end of the 1996-97 season, Van Exel and Harris were at each other's throats.

In Game 4 of the Lakers' second-round playoff series against the Utah Jazz, Harris pulled Van Exel off the floor 1 minute and 57 seconds into the game when Harris thought the guard wasn't following instructions. The two then engaged in a very loud, very public "discussion."

Van Exel eventually got back into the game, but never totally back into Harris' good graces.

In the season-ending overtime loss to the Jazz in Game 5, Van Exel had a team-high 26 points in 51 minutes.

But afterward Van Exel criticized Harris for allowing Kobe Bryant to take the last shot in regulation time, an airball.

And Van Exel warned that he could no longer coexist with Harris.

"I felt like I wanted to take the last shot," Van Exel said. "But he [Harris] wanted to go to Kobe."

That brought West into the fray.

"We can't have a player complaining about a coach," West said, "when maybe he should look in the mirror himself.... . This is not going to be easy to resolve." Harris and Van Exel tried to rebuild their relationship in the 1997-98 season.

But by then, another Van Exel problem had grown worse. He had arthroscopic surgery on his right knee in February.

When Van Exel returned, his knee still hurting, he asked that his replacement, Derek Fisher, remain in the starting lineup with Van Exel coming off the bench. And that's the way it stayed into the playoffs. Even with Fisher struggling and the Lakers in danger of being swept out of the Western Conference Finals by the Jazz, Van Exel didn't start.

Asked before Game 3 if he'd consider again making Van Exel a starter, Harris said, "Why would I react like some moron and panic?"

Harris was called worse things than a moron by his critics when the Lakers were swept by the Jazz.

He survived the criticism, but Van Exel, who shot 33.% from the field in the playoffs, did not.

On the day of the 1998 draft, the Lakers traded Van Exel to the Denver Nuggets for guard Tyronn Lue of Nebraska, the No. 23 selection that day, and reserve power forward Tony Battie.

"I just think," West said, "a change of scenery will be good for everyone." Added West a day later, "Derek Fisher is not as good as [Van Exel]. But Derek Fisher is steadier than Nick and not as volatile."

Vincent, Jay Fletcher (1959-) ▶ Vincent was responsible for engineering a victory over Magic Johnson's team that brought Johnson to tears. It was tough for Johnson to accept the fact that Vincent had beaten him.

But that happened only once, when both were in the ninth grade.

The two grew up at the same time in Lansing, Mich.

They were the same age, the same size, and at one time, the same in terms of basketball ability.

When they were in the 10th grade, Vincent playing for Eastern High and Johnson for Everett, their head-to-head meeting had to be moved from Eastern to a bigger gym to accommodate the huge crowd.

They were roommates and teammates at Michigan State.

The next time they were teammates, it was on the Lakers. It was the 1989-90 season and, of course, by then, nobody was comparing them in terms of basketball ability.

Vincent had had a respectable NBA career, seven seasons scoring in double figures, but he was in his ninth and final season by the time he joined the Lakers. Vincent averaged 3.8 points and 1.1 rebounds in 24 games for the Lakers, who renounced their rights to him at the end of the season.

The man who'd once been the equal of Magic Johnson had played out his NBA career.

Vitti, Gary ▶ He has been the Laker trainer since the 1984-85 season. He has worked with hundreds of athletes, taped thousands of ankles and wrists and treated countless aches, pains, scratches and bruises.

But for Vitti, one moment stands out as his most memorable with the Lakers, a moment that turned from the routine into the bizarre.

On Oct. 30, 1992, the Lakers were playing an exhibition against the Cleveland Cavaliers at the University of North Carolina, in Chapel Hill. It had been a year since Magic Johnson had announced his retirement after testing positive for HIV, the virus that causes AIDS. Johnson was trying to make a comeback.

Jerry Colangelo, president of the Phoenix Suns, and Karl Malone, a power forward for the Utah Jazz, had publicly questioned the advisability of Johnson's return to the court because of the virus. Despite medical research to the contrary, fears were being expressed that the disease could be spread by Johnson in a game as physical as basketball.

On that night, the fear turned ugly.

Sean Higgins, a Laker reserve, told Vitti during the game that he thought he saw Johnson get cut by a fingernail. Vitti alerted a nearby referee, who couldn't see

Trainer Gary Vitti treats a fallen Magic Johnson during a game.

any damage to Johnson's arm.

But during a timeout, Vitti found a small cut on Johnson's forearm. "The referee hadn't even seen it," Vitti said. "That's how small it was."

There was no blood, but Vitti knew what he had to do.

He had written the league's new procedures for treating wounds on the court, having studied extensively about HIV and AIDS over the previous year because of Johnson's condition. Under those new rules, Vitti was obligated to bandage the broken skin even though there was no bleeding and to protect himself with medical gloves before treating Johnson.

But as Vitti reached into his back pocket to get those gloves, another thought crossed his mind.

"What people didn't know," Vitti said, "was that while Colangelo and Malone had spoken out publicly, some of the Laker players had come to me privately, worried about getting the virus. Malone played against Earvin a couple of times a season. Our guys had to practice against him every day. I assured the players that there was no problem. I believed in my heart that nothing could happen.

"I was more concerned about what other people could give Magic, which would have compromised his immune system. I would tell him, "Stay away from this guy because he's got a 'cold,' or 'That guy has the flu.'

"But now, if I put those gloves on, one of the players might say, "Hey, Gary, what is this? You said we can't get it, and now you're putting gloves on. He can bleed on me, but he can't bleed on you.' Is that a mixed message or what?"

So instead, Vitti's message turned out to be that he wasn't worried about catching the virus from Johnson. He kept the gloves in his pocket, treated the cut and put a bandage on without touching the injured area.

But after a picture of Vitti treating Johnson ran in papers all over the world, the debate over the likelihood of other players catching the disease from Johnson intensified.

A player's wife, who asked that she not be identified said, "If Magic wants to score a basket, all he has to do is slash his wrist and dribble down the middle. Nobody will touch him."

Three days after the incident, Johnson retired again, not to appear again in a Laker uniform for $3\frac{1}{2}$ years.

OSHA, the Occupational Safety and Health Administration, acting on a complaint from a physician in Rhode Island, began an investigation of Vitti and the Lakers. The investigation, which lasted nearly 12 months, failed to turn up any major violations by the Lakers, vindicating Vitti, but it left a scar.

"Because of my actions, altruistic as they may have been," Vitti said, "I had opened up a Pandora's Box for Dr. [Jerry] Buss. I felt like I had stood on principle and had been kicked in the behind for it.

"This whole thing taught me what life is all about. It's a test of character."

SEE ALSO • *Johnson, Magic.*

Wagner, Milton "Milt" (1963-) ▶
Wagner knew something about winning championships.

He was a member of New Jersey's Camden High School team when it won a state basketball title. He was a member of the Louisville Cardinals when they won an NCAA basketball title in 1986, the culmination of a successful run in which Louisville reached the Final Four three times in four seasons with Wagner on the roster. He was a member of the Lakers' Southern California summer league team when it won the league championship in 1987 with Wagner scoring a game-high 43 points in the title game. Wagner was also a member of the Rockford Lightning when it reached the Continental Basketball Assn. title game in 1987.

And he was the only rookie on the roster when the Lakers won an NBA title in 1987-88 by beating the Detroit Pistons.

However, the 6-foot-5, 185-pound guard's contribution to the Lakers was considerably less than it had been for the other championship teams. In 40 games, he averaged only 9.5 minutes, 3.8 points and 1.5 assists.

And at the start of the 1988-89 season, he was waived by the Lakers. Still, he had been part of yet another championship, this one at the highest level.

War of Words ▶ They were two of the game's dominating centers. They both played for the Lakers. They were even friendly at one point. But, overall, the relationship between Kareem Abdul-Jabbar and Wilt Chamberlain was not a warm one.

Throughout most of the years Abdul-Jabbar played for the Lakers, he was the target of insults from the former Laker center, many of which focused on Abdul-Jabbar's rebounding totals which were poor when compared to those of Chamberlain, the NBA's career rebound leader.

At first, Abdul-Jabbar did not to respond publicly to the gibes from his childhood idol.

After all, when Abdul-Jabbar was still in high school, Chamberlain had befriended the youngster, inviting him to New York and allowing him to pal around the city with him.

They eventually faced each other in the NBA, when Abdul-Jabbar was a member of the Milwaukee Bucks and

A young Kareem, then of the Milwaukee Bucks, and Wilt go one-on-on during a 1970 game. Wilt won this match-up. (AP photo)

Chamberlain was playing for the Lakers.

By the time Abdul-Jabbar became a Laker in the 1975-76 season, Chamberlain was retired–and lashing out at his successor, often qualifying compliments with demeaning comments.

"I feel sorry for Kareem," Chamberlain said in PhillySport Magazine in 1982. "One thing for sure. He was blessed with a magnificent body and magnificent talent. Not to say he loafed, but he never pushed himself to the limit.

"I'm not here to chastise Kareem. He was the greatest offensive force I ever faced on a basketball court, by far. The only time I ever saw him really push himself was against me."

In 1991, Chamberlain took another few jabs at Abdul–Jabbar while discussing his dog, Careem.

Chamberlain insisted that those who thought he had named the Great Dane after Abdul-Jabbar were wrong.

"It came off that way," Chamberlain said. "It really wasn't. [Abdul-Jabbar] should have been so lucky to have had the properties of that dog. This dog was quite an animal. He was quite a stud."

Chamberlain never said after whom the dog was named.

There were other things that bothered Chamberlain about Abdul-Jabbar, such as the publicity Abdul-Jabbar received for the consecutive number of times he scored 10 or more points in a game.

"They give you that thing," Chamberlain said, "about 700-plus games he's had in double figures. I mean, what is that supposed to mean? I went through a whole career in double figures... .So Kareem scores 10 points. I've never seen a center cherry-picking for a basket in my life until I saw Kareem."

Chamberlain also made it plain that he was hurt that gifts and accolades were heaped upon Abdul-Jabbar for breaking the league scoring record previously held by Chamberlain. Abdul-Jabbar finished his career with 38,387 points, Chamberlain is second with 31,419.

"They gave Kareem a $65,000 Mercedes [for breaking the scoring record].... . I didn't get nothing when I did it," Chamberlain said. "I mean, if this record was so sensational nobody could even tell what the record was when I had it.... . I mean I never even got a card from anybody about holding the record, you understand?"

Abdul-Jabbar wrote about Chamberlain in his 1983 autobiography, "Giant Steps." "I think that Wilt feels, that

beyond playing hard, I tried to embarrass him," Abdul-Jabbar wrote, "somehow to build my reputation at his expense, pull him down from his greatness. Make him look small... . And sometimes, on the court, I did embarrass him, though never intentionally.

"I started to lose my reverence for him when he supported Richard Nixon for president in 1968. Harlem was in an uproar. Black people were struggling for basic human rights and Wilt was throwing his weight behind an obvious crook who had no regard for us. [Wilt] was a high-profile, jet-set, trickle-down Republican and I was a private, community-oriented, share-the-wealth Muslim. Our differences were made perfectly clear when he published his autobiography and, in it, declared that black women were inferior sexual partners, were generally socially inferior because they were unsophisticated. I knew that was b.s. and, though I should have assumed it would cause trouble, I said so in public."

The tension between the two finally started to lift when they filmed a television commercial together in 1993.

As grunts and nods of the head turned into a conversation, each told the other how he had felt. And those words finally ended the "war of words."

SEE ALSO • *Abdul-Jabbar, Kareem; Chamberlain, Wilt.*

Warner, Cornell (1948-) ➤ Pete Newell was always a great admirer of defense. That's how he built his teams as head coach at California. And that's how he tried to fortify the Lakers in his days as the team's general manager.

So, when he saw a chance to obtain the 6-foot-9, 225-pound Warner on the eve of the 1975-76 Laker opener, Newell jumped at it.

Newell called Warner "the type of defensive front-line man that we've lacked for two years."

Such talk was fine with Warner, who had averaged 10.3 rebounds with Milwaukee in the 1974-75 season. But he also wanted to be known as an offensive player. Warner had shot 51.2% in the 1974 NBA Finals with the Bucks.

"Funny," he said, "the other coaches said I couldn't shoot."

Warner shot 47.8% from the field for the Lakers in 95 games and averaged 6.8 points.

He was waived after the 1976-77 season.

Washington, Kermit Alan (1951-)▶

It was only one punch. But it was as devastating as any ever thrown by Mike Tyson or George Foreman.

With one blow, Washington effectively ended his Laker career and nearly ended the career of Rudy Tomjanovich.

On Dec 9, 1977, Washington and the Lakers were playing Tomjanovich and the Houston Rockets.

Tomjanovich was a merely spectator when Washington and Houston's Kevin Kunnert got into a fight heading upcourt. Kunnert threw the first punch.

Washington, a 6-foot-9 forward known for his fighting ability, got in the last few punches, sending Kunnert to one knee.

The 6-8 Tomjanovich, the team's captain and peacemaker, entered the fray to try to stop Washington. Washington later said all he saw was "a blur" in a Rocket uniform rushing toward him from behind.

Washington, claiming he instinctively acted in self-defense, planted his feet and landed a punch squarely to the face of the onrushing Tomjanovich.

The Rocket forward fell, his head banging against the hardwood floor. Tomjanovich sustained a broken nose, a double fracture of the jaw, an eye injury, a concussion, facial cuts and heavy swelling in his head.

Tomjanovich's injuries led to three operations. He later said, "I remember thinking that the scoreboard must have fallen on me."

Washington told the Los Angeles Times at the time, "My God, I don't want to hurt anyone. I'm just trying to earn a living. Maybe I ought to just be a teacher."

And he told the New York Times, "I'm very sorry it happened, but it was just an honest mistake."

And a costly one.

Washington was fined a then-record $10,000 and suspended for 60 days by NBA Commissioner Larry O'Brien.

Eighteen days after the incident, Washington's Laker career ended after 4 1/2 seasons when he was shipped to the Boston Celtics with Don Chaney and a first-round draft choice for Charlie Scott.

Washington would also play for the San Diego Clippers, Portland Trail Blazers and Golden State Warriors, lasting five more seasons and averaging 9.2 points and 8.3 rebounds for his career.

Tomjanovich didn't return that season, but he played in the next three for Houston and eventually became the Rockets' coach, leading them to back-to-back NBA titles in the 1990s.

But no matter either man's eventual accomplishments, the punch, for many, remains the single most memorable event of their careers.

SEE ALSO • *Chaney; Don; Scott, Charlie.*

Wesley, Walter "Walt" (1945-) ▶

Wesley had played nine seasons in the NBA, was 6 feet 11 and weighed 230 pounds, and had averaged 17.7 points and 8.7 rebounds one season with the Cleveland Cavaliers.

But his arrival with the Lakers in June 1975 went almost unnoticed. Wesley was lost in the shadow of the man who accompanied him from Milwaukee in a six-player trade, a center named Kareem Abdul-Jabbar.

The Lakers gave up Elmore Smith, Brian Winters, Dave Meyers and Junior Bridgeman to get Abdul-Jabbar, who would help them win five NBA titles.

Wesley? He lasted one game, playing seven minutes, before being cut Oct. 30, 1975.

SEE ALSO • *Abdul-Jabbar, Kareem; Bridgeman, Junior; Meyers, Dave; Smith, Elmore; Winters, Brian.*

West, Jerome Alan "Jerry," "Mr. Clutch" (1938-) ▶

He became a Laker the year they became the Los Angeles Lakers.

And he has been one ever since, moving up the ladder from player to coach to consultant to general manager to executive vice president.

He went from one of the game's greatest guards to one of its best general managers.

As a player, he made clutch plays that earned him his nickname, including:

* A steal and dribble from midcourt in the final two seconds to score the winning basket against the Boston Celtics in the third game of the 1962 NBA Finals.

*An average of 46.3 points per game against the Baltimore Bullets in a 1965 six-game playoff series, an all-time record for a postseason series.

Jerry West drives down court as Wilt Chamberlain holds back traffic during a 1973 game against the Chicago Bulls.

* A 60-foot shot at the buzzer against the New York Knicks to force an overtime in Game 3 of the 1970 NBA Finals.

* A total of 840 successful free throws in the 1965-66 regular season, still the league record.

West's statistical accomplishments alone could fill pages, but that ignores his other talents, for which there are no entries in the NBA record book.

Former Boston Celtic star Bill Sharman, whose last season as a player was West's first, said that, although no records were kept on steals until the end of West's career, Sharman is sure there are games in which West got as many as 10.

Hot Rod Hundley, who played with West both at West Virginia and with the Lakers, remembered West's incredible defensive skills.

"He was the only guy I ever saw who could stop a bounce pass by an opposing player by catching it in midair when it was thrown from an inch away," Hundley said. "He could also do that with an overhead pass. You would try to throw it with Jerry in your face and he would catch it.

"According to the scouting report at the time on West, players were told that if they were coming down the court with the ball in the middle on a three-on-one, and West was the one, the guy with the ball should shoot it, because if he tried to pass it, West would get it and be going back the other way."

West, a 6-foot-2 1/2, 180-pounder, was blessed with long arms, extreme quickness and great jumping ability.

Announcer Chick Hearn said that West also must have had a clock in his head; that was the only way to explain

Now a Laker VP, West watches a 1997 game courtside. (AP photo)

how West repeatedly came down court with time running out and launched a shot, without looking at the clock, just before the buzzer sounded.

Once asked what his coach, Fred Schaus, did to get him out of a slump, West replied, "I never had a slump."

West meant that when he experienced stretches in which his sure-fire shot was not so sure, he found other ways to help his team–ballhandling, rebounding, defense.

A fiery competitor as a player, West, as an executive, finds it tough to sit and watch his team. Often, he paces up and down the tunnel in the Forum during games, frustrated that he can't change a game's outcome.

As a player, West knew frustration too, losing in the NBA Finals seven times before finally winning his only championship as a player in the 1971-72 season.

Six of those championship-round setbacks were to the Celtics. West would have to wait until he was a Laker executive to finally beat his rivals from Boston, in 1985.

West quit playing in the 1973-74 season, his 14th. At 36, he was still averaging 20.3 points and 6.6 assists, but didn't believe he could perform any longer at his standards.

West was elected to the Basketball Hall of Fame in 1979 and has been named to the NBA's list of the 50 greatest players of all time. His No. 44 Laker jersey has been retired. West played in 12 All-Star games, was named to the All-NBA first team 10 times and the all-defensive first team four times.

West coached the Lakers for three seasons after he retired as a player but never had any great love for it. The team was 145-101 under him. When Jerry Buss bought the Lakers in 1979, West found his niche as the team's general manager.

It was owner Jack Kent Cooke, not West, who insisted the team draft a kid out of Michigan State named Magic Johnson rather than Sidney Moncrief, another hot prospect.

But West soon set standards of excellence in the front office as his club won five NBA title in the 1980s.

Two of his moves stand out. In 1982, with the No. 1 overall pick, West drafted James Worthy over Dominique Wilkins and Terry Cummings, two other highly prized collegiate stars. In 1996, West traded center Vlade Divac in a move that helped him land the man he wanted, Shaquille O'Neal.

Not every move worked. In 1993, West traded Sam Perkins to the Seattle SuperSonics for Doug Christie and Benoit Benjamin, neither of whom lasted long. But overall, as when he played, West has hit far more often than he has missed.

He has been with the team for nearly four decades, and the Lakers have been a championship contender for much of that time. It's no co-incidence.

SEE ALSO • *Benjamin, Benoit; Buss, Jerry; Christie, Doug; Cooke, Jack Kent; Divac, Vlade; Hearn, Chick; Hundley, Hot Rod; Johnson, Magic; O'Neal, Shaquille; Perkins, Sam; Schaus, Fred; Sharman, Bill; Worthy, James.*

Westhead, Paul (1939-) ▶

The very substance of the ambitious is merely the shadow of a dream. – From "Hamlet," William Shakespeare

For Westhead, the dream was born of ambition. Tragedy turned the dream into reality. Ambition turned the reality into a nightmare.

It was all so Shakespearean.

And that was so fitting because Shakespeare was one of the two great passions in Westhead's life; the other was basketball. He could straddle the two worlds like few others.

Westhead was a Shakespearean scholar at the University of Dayton, St. Joseph's and La Salle.

But his dream was to be a basketball coach in the NBA.

He got that opportunity under the most unlikely of circumstances. In nine years as the head coach at La Salle, he twice got the school into the NCAA tournament and once into the NIT.

But it probably wouldn't have happened without Jack McKinney. McKinney was the guiding force in Westhead's coaching career.

He hired Westhead as an assistant at St. Joseph's when he was the head coach. He recommended Westhead for several international basketball assignments. And he brought Westhead into the NBA as his assistant when McKinney was named head coach of the Lakers for the 1979-80 season.

Thirteen games into that season, as McKinney was cycling his way to a tennis game with Westhead, he fell off his bicycle and suffered major head injuries.

Westhead took over the team, comparing his position to that of a substitute teacher.

But as the months went by and McKinney's condition failed to improve sufficiently for him to return, it was the substitute who took the class of 1979-80 to the highest of honors as the Lakers won the NBA title.

Owner Jerry Buss told Westhead that his good friend, McKinney, was not going to get his job back.

Did Westhead want it?

With his dream position dangled in front of him, his friend already out in the cold, Westhead grabbed the opportunity, shattering what had been a strong bond between the McKinney and Westhead families.

For a while, Westhead was a breath of fresh air in a profession sometimes buried under a mountain of cliches and old ideas.

In one game, with the Lakers behind and little time left, Westhead, during a timeout, exhorted his players with a line never heard before or since in an NBA huddle.

"If it were done when 'tis done, then 'twere well it were done quickly," he said, quoting from "Macbeth."

While some players sat there stunned, Magic Johnson responded.

"You want me to get it into the Big Fella?" he asked Westhead, looking toward Kareem Abdul-Jabbar.

But the relationship soon soured between Westhead and his players, especially Johnson.

The concerns first surfaced in 1980-81, Westhead's first full season, when he unveiled something he called the Balance of Energy. All he had really done was change the starting lineup to shake his team up. It would have been fine except Westhead failed to tell the players being taken out of the starting lineup–forward Jim Chones and guard Michael Cooper–until just before tipoff. That failure to communicate, coupled with the fancy name he came up with for the switch, angered some players who believed Westhead was more concerned with making himself look clever than he was with making the team better.

That perception grew at the start of the 1981-82 season when Sports Illustrated ran a shot of Westhead in a classroom acting as the professor while the players were in seats portrayed as the students.

Dissatisfaction turned into open revolt when Westhead shook up the offense. Some believed he was slowing down the Lakers' running game, the best in basketball, because he wanted to be in control. The players said Westhead was taking the decision-making away from Johnson, the best point guard in the game, because Westhead had to be seen as the genius who was pulling the strings behind Showtime.

But it wasn't only the players who were upset. Buss said he had already decided to fire Westhead by the time the team departed for Utah in November.

The Lakers weren't doing badly. They beat the Jazz in

that game to give them a five-game winning streak.

But the tension exploded in a small equipment room after the final buzzer when Westhead ripped into Johnson, accusing him of not paying attention in the huddle and not being plugged into the game plan.

That was it.

Johnson went into the locker room and told reporters he wanted to be traded. About 15 hours later, Westhead was fired, replaced by Pat Riley.

What hurt Westhead the most, he often said, was that he was fired for not being a running coach. For the rest of his career, which included head coaching jobs with the Chicago Bulls and Denver Nuggets in the NBA and Loyola Marymount and George Mason at the college level, he sometimes designed wide-open offenses, run-like-hell offenses, the hell-with-defense offenses that racked up huge point totals, but didn't leave Westhead's teams on the winning end often enough.

Alex Hannum, a coach who won a few NBA titles himself, once labeled Westhead's offense "crap-a-doodle."

Shakespeare might have been more literate, but not necessarily more complimentary.

SEE ALSO • *Balance of Energy; Buss, Jerry; Johnson, Magic; McKinney, Jack; Strangest Press Conference.*

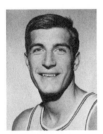

Wetzel, John Francis (1944-) ➤

Wetzel had two shots at making the Lakers. The first was in 1966 after a successful career at Virginia Tech, where he was a good shooter and a strong defensive player.

But while putting on an impressive show in the Lakers' training camp, Wetzel broke his right wrist, which he had already broken once in college.

A year later, he was back in Laker camp and, this time, he made the team. After averaging 3.7 points and 1.3 assists, Wetzel was taken by the Phoenix Suns in the expansion draft.

Wiley, Eugene "Gene" (1937-) ➤ A 6-foot-10, 220-
pounder, Wiley spent four seasons with the Lakers beginning in 1962-63. He was never a scoring force, but he could be a factor on the boards, averaging 7.3 rebounds, his best season being 1964-65 when he averaged 8.6 rebounds.

Wiley, an artist away from the game, was a graceful

player, exceptionally athletic for his size.

Teammate Rudy LaRusso referred to Wiley as being "like Bambi, and he could leap to the moon."

Wiley's athletic ability sometimes surprised even the officials.

One night, he had the task of guarding Wilt Chamberlain. The 7-1, 275-pound Chamberlain went up for one of his dunks, but Wiley blocked it.

Laker teammates later agreed that Wiley had fouled Chamberlain. But the official was too stunned at Wiley's ability to foil the seemingly unstoppable Chamberlain to make the call.

Back came the ball to Chamberlain. Up he went. Up went Wiley. Another block. Probably another foul.

Again, no call.

The same sequence was repeated a third time.

Finally, there was a call: Jump ball. It was a moment for the Lakers to savor. If, for only an instant, someone had finally gotten the better of Chamberlain.

SEE ALSO • *Chamberlain, Wilt, LaRusso, Rudy.*

Wilkes, Jamaal "Silk" (1953-) ➤
Coach Paul Westhead referred to Wilkes' shot as "snow falling off a bamboo leaf " because the release was so soft.

Announcer Chick Hearn referred to his jump shot as a 20-foot layup because he shot it with such accuracy. He got his nickname because he was so smooth on the court.

On a Laker team in the 1980s with such spotlight performers as Magic Johnson and Kareem Abdul-Jabbar, the soft-spoken, humble Wilkes felt more comfortable in the background.

And that's where he often stayed. It was almost easy to forget he was there–until one looked at a score sheet.

Most basketball fans of that era remember Johnson's spectacular performance in Game 6 of the 1980 NBA Finals. He played all five positions, scored 42 points and led the Lakers past the Philadelphia 76ers to the championship-clinching victory.

But Wilkes scored 37 points and was the one who kept the Lakers in the game by scoring 16 points in the third quarter.

It seemed typical of Wilkes' understated career that he would have the biggest game of his career the same night

Magic Johnson had his greatest all-around performance.

On the great UCLA teams that won NCAA titles in 1972 and 1973 and reached the Final Four in 1974, the Bruin most remembered is center Bill Walton. But Wilkes, whose name was then Keith Wilkes, was also a key member of the 1972-74 teams.

The 1974-75 Golden State State Warriors won the NBA title by sweeping the Washington Bullets in the finals. Rick Barry was the high-profile Warrior.

But Wilkes was also an important member of that club, averaging 15 points and seven rebounds in the postseason.

Wilkes was with the Lakers for eight seasons. He averaged 20 or more points three consecutive seasons, and 17.3 or higher for six seasons. He shot more than 50% from the field for six straight seasons.

When the Lakers needed a big shot, a teammate, usually Johnson, would pass the ball to Wilkes, who would set up somewhere within his 20-foot range, cock the ball behind his right ear and let loose with one of the most dependable shots in the game. His eighth Laker season ended because of a knee injury. In Wilkes' absence, the small forward position was taken over by a flashy, rising star named James Worthy.

Wilkes tried to play one more season, as a member of the Clippers, but he lasted only 13 games.

And then, he slipped away as silently as he had played.

Forgotten once again?

Not by those who saw him in his prime and appreciated the fact that, in the company of the greatest players of his era, Wilkes could be as smooth and effective as any of them.

SEE ALSO • *Biggest games; Johnson, Magic, Worthy, James.*

Williams, Ronald, Robert "Ron" "Fritz" (1944-) ➤

The nickname Fritz came from frisky, a label Williams picked up at Weirton High in West Virginia where his speed enabled him to star in track as well as basketball.

It was that speed that prompted the Dallas Cowboys to draft Williams in 1968 when he was coming out of West Virginia University even though Williams hadn't played a minute of college football.

The Cowboys had a tradition of taking speedsters like Bob Hayes and turning them into football players. The Cowboys saw Williams as a defensive back.

He saw himself as a professional basketball player. So when the Golden State Warriors made Williams a first-round pick in the 1968 draft, he turned his back on the Cowboys after attending their training camp and began an NBA career that would include five seasons with the Warriors and two with the Milwaukee Bucks before he arrived in Los Angeles, traded by the Bucks for a fifth-round draft choice.

Williams played in only nine games for the Lakers in the 1975-76 season before being put on waivers Nov. 25.

Nobody claimed him.

Wilson, Trevor (1968-) ➤ Wilson is another Laker whose greatest basketball moments in Los Angeles came before he turned professional.

After leading Cleveland High School in Reseda to the Los Angeles City 4-A championship, Wilson went to UCLA, where he became the third-leading scorer in school history with 1,798 points, trailing only Lew Alcindor and Reggie Miller. Wilson was All-Pacific 10 Conference three times.

The pros, however, were a different matter.

After a season with the Atlanta Hawks, who had made him a second-round draft choice in 1990, and two seasons in Spain, Wilson was signed as a free agent by the Lakers in the summer of 1993. But his return to Los Angeles was short and not so sweet. He appeared in only five games before being waived.

Winter, Max (1903-1996) ➤ Born in Austria, Winter knew nothing about American sports as a young boy.

But he arrived in this country at age 10 and learned quickly. By time he reached adulthood, Winter was teaching others the do's and don'ts of professional sports.

He was a boxing promoter and manager and promoted Harlem Globetrotter games before becoming general manager of the Minneapolis Lakers in 1947.

He resigned after the 1954-55 season, leaving an extraordinary legacy. Under Winter, the Lakers won six titles in seven seasons in three leagues.

They won the National Basketball League title in 1947-1948 and the Basketball Assn. of America in 1948-49.

Even when the two leagues merged to become the

NBA for the 1949-50 season, and the Lakers kept on winning.

Upon leaving the club, Winter sold his stock to center George Mikan, the Lakers' first superstar. But Winter wasn't finished. He went on to found the NFL's Minnesota Vikings, a team that while reaching the Super Bowl four times under his guidance, lost in all four appearances.

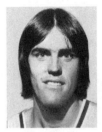

Winters, Brian Joseph (1952-) ➤

It may be small consolation to the Milwaukee Bucks, but they got an awful lot of good basketball out of Brian Winters. He played eight years for them, never averaged less than double figures in scoring, had three straight seasons in which he averaged more than 19 points a game, and had seven straight seasons in which he made at least 46% of his shots from the field.

Of course, those totals pale in comparison to the numbers racked up by Kareem Abdul-Jabbar, the man the Bucks gave up with Walt Wesley in 1975 in a trade with the Lakers for Winters, Elmore Smith, Junior Bridgeman and Dave Meyers.

But the Bucks weren't going to keep Abdul-Jabbar anyway. He had made up his mind to leave the small Midwestern market of Milwaukee, where he never really fit in. And at least in Winters, the Bucks got a player who lived up to the billing given him by Laker General Manager Pete Newell, who called Winters "the 1974 college crop's best outside shooting guard."

Winters was a first-round draft choice of the Lakers in 1974, the 12th player taken overall, after leading a South Carolina team that went 22-5.

Woolridge, Orlando Vernada

(1959-) ➤ Woolridge came to the Lakers desperately seeking a comeback. But it had nothing to do with his fortunes on the court. Woolridge cut short his seventh NBA season, leaving the New Jersey Nets in February 1988 to voluntarily enter a drug rehabilitation center in Van Nuys.

The next August, Woolridge signed with the Lakers and averaged 11.1 points and 3.3 rebounds in 136 games over two seasons with the club.

Woolridge's professional career had begun when the Chicago Bulls drafted him out of Notre Dame on the first round in 1981. Woolridge once scored 44 points in a game for the Bulls and twice averaged more than 20 points a game with them.

In August of 1990, the Lakers traded Woolridge to the Denver Nuggets for two second-round draft choices, and in his one season in Denver, he averaged 25.1 points. He finished his career with an average of 16.0 points a game.

Worthy, James Ager "Big Game
James" (1961-) ➤ Looking at Worthy's accomplishments, at his retired jersey on the Forum wall, it might be hard to believe there was any doubt the Lakers would use the first pick in the 1982 draft to take him.

But the choice was a lot less clear at the time.

Also available were Georgia's Dominique Wilkins, whose spectacular play had earned him the nickname "the Human Highlight Film."

There was the solid DePaul power forward, Terry Cummings.

And there was also the temptation for the Lakers to deal the 1982 top choice in order to try to land the top pick in 1983, which they could use to obtain Virginia center Ralph Sampson, thought by some to be the next dominating player in the NBA. Instead, the Lakers went for Worthy, a man Bill Sharman, then the Laker general manager, called an "electrifying player who will fit right in."

How right Sharman was.

Sampson never lived up to expectations. Cummings who has an average so far in his career of 17.7 points a game, didn't have the kind of speed to mesh with the Laker offense of the time. And Wilkins, while a great individual player, struggled to balance his talent with the needs of the teams he was on. Worthy was a smooth fit on a Laker squad loaded with talent, beginning with Magic Johnson and Kareem Abdul-Jabbar.

The Lakers had already won two NBA titles in the 1980s when Worthy arrived, and Jamaal Wilkes was established as the small forward, but, with Worthy soon replacing him, the team went on to win three more titles before the decade was done. Worthy had been in the national spotlight at North Carolina, where he had led the Tar Heels to a 63-62 win over Georgetown in the 1982

NCAA title game to conclude his junior year. Worthy was named most valuable player of the tournament after scoring a game-high 28 points in the title game.

Saving his best performances for the biggest games was a pattern Worthy followed throughout his career.

He played with confidence and maturity, traits he had early in life and maintained even as a rookie on a Laker team of hardened veterans.

His father, Ervin, remembered seeing that confidence when James was a young boy.

"What I remember most clearly was sitting at the dining room table one night and looking at all my bills," the elder Worthy told the Washington Post. "James... came in and said to me, 'Daddy, when I go to college, you won't have to worry about having to pay for me because I'm going to get a scholarship.' "

And, as it turned out, a lot more.

Worthy had great speed and sure hands that made him the ideal receiver on the end of the bullet passes thrown by Johnson, the quarterback of the Laker offense. Quickly becoming a key element in the Lakers' famed fastbreak, Worthy was the best finisher in the league. If he could get his hands on a Johnson pass while racing down the floor at full speed, there wasn't a defender who could stop him.

And Worthy could also generate offense. In his rookie season, playing in Oakland against the Warriors, he went up for a hook shot, saw that it wasn't going to work, made a 360-degree spin–he hadn't come back to the floor yet–and put the ball in.

Johnson named Worthy's shot a "dipsy-doo-360-clutch-skin-and-in."

There were two incidents that could have slowed Worthy's high-flying career, one on the court and one off it.

On the court, there was Game 2 of the 1984 NBA Finals against the Celtics in Boston. With victory seemingly assured for the Lakers, who had a two-point lead with seconds to play, Worthy threw a pass from under the Celtic basket in Boston Garden that was intercepted by Gerald Henderson.

Henderson scored on the play, and Boston went on to win the game in overtime and, ultimately, the series in seven games. That mental error by Worthy was considered the pivotal play in a turnaround that enabled the Celtics to get back into the series. Had the Lakers won, they would have returned to Los Angeles having swept the first two games in Boston Garden.

Off the court, Worthy was arrested while on a trip in Houston for soliciting a prostitute. He eventually pleaded no contest and acknowledged that he had made a serious mistake.

But neither incident could diminish what would become one of the most memorable careers in Laker history.

Two of his biggest games were two of the biggest for the team as well.

One came in the title-clinching game of the 1987 NBA Finals against the Celtics. With the Lakers trailing by a point early in the third quarter of Game 6, Worthy stole a pass by Kevin McHale.

Too close to the sideline, Worthy lost his balance and was about to tumble out of bounds.

He did, but not before he shoveled the ball to Johnson, who completed the break to give the Lakers the lead.

Laker Coach Pat Riley called that memorable exchange the turning point of a game that resulted in another Laker title.

A year later, in Game 7 of the 1988 finals, Worthy led the Lakers to victory over the Detroit Pistons with the first triple-double of his career, scoring 36 points, pulling down 16 rebounds and handing out 10 assists.

Worthy averaged 17.6 points, 5.1 rebounds and 3.0 assists over 12 seasons with the Lakers, and each of those statistics was better in the playoffs: 21.1 points, 5.2 rebounds and 3.2 assists–and three NBA championships.

Anybody out there still wonder if the Lakers made the right choice in the 1982 draft?

SEE ALSO • *Smithsonian Institution; Coin Flip That Could Have Changed History;*

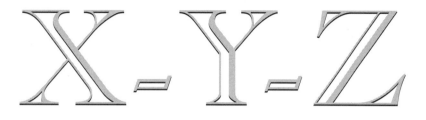

X-Factor ➤ Xavier McDaniel was never a Laker, but the smooth-shooting forward did his best to shoot down the team's run at back-to-back NBA championships at the end of the '80s.

All McDaniel got for his efforts, however, was a spot in the Laker record book. In May 1987, after having beaten the Denver Nuggets and the Golden State Warriors in the playoffs, the Lakers led the Seattle SuperSonics, 2-0, in the Western Conference finals. They were on their way to what they hoped would be another meeting in the NBA Finals against the Boston Celtics.

But in Game 3 in Seattle, McDaniel came up with one of the greatest postseason performances ever against the Lakers, scoring 42 points, including 20 in the final quarter. The 20 field goals he made that day, in 29 attempts, are still a postseason record for a Laker opponent.

But it wasn't enough.

James Worthy scored 39 points, the Lakers squeaked by, 122-121, went on to sweep the series, beat the Celtics for the NBA title and then repeat the next year. Said Laker guard Michael Cooper: "X and James X'd each other out."

Yates, Wayne E. (1937-) ➤ Yates was the Lakers' first pick in the 1961 draft, the first after the Lakers had moved to Los Angeles. Yates, the fifth pick overall, struggled to earn a spot on the roster. A 6-foot-8, 235-pounder from Memphis State, Yates lasted only one year in the league.

Yates made only 29.5% of his shots from the field in the NBA, partially because he took too many shots that were beyond his effective range.

The most memorable incident in Yates' season occurred off the court.

In a bar one night during a Laker trip, he got into a scuffle and staggered out of it pretty badly beaten up.

While heading back to his hotel in a cab, Yates told the cab driver what had happened. When he described the man he had fought, the cabbie nodded.

"Oh that guy is a pro fighter," he said. "That's what he does around here, keeps the peace."

Yates' jaw was so badly damaged, it had to be wired shut.

Zeke From Cabin Creek ➤ Elgin Baylor was the leader of the Laker team that came to Los Angeles in 1960, on and off the court.

He scored the most points, pulled down the most rebounds, put people in the seats and the Lakers in the public consciousness.

Baylor also organized the team's leisure-time activities–primarily around-the-clock poker games on the road–and provided nicknames for incoming players.

The team's No. 1 draft choice in 1960 was Jerry West. He was an exceptional player, an All-American and an Olympian, but with his West Virginia twang and shy personality, he was an easy target for Baylor's needles.

So after West arrived, and Baylor heard his accent, the West Virginia star became Zeke From Cabin Creek.

West didn't see the humor in the name. But it stuck long after he had shed his accent and become a fixture not only on the court in Los Angeles, but in the Laker front office and on the most exclusive golf courses in Southern California. West became a sharp-dressing resident of the Bel Air community, but, to a few, he would always be Zeke From Cabin Creek.

SEE ALSO • *Baylor, Elgin; NBA Logo; West Jerry.*

PLAYER STATISTICS

Abdul-Jabbar, Kareem

Height	7-2
Weight	267
Born	4-16-47
College	UCLA

SEASON	TEAM	G	FGM	FGA	PCT	FTM	FTA	PCT	REB	RPG	AST	APG	STL	BLK	PTS	PPG
1969-1970	MILWAUKEE	82	938	1810	.518	485	743	.653	1190	14.5	337	4.1	N/A	N/A	2361	28.8
1970-1971	MILWAUKEE	82	1063	1843	.577	470	681	.690	1311	16.0	272	3.3	N/A	N/A	2596	31.7
1971-1972	MILWAUKEE	81	1159	2019	.574	504	732	.689	1346	16.6	370	4.6	N/A	N/A	2822	34.8
1972-1973	MILWAUKEE	76	982	1772	.554	328	460	.713	1224	16.1	379	5.0	N/A	N/A	2292	30.2
1973-1974	MILWAUKEE	81	948	1759	.539	295	420	.702	1178	14.5	386	4.8	112	283	2191	27.0
1974-1975	MILWAUKEE	65	812	1584	.513	325	426	.763	912	14.0	264	4.1	65	212	1949	30.0
1975-1976	LOS ANGELES	82	914	1728	.529	447	636	.703	1383	16.9	413	5.0	119	338	2275	27.7
1976-1977	LOS ANGELES	82	888	1533	.579	376	536	.702	1090	13.3	319	3.9	101	261	2152	26.2
1977-1978	LOS ANGELES	62	663	1205	.550	274	350	.783	801	12.9	269	4.3	103	185	1600	25.8
1978-1979	LOS ANGELES	80	777	1347	.577	349	474	.736	1025	12.8	431	5.4	76	316	1903	23.8
1979-1980	LOS ANGELES	82	835	1383	.604	364	476	.765	886	10.8	371	4.5	81	280	2034	24.8
1980-1981	LOS ANGELES	80	836	1457	.574	423	552	.766	821	10.3	272	3.4	59	228	2095	26.2
1981-1982	LOS ANGELES	76	753	1301	.579	312	442	.706	659	8.7	225	3.0	63	207	1818	23.9
1982-1983	LOS ANGELES	79	722	1228	.588	278	371	.749	592	7.5	200	2.5	61	170	1722	21.8
1983-1984	LOS ANGELES	80	716	1238	.578	285	394	.723	587	7.3	211	2.6	55	143	1717	21.5
1984-1985	LOS ANGELES	79	723	1207	.599	289	395	.732	622	7.9	249	3.2	63	162	1735	22.0
1985-1986	LOS ANGELES	79	755	1338	.564	336	439	.765	478	6.1	280	3.5	67	130	1846	23.4
1986-1987	LOS ANGELES	78	560	993	.564	245	343	.714	523	6.7	203	2.6	49	97	1366	17.5
1987-1988	LOS ANGELES	80	480	903	.532	205	269	.762	478	6.0	135	1.7	48	92	1165	14.6
1988-1989	LOS ANGELES	74	313	659	.475	122	165	.739	334	4.5	74	1.0	38	85	748	10.1
NBA CAREER TOTALS		1560	15837	28307	.559	6712	9304	.721	17440	11.2	5660	3.6	1160	3189	38387	24.6
NBA PLAYOFF TOTALS		237	2356	4422	.533	1050	1419	.740	2481	10.5	767	3.2	189	476	5762	24.3

Abernethy,Thomas Craig

Height	6-7
Weight	220
Born	5-6-54
College	Indiana

SEASON	TEAM	G	FGM	FGA	PCT	FTM	FTA	PCT	REB	RPG	AST	APG	STL	BLK	PTS	PPG
1976-1977	LOS ANGELES	70	169	349	.484	101	134	.754	291	4.2	98	1.4	49	10	439	6.3
1977-1978	LOS ANGELES	73	201	404	.498	91	111	.820	265	3.6	101	1.4	55	22	493	6.8
1978-1979	GOLDEN STATE	70	176	342	.515	70	94	.745	216	3.1	79	1.1	39	13	422	6.0
1979-1980	GOLDEN STATE	67	153	318	.481	56	82	.683	191	2.9	87	1.3	35	12	362	5.4
1980-1981	G.S.-INDIANA	39	25	59	.424	13	22	.591	48	1.2	19	0.5	7	3	63	1.6
NBA CAREER TOTALS		319	724	1472	.492	331	443	.747	1011	3.2	384	1.2	185	60	1779	5.6
NBA PLAYOFF TOTALS		13	22	54	.407	24	29	.828	42	3.2	23	1.8	7	2	68	5.2

Alcorn, Gary R.

Height	6-9
Weight	225
Born	10-8-36
College	Fresno St

SEASON	TEAM	G	FGM	FGA	PCT	FTM	FTA	PCT	REB	RPG	AST	APG	STL	BLK	PTS	PPG
1959-1960	DETROIT	58	91	312	.292	48	84	.571	279	4.8	22	0.4	N/A	N/A	230	4.0
1960-1961	LOS ANGELES	20	12	40	.300	7	8	.875	50	2.5	2	0.1	N/A	N/A	31	1.6
NBA CAREER TOTALS		78	103	352	.293	55	92	.598	329	4.2	24	0.3	N/A	N/A	261	3.3

Allen, Lucius Oliver, Jr.

SEASON	TEAM	G	FGM	FGA	PCT	FTM	FTA	PCT	REB	RPG	AST	APG	STL	BLK	PTS	PPG
1969-1970	SEATTLE	81	306	692	.442	182	249	.731	211	2.6	342	4.2	N/A	N/A	794	9.8
1970-1971	MILWAUKEE	61	178	398	.447	77	110	.700	152	2.5	161	2.6	N/A	N/A	433	7.1
1971-1972	MILWAUKEE	80	441	874	.505	198	259	.764	254	3.2	333	4.2	N/A	N/A	1080	13.5
1972-1973	MILWAUKEE	80	547	1130	.484	143	200	.715	279	3.5	426	5.3	N/A	N/A	1237	15.5
1973-1974	MILWAUKEE	72	526	1062	.495	216	274	.788	291	4.0	374	5.2	137	22	1268	17.6
1974-1975	MILW.-L.A.	66	511	1170	.437	238	306	.778	278	4.2	372	5.6	136	29	1260	19.1
1975-1976	LOS ANGELES	76	461	1004	.459	197	254	.776	214	2.8	357	4.7	101	20	1119	14.7
1976-1977	LOS ANGELES	78	472	1035	.456	195	252	.774	251	3.2	405	5.2	116	19	1139	14.6
1977-1978	KANSAS CITY	77	373	846	.441	174	220	.791	229	3.0	360	4.7	93	28	920	11.9
1978-1979	KANSAS CITY	31	69	174	.397	19	33	.576	46	1.5	44	1.4	21	6	157	5.1
NBA CAREER TOTALS		702	3884	8385	.463	1639	2157	.760	2205	3.1	3174	4.5	604	124	9407	13.4
NBA PLAYOFF TOTALS		43	202	450	.449	102	135	.756	133	3.1	142	3.3	13	4	506	11.8

Height	6-2
Weight	175
Born	9-26-47
College	UCLA

Anderson, Clifford V.

SEASON	TEAM	G	FGM	FGA	PCT	FTM	FTA	PCT	REB	RPG	AST	APG	STL	BLK	PTS	PPG
1967-1968	LOS ANGELES	18	7	29	.241	12	28	.429	11	0.6	17	0.9	N/A	N/A	26	1.4
1968-1969	LOS ANGELES	35	44	108	.407	47	82	.573	44	1.3	31	0.9	N/A	N/A	135	3.9
1969-1970	DENVER (A)	3	2	4	.500	2	6	.333	4	1.3	4	1.3	N/A	N/A	6	2.0
1970-1971	CLEV.-PHIL.	28	20	65	.308	46	67	.687	48	1.7	20	0.7	N/A	N/A	86	3.1
NBA CAREER TOTALS		81	71	202	.351	105	177	.593	103	1.3	68	0.8	N/A	N/A	247	3.0
NBA PLAYOFF TOTALS		3	2	5	.400	0	0	N/A	1	0.3	N/A	0.0	N/A	N/A	4	1.3

Height	6-5
Weight	200
Born	9-7-44
College	St. Joseph

Barnes, V. James

SEASON	TEAM	G	FGM	FGA	PCT	FTM	FTA	PCT	REB	RPG	AST	APG	STL	BLK	PTS	PPG
1964-1965	New York	75	454	1070	.424	251	379	.662	729	9.7	93	1.2	N/A	N/A	1159	15.5
1965-1966	N.Y.-Balt.	73	348	818	.425	212	310	.684	755	10.3	94	1.3	N/A	N/A	908	12.4
1966-1967	Los Angeles	80	217	497	.437	128	187	.684	450	5.6	47	0.6	N/A	N/A	562	7.0
1967-1968	L.A.-Chicago	79	221	499	.443	133	191	.696	415	5.3	55	0.7	N/A	N/A	575	7.3
1968-1969	Chicago-Boston	59	115	261	.441	75	111	.676	224	3.8	28	0.5	N/A	N/A	305	5.2
1969-1970	Boston	77	178	434	.410	95	128	.742	350	4.5	52	0.7	N/A	N/A	451	5.9
1970-1971	Baltimore	11	15	28	.536	7	11	.636	16	1.5	8	0.7	N/A	N/A	37	3.4
NBA CAREER TOTALS		454	1548	3607	.429	901	1317	.684	2939	6.5	377	0.8	N/A	N/A	3997	8.8
NBA PLAYOFF TOTALS		11	26	63	.413	12	18	.667	61	5.5	6	0.5	N/A	N/A	64	5.8

Height	6-8
Weight	240
Born	4-14-41
College	UTEP

Barnett, Richard

SEASON	TEAM	G	FGM	FGA	PCT	FTM	FTA	PCT	REB	RPG	AST	APG	STL	BLK	PTS	PPG
1959-1960	Syracuse	57	289	701	.412	128	180	.711	155	2.7	160	2.8	N/A	N/A	706	12.4
1960-1961	Syracuse	78	540	1194	.452	240	337	.712	283	3.6	218	2.8	N/A	N/A	1320	16.9
1962-1963	Los Angeles	80	547	1162	.471	343	421	.815	242	3.0	224	2.8	N/A	N/A	1437	18.0
1963-1964	Los Angeles	78	541	1197	.452	351	454	.773	250	3.2	238	3.1	N/A	N/A	1433	18.4
1964-1965	Los Angeles	74	375	908	.413	270	338	.799	200	2.7	159	2.1	N/A	N/A	1020	13.8
1965-1966	New York	75	631	1344	.469	467	605	.772	310	4.1	259	3.5	N/A	N/A	1729	23.1
1966-1967	New York	67	454	949	.478	231	295	.783	226	3.4	161	2.4	N/A	N/A	1139	17.0
1967-1968	New York	81	559	1159	.482	343	440	.780	238	2.9	242	3.0	N/A	N/A	1461	18.0
1968-1969	New York	82	565	1220	.463	312	403	.774	251	3.1	291	3.5	N/A	N/A	1442	17.6
1969-1970	New York	82	494	1039	.475	232	325	.714	221	2.7	298	3.6	N/A	N/A	1220	14.9
1970-1971	New York	82	540	1184	.456	193	278	.694	238	2.9	225	2.7	N/A	N/A	1273	15.5
1971-1972	New York	79	401	918	.437	162	215	.753	153	1.9	198	2.5	N/A	N/A	964	12.2
1972-1973	New York	51	88	226	.389	16	30	.533	41	0.8	50	1.0	N/A	N/A	192	3.8
1973-1974	New York	5	10	26	.385	2	3	.667	4	0.8	6	1.2	1	0	22	4.4
NBA CAREER TOTALS		971	6034	13227	.456	3290	4324	.761	2812	2.9	2729	2.8	1	0	15358	15.8
NBA PLAYOFF TOTALS		102	603	1317	.458	333	445	.748	273	2.7	247	2.4	0	0	1539	15.1

Height   6-4
Weight   190
Born   10-2-36
College   Tenn St

Barry, Jon

SEASON	TEAM	G	FGM	FGA	PCT	FTM	FTA	PCT	REB	RPG	AST	APG	STL	BLK	PTS	PPG
1992-1993	MILWAUKEE	47	76	206	.369	33	49	.673	43	0.9	68	1.4	35	3	206	4.4
1993-1994	MILWAUKEE	72	158	382	.414	97	122	.795	146	2.0	168	2.3	102	17	445	6.2
1994-1995	MILWAUKEE	52	57	134	.425	61	80	.763	49	0.9	85	1.6	30	4	191	3.7
1995-1996	GOLDEN STATE	68	91	185	.492	31	37	.838	63	0.9	85	1.3	33	11	257	3.8
1996-1997	ATLANTA	58	100	246	.407	37	46	.804	99	1.7	115	2.0	55	3	285	4.9
1997-1998	LOS ANGELES	49	38	104	.365	27	29	.931	37	0.8	51	1.0	24	3	121	2.5
NBA CAREER TOTALS		346	520	1257	.414	286	363	.788	437	1.2	572	1.6	279	41	1505	4.3
NBA PLAYOFF TOTALS		7	0	8	.000	0	0	.000	2	0.3	0	0.0	1	0	0	0.0

Height   6-5
Weight   210
Born   7-25-69
College   Georgia Tech

Bates, Billy Ray

SEASON	TEAM	G	FGM	FGA	PCT	FTM	FTA	PCT	REB	RPG	AST	APG	STL	BLK	PTS	PPG
1979-1980	Portland	16	72	146	.493	28	39	.718	29	1.8	31	1.9	14	2	180	11.3
1980-1981	Portland	77	439	902	.487	170	199	.854	157	2.0	196	2.5	82	6	1062	13.8
1981-1982	Portland	75	327	692	.473	166	211	.787	108	1.4	111	1.5	41	5	832	11.1
1982-1983	Wash.-L. A.	19	55	145	.379	11	22	.500	19	1.0	14	0.7	14	3	123	6.5
NBA CAREER		187	893	1885	.474	375	471	.796	313	1.7	352	1.9	151	16	2197	11.7
NBA PLAYOFF TOTALS		6	66	121	.545	25	31	.806	17	2.8	25	4.2	10	2	160	26.7

Height   6-4
Weight   210
Born   5-31-56
College   Kentucky St

Baylor, Elgin Gay

SEASON	TEAM	G	FGM	FGA	PCT	FTM	FTA	PCT	REB	RPG	AST	APG	STL	BLK	PTS	PPG
1958-1959	Minneapolis	70	605	1482	.408	532	685	.777	1050	15.0	287	4.1	N/A	N/A	1742	24.9
1959-1960	Minneapolis	70	755	1781	.424	564	770	.732	1150	16.4	243	3.5	N/A	N/A	2074	29.6
1960-1961	Los Angeles	73	931	2166	.430	676	863	.783	1447	19.8	371	5.1	N/A	N/A	2538	34.8
1961-1962	Los Angeles	48	680	1588	.428	476	631	.754	892	18.6	222	4.6	N/A	N/A	1836	38.3
1962-1963	Los Angeles	80	1029	2273	.453	661	790	.837	1146	14.3	386	4.8	N/A	N/A	2719	34.0
1963-1964	Los Angeles	78	756	1778	.425	471	586	.804	936	12.0	347	4.4	N/A	N/A	1983	25.4
1964-1965	Los Angeles	74	763	1903	.401	483	610	.792	950	12.8	280	3.8	N/A	N/A	2009	27.1
1965-1966	Los Angeles	65	415	1034	.401	249	337	.739	621	9.6	224	3.4	N/A	N/A	1079	16.6
1966-1967	Los Angeles	70	711	1658	.429	440	541	.813	898	12.8	215	3.1	N/A	N/A	1862	26.6
1967-1968	Los Angeles	77	757	1709	.443	488	621	.786	941	12.2	355	4.6	N/A	N/A	2002	26.0
1968-1969	Los Angeles	76	730	1632	.447	421	567	.743	805	10.6	408	5.4	N/A	N/A	1881	24.8
1969-1970	Los Angeles	54	511	1051	.486	276	357	.773	559	10.4	292	5.4	N/A	N/A	1298	24.0
1970-1971	Los Angeles	2	8	19	.421	4	6	.667	11	5.5	2	1.0	N/A	N/A	20	10.0
1971-1972	Los Angeles	9	42	97	.433	22	27	.815	57	6.3	18	2.0	N/A	N/A	106	11.8
NBA CAREER TOTALS		846	8693	20171	.431	5763	7391	.780	11463	13.5	3650	4.3	N/A	N/A	23149	27.4
NBA PLAYOFF TOTALS		134	1388	3161	.439	847	1098	.771	1724	12.9	541	4.0	N/A	N/A	3623	27.0

Height	6-5
Weight	225
Born	9-16-34
College	Seattle

Beaty, Zelmo, Jr.

SEASON	TEAM	G	FGM	FGA	PCT	FTM	FTA	PCT	REB	RPG	AST	APG	STL	BLK	PTS	PPG
1962-1963	St. Louis	80	297	677	.439	220	307	.717	665	8.3	85	1.1	N/A	N/A	814	10.2
1963-1964	St. Louis	59	287	647	.444	200	270	.741	633	10.7	79	1.3	N/A	N/A	774	13.1
1964-1965	St. Louis	80	505	1047	.482	341	477	.715	966	12.1	111	1.4	N/A	N/A	1351	16.9
1965-1966	St. Louis	80	616	1301	.473	424	559	.758	1086	13.6	125	1.6	N/A	N/A	1656	20.7
1966-1967	St. Louis	48	328	694	.473	197	260	.758	515	10.7	60	1.3	N/A	N/A	853	17.8
1967-1968	St. Louis	82	639	1310	.488	455	573	.794	959	11.7	174	2.1	N/A	N/A	1733	21.1
1968-1969	Atlanta	72	588	1251	.470	370	506	.731	798	11.1	131	1.8	N/A	N/A	1546	21.5
1970-1971	Utah (A)	76	661	1192	.555	420	531	.791	1190	15.7	148	1.9	N/A	N/A	1744	22.9
1971-1972	Utah (A)	84	729	1353	.539	522	630	.829	1110	13.2	125	1.5	N/A	N/A	1980	23.6
1972-1973	Utah (A)	82	521	1002	.520	306	381	.803	801	9.8	125	1.5	N/A	79	1348	16.4
1973-1974	Utah (A)	77	417	796	.524	194	244	.795	615	8.0	128	1.7	62	64	1028	13.4
1974-1975	Los Angeles	69	136	310	.439	108	135	.800	327	4.7	74	1.1	45	29	380	5.5
NBA CAREER TOTALS		570	3396	7237	.469	2315	3087	.750	5949	10.4	839	1.5	45	29	9107	16.0
NBA PLAYOFF TOTALS		63	399	857	.466	273	370	.738	696	11.0	98	1.6	0	0	1071	17.0

Height	6-9
Weight	235
Born	10-25-39
Col	Prairie View A&M

Benjamin, Benoit

SEASON	TEAM	G	FGM	FGA	PCT	FTM	FTA	PCT	REB	RPG	AST	APG	STL	BLK	PTS	PPG
1985-1986	Clippers	79	324	661	.490	229	307	.746	600	7.6	79	1.0	64	206	878	11.1
1986-1987	Clippers	72	320	713	.449	188	263	.715	586	8.1	135	1.9	60	187	828	11.5
1987-1988	Clippers	66	340	693	.491	180	255	.706	530	8.0	172	2.6	50	225	860	13.0
1988-1989	Clippers	79	491	907	.541	317	426	.744	696	8.8	157	2.0	57	221	1299	16.4
1989-1990	Clippers	71	362	688	.526	235	321	.732	657	9.3	159	2.2	59	187	959	13.5
1990-1991	Clippers-Seattle	70	386	778	.496	210	295	.712	723	10.3	119	1.7	54	145	982	14.0
1991-1992	Seattle	63	354	740	.478	171	249	.687	513	8.1	76	1.2	39	118	879	14.0
1992-1993	Seattle-L.A.	59	133	271	.491	69	104	.663	209	3.5	22	0.4	31	48	335	5.7
1993-1994	New Jersey	77	283	589	.480	152	214	.710	499	6.5	44	0.6	35	90	718	9.3
1994-1995	New Jersey	61	271	531	.510	133	175	.760	440	7.2	38	0.6	23	64	675	11.1
1995-1996	Van.-Mil.	83	294	590	.498	140	194	.722	539	6.5	64	0.8	45	85	728	8.8
1996-1997	Toronto	4	5	12	.417	3	4	.750	9	2.3	1	0.3	1	0	13	3.3
1997-1998	Philadelphia	14	22	41	.537	19	30	.633	53	3.8	3	0.2	4	4	63	4.5
NBA CAREER TOTALS		798	3585	7214	.497	2046	2837	.721	6054	7.6	1069	1.4	522	1580	9217	11.6
NBA PLAYOFF TOTALS		18	50	99	.505	45	58	.776	100	5.6	7	0.4	10	34	145	8.1

Height	7-0
Weight	265
Born	11-22-64
College	Creighton

Bennett, Mario

SEASON	TEAM	G	FGM	FGA	PCT	FTM	FTA	PCT	REB	RPG	AST	APG	STL	BLK	PTS	PPG
1997-1998	Los Angeles	45	80	135	.593	16	44	.364	126	2.8	18	0.4	19	11	177	3.9
NBA CAREER TOTALS		45	80	135	.593	16	44	.364	126	2.8	18	0.4	19	11	177	3.9

Height	6-9
Weight	235
Born	8-1-73
College	Arizona St

Blackwell, Robert Alexander

SEASON	TEAM	G	FGM	FGA	PCT	FTM	FTA	PCT	REB	RPG	AST	APG	STL	BLK	PTS	PPG
1992-1993	Los Angeles	27	14	42	.333	6	8	.750	23	0.9	7	0.3	4	2	34	1.3
NBA CAREER TOTALS		27	14	42	.333	6	8	.750	23	0.9	7	0.3	4	2	34	1.3

Height	6-6
Weight	255
Born	6-27-70
College	Monmouth

Block, John William, Jr.

SEASON	TEAM	G	FGM	FGA	PCT	FTM	FTA	PCT	REB	RPG	AST	APG	STL	BLK	PTS	PPG
1966-1967	Los Angeles	22	20	52	.385	24	34	.706	45	2.0	5	0.2	N/A	N/A	64	2.9
1967-1968	San Diego	52	366	865	.423	316	394	.802	571	11.0	71	1.4	N/A	N/A	1048	20.2
1968-1969	San Diego	78	448	1061	.422	299	400	.748	703	9.0	141	1.8	N/A	N/A	1195	15.3
1969-1970	San Diego	82	453	1025	.442	287	367	.782	609	7.4	137	1.7	N/A	N/A	1193	14.5
1970-1971	San Diego	73	245	584	.420	212	270	.785	442	6.1	98	1.3	N/A	N/A	702	9.6
1971-1972	Milwaukee	79	233	530	.440	206	275	.749	410	5.2	95	1.2	N/A	N/A	672	8.5
1972-1973	Phil.-K.C.-Omaha	73	391	886	.441	300	378	.794	562	7.7	113	1.5	N/A	N/A	1082	14.8
1973-1974	Kansas City-Omaha	82	275	634	.434	164	206	.796	389	4.7	94	1.1	68	35	714	8.7
1974-1975	N.O.-Chicago	54	159	346	.460	114	144	.792	232	4.3	51	0.9	42	32	432	8.0
1975-1976	Chicago	2	2	4	.500	0	2	.000	2	1.0	0	0.0	1	0	4	2.0
NBA CAREER TOTALS		597	2592	5987	.433	1922	2470	.778	3965	6.6	805	1.3	111	67	7106	11.9
NBA PLAYOFF TOTALS		21	50	112	.446	30	39	.769	75	3.6	9	0.4	4	0	130	6.2

Height	6-9
Weight	210
Born	4-16-44
College	USC

Blount, Corie

SEASON	TEAM	G	FGM	FGA	PCT	FTM	FTA	PCT	REB	RPG	AST	APG	STL	BLK	PTS	PPG
1993-1994	CHICAGO	67	76	174	.437	46	75	.613	194	2.9	56	0.8	19	33	198	3.0
1994-1995	CHICAGO	68	100	210	.476	38	67	.567	240	3.5	60	0.9	26	33	238	3.5
1995-1996	LOS ANGELES	57	79	167	.473	25	44	.568	170	3.0	42	0.7	25	35	183	3.2
1996-1997	LOS ANGELES	58	92	179	.514	56	83	.675	276	4.8	35	0.6	22	26	241	4.2
1997-1998	LOS ANGELES	70	107	187	.572	39	78	.500	298	4.3	37	0.5	29	25	253	3.6
NBA CAREER TOTALS		320	454	917	.495	204	347	.588	1178	3.7	230	0.7	121	152	1113	3.5
NBA PLAYOFF TOTALS		23	13	28	.464	8	13	.615	71	3.1	8	0.3	6	4	34	1.5

Height	6-10
Weight	242
Born	1-4-69
College	Cincinnati

Boone, Ronald Bruce

SEASON	TEAM	G	FGM	FGA	PCT	FTM	FTA	PCT	REB	RPG	AST	APG	STL	BLK	PTS	PPG
1968-1969	DALLAS (A)	78	520	1197	.434	436	537	.812	394	5.1	279	3.6	N/A	N/A	1478	18.9
1969-1970	DALLAS (A)	84	423	980	.432	300	382	.785	366	4.4	272	3.2	N/A	N/A	1163	13.8
1970-1971	TEXAS-UTAH (A)	86	610	1395	.437	278	357	.779	564	6.6	256	3.0	N/A	N/A	1547	18.0
1971-1972	UTAH (A)	84	404	962	.420	271	341	.795	393	4.7	233	2.8	N/A	N/A	1092	13.0
1972-1973	UTAH (A)	84	566	1136	.498	415	479	.866	425	5.1	353	4.2	N/A	N/A	1557	18.5
1973-1974	UTAH (A)	84	587	1188	.494	300	343	.875	435	5.2	417	5.0	123	22	1480	17.6
1974-1975	UTAH (A)	84	872	1776	.491	363	422	.860	406	4.8	372	4.4	126	34	2117	25.2
1975-1976	UTAH-ST.L. (A)	78	713	1467	.486	277	318	.871	319	4.1	387	5.0	154	15	1719	22.0
1976-1977	KANSAS CITY	82	747	1577	.474	324	384	.844	321	3.9	338	4.1	119	19	1818	22.2
1977-1978	KANSAS CITY	82	563	1271	.443	322	377	.854	269	3.3	311	3.8	105	11	1448	17.7
1978-1979	LOS ANGELES	82	259	569	.455	90	104	.865	145	1.8	154	1.9	66	11	608	7.4
1979-1980	L.A.-UTAH	81	405	915	.443	175	196	.893	227	2.8	309	3.8	97	3	1004	12.4
1980-1981	UTAH	52	160	371	.431	75	94	.798	84	1.6	161	3.1	33	8	406	7.8
NBA CAREER TOTALS		379	2134	4703	.454	986	1155	.854	1046	2.8	1273	3.4	420	52	5284	13.9
NBA PLAYOFF TOTALS		8	37	77	.481	20	21	.952	15	1.9	14	1.8	9	0	94	11.8

Height	6-2
Weight	200
Born	9-6-46
College	Idaho St

Boozer, Robert Lewis

SEASON	TEAM	G	FGM	FGA	PCT	FTM	FTA	PCT	REB	RPG	AST	APG	STL	BLK	PTS	PPG
1960-1961	CINCINNATI	79	250	603	.415	166	247	.672	488	6.2	109	1.4	N/A	N/A	666	8.4
1961-1962	CINCINNATI	79	410	936	.438	263	372	.707	804	10.2	130	1.6	N/A	N/A	1083	13.7
1962-1963	CINCINNATI	79	440	992	.444	252	353	.714	878	11.1	102	1.3	N/A	N/A	1132	14.3
1963-1964	CIN.-N.Y.	81	468	1096	.427	272	376	.723	596	7.4	96	1.2	N/A	N/A	1208	14.9
1964-1965	NEW YORK	80	424	963	.440	288	375	.768	604	7.6	108	1.4	N/A	N/A	1136	14.2
1965-1966	LOS ANGELES	78	365	754	.484	225	289	.779	548	7.0	87	1.1	N/A	N/A	955	12.2
1966-1967	CHICAGO	80	538	1104	.487	360	461	.781	679	8.5	90	1.1	N/A	N/A	1436	18.0
1967-1968	CHICAGO	77	622	1265	.492	411	535	.768	756	9.8	121	1.6	N/A	N/A	1655	21.5
1968-1969	CHICAGO	79	661	1375	.481	394	489	.806	614	7.8	156	2.0	N/A	N/A	1716	21.7
1969-1970	SEATTLE	82	493	1005	.491	263	320	.822	717	8.7	110	1.3	N/A	N/A	1249	15.2
1970-1971	MILWAUKEE	80	290	645	.450	148	181	.818	435	5.4	128	1.6	N/A	N/A	728	9.1
NBA CAREER TOTALS		874	4961	10738	.462	3042	3998	.761	7119	8.1	1237	1.4	N/A	N/A	12964	14.8
NBA PLAYOFF TOTALS		48	213	456	.467	130	176	.739	341	7.1	58	1.2	N/A	N/A	556	11.6

Height	6-8
Weight	220
Born	4-26-37
College	Kansas St

Bowie, Samuel Paul

SEASON	TEAM	G	FGM	FGA	PCT	FTM	FTA	PCT	REB	RPG	AST	APG	STL	BLK	PTS	PPG
1984-1985	PORTLAND	76	299	557	.537	160	225	.711	656	8.6	215	2.8	55	203	758	10.0
1985-1986	PORTLAND	38	167	345	.484	114	161	.708	327	8.6	99	2.6	21	96	448	11.8
1986-1987	PORTLAND	5	30	66	.455	20	30	.667	33	6.6	9	1.8	1	10	80	16.0
1988-1989	PORTLAND	20	69	153	.451	28	49	.571	106	5.3	36	1.8	7	33	171	8.6
1989-1990	NEW JERSEY	68	347	834	.416	294	379	.776	690	10.1	91	1.3	38	121	998	14.7
1990-1991	NEW JERSEY	62	314	723	.434	169	231	.732	480	7.7	147	2.4	43	90	801	12.9
1991-1992	NEW JERSEY	71	421	947	.445	212	280	.757	578	8.1	186	2.6	41	120	1062	15.0
1992-1993	NEW JERSEY	79	287	638	.450	141	181	.779	556	7.0	127	1.6	32	128	717	9.1
1993-1994	LOS ANGELES	25	75	172	.436	72	83	.867	131	5.2	47	1.9	4	28	223	8.9
NBA CAREER TOTALS		444	2009	4435	.453	1210	1619	.747	3557	8.0	957	2.2	242	829	5258	11.8
NBA PLAYOFF TOTALS		19	56	129	.434	30	47	.638	127	6.7	35	1.8	13	32	144	7.6

Height	7-1
Weight	260
Born	3-17-61
College	Kentucky

Branch, Adrian Francis

SEASON	TEAM	G	FGM	FGA	PCT	FTM	FTA	PCT	REB	RPG	AST	APG	STL	BLK	PTS	PPG
1986-1987	LOS ANGELES	32	48	96	1	42	54	1	53	2	16	1	16	3	138	4
1987-1988	NEW JERSEY	20	56	134	0	20	23	1	48	2	16	1	16	11	133	7
1988-1989	PORTLAND	67	202	436	0	87	120	1	132	2	60	1	45	3	498	7
1989-1990	MINNESOTA	11	25	61	0	14	22	1	20	2	4	0	6	0	65	6
NBA CAREER TOTALS		130	331	727	0	163	219	1	253	2	96	1	83	17	834	6
NBA PLAYOFF TOTALS		12	4	24	0	8	14	1	11	1	7	1	2	0	16	1

Height	6-8
Weight	185
Born	11-17-63
College	Maryland

Brewer, James Turner

SEASON	TEAM	G	FGM	FGA	PCT	FTM	FTA	PCT	REB	RPG	AST	APG	STL	BLK	PTS	PPG
1973-1974	CLEVELAND	82	210	548	.383	80	123	.650	524	6.4	149	1.8	46	35	500	6.1
1974-1975	CLEVELAND	82	291	639	.455	103	159	.648	509	6.2	128	1.6	77	43	685	8.4
1975-1976	CLEVELAND	82	400	874	.458	140	214	.654	891	10.9	209	2.5	94	89	940	11.5
1976-1977	CLEVELAND	81	296	657	.451	97	178	.545	762	9.4	195	2.4	94	82	689	8.5
1977-1978	CLEVELAND	80	175	390	.449	46	100	.460	495	6.2	98	1.2	60	48	396	5.0
1978-1979	CLEV.-DETROIT	80	141	319	.442	26	63	.413	475	5.9	87	1.1	61	66	308	3.9
1979-1980	PORTLAND	67	90	184	.489	14	29	.483	257	3.8	75	1.1	42	43	194	2.9
1980-1981	LOS ANGELES	78	101	197	.513	15	40	.375	281	3.6	55	0.7	43	58	217	2.8
1981-1982	LOS ANGELES	71	81	175	.463	7	19	.368	264	3.7	42	0.6	39	46	170	2.4
NBA CAREER TOTALS		703	1785	3983	.448	528	925	.571	4458	6.3	1038	1.5	556	510	4099	5.8
NBA PLAYOFF TOTALS		31	68	145	.469	28	54	.519	204	6.6	49	1.6	24	24	164	5.3

Height	6-8
Weight	185
Born	11-17-63
College	Maryland

Brickowski, Francis Anthony

SEASON	TEAM	G	FGM	FGA	PCT	FTM	FTA	PCT	REB	RPG	AST	APG	STL	BLK	PTS	PPG
1984-1985	SEATTLE	78	150	305	.492	85	127	.669	280	3.3	100	1.3	34	15	385	4.9
1985-1986	SEATTLE	40	30	58	.517	18	27	.667	54	1.4	21	0.5	11	7	78	2.0
1986-1987	L.A.-SAN ANTONIO	44	63	124	.508	50	70	.714	116	2.6	17	0.4	20	6	176	4.0
1987-1988	SAN ANTONIO	70	425	805	.528	268	349	.768	483	6.9	266	3.8	74	36	1119	16.0
1988-1989	SAN ANTONIO	64	337	654	.515	201	281	.715	408	6.3	131	2.0	102	35	875	13.7
1989-1990	SAN ANTONIO	78	211	387	.545	95	141	.674	327	4.2	105	1.3	66	37	517	6.6
1990-1991	MILWAUKEE	75	372	706	.527	198	248	.798	426	5.7	131	1.7	86	43	942	12.6
1991-1992	MILWAUKEE	65	306	584	.524	125	163	.767	344	5.3	122	1.9	60	23	740	11.4
1992-1993	MILWAUKEE	66	456	836	.545	195	268	.728	405	6.1	196	3.0	80	44	1115	16.9
1993-1994	MILW.-CHA.	71	368	754	.488	195	254	.768	404	5.7	222	3.1	80	27	935	13.2
NBA CAREER TOTALS		651	2718	5213	.521	1430	1928	.742	3225	5.0	1311	2.0	613	273	6882	10.6
NBA PLAYOFF TOTALS		16	77	143	.538	37	59	.627	92	5.8	28	1.8	15	5	192	12.0

Height	6-9
Weight	245
Born	8-14-59
College	Penn St

Bridges, William C.

SEASON	TEAM	G	FGM	FGA	PCT	FTM	FTA	PCT	REB	RPG	AST	APG	STL	BLK	PTS	PPG
1962-1963	ST. LOUIS	27	66	160	.413	32	51	.627	144	5.3	23	0.9	N/A	N/A	164	6.1
1963-1964	ST. LOUIS	80	268	675	.397	146	224	.652	680	8.5	181	2.3	N/A	N/A	682	8.5
1964-1965	ST. LOUIS	79	362	938	.386	186	275	.676	853	10.8	187	2.4	N/A	N/A	910	11.5
1965-1966	ST. LOUIS	78	377	927	.407	257	364	.706	951	12.2	208	2.7	N/A	N/A	1011	13.0
1966-1967	ST. LOUIS	79	503	1106	.455	367	523	.702	1190	15.1	222	2.8	N/A	N/A	1373	17.4
1967-1968	ST. LOUIS	82	466	1009	.462	347	484	.717	1102	13.4	253	3.1	N/A	N/A	1279	15.6
1968-1969	ATLANTA	80	351	775	.453	239	353	.677	1132	14.2	298	3.7	N/A	N/A	941	11.8
1969-1970	ATLANTA	82	443	932	.475	331	451	.734	1181	14.4	345	4.2	N/A	N/A	1217	14.8
1970-1971	ATLANTA	82	382	834	.458	211	330	.639	1233	15.0	240	2.9	N/A	N/A	975	11.9
1971-1972	ATLANTA-PHIL.	78	379	779	.487	222	316	.703	1051	13.5	198	2.5	N/A	N/A	980	12.6
1972-1973	PHIL.-LOS ANGELES	82	333	722	.461	179	255	.702	904	11.0	219	2.7	N/A	N/A	845	10.3
1973-1974	LOS ANGELES	65	216	513	.421	116	164	.707	499	7.7	148	2.3	58	31	548	8.4
1974-1975	LOS ANGELES-G.S.	32	35	93	.376	17	34	.500	134	4.2	31	1.0	11	5	87	2.7
NBA CAREER TOTALS		926	4181	9463	.442	2650	3824	.693	11054	11.9	2553	2.8	69	36	11012	11.9
NBA PLAYOFF TOTALS		113	475	1135	.419	235	349	.673	1305	11.5	219	1.9	16	4	1185	10.5

Height	6-5
Weight	230
Born	4-4-39
College	Kansas

Brown, Anthony William

SEASON	TEAM	G	FGM	FGA	PCT	FTM	FTA	PCT	REB	RPG	AST	APG	STL	BLK	PTS	PPG
1984-1985	INDIANA	82	214	465	.460	116	171	.678	288	3.5	159	1.9	59	12	544	6.6
1985-1986	CHICAGO	10	18	41	.439	9	13	.692	16	1.6	14	1.4	5	1	45	4.5
1986-1987	NEW JERSEY	77	358	810	.442	152	206	.738	219	2.8	259	3.4	89	14	873	11.3
1988-1989	HOUSTON-MILW.	43	50	118	.424	24	31	.774	44	1.0	26	0.6	15	4	128	3.0
1989-1990	MILWAUKEE	61	88	206	.427	38	56	.679	72	1.2	41	0.7	32	4	219	3.6
1990-1991	L.A.-UTAH	30	30	80	.375	20	23	.870	43	1.4	16	0.5	4	0	83	2.8
1991-1992	CLIPPERS-SEATTLE	56	102	249	.410	48	66	.727	84	1.5	48	0.9	30	5	271	4.8
NBA CAREER TOTALS		359	860	1969	.437	407	566	.719	766	2.1	563	1.6	234	40	2163	6.0
NBA PLAYOFF TOTALS		17	11	28	.393	7	11	.636	12	0.7	9	0.5	4	0	32	1.9

Height	6-6
Weight	200
Born	7-29-60
College	Arkansas

Brown, Clarence

SEASON	TEAM	G	FGM	FGA	PCT	FTM	FTA	PCT	REB	RPG	AST	APG	STL	BLK	PTS	PPG
1989-1990	CLEVELAND	75	210	447	.470	125	164	.762	231	3.1	50	0.7	33	26	545	7.3
1990-1991	CLEVELAND	74	263	502	.524	101	144	.701	213	2.9	80	1.1	26	24	627	8.5
1991-1992	CLEV.-LOS ANGELES	42	60	128	.469	30	49	.612	82	2.0	26	0.6	12	7	150	3.6
1992-1993	NEW JERSEY	77	160	331	.483	71	98	.724	232	3.0	51	0.7	20	24	391	5.1
1993-1994	DALLAS	1	1	1	1.000	1	1	1.000	1	1.0	0	0.0	0	0	3	3.0
NBA CAREER TOTALS		269	694	1409	.493	328	456	.719	759	2.8	207	0.8	91	81	1716	6.4
NBA PLAYOFF TOTALS		7	17	41	.415	9	13	.692	20	2.9	3	0.4	3	5	43	6.1

Height	6-8
Weight	215
Born	2-29-68
College	N Carolina St

Brown, W. Roger

SEASON	TEAM	G	FGM	FGA	PCT	FTM	FTA	PCT	REB	RPG	AST	APG	STL	BLK	PTS	PPG
1972-1973	LOS ANGELES	1	0	0	N/A	1	3	.333	0	0.0	0	0.0	N/A	N/A	1	1.0
1972-1973	CAROLINA (A)	62	59	129	.457	28	51	.549	178	2.9	25	0.4	N/A	N/A	146	2.4
1973-1974	SAN ANTONIO-VIR. (A)	63	98	260	.377	34	56	.607	352	5.6	46	0.7	23	62	230	3.7
1975-1976	DETROIT	29	29	72	.403	14	18	.778	130	4.5	12	0.4	6	25	72	2.5
1975-1976	DENVER (A)	37	28	61	.459	16	24	.667	75	2.0	22	0.6	8	22	74	2.0
1976-1977	DETROIT	43	21	56	.375	18	26	.692	90	2.1	12	0.3	15	18	60	1.4
1979-1980	CHICAGO	4	1	3	.333	0	0	N/A	10	2.5	1	0.3	0	3	2	0.5
NBA CAREER TOTALS		77	51	131	.389	33	47	.702	230	3.0	25	0.3	21	46	135	1.8
NBA PLAYOFF TOTALS		11	4	10	.400	2	4	.500	14	1.3	2	0.2	0	2	10	0.9

Height	6-11
Weight	230
Born	2-23-50
College	Kansas

Bryant, Kobe

SEASON	TEAM	G	FGM	FGA	PCT	FTM	FTA	PCT	REB	RPG	AST	APG	STL	BLK	PTS	PPG
1996-1997	LOS ANGELES	71	176	422	.417	136	166	.819	132	1.9	91	1.3	49	23	539	7.6
1997-1998	LOS ANGELES	79	391	913	.428	363	457	.794	242	3.1	199	2.5	74	40	1220	15.4
NBA CAREER TOTALS		150	567	1335	.424	499	623	.801	374	2.5	290	1.9	123	63	1759	11.7
NBA PLAYOFF TOTALS		20	52	131	.397	57	75	.760	32	1.6	27	1.3	6	10	170	8.5

Height	6-7
Weight	210
Born	8-23-78
College	None

Bucknall, Steven Lee

SEASON	TEAM	G	FGM	FGA	PCT	FTM	FTA	PCT	REB	RPG	AST	APG	STL	BLK	PTS	PPG
1989-1990	LOS ANGELES	18	9	33	.273	5	6	.833	7	0.4	10	0.6	2	1	23	1.3
NBA CAREER TOTALS		18	9	33	.273	5	6	.833	7	0.4	10	0.6	2	1	23	1.3

Height	6-6
Weight	215
Born	3-17-66
College	N Carolina

Byrnes, Martin William

SEASON	TEAM	G	FGM	FGA	PCT	FTM	FTA	PCT	REB	RPG	AST	APG	STL	BLK	PTS	PPG
1978-1979	PHOENIX-N.O.	79	187	389	.481	106	154	.688	191	2.4	104	1.3	27	10	480	6.1
1979-1980	LOS ANGELES	32	25	50	.500	13	15	.867	27	0.8	13	0.4	5	1	63	2.0
1980-1981	DALLAS	72	216	451	.479	120	157	.764	177	2.5	113	1.6	29	17	561	7.8
1982-1983	INDIANA	80	157	374	.420	71	95	.747	191	2.4	179	2.2	41	6	391	4.9
NBA CAREER TOTALS		263	585	1264	.463	310	421	.736	586	2.2	409	1.6	102	34	1495	5.7
NBA PLAYOFF TOTALS		4	1	3	.333	4	6	.667	1	0.3	1	0.3	0	0	6	1.5

Height	6-7
Weight	220
Born	4-30-56
College	Syracuse

Calhoun, David L.

SEASON	TEAM	G	FGM	FGA	PCT	FTM	FTA	PCT	REB	RPG	AST	APG	STL	BLK	PTS	PPG
1972-1973	PHOENIX	82	211	450	.469	71	96	.740	338	4.1	76	0.9	N/A	N/A	493	6.0
1973-1974	PHOENIX	77	268	581	.461	98	129	.760	407	5.3	135	1.8	71	30	634	8.2
1974-1975	PHOENIX-L.A.	70	132	318	.415	58	77	.753	269	3.8	79	1.1	55	25	322	4.6
1975-1976	LOS ANGELES	76	172	368	.467	65	83	.783	341	4.5	85	1.1	62	35	409	5.4
1976-1977	PORTLAND	70	85	183	.464	66	85	.776	144	2.1	35	0.5	24	8	236	3.4
1977-1978	PORTLAND	79	175	365	.479	66	76	.868	215	2.7	87	1.1	42	15	416	5.3
1978-1979	INDIANA	81	153	335	.457	72	86	.837	238	2.9	104	1.3	37	19	378	4.7
1979-1980	INDIANA	7	4	9	.444	0	2	.000	10	1.4	0	0.0	2	0	8	1.1
NBA CAREER TOTALS		542	1200	2609	.460	496	634	.782	1962	3.6	601	1.1	293	132	2896	5.3
NBA PLAYOFF TOTALS		18	28	54	.519	6	10	.600	28	1.6	7	0.4	6	3	62	3.4

Height	6-7
Weight	210
Born	11-1-50
College	Pennsylvania

Calip, Demetrius

SEASON	TEAM	G	FGM	FGA	PCT	FTM	FTA	PCT	REB	RPG	AST	APG	STL	BLK	PTS	PPG
1991-1992	LOS ANGELES	7	4	18	.222	2	3	.667	5	0.7	12	1.7	1	0	11	1.6
NBA CAREER TOTALS		7	4	18	.222	2	3	.667	5	0.7	12	1.7	1	0	11	1.6

Height	6-1
Weight	165
Born	11-18-69
College	Michigan

Calvin, Mack

SEASON	TEAM	G	FGM	FGA	PCT	FTM	FTA	PCT	REB	RPG	AST	APG	STL	BLK	PTS	PPG
1969-1970	LOS ANGELES (A)	84	441	1047	.421	529	642	.824	294	3.5	478	5.7	N/A	N/A	1414	16.8
1970-1971	FLORIDIANS (A)	81	744	1728	.431	696	805	.865	283	3.5	619	7.6	N/A	N/A	2201	27.2
1971-1972	FLORIDIANS (A)	82	552	1253	.441	611	701	.872	274	3.3	481	5.9	N/A	N/A	1726	21.0
1972-1973	CAROLINA (A)	84	478	944	.506	500	582	.859	215	2.6	301	3.6	N/A	N/A	1467	17.5
1973-1974	CAROLINA (A)	83	498	1078	.462	490	560	.875	243	2.9	347	4.2	135	7	1496	18.0
1974-1975	DENVER (A)	74	483	996	.485	475	530	.896	210	2.8	570	7.7	140	8	1444	19.5
1975-1976	VIRGINIA (A)	45	306	717	.427	253	285	.888	128	2.8	271	6.0	71	1	872	19.4
1976-1977	L.A.-S.A.-DENVER	76	220	544	.404	287	338	.849	96	1.3	240	3.2	61	3	727	9.6
1977-1978	DENVER	77	147	333	.441	173	206	.840	84	1.1	148	1.9	46	5	467	6.1
1979-1980	UTAH	48	100	227	.441	105	117	.897	84	1.8	134	2.8	27	0	306	6.4
1980-1981	CLEVELAND	21	13	39	.333	25	35	.714	12	0.6	28	1.3	5	0	52	2.5
NBA CAREER TOTALS		222	480	1143	.420	590	696	.848	276	1.2	550	2.5	139	8	1552	7.0
NBA PLAYOFF TOTALS		18	38	82	.463	51	58	.879	17	0.9	34	1.9	8	0	127	7.1

Height	6-0
Weight	170
Born	7-27-47
College	USC

Campbell, Anthony

SEASON	TEAM	G	FGM	FGA	PCT	FTM	FTA	PCT	REB	RPG	AST	APG	STL	BLK	PTS	PPG
1984-1985	DETROIT	56	130	262	.496	56	70	.800	89	1.6	24	0.4	28	3	316	5.6
1985-1986	DETROIT	82	294	608	.484	58	73	.795	236	2.9	45	0.5	62	7	648	7.9
1986-1987	DETROIT	40	57	145	.393	24	39	.615	58	1.5	19	0.5	12	1	138	3.5
1987-1988	LOS ANGELES	13	57	101	.564	28	39	.718	27	2.1	15	1.2	11	2	143	11.0
1988-1989	LOS ANGELES	63	158	345	.458	70	83	.843	130	2.1	47	0.7	37	6	388	6.2
1989-1990	MINNESOTA	82	723	1581	.457	448	569	.787	451	5.5	213	2.6	111	31	1903	23.2
1990-1991	MINNESOTA	77	652	1502	.434	358	446	.803	346	4.5	214	2.8	121	48	1678	21.8
1991-1992	MINNESOTA	78	527	1137	.464	240	299	.803	286	3.7	229	2.9	84	31	1307	16.8
1992-1993	NEW YORK	58	194	396	.490	59	87	.678	155	2.7	62	1.1	34	5	449	7.7
1993-1994	N.Y.-DALLAS	63	227	512	.443	94	120	.783	186	3.0	82	1.3	50	15	555	8.8
NBA CAREER TOTALS		612	3019	6589	.458	1435	1825	.786	1964	3.2	950	1.6	550	149	7525	12.3
NBA PLAYOFF TOTALS		34	49	102	.480	36	50	.720	35	1.0	14	0.4	7	0	137	4.0

Height	6-7
Weight	215
Born	5-7-62
College	Ohio St

Campbell, Elden Jerome

SEASON	TEAM	G	FGM	FGA	PCT	FTM	FTA	PCT	REB	RPG	AST	APG	STL	BLK	PTS	PPG
1990-1991	LOS ANGELES	52	56	123	.455	32	49	.653	96	1.8	10	0.2	11	38	144	2.8
1991-1992	LOS ANGELES	81	220	491	.448	138	223	.619	423	5.2	59	0.7	53	159	578	7.1
1992-1993	LOS ANGELES	79	238	520	.458	130	204	.637	332	4.2	48	0.6	59	100	606	7.7
1993-1994	LOS ANGELES	76	373	808	.462	188	273	.689	519	6.8	86	1.1	64	146	934	12.3
1994-1995	LOS ANGELES	73	360	785	.459	193	290	.666	445	6.1	92	1.3	69	132	913	12.5
1995-1996	LOS ANGELES	82	447	888	.503	249	349	.713	623	7.6	181	2.2	88	212	1143	13.9
1996-1997	LOS ANGELES	77	442	942	.469	263	370	.711	615	8.0	126	1.6	46	117	1148	14.9
1997-1998	LOS ANGELES	81	289	524	.463	237	342	.693	455	5.6	78	0.9	35	102	816	10.1
NBA CAREER TOTALS		601	2425	5181	.468	1430	2100	.681	3508	5.8	680	1.1	425	1006	6282	10.5
NBA PLAYOFF TOTALS		59	212	459	.461	121	189	.640	285	4.8	57	0.9	30	90	546	9.2

Height	7-0
Weight	255
Born	7-23-68
College	Clemson

Carr, Kenneth Alan

SEASON	TEAM	G	FGM	FGA	PCT	FTM	FTA	PCT	REB	RPG	AST	APG	STL	BLK	PTS	PPG
1977-1978	LOS ANGELES	52	134	302	.444	55	85	.647	208	4.0	26	0.5	18	14	323	6.2
1978-1979	LOS ANGELES	72	225	450	.500	83	137	.606	292	4.1	60	0.8	38	31	533	7.4
1979-1980	L.A.-CLEV.	79	378	768	.492	173	263	.658	588	7.4	77	1.0	66	52	929	11.8
1980-1981	CLEVELAND	81	469	918	.511	292	409	.714	835	10.3	192	2.4	76	42	1230	15.2
1981-1982	CLEV.-DETROIT	74	348	692	.503	198	302	.656	531	7.2	86	1.2	64	22	895	12.1
1982-1983	PORTLAND	82	362	717	.505	255	366	.697	589	7.2	116	1.4	62	42	981	12.0
1983-1984	PORTLAND	82	518	923	.561	247	367	.673	642	7.8	157	1.9	68	33	1283	15.6
1984-1985	PORTLAND	48	190	363	.523	118	164	.720	323	6.7	56	1.2	25	17	498	10.4
1985-1986	PORTLAND	55	232	466	.498	149	217	.687	492	8.9	70	1.3	38	30	613	11.1
1986-1987	PORTLAND	49	201	399	.504	126	169	.746	499	10.2	83	1.7	29	13	528	10.8
NBA CAREER TOTALS		674	3057	5998	.510	1696	2479	.684	4999	7.4	923	1.4	484	296	7813	11.6
NBA PLAYOFF TOTALS		35	153	299	.512	62	85	.729	230	6.6	37	1.1	18	12	368	10.5

Height	6-7
Weight	220
Born	8-15-55
Coll	N Carolina St

Carter, Clarence Eugene, Jr.

SEASON	TEAM	G	FGM	FGA	PCT	FTM	FTA	PCT	REB	RPG	AST	APG	STL	BLK	PTS	PPG
1980-1981	LOS ANGELES	54	114	247	.462	70	95	.737	65	1.2	52	1.0	23	1	301	5.6
1981-1982	INDIANA	75	188	402	.468	58	70	.829	79	1.1	60	0.8	34	11	442	5.9
1982-1983	INDIANA	81	354	706	.501	124	154	.805	150	1.9	194	2.4	78	13	849	10.5
1983-1984	INDIANA	73	413	862	.479	136	178	.764	153	2.1	206	2.8	128	13	977	13.4
1984-1985	NEW YORK	69	214	476	.450	109	134	.813	95	1.4	167	2.4	57	5	548	7.9
1985-1986	N.Y.-PHIL.	9	7	24	.292	6	7	.857	4	0.4	4	0.4	1	0	20	2.2
NBA CAREER TOTALS		361	1290	2717	.475	503	638	.788	546	1.5	683	1.9	321	43	3137	8.7

Height	6-5
Weight	180
Born	6-11-58
College	Indiana

Carter, Ronald, Jr.

SEASON	TEAM	G	FGM	FGA	PCT	FTM	FTA	PCT	REB	RPG	AST	APG	STL	BLK	PTS	PPG
1978-1979	LOS ANGELES	46	54	124	.435	36	54	.667	45	1.0	25	0.5	17	7	144	3.1
1979-1980	INDIANA	13	15	37	.405	2	7	.286	19	1.5	9	0.7	2	3	32	2.5
NBA CAREER TOTALS		59	69	161	.429	38	61	.623	64	1.1	34	0.6	19	10	176	3.0
NBA PLAYOFF TOTALS		2	0	1	.000	0	0	N/A	0	0.0	N/A	0.0	0	0	0	0.0

Height	6-5
Weight	190
Born	8-31-56
College	VMI

Carty, Jay J., Jr.

SEASON	TEAM	G	FGM	FGA	PCT	FTM	FTA	PCT	REB	RPG	AST	APG	STL	BLK	PTS	PPG
1968-1969	LOS ANGELES	28	34	89	.382	8	11	.727	58	2.1	11	0.4	N/A	N/A	76	2.7
NBA CAREER TOTALS		28	34	89	.382	8	11	.727	58	2.1	11	0.4	N/A	N/A	76	2.7
NBA PLAYOFF TOTALS		3	0	2	.000	1	3	.333	2	0.7	1	0.3	N/A	N/A	1	0.3

Height	6-7
Weight	220
Born	7-4-41
College	Oregon St

Ceballos, Cedric

SEASON	TEAM	G	FGM	FGA	PCT	FTM	FTA	PCT	REB	RPG	AST	APG	STL	BLK	PTS	PPG
1990-1991	PHOENIX	63	204	419	.487	110	166	.663	150	2.4	35	0.6	22	5	519	8.2
1991-1992	PHOENIX	64	176	365	.482	109	148	.736	152	2.4	50	0.8	16	11	462	7.2
1992-1993	PHOENIX	74	381	662	.576	187	258	.725	408	5.5	77	1.0	54	28	949	12.8
1993-1994	PHOENIX	53	425	795	.535	160	221	.724	344	6.5	91	1.7	59	23	1010	19.1
1994-1995	LOS ANGELES	58	497	977	.509	209	292	.716	464	8.0	105	1.8	60	19	1261	21.7
1995-1996	LOS ANGELES	78	638	1203	.530	329	409	.804	536	6.9	119	1.5	94	22	1656	21.2
1996-1997	LOS ANGELES-PHO.	50	282	617	.457	139	186	.747	330	6.6	64	1.3	33	23	729	14.6
1997-1998	PHOENIX-DALLAS	47	204	415	.492	107	145	.738	221	4.7	60	1.3	33	16	536	11.4
NBA CAREER TOTALS		487	2807	5453	.515	1350	1825	.739	2605	5.3	601	1.2	371	147	7122	14.6
NBA PLAYOFF TOTALS		56	223	476	.468	100	134	.746	257	4.6	61	1.1	41	26	572	10.2

Height	6-7
Weight	225
Born	8-2-69
Coll	Cal St Fullerton

Chamberlain, Wilton

SEASON	TEAM	G	FGM	FGA	PCT	FTM	FTA	PCT	REB	RPG	AST	APG	STL	BLK	PTS	PPG
1959-1960	PHILADELPHIA	72	1065	2311	.461	577	991	.582	1941	27.0	168	2.3	N/A	N/A	2707	37.6
1960-1961	PHILADELPHIA	79	1251	2457	.509	531	1054	.504	2149	27.2	148	1.9	N/A	N/A	3033	38.4
1961-1962	PHILADELPHIA	80	1597	3159	.506	835	1363	.613	2052	25.7	192	2.4	N/A	N/A	4029	50.4
1962-1963	SAN FRANCISCO	80	1463	2770	.528	660	1113	.593	1946	24.3	275	3.4	N/A	N/A	3586	44.8
1963-1964	SAN FRANCISCO	80	1204	2298	.524	540	1016	.531	1787	22.3	403	5.0	N/A	N/A	2948	36.9
1964-1965	S.F.-PHIL.	73	1063	2083	.510	408	880	.464	1673	22.9	250	3.4	N/A	N/A	2534	34.7
1965-1966	PHILADELPHIA	79	1074	1990	.540	501	976	.513	1943	24.6	414	5.2	N/A	N/A	2649	33.5
1966-1967	PHILADELPHIA	81	785	1150	.683	386	875	.441	1957	24.2	630	7.8	N/A	N/A	1956	24.1
1967-1968	PHILADELPHIA	82	819	1377	.595	354	932	.380	1952	23.8	702	8.6	N/A	N/A	1992	24.3
1968-1969	LOS ANGELES	81	641	1099	.583	382	857	.446	1712	21.1	366	4.5	N/A	N/A	1664	20.5
1969-1970	LOS ANGELES	12	129	227	.568	70	157	.446	221	18.4	49	4.1	N/A	N/A	328	27.3
1970-1971	LOS ANGELES	82	668	1226	.545	360	669	.538	1493	18.2	352	4.3	N/A	N/A	1696	20.7
1971-1972	LOS ANGELES	82	496	764	.649	221	524	.422	1572	19.2	329	4.0	N/A	N/A	1213	14.8
1972-1973	LOS ANGELES	82	426	586	.727	232	455	.510	1526	18.6	365	4.5	N/A	N/A	1084	13.2
NBA CAREER TOTALS		1045	12681	23497	.540	6057	11862	.511	23924	22.9	4643	4.4	N/A	N/A	31419	30.1
NBA PLAYOFF TOTALS		160	1425	2728	.522	757	1627	.465	3913	24.5	673	4.2	N/A	N/A	3607	22.5

Height	7-1
Weight	275
Born	8-21-36
College	Kansas

Chambers, Jerome Purcell

SEASON	TEAM	G	FGM	FGA	PCT	FTM	FTA	PCT	REB	RPG	AST	APG	STL	BLK	PTS	PPG
1966-1967	LOS ANGELES	68	224	496	.452	68	93	.731	208	3.1	44	0.6	N/A	N/A	516	7.6
1969-1970	PHOENIX	79	283	658	.430	91	125	.728	219	2.8	54	0.7	N/A	N/A	657	8.3
1970-1971	ATLANTA	65	237	526	.451	106	134	.791	245	3.8	61	0.9	N/A	N/A	580	8.9
1971-1972	BUFFALO	26	78	180	.433	22	32	.688	67	2.6	23	0.9	N/A	N/A	178	6.8
1972-1973	SAN DIEGO (A)	43	199	468	.425	112	130	.862	190	4.4	46	1.1	N/A	N/A	512	11.9
1973-1974	SAN ANTONIO (A)	38	94	206	.456	36	48	.750	103	2.7	42	1.1	11	3	224	5.9
NBA CAREER TOTALS		238	822	1860	.442	287	384	.747	739	3.1	182	0.8	N/A	N/A	1931	8.1
NBA PLAYOFF TOTALS		14	29	69	.420	13	17	.765	30	2.1	8	0.6	N/A	N/A	71	5.1

Height	6-5
Weight	185
Born	7-18-43
College	Utah

Chaney, Donald R.

SEASON	TEAM	G	FGM	FGA	PCT	FTM	FTA	PCT	REB	RPG	AST	APG	STL	BLK	PTS	PPG
1968-1969	BOSTON	20	36	113	.319	8	20	.400	46	2.3	19	1.0	N/A	N/A	80	4.0
1969-1970	BOSTON	63	115	320	.359	82	109	.752	152	2.4	72	1.1	N/A	N/A	312	5.0
1970-1971	BOSTON	81	348	766	.454	234	313	.748	463	5.7	235	2.9	N/A	N/A	930	11.5
1971-1972	BOSTON	79	373	786	.475	197	255	.773	395	5.0	202	2.6	N/A	N/A	943	11.9
1972-1973	BOSTON	79	414	859	.482	210	267	.787	449	5.7	221	2.8	N/A	N/A	1038	13.1
1973-1974	BOSTON	81	348	750	.464	149	180	.828	378	4.7	176	2.2	83	62	845	10.4
1974-1975	BOSTON	82	321	750	.428	133	165	.806	370	4.5	181	2.2	122	66	775	9.5
1975-1976	ST. LOUIS (A)	48	191	457	.418	64	82	.780	234	4.9	169	3.5	66	36	447	9.3
1976-1977	LOS ANGELES	81	213	522	.408	70	94	.745	330	4.1	308	3.8	140	33	496	6.1
1977-1978	L.A.-BOSTON	51	104	269	.387	38	45	.844	116	2.3	66	1.3	44	13	246	4.8
1978-1979	BOSTON	65	174	414	.420	36	42	.857	141	2.2	75	1.2	72	11	384	5.9
1979-1980	BOSTON	60	67	189	.354	32	42	.762	73	1.2	38	0.6	31	11	167	2.8
NBA CAREER TOTALS		742	2513	5738	.438	1189	1532	.776	2913	3.9	1593	2.1	492	196	6216	8.4
NBA PLAYOFF TOTALS		70	230	511	.450	110	142	.775	250	3.6	156	2.2	66	17	570	8.1

Height	6-5
Weight	210
Born	3-22-46
College	Houston

Chones, James Bernett

SEASON	TEAM	G	FGM	FGA	PCT	FTM	FTA	PCT	REB	RPG	AST	APG	STL	BLK	PTS	PPG
1972-1973	NEW YORK (A)	82	395	769	.514	142	240	.592	586	7.1	95	1.2	N/A	N/A	932	11.4
1973-1974	CAROLINA (A)	83	535	1017	.526	155	252	.615	645	7.8	118	1.4	59	131	1225	14.8
1974-1975	CLEVELAND	72	446	916	.487	152	224	.679	677	9.4	132	1.8	49	120	1044	14.5
1975-1976	CLEVELAND	82	563	1258	.448	172	260	.662	739	9.0	163	2.0	42	93	1298	15.8
1976-1977	CLEVELAND	82	450	972	.463	155	212	.731	688	8.4	104	1.3	32	77	1055	12.9
1977-1978	CLEVELAND	82	525	1113	.472	180	250	.720	844	10.3	131	1.6	52	58	1230	15.0
1978-1979	CLEVELAND	82	472	1073	.440	158	215	.735	842	10.3	181	2.2	47	102	1102	13.4
1979-1980	LOS ANGELES	82	372	760	.489	125	169	.740	564	6.9	151	1.8	56	65	869	10.6
1980-1981	LOS ANGELES	82	378	751	.503	126	193	.653	657	8.0	153	1.9	39	96	882	10.8
1981-1982	WASHINGTON	59	74	171	.433	36	46	.783	185	3.1	64	1.1	15	32	184	3.1
NBA CAREER TOTALS		623	3280	7014	.468	1104	1569	.704	5196	8.3	1079	1.7	332	643	7664	12.3
NBA PLAYOFF TOTALS		36	136	312	.436	50	78	.641	223	6.2	47	1.3	13	20	322	8.9

Height	6-11
Weight	220
Born	11-30-49
College	Marquette

Christie, Douglas Dale

SEASON	TEAM	G	FGM	FGA	PCT	FTM	FTA	PCT	REB	RPG	AST	APG	STL	BLK	PTS	PPG
1992-1993	LOS ANGELES	23	45	106	.425	50	66	.758	51	2.2	53	2.3	22	5	142	6.2
1993-1994	LOS ANGELES	65	244	562	.434	145	208	.697	235	3.6	136	2.1	89	28	672	10.3
1994-1995	NEW YORK	12	5	22	.227	4	5	.800	13	1.1	8	0.7	2	1	15	1.3
1995-1996	N.Y.-TOR.	55	150	337	.445	69	93	.742	154	2.8	117	2.1	70	19	415	7.5
1996-1997	TORONTO	81	396	949	.417	237	306	.775	432	5.3	315	3.9	201	45	1176	14.5
1997-1998	TORONTO	78	458	1071	.428	271	327	.829	404	5.2	282	3.6	190	57	1287	16.5
NBA CAREER TOTALS		314	1298	3047	.425	776	1005	.772	1289	4.1	911	2.9	574	155	3707	11.8
NBA PLAYOFF TOTALS		7	4	15	.267	0	0	N/A	4	0.6	6	0.9	2	2	9	1.3

Height	6-6
Weight	205
Born	5-9-70
College	Pepperdine

Clark, Archie L.

SEASON	TEAM	G	FGM	FGA	PCT	FTM	FTA	PCT	REB	RPG	AST	APG	STL	BLK	PTS	PPG
1966-1967	LOS ANGELES	76	331	732	.452	136	192	.708	218	2.9	205	2.7	N/A	N/A	798	10.5
1967-1968	LOS ANGELES	81	628	1309	.480	356	481	.740	342	4.2	353	4.4	N/A	N/A	1612	19.9
1968-1969	PHILADELPHIA	82	444	928	.478	219	314	.697	265	3.2	296	3.6	N/A	N/A	1107	13.5
1969-1970	PHILADELPHIA	76	594	1198	.496	311	396	.785	301	4.0	380	5.0	N/A	N/A	1499	19.7
1970-1971	PHILADELPHIA	82	662	1334	.496	422	536	.787	391	4.8	440	5.4	N/A	N/A	1746	21.3
1971-1972	PHIL.-BALT.	77	712	1516	.470	514	667	.771	268	3.5	613	8.0	N/A	N/A	1938	25.2
1972-1973	BALTIMORE	39	302	596	.507	111	137	.810	129	3.3	275	7.1	N/A	N/A	715	18.3
1973-1974	CAPITAL	56	315	675	.467	103	131	.786	141	2.5	285	5.1	59	6	733	13.1
1974-1975	SEATTLE	77	455	919	.495	161	193	.834	235	3.1	433	5.6	110	5	1071	13.9
1975-1976	DETROIT	79	250	577	.433	100	116	.862	137	1.7	218	2.8	62	4	600	7.6
NBA CAREER TOTALS		725	4693	9784	.480	2433	3163	.769	2427	3.3	3498	4.8	231	15	11819	16.3
NBA PLAYOFF TOTALS		71	444	977	.454	237	307	.772	229	3.2	297	4.2	17	1	1125	15.8

Height	6-2
Weight	175
Born	7-15-41
College	Minnesota

Cleamons, James Mitchell

SEASON	TEAM	G	FGM	FGA	PCT	FTM	FTA	PCT	REB	RPG	AST	APG	STL	BLK	PTS	PPG
1971-1972	LOS ANGELES	38	35	100	.350	28	36	.778	39	1.0	35	0.9	N/A	N/A	98	2.6
1972-1973	CLEVELAND	80	192	423	.454	75	101	.743	167	2.1	205	2.6	N//A	N/A	459	5.7
1973-1974	CLEVELAND	81	236	545	.433	93	133	.699	230	2.8	227	2.8	61	17	565	7.0
1974-1975	CLEVELAND	74	369	768	.480	144	181	.796	329	4.4	381	5.1	84	21	882	11.9
1975-1976	CLEVELAND	82	413	887	.466	174	218	.798	354	4.3	428	5.2	124	20	1000	12.2
1976-1977	CLEVELAND	60	257	592	.434	112	148	.757	273	4.6	308	5.1	66	23	626	10.4
1977-1978	NEW YORK	79	215	448	.480	81	103	.786	212	2.7	283	3.6	68	17	511	6.5
1978-1979	NEW YORK	79	311	657	.473	130	171	.760	225	2.8	376	4.8	73	11	752	9.5
1979-1980	N.Y.-WASH.	79	214	450	.476	84	113	.743	152	1.9	288	3.6	57	11	519	6.6
NBA CAREER TOTALS		652	2242	4870	.460	921	1204	.765	981	3.0	2531	3.9	533	120	5412	8.3
NBA PLAYOFF TOTALS		27	91	230	.396	39	46	.848	89	3.3	89	3.3	12	3	221	8.2

Height	6-3
Weight	185
Born	9-13-49
College	Ohio St

Connor, Lester Allen

Height	6-4
Weight	185
Born	9-17-59
College	Oregon St

SEASON	TEAM	G	FGM	FGA	PCT	FTM	FTA	PCT	REB	RPG	AST	APG	STL	BLK	PTS	PPG
1982-1983	GOLDEN STATE	75	145	303	.479	79	113	.699	221	2.9	253	3.4	116	7	369	4.9
1983-1984	GOLDEN STATE	82	360	730	.493	186	259	.718	305	3.7	401	4.9	162	12	907	11.1
1984-1985	GOLDEN STATE	79	246	546	.451	144	192	.750	246	3.1	369	4.7	161	13	640	8.1
1985-1986	GOLDEN STATE	36	51	136	.375	40	54	.741	62	1.7	43	1.2	24	1	144	4.0
1987-1988	HOUSTON	52	50	108	.463	32	41	.780	38	0.7	59	1.1	38	1	132	2.5
1988-1989	NEW JERSEY	82	309	676	.457	212	269	.788	355	4.3	604	7.4	181	5	843	10.3
1989-1990	NEW JERSEY	82	237	573	.414	172	214	.804	265	3.2	385	4.7	172	8	648	7.9
1990-1991	N.J.-MILW.	74	96	207	.464	68	94	.723	112	1.5	165	2.2	85	2	260	3.5
1991-1992	MILWAUKEE	81	103	239	.431	81	115	.704	184	2.3	294	3.6	97	10	287	3.5
1992-1993	CLIPPERS	31	28	62	.452	18	19	.947	49	1.6	65	2.1	34	4	74	2.4
1993-1994	INDIANA	11	14	38	.368	3	6	.500	24	2.2	31	2.8	14	1	31	2.8
1994-1995	LOS ANGELES	2	0	0	N/A	2	2	1.000	0	0.0	0	0.0	1	0	2	1.0
NBA CAREER TOTALS		689	1639	3618	.453	1039	1380	.733	1861	2.7	2669	3.9	1086	64	4339	6.3
NBA PLAYOFF TOTALS		13	12	18	.667	6	7	.857	13	1.0	13	1.0	5	1	31	2.4

Cooper, Joseph Edward

Height	6-10
Weight	230
Born	9-1-57
College	Colorado

SEASON	TEAM	G	FGM	FGA	PCT	FTM	FTA	PCT	REB	RPG	AST	APG	STL	BLK	PTS	PPG
1981-1982	NEW JERSEY	1	1	2	.500	0	0	N/A	2	2.0	0	0.0	0	0	2	2.0
1982-1983	L.A.-WASH.-S.D.	20	37	72	.514	16	29	.552	86	4.3	17	0.9	9	20	90	4.5
1984-1985	SEATTLE	3	7	15	.467	3	6	.500	9	3.0	2	0.7	2	1	17	5.7
NBA CAREER TOTALS		24	45	89	.506	19	35	.543	97	4.0	19	0.8	11	21	109	4.5

Cooper, Michael Jerome

Height	6-7
Weight	170
Born	4-15-56
College	New Mexico

SEASON	TEAM	G	FGM	FGA	PCT	FTM	FTA	PCT	REB	RPG	AST	APG	STL	BLK	PTS	PPG
1978-1979	LOS ANGELES	3	3	6	.500	0	0	N/A	0	0.0	0	0.0	1	0	6	2.0
1979-1980	LOS ANGELES	82	303	578	.524	111	143	.776	229	2.8	221	2.7	86	38	722	8.8
1980-1981	LOS ANGELES	81	321	654	.491	117	149	.785	336	4.1	332	4.1	133	78	763	9.4
1981-1982	LOS ANGELES	76	383	741	.517	139	171	.813	269	3.5	230	3.0	120	61	907	11.9
1982-1983	LOS ANGELES	82	266	497	.535	102	130	.785	274	3.3	315	3.8	115	50	639	7.8
1983-1984	LOS ANGELES	82	273	549	.497	155	185	.838	262	3.2	482	5.9	113	67	739	9.0
1984-1985	LOS ANGELES	82	276	593	.465	115	133	.865	255	3.1	429	5.2	93	49	702	8.6
1985-1986	LOS ANGELES	82	274	606	.452	147	170	.865	244	3.0	466	5.7	89	43	758	9.2
1986-1987	LOS ANGELES	82	322	736	.438	126	148	.851	254	3.1	373	4.5	78	43	859	10.5
1987-1988	LOS ANGELES	61	189	482	.392	97	113	.858	228	3.7	289	4.7	66	26	532	8.7
1988-1989	LOS ANGELES	80	213	494	.431	81	93	.871	191	2.4	314	3.9	72	32	587	7.3
1989-1990	LOS ANGELES	80	191	493	.387	83	94	.883	227	2.8	215	2.7	67	36	515	6.4
NBA CAREER TOTALS		873	3014	6429	.469	1273	1529	.833	2769	3.2	3666	4.2	1033	523	7729	8.9
NBA PLAYOFF TOTALS		168	582	1244	.468	293	355	.825	574	3.4	703	4.2	203	96	1581	9.4

Cooper, Samuel Duane

SEASON	TEAM	G	FGM	FGA	PCT	FTM	FTA	PCT	REB	RPG	AST	APG	STL	BLK	PTS	PPG
1992-1993	LOS ANGELES	65	62	158	.392	25	35	.714	50	0.8	150	2.3	18	2	156	2.4
1993-1994	PHOENIX	23	18	41	.439	11	15	.733	9	0.4	28	1.2	3	0	48	2.1
NBA CAREER TOTALS		88	80	199	.402	36	50	.720	59	0.7	178	2.0	21	2	204	2.3
NBA PLAYOFF TOTALS		2	0	6	.000	0	0	N/A	2	1.0	1	0.5	0	0	0	0.0

Height	6-1
Weight	185
Born	6-25-69
College	USC

Counts, Mel Grant

SEASON	TEAM	G	FGM	FGA	PCT	FTM	FTA	PCT	REB	RPG	AST	APG	STL	BLK	PTS	PPG
1964-1965	BOSTON	54	100	272	.368	58	74	.789	265	4.9	19	0.4	N/A	N/A	258	4.8
1965-1966	BOSTON	67	221	549	.403	120	145	.828	432	6.4	50	0.7	N/A	N/A	562	8.4
1966-1967	BALT.-L.A.	56	177	419	.422	69	94	.734	344	6.1	52	0.9	N/A	N/A	423	7.6
1967-1968	LOS ANGELES	82	384	808	.475	190	254	.748	732	8.9	139	1.7	N/A	N/A	958	11.7
1968-1969	LOS ANGELES	77	390	867	.450	178	221	.805	600	7.8	109	1.4	N/A	N/A	958	12.4
1969-1970	LOS ANGELES	81	434	1017	.427	156	201	.776	683	8.4	160	2.0	N/A	N/A	1024	12.6
1970-1971	PHOENIX	80	365	799	.457	149	198	.753	503	6.3	136	1.7	N/A	N/A	879	11.0
1971-1972	PHOENIX	76	147	344	.427	101	140	.721	257	3.4	96	1.3	N/A	N/A	395	5.2
1972-1973	PHIL.-L.A.	66	132	294	.449	39	58	.672	253	3.8	65	1.0	N/A	N/A	303	4.6
1973-1974	LOS ANGELES	45	61	167	.365	24	33	.727	146	3.2	54	1.2	20	23	146	3.2
1974-1975	NEW ORLEANS	75	217	495	.438	86	113	.761	441	5.9	182	2.4	49	43	520	6.9
1975-1976	NEW ORLEANS	30	37	91	.407	16	21	.762	100	3.3	38	1.3	16	8	90	3.0
NBA CAREER TOTALS		789	2665	6122	.435	1186	1552	.764	4756	6.0	1100	1.4	85	74	6516	8.3
NBA PLAYOFF TOTALS		85	255	599	.426	138	178	.775	519	6.1	100	1.2	2	2	648	7.6

Height	7-0
Weight	230
Born	10-16-41
College	Oregon St

Crawford, Frederick Russell, Jr.

SEASON	TEAM	G	FGM	FGA	PCT	FTM	FTA	PCT	REB	RPG	AST	APG	STL	BLK	PTS	PPG
1966-1967	NEW YORK	19	44	116	.379	24	38	.632	48	2.5	12	0.6	N/A	N/A	112	5.9
1967-1968	N.Y.-L.A.	69	224	507	.442	111	179	.620	195	2.8	141	2.0	N/A	N/A	559	8.1
1968-1969	LOS ANGELES	81	211	454	.465	83	154	.539	215	2.7	154	1.9	N/A	N/A	505	6.2
1969-1970	MILWAUKEE	77	243	506	.480	101	148	.682	184	2.4	225	2.9	N/A	N/A	587	7.6
1970-1971	BUFFALO-PHIL.	51	110	281	.391	48	98	.490	104	2.0	78	1.5	N/A	N/A	268	5.3
NBA CAREER TOTALS		297	832	1864	.446	367	617	.595	746	2.5	610	2.1	N/A	N/A	2031	6.8
NBA PLAYOFF TOTALS		35	105	252	.417	48	76	.632	97	2.8	73	2.1	N/A	N/A	258	7.4

Height	6-4
Weight	195
Born	12-23-40
Coll	St. Bonaventure

Daniels, Lloyd

SEASON	TEAM	G	FGM	FGA	PCT	FTM	FTA	PCT	REB	RPG	AST	APG	STL	BLK	PTS	PPG
1992-1993	SAN ANTONIO	77	285	644	.443	72	99	.727	216	2.8	148	1.9	38	30	701	9.1
1993-1994	SAN ANTONIO	65	140	372	.376	46	64	.719	111	1.7	94	1.4	29	16	370	5.7
1994-1995	PHIL.-LOS ANGELES	30	80	209	.383	22	27	.815	63	2.1	40	1.3	22	10	208	6.9
1996-1997	SAC.-N.J.	22	36	119	.303	5	6	.833	43	2.0	26	1.2	10	3	98	4.5
1996-1997	SAC.-N.J.	22	36	119	.303	5	6	.833	43	2.0	26	1.2	10	3	98	4.5
1997-1998	TORONTO	6	12	29	.414	8	10	.800	7	1.2	4	0.7	3	2	34	5.7
NBA CAREER TOTALS		200	553	1373	.403	153	206	.743	440	2.2	312	1.6	102	61	1411	7.1
NBA PLAYOFF TOTALS		12	19	50	.380	7	8	.875	24	2.0	5	0.4	3	1	50	4.2

Height	6-7
Weight	205
Born	9-4-67
Coll	Mt. San Antonio

Dantley, Adrian

Height	6-5
Weight	208
Born	2-28-56
College	Notre Dame

SEASON	TEAM	G	FGM	FGA	PCT	FTM	FTA	PCT	REB	RPG	AST	APG	STL	BLK	PTS	PPG
1976-1977	BUFFALO	77	544	1046	.520	476	582	.818	587	7.6	144	1.9	91	15	1564	20.3
1977-1978	IND.-L.A.	79	578	1128	.512	541	680	.796	620	7.8	253	3.2	118	24	1697	21.5
1978-1979	LOS ANGELES	60	374	733	.510	292	342	.854	342	5.7	138	2.3	63	12	1040	17.3
1979-1980	UTAH	68	730	1267	.576	443	526	.842	516	7.6	191	2.8	96	14	1903	28.0
1980-81	UTAH	80	909	1627	.559	632	784	.806	509	6.4	322	4.0	5			
1980-1981	UTAH	80	909	1627	.559	632	784	.806	509	6.4	322	4.0	109	18	2452	30.7
1981-1982	UTAH	81	904	1586	.570	648	818	.792	514	6.3	324	4.0	95	14	2457	30.3
1982-1983	UTAH	22	233	402	.580	210	248	.847	140	6.4	105	4.8	20	0	676	30.7
1983-1984	UTAH	79	802	1438	.558	813	946	.859	448	5.7	310	3.9	61	4	2418	30.6
1984-1985	UTAH	55	512	964	.531	438	545	.804	323	5.9	186	3.4	57	8	1462	26.6
1985-1986	UTAH	76	818	1453	.563	630	796	.791	395	5.2	264	3.5	64	4	2267	29.8
1986-1987	DETROIT	81	601	1126	.534	539	664	.812	332	4.1	162	2.0	63	7	1742	21.5
1987-1988	DETROIT	69	444	863	.514	492	572	.860	227	3.3	171	2.5	39	10	1380	20.0
1988-1989	DETROIT-DAL.	73	470	954	.493	460	568	.810	317	4.3	171	2.3	43	13	1400	19.2
1989-1990	DALLAS	45	231	484	.477	200	254	.787	172	3.8	80	1.8	20	7	662	14.7
1990-1991	MILWAUKEE	10	19	50	.380	18	26	.692	13	1.3	9	0.9	5	0	57	5.7
NBA CAREER TOTALS		955	8169	15121	.540	6832	8351	.818	5455	5.7	2830	3.0	944	150	23177	24.3
NBA PLAYOFF TOTALS		73	531	1012	.525	496	623	.796	395	5.4	169	2.3	69	6	1558	21.3

Davis, Bradley Ernest

Height	6-3
Weight	180
Born	12-17-55
College	Maryland

SEASON	TEAM	G	FGM	FGA	PCT	FTM	FTA	PCT	REB	RPG	AST	APG	STL	BLK	PTS	PPG
1977-1978	LOS ANGELES	33	30	72	.417	22	29	.759	35	1.1	83	2.5	15	2	82	2.5
1978-1979	L.A.-INDIANA	27	31	55	.564	16	23	.696	17	0.6	52	1.9	16	2	78	2.9
1979-1980	INDIANA-UTAH	18	35	63	.556	13	16	.813	17	0.9	50	2.8	13	1	83	4.6
1980-1981	DALLAS	56	230	410	.561	163	204	.799	151	2.7	385	6.9	52	11	626	11.2
1981-1982	DALLAS	82	397	771	.515	185	230	.804	226	2.8	509	6.2	73	6	993	12.1
1982-1983	DALLAS	79	359	628	.572	186	220	.845	198	2.5	565	7.2	80	11	915	11.6
1983-1984	DALLAS	81	345	651	.530	199	238	.836	187	2.3	561	6.9	94	13	896	11.1
1984-1985	DALLAS	82	310	614	.505	158	178	.888	193	2.4	581	7.1	91	10	825	10.1
1985-1986	DALLAS	82	267	502	.532	198	228	.868	146	1.8	467	5.7	57	15	764	9.3
1986-1987	DALLAS	82	199	436	.456	147	171	.860	114	1.4	373	4.5	63	10	577	7.0
1987-1988	DALLAS	75	208	415	.501	91	108	.843	102	1.4	303	4.0	51	18	537	7.2
1988-1989	DALLAS	78	183	379	.483	99	123	.805	108	1.4	242	3.1	48	18	497	6.4
1989-1990	DALLAS	73	179	365	.490	77	100	.770	93	1.3	242	3.3	47	9	470	6.4
1990-1991	DALLAS	80	159	373	.426	91	118	.771	118	1.5	230	2.9	45	17	431	5.4
1991-1992	DALLAS	33	38	86	.442	11	15	.733	33	1.0	66	2.0	11	3	92	2.8
NBA CAREER TOTALS		961	2970	5820	.510	1656	2001	.828	1738	1.8	4709	4.9	756	146	7866	8.2
NBA PLAYOFF TOTALS		45	125	236	.530	77	91	.846	75	1.7	167	3.7	16	6	341	7.6

DiGregorio, Ernest

Height	6-0
Weight	180
Born	1-15-51
College	Providence

SEASON	TEAM	G	FGM	FGA	PCT	FTM	FTA	PCT	REB	RPG	AST	APG	STL	BLK	PTS	PPG
1973-1974	BUFFALO	81	530	1260	.421	174	193	.902	219	2.7	663	8.2	59	9	1234	15.2
1974-1975	BUFFALO	31	103	234	.440	35	45	.778	45	1.5	151	4.9	19	0	241	7.8
1975-1976	BUFFALO	67	182	474	.384	86	94	.915	112	1.7	265	4.0	37	1	450	6.7
1976-1977	BUFFALO	81	365	875	.417	138	146	.945	184	2.3	378	4.7	57	3	868	10.7
1977-1978	L.A.-BOSTON	52	88	209	.421	28	33	.848	50	1.0	137	2.6	18	1	204	3.9
NBA CAREER TOTALS		312	1268	3052	.415	461	511	.902	610	2.0	1594	5.1	190	14	2997	9.6
NBA PLAYOFF TOTALS		15	67	148	.453	16	17	.941	29	1.9	97	6.5	6	2	150	10.0

Divac, Vlade

SEASON	TEAM	G	FGM	FGA	PCT	FTM	FTA	PCT	REB	RPG	AST	APG	STL	BLK	PTS	PPG
1989-1990	LOS ANGELES	82	274	549	.499	153	216	.708	512	6.2	75	0.9	79	114	701	8.5
1990-1991	LOS ANGELES	82	360	637	.565	196	279	.703	666	8.1	92	1.1	106	127	921	11.2
1991-1992	LOS ANGELES	36	157	317	.495	86	112	.768	247	6.9	60	1.7	55	35	405	11.3
1992-1993	LOS ANGELES	82	397	819	.485	235	341	.689	729	8.9	232	2.8	128	140	1050	12.8
1993-1994	LOS ANGELES	79	453	895	.506	208	303	.686	851	10.8	307	3.9	92	112	1123	14.2
1994-1995	LOS ANGELES	80	485	957	.507	297	382	.777	829	10.4	329	4.1	109	174	1277	16.0
1995-1996	LOS ANGELES	79	414	807	.513	189	295	.641	679	8.6	261	3.3	76	131	1020	12.9
1996-1997	CHARLOTTE	81	418	847	.494	177	259	.683	725	9.0	301	3.7	103	180	1024	12.6
1997-1998	CHARLOTTE	64	267	536	.498	130	188	.691	518	8.1	172	2.7	83	94	667	10.4
NBA CAREER TOTALS		665	3225	6364	.507	1671	2375	.704	5756	8.7	1829	2.8	831	1107	8188	12.3
NBA PLAYOFF TOTALS		58	295	571	.516	158	218	.724	417	7.2	140	2.4	59	99	757	13.1

Height	7-1
Weight	260
Born	2-3-68
College	None

Drew, Larry Donnell

SEASON	TEAM	G	FGM	FGA	PCT	FTM	FTA	PCT	REB	RPG	AST	APG	STL	BLK	PTS	PPG
1980-1981	DETROIT	76	197	484	.407	106	133	.797	120	1.6	249	3.3	88	7	504	6.6
1981-1982	KANSAS CITY	81	358	757	.473	150	189	.794	149	1.8	419	5.2	110	1	874	10.8
1982-1983	KANSAS CITY	75	599	1218	.492	310	378	.820	207	2.8	610	8.1	126	10	1510	20.1
1983-1984	KANSAS CITY	73	474	1026	.462	243	313	.776	146	2.0	558	7.6	121	10	1194	16.4
1984-1985	KANSAS CITY	72	457	913	.501	154	194	.794	164	2.3	484	6.7	93	8	1075	14.9
1985-1986	SACRAMENTO	75	376	776	.485	128	161	.795	125	1.7	338	4.5	66	2	890	11.9
1986-1987	CLIPPERS	60	295	683	.432	139	166	.837	103	1.7	326	5.4	60	2	741	12.4
1987-1988	CLIPPERS	74	328	720	.456	83	108	.769	119	1.6	383	5.2	65	0	765	10.3
1989-1990	LOS ANGELES	80	170	383	.444	46	60	.767	98	1.2	217	2.7	47	4	418	5.2
1990-1991	LOS ANGELES	48	54	125	.432	17	22	.773	34	0.7	118	2.5	15	1	139	2.9
NBA CAREER TOTALS		714	3308	7085	.467	1376	1724	.798	1265	1.8	3702	5.2	791	45	8110	11.4
NBA PLAYOFF TOTALS		31	38	85	.447	14	17	.824	15	0.5	50	1.6	11	0	95	3.1

Height	6-1
Weight	175
Born	4-2-58
College	Missouri

Edwards, James Franklin

SEASON	TEAM	G	FGM	FGA	PCT	FTM	FTA	PCT	REB	RPG	AST	APG	STL	BLK	PTS	PPG
1977-1978	L.A.-INDIANA	83	495	1093	.453	272	421	.646	615	7.4	85	1.0	53	78	1262	15.2
1978-1979	INDIANA	82	534	1065	.501	298	441	.676	693	8.5	92	1.1	60	109	1366	16.7
1979-1980	INDIANA	82	528	1032	.512	231	339	.681	578	7.0	127	1.5	55	104	1287	15.7
1980-1981	INDIANA	81	511	1004	.509	244	347	.703	571	7.0	212	2.6	32	128	1266	15.6
1981-1982	CLEVELAND	77	528	1033	.511	232	339	.684	581	7.5	123	1.6	24	117	1288	16.7
1982-1983	CLEV.-PHOENIX	31	128	263	.487	69	108	.639	155	5.0	40	1.3	12	19	325	10.5
1983-1984	PHOENIX	72	438	817	.536	183	254	.720	348	4.8	184	2.6	23	30	1059	14.7
1984-1985	PHOENIX	70	384	766	.501	276	370	.746	387	5.5	153	2.2	26	52	1044	14.9
1985-1986	PHOENIX	52	318	587	.542	212	302	.702	301	5.8	74	1.4	23	29	848	16.3
1986-1987	PHOENIX	14	57	110	.518	54	70	.771	60	4.3	19	1.4	6	7	168	12.0
1987-1988	PHOENIX-DETROIT	69	302	643	.470	210	321	.654	412	6.0	78	1.1	16	37	814	11.8
1988-1989	DETROIT	76	211	422	.500	133	194	.686	231	3.0	49	0.6	11	31	555	7.3
1989-1990	DETROIT	82	462	928	.498	265	354	.749	345	4.2	63	0.8	23	37	1189	14.5
1990-1991	DETROIT	72	383	792	.484	215	295	.729	277	3.8	65	0.9	12	30	982	13.6
1991-1992	CLIPPERS	72	250	538	.465	198	271	.731	202	2.8	53	0.7	24	33	698	9.7
1992-1993	LOS ANGELES	52	122	270	.452	84	118	.712	100	1.9	41	0.8	10	7	328	6.3
1993-1994	LOS ANGELES	45	78	168	.464	54	79	.684	65	1.4	22	0.5	4	3	210	4.7
NBA CAREER TOTALS		1112	5729	11531	.497	3230	4623	.699	5921	5.3	480	1.3	414	851	14689	13.2
NBA PLAYOFF TOTALS		104	395	843	.469	229	336	.682	350	3.4	84	0.8	17	46	1019	9.8

Height	7-1
Weight	255
Born	11-22-55
College	Washington

Egan, John Francis

SEASON	TEAM	G	FGM	FGA	PCT	FTM	FTA	PCT	REB	RPG	AST	APG	STL	BLK	PTS	PPG
1961-1962	DETROIT	58	128	301	.425	64	84	.762	86	1.5	102	1.8	N/A	N/A	320	5.5
1962-1963	DETROIT	46	110	296	.372	53	69	.768	59	1.3	114	2.5	N/A	N/A	273	5.9
1963-1964	DETROIT-N.Y.	66	334	758	.441	193	243	.794	191	2.9	358	5.4	N/A	N/A	861	13.0
1964-1965	NEW YORK	74	258	529	.488	162	199	.814	143	1.9	252	3.4	N/A	N/A	678	9.2
1965-1966	N.Y.-BALT.	76	259	574	.451	173	227	.762	183	2.4	273	3.6	N/A	N/A	691	9.1
1966-1967	BALTIMORE	71	267	624	.428	185	219	.845	180	2.5	275	3.9	N/A	N/A	719	10.1
1967-1968	BALTIMORE	67	163	415	.393	142	183	.776	112	1.7	134	2.0	N/A	N/A	468	7.0
1968-1969	LOS ANGELES	82	246	597	.412	204	240	.850	147	1.8	215	2.6	N/A	N/A	696	8.5
1969-1970	LOS ANGELES	72	215	491	.438	99	121	.818	104	1.4	216	3.0	N/A	N/A	529	7.3
1970-1971	CLEV.-S.D.	62	67	178	.376	42	51	.824	63	1.0	112	1.8	N/A	N/A	176	2.8
1971-1972	HOUSTON	38	42	104	.404	26	32	.813	26	0.7	51	1.3	N/A	N/A	110	2.9
NBA CAREER TOTALS		712	2089	4867	.429	1343	1668	.805	1294	1.8	2102	3.0	N/A	N/A	5521	7.8
NBA PLAYOFF TOTALS		42	165	369	.447	93	117	.795	67	1.6	131	3.1	N/A	N/A	423	10.1

Height 6-0
Weight 180
Born 1-31-39
College Providence

Ellis, Leroy B.

SEASON	TEAM	G	FGM	FGA	PCT	FTM	FTA	PCT	REB	RPG	AST	APG	STL	BLK	PTS	PPG
1962-1963	LOS ANGELES	80	222	530	.419	133	202	.658	518	6.5	46	0.6	N/A	N/A	577	7.2
1963-1964	LOS ANGELES	78	200	473	.423	112	170	.659	498	6.4	41	0.5	N/A	N/A	512	6.6
1964-1965	LOS ANGELES	80	311	700	.444	198	284	.697	652	8.2	49	0.6	N/A	N/A	820	10.3
1965-1966	LOS ANGELES	80	393	927	.424	186	256	.727	735	9.2	74	0.9	N/A	N/A	972	12.2
1966-1967	BALTIMORE	81	496	1166	.425	211	286	.738	970	12.0	170	2.1	N/A	N/A	1203	14.9
1967-1968	BALTIMORE	78	380	800	.475	207	286	.724	862	11.1	158	2.0	N/A	N/A	967	12.4
1968-1969	BALTIMORE	80	229	527	.435	117	155	.755	510	6.4	73	0.9	N/A	N/A	575	7.2
1969-1970	BALTIMORE	72	194	414	.469	86	116	.741	376	5.2	47	0.7	N/A	N/A	474	6.6
1970-1971	PORTLAND	74	485	1095	.443	209	261	.801	907	12.3	235	3.2	N/A	N/A	1179	15.9
1971-1972	LOS ANGELES	74	138	300	.460	66	95	.695	310	4.2	46	0.6	N/A	N/A	342	4.6
1972-1973	L.A.-PHIL.	79	421	969	.434	129	161	.801	777	9.8	139	1.8	N/A	N/A	971	12.3
1973-1974	PHILADELPHIA	81	326	722	.452	147	196	.750	890	11.0	189	2.3	86	87	799	9.9
1974-1975	PHILADELPHIA	82	287	623	.461	72	99	.727	582	7.1	117	1.4	44	55	646	7.9
1975-1976	PHILADELPHIA	29	61	132	.462	17	28	.607	122	4.2	21	0.7	16	9	139	4.8
NBA CAREER TOTALS		1048	4143	9378	.442	1890	2595	.728	8709	8.3	1405	1.3	146	151	10176	9.7
NBA PLAYOFF TOTALS		64	175	424	.413	113	163	.693	462	7.2	44	0.7	0	0	463	7.2

Height 6-11
Weight 210
Born 3-10-40
College St. John's

Erickson, Keith Raymond

SEASON	TEAM	G	FGM	FGA	PCT	FTM	FTA	PCT	REB	RPG	AST	APG	STL	BLK	PTS	PPG
1965-1966	SAN FRANCISCO	64	95	267	.356	43	65	.662	162	2.5	38	0.6	N/A	N/A	233	3.6
1966-1967	CHICAGO	76	235	641	.367	117	159	.736	338	4.4	119	1.6	N/A	N/A	587	7.7
1967-1968	CHICAGO	78	377	940	.401	194	257	.755	423	5.4	267	3.4	N/A	N/A	948	12.2
1968-1969	LOS ANGELES	77	264	629	.420	120	175	.686	308	4.0	194	2.5	N/A	N/A	648	8.4
1969-1970	LOS ANGELES	68	258	563	.458	91	122	.746	304	4.5	209	3.1	N/A	N/A	607	8.9
1970-1971	LOS ANGELES	73	369	783	.471	85	112	.759	404	5.5	223	3.1	N/A	N/A	823	11.3
1971-1972	LOS ANGELES	15	40	83	.482	6	7	.857	39	2.6	35	2.3	N/A	N/A	86	5.7
1972-1973	LOS ANGELES	76	299	696	.430	89	110	.809	337	4.4	242	3.2	N/A	N/A	687	9.0
1973-1974	PHOENIX	66	393	824	.477	177	221	.801	414	6.3	205	3.1	63	20	963	14.6
1974-1975	PHOENIX	49	237	557	.425	130	156	.833	243	5.0	170	3.5	50	12	604	12.3
1975-1976	PHOENIX	74	305	649	.470	134	157	.854	332	4.5	185	2.5	79	6	744	10.1
1976-1977	PHOENIX	50	142	294	.483	37	50	.740	144	2.9	104	2.1	30	7	321	6.4
NBA CAREER TOTALS		766	3014	6926	.435	1223	1591	.769	3448	4.5	1991	2.6	222	45	7251	9.5
NBA PLAYOFF TOTALS		87	364	806	.452	144	189	.762	386	4.4	216	2.5	11	4	872	10.0

Height 6-5
Weight 195
Born 4-19-44
College UCLA

Fairchild, John Russell

SEASON	TEAM	G	FGM	FGA	PCT	FTM	FTA	PCT	REB	RPG	AST	APG	STL	BLK	PTS	PPG
1965-1966	LOS ANGELES	30	23	89	.258	14	20	.700	45	1.5	11	0.4	N/A	N/A	60	2.0
1967-1968	ANAHEIM (A)	62	271	620	.437	135	200	.675	332	5.4	63	1.0	N/A	N/A	678	10.9
1968-1969	DENVER-INDIANA (A)	63	113	294	.384	89	127	.701	129	2.0	37	0.6	N/A	N/A	325	5.2
1969-1970	INDIANA-KEN. (A)	10	7	23	.304	5	10	.500	17	1.7	4	0.4	N/A	N/A	22	2.2
NBA CAREER TOTALS		30	23	89	.258	14	20	.700	45	1.5	11	0.4	N/A	N/A	60	2.0

Height	6-7
Weight	205
Born	4-28-43
College	BYU

Felix, Raymond Darlington

SEASON	TEAM	G	FGM	FGA	PCT	FTM	FTA	PCT	REB	RPG	AST	APG	STL	BLK	PTS	PPG
1953-1954	BALTIMORE	72	410	983	.417	449	704	.638	958	13.3	82	1.1	N/A	N/A	1269	17.6
1954-1955	NEW YORK	72	364	832	.438	310	498	.622	818	11.4	67	0.9	N/A	N/A	1038	14.4
1955-1956	NEW YORK	72	277	668	.415	331	469	.706	623	8.7	47	0.7	N/A	N/A	885	12.3
1956-1957	NEW YORK	72	295	709	.416	277	371	.747	587	8.2	36	0.5	N/A	N/A	867	12.0
1957-1958	NEW YORK	72	304	688	.442	271	389	.697	747	10.4	52	0.7	N/A	N/A	879	12.2
1958-1959	NEW YORK	72	260	700	.371	229	321	.713	569	7.9	49	0.7	N/A	N/A	749	10.4
1959-1960	N.Y.-MINN.	47	136	355	.383	70	112	.625	338	7.2	23	0.5	N/A	N/A	342	7.3
1960-1961	LOS ANGELES	78	189	508	.372	135	193	.699	539	6.9	37	0.5	N/A	N/A	513	6.6
1961-1962	LOS ANGELES	80	171	398	.430	90	130	.692	473	5.9	55	0.7	N/A	N/A	432	5.4
NBA CAREER TOTALS		637	2406	5841	.412	2162	3187	.678	5652	8.9	448	0.7	N/A	N/A	6974	10.9
NBA PLAYOFF TOTALS		38	106	248	.427	89	127	.701	290	7.6	29	0.8	N/A	N/A	301	7.9

Height	6-11
Weight	220
Born	12-10-30
College	Long Island U

Finkel, Henry J.

SEASON	TEAM	G	FGM	FGA	PCT	FTM	FTA	PCT	REB	RPG	AST	APG	STL	BLK	PTS	PPG
1966-1967	LOS ANGELES	27	17	47	.362	7	12	.583	64	2.4	5	0.2	N/A	N/A	41	1.5
1967-1968	SAN DIEGO	53	242	492	.492	131	191	.686	375	7.1	72	1.4	N/A	N/A	615	11.6
1968-1969	SAN DIEGO	35	49	111	.441	31	41	.756	107	3.1	21	0.6	N/A	N/A	129	3.7
1969-1970	BOSTON	80	310	683	.454	156	233	.670	613	7.7	103	1.3	N/A	N/A	776	9.7
1970-1971	BOSTON	80	214	489	.438	93	127	.732	343	4.3	79	1.0	N/A	N/A	521	6.5
1971-1972	BOSTON	78	103	254	.406	43	74	.581	251	3.2	61	0.8	N/A	N/A	249	3.2
1972-1973	BOSTON	76	78	173	.451	28	52	.538	151	2.0	26	0.3	N/A	N/A	184	2.4
1973-1974	BOSTON	60	60	130	.462	28	43	.651	135	2.3	27	0.5	3	7	148	2.5
1974-1975	BOSTON	62	52	129	.403	23	43	.535	112	1.8	32	0.5	7	3	127	2.0
NBA CAREER TOTALS		551	1125	2508	.449	540	816	.662	2151	3.9	426	0.8	10	10	2790	5.1
NBA PLAYOFF TOTALS		33	27	59	.458	4	6	.667	53	1.6	13	0.4	1	0	58	1.8

Height	7-0
Weight	240
Born	4-20-42
College	Dayton

Fisher, Derek

SEASON	TEAM	G	FGM	FGA	PCT	FTM	FTA	PCT	REB	RPG	AST	APG	STL	BLK	PTS	PPG
1996-1997	LOS ANGELES	80	104	262	.397	79	120	.658	97	1.2	119	1.5	41	5	309	3.9
1997-1998	LOS ANGELES	82	164	378	.434	115	152	.757	193	2.4	333	4.1	75	5	474	5.8
NBA CAREER TOTALS		162	268	640	.419	194	272	.713	290	1.8	452	2.8	116	10	783	4.8
NBA PLAYOFF TOTALS		19	30	79	.379	20	32	.625	28	1.5	55	3.1	18	0	86	4.5

Height	6-1
Weight	200
Born	8-9-74
College	Arkansas

Ford, Donald J.

SEASON	TEAM	G	FGM	FGA	PCT	FTM	FTA	PCT	REB	RPG	AST	APG	STL	BLK	PTS	PPG
1975-1976	LOS ANGELES	76	311	710	.438	104	139	.748	333	4.4	111	1.5	50	14	726	9.6
1976-1977	LOS ANGELES	82	262	570	.460	73	102	.716	353	4.3	133	1.6	60	21	597	7.3
1977-1978	LOS ANGELES	79	272	576	.472	68	90	.756	353	4.5	142	1.8	68	46	612	7.7
1978-1979	LOS ANGELES	79	228	450	.507	72	89	.809	268	3.4	101	1.3	51	25	528	6.7
1979-1980	L.A.-CLEV.	73	131	274	.478	45	53	.849	185	2.5	65	0.9	22	21	308	4.2
1980-1981	CLEVELAND	64	100	224	.446	22	24	.917	164	2.6	84	1.3	15	12	222	3.5
1981-1982	CLEVELAND	21	9	24	.375	5	6	.833	35	1.7	11	0.5	8	0	23	1.1
NBA CAREER TOTALS		474	1313	2828	.464	389	503	.773	1691	3.6	647	1.4	274	139	3016	6.4
NBA PLAYOFF TOTALS		20	58	131	.443	28	39	.718	85	4.3	44	2.2	21	6	144	7.2

Height	6-8
Weight	215
Born	12-31-52
College	UCSB

Fox, Rick

SEASON	TEAM	G	FGM	FGA	PCT	FTM	FTA	PCT	REB	RPG	AST	APG	STL	BLK	PTS	PPG
1991-1992	BOSTON	81	241	525	.459	139	184	.755	220	2.7	126	1.6	78	30	644	8.0
1992-1993	BOSTON	71	184	380	.484	81	101	.802	159	2.2	113	1.6	61	21	453	6.4
1993-1994	BOSTON	82	340	728	.467	174	230	.757	355	4.3	217	2.6	81	52	887	10.8
1994-1995	BOSTON	53	169	351	.481	95	123	.772	155	2.9	139	2.6	52	19	464	8.8
1995-1996	BOSTON	81	421	928	.454	196	254	.772	450	5.6	369	4.6	113	41	1137	14.0
1996-1997	BOSTON	76	433	950	.456	207	263	.787	394	5.2	286	3.8	167	40	1174	15.4
1997-1998	LOS ANGELES	82	363	771	.471	171	230	.743	358	4.4	276	3.4	100	48	983	12.0
NBA CAREER TOTALS		526	2151	4633	.464	1043	1385	.753	2091	4.0	1526	2.9	652	251	5742	10.9
NBA PLAYOFF TOTALS		25	69	162	.426	25	29	.862	83	3.3	60	2.4	7	11	142	5.7

Height	6-7
Weight	240
Born	7-24-69
College	N Carolina

Freeman, Donald E.

SEASON	TEAM	G	FGM	FGA	PCT	FTM	FTA	PCT	REB	RPG	AST	APG	STL	BLK	PTS	PPG
1967-1968	MINNESOTA (A)	69	414	1013	.409	296	414	.715	326	4.7	190	2.8	N/A	N/A	1124	16.3
1968-1969	MIAMI (A)	78	651	1346	.484	420	534	.787	285	3.7	501	6.4	N/A	N/A	1724	22.1
1969-1970	MIAMI (A)	79	766	1684	.455	626	762	.822	400	5.1	291	3.7	N/A	N/A	2163	27.4
1970-1971	UTAH-TEXAS (A)	66	596	1235	.483	367	459	.800	324	4.9	332	5.0	N/A	N/A	1559	23.6
1971-1972	DALLAS (A)	72	628	1336	.470	475	576	.825	206	2.9	245	3.4	N/A	N/A	1733	24.1
1972-1973	INDIANA (A)	77	412	933	.442	277	343	.808	219	2.8	195	2.5	N/A	N/A	1103	14.3
1973-1974	INDIANA (A)	66	383	839	.456	177	222	.797	168	2.5	165	2.5	48	22	943	14.3
1974-1975	SAN ANTONIO (A)	77	453	1012	.448	289	352	.821	184	2.4	202	2.6	65	15	1195	15.5
1975-1976	LOS ANGELES	64	263	606	.434	163	199	.819	180	2.8	171	2.7	57	11	689	10.8
NBA CAREER TOTALS		64	263	606	.434	163	199	.819	180	2.8	171	2.7	57	11	689	10.8

Height	6-3
Weight	185
Born	7-18-44
College	Illinois

Garrett, Calvin Eugene

SEASON	TEAM	G	FGM	FGA	PCT	FTM	FTA	PCT	REB	RPG	AST	APG	STL	BLK	PTS	PPG
1980-1981	HOUSTON	70	188	415	.453	50	62	.806	264	3.8	132	1.9	50	10	427	6.1
1981-1982	HOUSTON	51	105	242	.434	17	26	.654	94	1.8	76	1.5	32	6	230	4.5
1982-1983	HOUSTON	4	4	11	.364	2	2	1.000	7	1.8	3	0.8	0	0	10	2.5
1983-1984	LOS ANGELES	41	78	152	.513	30	39	.769	71	1.7	31	0.8	12	2	188	4.6
NBA CAREER TOTALS		166	375	820	.457	99	129	.767	436	2.6	242	1.5	94	18	855	5.2
NBA PLAYOFF TOTALS		14	9	22	.409	7	8	.875	15	1.1	6	0.4	5	1	25	1.8

Height	6-7
Weight	190
Born	7-11-56
College	Oral Roberts

Garrett, Eldo "Dick"

SEASON	TEAM	G	FGM	FGA	PCT	FTM	FTA	PCT	REB	RPG	AST	APG	STL	BLK	PTS	PPG
1969-1970	LOS ANGELES	73	354	816	.434	138	162	.852	235	3.2	180	2.5	N/A	N/A	846	11.6
1970-1971	BUFFALO	75	373	902	.414	218	251	.869	295	3.9	264	3.5	N/A	N/A	964	12.9
1971-1972	BUFFALO	73	325	735	.442	136	157	.866	225	3.1	165	2.3	N/A	N/A	786	10.8
1972-1973	BUFFALO	78	341	813	.419	96	110	.873	209	2.7	217	2.8	N/A	N/A	778	10.0
1973-1974	N.Y.-MILW.	40	43	126	.341	15	19	.789	40	1.0	23	0.6	10	1	101	2.5
NBA CAREER TOTALS		339	1436	3392	.423	603	699	.863	1004	3.0	849	2.5	10	1	3475	10.3
NBA PLAYOFF TOTALS		26	103	205	.502	30	36	.833	55	2.1	46	1.8	2	0	236	9.1

Height	6-3
Weight	185
Born	1-31-47
College	S Illinois

Gibson, Melvin L.

SEASON	TEAM	G	FGM	FGA	PCT	FTM	FTA	PCT	REB	RPG	AST	APG	STL	BLK	PTS	PPG
1963-1964	LOS ANGELES	9	6	20	.300	1	2	.500	4	0.4	6	0.7	N/A	N/A	13	1.4
NBA CAREER TOTALS		9	6	20	.300	1	2	.500	4	0.4	6	0.7	N/A	N/A	13	1.4

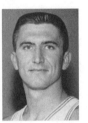

Height	6-3
Weight	180
Born	12-31-40
College	W Carolina

Goodrich, Gail

SEASON	TEAM	G	FGM	FGA	PCT	FTM	FTA	PCT	REB	RPG	AST	APG	STL	BLK	PTS	PPG
1965-1966	LOS ANGELES	65	203	503	.404	103	149	.691	130	2.0	103	1.6	N/A	N/A	509	7.8
1966-1967	LOS ANGELES	77	352	776	.454	253	337	.751	251	3.3	210	2.7	N/A	N/A	957	12.4
1967-1968	LOS ANGELES	79	395	812	.486	302	392	.770	199	2.5	205	2.6	N/A	N/A	1092	13.8
1968-1969	PHOENIX	81	718	1746	.411	495	663	.747	437	5.4	518	6.4	N/A	N/A	1931	23.8
1969-1970	PHOENIX	81	568	1251	.454	488	604	.808	340	4.2	605	7.5	N/A	N/A	1624	20.0
1970-1971	LOS ANGELES	79	558	1174	.475	264	343	.770	260	3.3	380	4.8	N/A	N/A	1380	17.5
1971-1972	LOS ANGELES	82	826	1695	.487	475	559	.850	295	3.6	365	4.5	N/A	N/A	2127	25.9
1972-1973	LOS ANGELES	76	750	1615	.464	314	374	.840	263	3.5	332	4.4	N/A	N/A	1814	23.9
1973-1974	LOS ANGELES	82	784	1773	.442	508	588	.864	250	3.0	427	5.2	126	12	2076	25.3
1974-1975	LOS ANGELES	72	656	1429	.459	318	378	.841	219	3.0	420	5.8	102	6	1630	22.6
1975-1976	LOS ANGELES	75	583	1321	.441	293	346	.847	214	2.9	421	5.6	123	17	1459	19.5
1976-1977	NEW ORLEANS	27	136	305	.446	68	85	.800	61	2.3	74	2.7	22	2	340	12.6
1977-1978	NEW ORLEANS	81	520	1050	.495	264	332	.795	177	2.2	388	4.8	82	22	1304	16.1
1978-1979	NEW ORLEANS	74	382	850	.449	174	204	.853	183	2.5	357	4.8	90	13	938	12.7
NBA CAREER TOTALS		1031	7431	16300	.456	4319	5354	.807	3279	3.2	4805	4.7	545	72	19181	18.6
NBA PLAYOFF TOTALS		80	542	1227	.442	366	447	.819	250	3.1	333	4.2	7	1	1450	18.1

Height	6-1
Weight	170
Born	4-23-43
College	UCLA

Grant, Travis

SEASON	TEAM	G	FGM	FGA	PCT	FTM	FTA	PCT	REB	RPG	AST	APG	STL	BLK	PTS	PPG
1972-1973	LOS ANGELES	33	51	116	.440	23	26	.885	52	1.6	7	0.2	N/A	N/A	125	3.8
1973-1974	LOS ANGELES	3	1	4	.250	1	3	.333	1	0.3	0	0.0	0	0	3	1.0
1973-1974	SAN DIEGO (A)	56	357	681	.524	141	176	.801	298	5.3	63	1.1	46	12	856	15.3
1974-1975	SAN DIEGO (A)	53	576	1058	.544	182	218	.835	328	6.2	98	1.8	44	21	1335	25.2
1975-1976	KEN.-INDIANA (A)	56	198	398	.497	52	69	.754	140	2.5	43	0.8	16	18	448	8.0
NBA CAREER TOTALS		36	52	120	.433	24	29	.828	53	1.5	7	0.2	0	0	128	3.6
NBA PLAYOFF TOTALS		2	4	6	.667	0	0	N/A	4	2.0	N/A	0.0	0	0	8	4.0

Height	6-8
Weight	215
Born	1-1-50
College	Kentucky St

Green, A.C., Jr.

SEASON	TEAM	G	FGM	FGA	PCT	FTM	FTA	PCT	REB	RPG	AST	APG	STL	BLK	PTS	PPG
1985-1986	LOS ANGELES	82	209	388	.539	102	167	.611	381	4.6	54	0.7	49	49	521	6.4
1986-1987	LOS ANGELES	79	316	587	.538	220	282	.780	615	7.8	84	1.1	70	80	852	10.8
1987-1988	LOS ANGELES	82	322	640	.503	293	379	.773	710	8.7	93	1.1	87	45	937	11.4
1988-1989	LOS ANGELES	82	401	758	.529	282	359	.786	739	9.0	103	1.3	94	55	1088	13.3
1989-1990	LOS ANGELES	82	385	806	.478	278	370	.751	712	8.7	90	1.1	66	50	1061	12.9
1990-1991	LOS ANGELES	82	258	542	.476	223	302	.738	516	6.3	71	0.9	59	23	750	9.1
1991-1992	LOS ANGELES	82	382	803	.476	340	457	.744	762	9.3	117	1.4	91	36	1116	13.6
1992-1993	LOS ANGELES	82	379	706	.537	277	375	.739	711	8.7	116	1.4	88	39	1051	12.8
1993-1994	PHOENIX	82	465	926	.502	266	362	.735	753	9.2	137	1.7	70	38	1204	14.7
1994-1995	PHOENIX	82	311	617	.504	251	343	.732	669	8.2	127	1.5	55	31	916	11.2
1995-1996	PHOENIX	82	215	444	.484	168	237	.709	554	6.8	72	0.9	45	23	612	7.5
1996-1997	PHO.-DAL.	83	234	484	.483	128	197	.650	656	7.9	69	0.8	70	16	597	7.2
1997-1998	DALLAS	82	242	534	.453	116	162	.716	668	8.1	123	1.5	78	27	600	7.3
NBA CAREER TOTALS		1064	4119	8235	.500	2944	3992	.737	8466	7.9	1256	1.2	922	512	11305	10.6
NBA PLAYOFF TOTALS		127	417	865	.482	376	508	.740	984	7.7	115	0.9	85	43	1222	9.6

Height	6-9
Weight	230
Born	10-4-63
College	Oregon St

Grote, Jerry C.

SEASON	TEAM	G	FGM	FGA	PCT	FTM	FTA	PCT	REB	RPG	AST	APG	STL	BLK	PTS	PPG
1964-1965	LOS ANGELES	11	6	11	.545	2	2	1.000	4	0.4	4	0.4	N/A	N/A	14	1.3
NBA CAREER TOTALS		11	6	11	.545	2	2	1.000	4	0.4	4	0.4	N/A	N/A	14	1.3

Height	6-4
Weight	215
Born	12-28-40
College	LMU

Gudmundsson, Karl Petur

SEASON	TEAM	G	FGM	FGA	PCT	FTM	FTA	PCT	REB	RPG	AST	APG	STL	BLK	PTS	PPG
1981-1982	PORTLAND	68	83	166	.500	52	76	.684	186	2.7	59	0.9	13	30	219	3.2
1985-1986	LOS ANGELES	8	20	37	.541	18	27	.667	38	4.8	3	0.4	3	4	58	7.3
1987-1988	SAN ANTONIO	69	139	280	.496	117	145	.807	323	4.7	86	1.2	18	61	395	5.7
1988-1989	SAN ANTONIO	5	9	25	.360	3	4	.750	16	3.2	5	1.0	1	1	21	4.2
NBA CAREER TOTALS		150	251	508	.494	190	252	.754	563	3.8	153	1.0	35	96	693	4.6
NBA PLAYOFF TOTALS		14	16	29	.552	10	15	.667	26	1.9	4	0.3	3	4	42	3.0

Height	7-2
Weight	260
Born	10-30-58
College	Washington

Hairston, Harold

SEASON	TEAM	G	FGM	FGA	PCT	FTM	FTA	PCT	REB	RPG	AST	APG	STL	BLK	PTS	PPG
1964-1965	CINCINNATI	61	131	351	.373	110	165	.667	293	4.8	27	0.4	N/A	N/A	372	6.1
1965-1966	CINCINNATI	72	398	814	.489	220	321	.685	546	7.6	44	0.6	N/A	N/A	1016	14.1
1966-1967	CINCINNATI	79	461	962	.479	252	382	.660	631	8.0	62	0.8	N/A	N/A	1174	14.9
1967-1968	CIN.-DETROIT	74	481	987	.487	365	522	.699	617	8.3	95	1.3	N/A	N/A	1327	17.9
1968-1969	DETROIT	81	530	1131	.469	404	553	.731	959	11.8	109	1.3	N/A	N/A	1464	18.1
1969-1970	DETROIT-L.A.	70	483	973	.496	326	413	.789	775	11.1	121	1.7	N/A	N/A	1292	18.5
1970-1971	LOS ANGELES	80	574	1233	.466	337	431	.782	797	10.0	168	2.1	N/A	N/A	1485	18.6
1971-1972	LOS ANGELES	80	368	798	.461	311	399	.779	1045	13.1	193	2.4	N/A	N/A	1047	13.1
1972-1973	LOS ANGELES	28	158	328	.482	140	178	.787	370	13.2	68	2.4	N/A	N/A	456	16.3
1973-1974	LOS ANGELES	77	385	759	.507	343	445	.771	1040	13.5	208	2.7	64	17	1113	14.5
1974-1975	LOS ANGELES	74	271	536	.506	217	271	.801	946	12.8	173	2.3	52	11	759	10.3
NBA CAREER TOTALS		776	4240	8872	.478	3025	4080	.741	8019	10.3	1268	1.6	116	28	11505	14.8
NBA PLAYOFF TOTALS		69	307	690	.445	187	255	.733	559	8.1	121	1.8	5	1	801	11.6

Height	6-7
Weight	225
Born	5-31-42
College	NYU

Haley, Jack Kevin

SEASON	TEAM	G	FGM	FGA	PCT	FTM	FTA	PCT	REB	RPG	AST	APG	STL	BLK	PTS	PPG
1988-1989	CHICAGO	51	37	78	.474	36	46	.783	71	1.4	10	0.2	11	0	110	2.2
1989-1990	CHICAGO-N. J.	67	138	347	.398	85	125	.680	300	4.5	26	0.4	18	12	361	5.4
1990-1991	NEW JERSEY	78	161	343	.469	112	181	.619	356	4.6	31	0.4	20	21	434	5.6
1991-1992	LOS ANGELES	49	31	84	.369	14	29	.483	95	1.9	7	0.1	7	8	76	1.6
1992-1993	LOS ANGELES	DID NOT PLAY–INJURED														
1993-1994	SAN ANTONIO	28	21	48	.438	17	21	.810	24	0.9	1	0.0	0	0	59	2.1
1994-1995	SAN ANTONIO	31	26	61	.426	21	32	.656	27	0.9	2	0.1	3	5	73	2.4
1995-1996	CHICAGO	1	2	6	.333	1	2	.500	2	2.0	0	0.0	0	0	5	5.0
1996-1997	NEW JERSEY	20	13	37	.351	14	19	.737	32	1.6	5	0.3	1	1	40	2.0
1997-1998	NEW JERSEY	16	5	18	.278	12	21	.571	15	0.9	0	0.0	0	1	22	1.4
NBA CAREER TOTALS		341	434	1022	.424	312	476	.655	922	2.7	82	0.2	60	48	1180	3.5
NBA PLAYOFF TOTALS		14	8	22	.364	7	10	.700	15	1.1	4	0.3	0	1	23	1.6

Height	6-10
Weight	240
Born	1-27-64
College	UCLA

Hamilton, Dennis Eugene

SEASON	TEAM	G	FGM	FGA	PCT	FTM	FTA	PCT	REB	RPG	AST	APG	STL	BLK	PTS	PPG
1967-1968	LOS ANGELES	44	54	108	.500	13	13	1.000	72	1.6	30	0.7	N/A	N/A	121	2.8
1968-1969	ATLANTA	25	37	67	.552	2	5	.400	29	1.2	8	0.3	N/A	N/A	76	3.0
1969-1970	PITTSBURGH (A)	72	190	375	.507	76	100	.760	340	4.7	73	1.0	N/A	N/A	456	6.3
1970-1971	KENTUCKY (A)	3	1	2	.500	1	1	1.000	1	0.3	1	0.3	N/A	N/A	3	1.0
NBA CAREER TOTALS		69	91	175	.520	15	18	.833	101	1.5	38	0.6	N/A	N/A	197	2.9
NBA PLAYOFF TOTALS		2	1	3	.333	0	0	N/A	2	1.0	1	0.5	N/A	N/A	2	1.0

Height	6-8
Weight	210
Born	5-8-44
College	Arizona St

Hardy, Alan Timothy

SEASON	TEAM	G	FGM	FGA	PCT	FTM	FTA	PCT	REB	RPG	AST	APG	STL	BLK	PTS	PPG
1980-1981	LOS ANGELES	22	22	59	.373	7	10	.700	19	0.9	3	0.1	1	9	51	2.3
1981-1982	DETROIT	38	62	136	.456	18	29	.621	34	0.9	20	0.5	9	4	142	3.7
NBA CAREER TOTALS		60	84	195	.431	25	39	.641	53	0.9	23	0.4	10	13	193	3.2

Height	6-6
Weight	195
Born	5-25-57
College	Michigan

Harvey, Antonio

SEASON	TEAM	G	FGM	FGA	PCT	FTM	FTA	PCT	REB	RPG	AST	APG	STL	BLK	PTS	PPG
1993-1994	LOS ANGELES	27	29	79	.367	12	26	.462	59	2.2	5	0.2	8	19	70	2.6
1994-1995	LOS ANGELES	59	77	176	.438	24	45	.533	102	1.7	23	0.4	15	41	179	3.0
1995-1996	VAN.-CLIPPERS	55	83	224	.371	38	83	.458	200	3.6	15	0.3	27	47	204	3.7
1996-1997	SEATTLE	6	5	11	.455	5	6	.833	10	1.7	1	0.2	0	4	15	2.5
NBA CAREER TOTALS		147	194	490	.396	79	160	.494	371	2.5	44	0.3	50	111	468	3.2
NBA PLAYOFF TOTALS		3	0	0	N/A	0	0	N/A	1	0.3	0	0.0	0	0	0	0.0

Height	6-11
Weight	225
Born	7-9-70
College	Pfeiffer

Hawkins, Cornelius L.

SEASON	TEAM	G	FGM	FGA	PCT	FTM	FTA	PCT	REB	RPG	AST	APG	STL	BLK	PTS	PPG
1967-1968	PITTSBURGH (A)	70	635	1223	.519	603	789	.764	945	13.5	320	4.6	N/A	N/A	1875	26.8
1968-1969	MINNESOTA (A)	47	496	971	.511	425	554	.767	534	11.4	184	3.9	N/A	N/A	1420	30.2
1969-1970	PHOENIX	81	709	1447	.490	577	741	.779	846	10.4	391	4.8	N/A	N/A	1995	24.6
1970-1971	PHOENIX	71	512	1181	.434	457	560	.816	643	9.1	322	4.5	N/A	N/A	1481	20.9
1971-1972	PHOENIX	76	571	1244	.459	456	565	.807	633	8.3	296	3.9	N/A	N/A	1598	21.0
1972-1973	PHOENIX	75	441	920	.479	322	404	.797	641	8.5	304	4.1	N/A	N/A	1204	16.1
1973-1974	PHOENIX-L.A.	79	404	807	.501	191	251	.761	565	7.2	407	5.2	113	81	999	12.6
1974-1975	LOS ANGELES	43	139	324	.429	68	99	.687	198	4.6	120	2.8	51	23	346	8.0
1975-1976	ATLANTA	74	237	530	.447	136	191	.712	445	6.0	212	2.9	80	46	610	8.2
NBA CAREER TOTALS		499	3013	6453	.467	2207	2811	.785	3971	8.0	2052	4.1	244	150	8233	16.5
NBA PLAYOFF TOTALS		12	83	210	.395	66	81	.815	137	11.4	57	4.8	7	1	232	19.3

Height	6-8
Weight	215
Born	7-17-42
College	Iowa

Hawkins, Thomas Jerome

SEASON	TEAM	G	FGM	FGA	PCT	FTM	FTA	PCT	REB	RPG	AST	APG	STL	BLK	PTS	PPG
1959-1960	MINNEAPOLIS	69	220	579	.380	106	164	.646	428	6.2	54	0.8	N/A	N/A	546	7.9
1960-1961	LOS ANGELES	78	310	719	.431	140	235	.596	479	6.1	88	1.1	N/A	N/A	760	9.7
1961-1962	LOS ANGELES	79	289	704	.411	143	222	.644	514	6.5	95	1.2	N/A	N/A	721	9.1
1962-1963	CINCINNATI	79	299	635	.471	147	241	.610	543	6.9	100	1.3	N/A	N/A	745	9.4
1963-1964	CINCINNATI	73	256	580	.441	113	188	.601	435	6.0	74	1.0	N/A	N/A	625	8.6
1964-1965	CINCINNATI	79	220	538	.409	116	204	.569	475	6.0	80	1.0	N/A	N/A	556	7.0
1965-1966	CINCINNATI	79	273	604	.452	116	209	.555	575	7.3	99	1.3	N/A	N/A	662	8.4
1966-1967	LOS ANGELES	76	275	572	.481	82	173	.474	434	5.7	83	1.1	N/A	N/A	632	8.3
1967-1968	LOS ANGELES	78	389	779	.499	125	229	.546	458	5.9	117	1.5	N/A	N/A	903	11.6
1968-1969	LOS ANGELES	74	230	461	.499	62	151	.411	266	3.6	81	1.1	N/A	N/A	522	7.1
NBA CAREER TOTALS		764	2761	6171	.447	1150	2016	.570	4607	6.0	871	1.1	N/A	N/A	6672	8.7
NBA PLAYOFF TOTALS		96	311	677	.459	145	235	.617	537	5.6	106	1.1	N/A	N/A	767	8.0

Height	6-5
Weight	210
Born	12-22-36
College	Notre Dame

Hawthorne, Nate

SEASON	TEAM	G	FGM	FGA	PCT	FTM	FTA	PCT	REB	RPG	AST	APG	STL	BLK	PTS	PPG
1973-1974	LOS ANGELES	33	38	93	.409	30	48	.625	32	1.0	23	0.7	9	6	106	3.2
1974-1975	PHOENIX	50	118	287	.411	61	94	.649	92	1.8	39	0.8	30	21	297	5.9
1975-1976	PHOENIX	79	182	423	.430	115	170	.676	209	2.6	46	0.6	33	15	479	6.1
NBA CAREER TOTALS		162	338	803	.421	206	312	.660	333	2.1	108	0.7	72	42	882	5.4
NBA PLAYOFF TOTALS		18	10	33	.303	12	16	.750	18	1.0	6	0.3	6	2	32	1.8

Height 6-4
Weight 190
Born 1-15-50
College S Illinois

Haywood, Spencer

SEASON	TEAM	G	FGM	FGA	PCT	FTM	FTA	PCT	REB	RPG	AST	APG	STL	BLK	PTS	PPG
1970-71	SEATTLE	33	260	579	.449	160	218	.734	396	12.0	48	1.5	N/A	N/A	680	20.6
1971-72	SEATTLE	73	717	1557	.461	480	586	.819	926	12.7	148	2.0	N/A	N/A	1914	26.2
1972-73	SEATTLE	77	889	1868	.476	473	564	.839	995	12.9	196	2.5	N/A	N/A	2251	29.2
1973-74	SEATTLE	75	694	1520	.457	373	458	.814	1007	13.4	240	3.2	65	106	1761	23.5
1974-75	SEATTLE	68	608	1325	.459	309	381	.811	630	9.3	137	2.0	54	108	1525	22.4
1975-76	NEW YORK	78	605	1360	.445	339	448	.757	878	11.3	92	1.2	53	80	1549	19.9
1976-77	N. Y. KNICKS	31	202	449	.450	109	131	.832	280	9.0	50	1.6	14	29	513	16.5
1977-78	NEW YORK	67	412	852	.484	96	135	.711	442	6.6	126	1.9	37	72	920	13.7
1978-79	N. Y.-N. O.	68	595	1205	.494	231	292	.791	533	7.8	127	1.9	40	82	1421	20.9
1979-80	LOS ANGELES	76	288	591	.487	159	206	.772	346	4.6	93	1.2	35	57	736	9.7
1981-82	WASHINGTON	76	395	829	.476	219	260	.842	422	5.6	64	0.8	45	68	1009	13.3
1982-83	WASHINGTON	38	125	312	.401	63	87	.724	183	4.8	30	0.8	12	27	313	8.2
NBA CAREER TOTALS		760	5790	12447	.465	3011	3766	.800	7038	9.3	1351	1.8	355	629	14592	19.2
NBA PLAYOFF TOTALS		33	172	384	.448	97	123	.789	188	5.7	41	1.2	13	36	441	13.4

Height 6-8
Weight 225
Born 4-22-49
College Detroit

Hazzard, Walter Raphael, Jr.

SEASON	TEAM	G	FGM	FGA	PCT	FTM	FTA	PCT	REB	RPG	AST	APG	STL	BLK	PTS	PPG
1964-1965	LOS ANGELES	66	117	306	.382	46	71	.648	111	1.7	140	2.1	N/A	N/A	280	4.2
1965-1966	LOS ANGELES	80	458	1003	.457	182	257	.708	219	2.7	393	4.9	N/A	N/A	1098	13.7
1966-1967	LOS ANGELES	79	301	706	.426	129	177	.729	231	2.9	323	4.1	N/A	N/A	731	9.3
1967-1968	SEATTLE	79	733	1662	.441	428	553	.774	332	4.2	493	6.2	N/A	N/A	1894	24.0
1968-1969	ATLANTA	80	345	869	.397	208	294	.707	266	3.3	474	5.9	N/A	N/A	898	11.2
1969-1970	ATLANTA	82	493	1056	.467	267	330	.809	329	4.0	561	6.8	N/A	N/A	1253	15.3
1970-1971	ATLANTA	82	517	1126	.459	315	415	.759	300	3.7	514	6.3	N/A	N/A	1349	16.5
1971-1972	BUFFALO	72	450	998	.451	237	303	.782	213	3.0	406	5.6	N/A	N/A	1137	15.8
1972-1973	BUFFALO-G.S.	55	107	256	.418	47	57	.825	88	1.6	129	2.3	N/A	N/A	261	4.7
1973-1974	SEATTLE	49	76	180	.422	34	45	.756	57	1.2	122	2.5	26	6	186	3.8
NBA CAREER TOTALS		724	3597	8162	.441	1893	2502	.757	2146	3.0	3555	4.9	26	6	9087	12.6
NBA PLAYOFF TOTALS		58	268	649	.413	149	202	.738	169	2.9	242	4.2	0	0	685	11.8

Height 6-2
Weight 190
Born 4-15-42
College UCLA

Henderson, Jerome D.

SEASON	TEAM	G	FGM	FGA	PCT	FTM	FTA	PCT	REB	RPG	AST	APG	STL	BLK	PTS	PPG
1985-1986	LOS ANGELES	1	2	3	.667	0	0	N/A	1	1.0	0	0.0	0	0	4	4.0
1986-1987	MILWAUKEE	6	4	13	.308	4	4	1.000	7	1.2	0	0.0	1	1	12	2.0
NBA CAREER TOTALS		7	6	16	.375	4	4	1.000	8	1.1	0	0.0	1	1	16	2.3
NBA PLAYOFF TOTALS		1	0	0	N/A	0	0	N/A	0	0.0	N/A	0.0	0	0	0	0.0

Height	6-11
Weight	230
Born	10-5-59
College	New Mexico

Hetzel, Fred W.

SEASON	TEAM	G	FGM	FGA	PCT	FTM	FTA	PCT	REB	RPG	AST	APG	STL	BLK	PTS	PPG
1965-1966	SAN FRANCISCO	56	160	401	.399	63	92	.685	290	5.2	27	0.5	N/A	N/A	383	6.8
1966-1967	SAN FRANCISCO	77	373	932	.400	192	237	.810	639	8.3	111	1.4	N/A	N/A	938	12.2
1967-1968	SAN FRANCISCO	77	533	1287	.414	395	474	.833	546	7.1	131	1.7	N/A	N/A	1461	19.0
1968-1969	MILW.-CIN.	84	456	1047	.436	299	357	.838	613	7.3	112	1.3	N/A	N/A	1211	14.4
1969-1970	PHILADELPHIA	63	156	323	.483	71	85	.835	207	3.3	44	0.7	N/A	N/A	383	6.1
1970-1971	LOS ANGELES	59	111	256	.434	60	77	.779	149	2.5	37	0.6	N/A	N/A	282	4.8
NBA CAREER TOTALS		416	1789	4246	.421	1080	1322	.817	2444	5.9	462	1.1	N/A	N/A	4658	11.2
NBA PLAYOFF TOTALS		35	138	323	.427	83	102	.814	184	5.3	44	1.3	N/A	N/A	359	10.3

Height	6-8
Weight	230
Born	7-21-42
College	Davidson

Hewitt, William Severlyn

SEASON	TEAM	G	FGM	FGA	PCT	FTM	FTA	PCT	REB	RPG	AST	APG	STL	BLK	PTS	PPG
1968-1969	LOS ANGELES	75	239	528	.453	61	106	.575	332	4.4	76	1.0	N/A	N/A	539	7.2
1969-1970	L.A.-DETROIT	65	110	298	.369	54	94	.574	354	5.4	64	1.0	N/A	N/A	274	4.2
1970-1971	DETROIT	62	203	435	.467	69	120	.575	454	7.3	124	2.0	N/A	N/A	475	7.7
1971-1972	DETROIT	68	131	277	.473	41	82	.500	370	5.4	71	1.0	N/A	N/A	303	4.5
1972-1973	BUFFALO	73	152	364	.418	41	74	.554	368	5.0	110	1.5	N/A	N/A	345	4.7
1974-1975	CHICAGO	18	56	129	.434	14	23	.609	116	6.4	24	1.3	9	10	126	7.0
NBA CAREER TOTALS		361	891	2031	.439	280	499	.561	1994	5.5	469	1.3	9	10	2062	5.7
NBA PLAYOFF TOTALS		15	61	151	.404	18	29	.621	78	5.2	17	1.1	0	0	140	9.3

Height	6-7
Weight	210
Born	8-8-44
College	USC

Higgins, Michael S.

SEASON	TEAM	G	FGM	FGA	PCT	FTM	FTA	PCT	REB	RPG	AST	APG	STL	BLK	PTS	PPG
1989-1990	L.A.-DENVER	11	3	8	.375	8	10	.800	4	0.4	3	0.3	2	2	14	1.3
1990-1991	SACRAMENTO	7	6	10	.600	4	7	.571	5	0.7	2	0.3	0	2	16	2.3
NBA CAREER TOTALS		18	9	18	.500	12	17	.706	9	0.5	5	0.3	2	4	30	1.7

Height	6-9
Weight	220
Born	2-17-67
College	N Colorado

Holland, John Bradley

SEASON	TEAM	G	FGM	FGA	PCT	FTM	FTA	PCT	REB	RPG	AST	APG	STL	BLK	PTS	PPG
1979-1980	LOS ANGELES	38	44	104	.423	15	16	.938	17	0.4	22	0.6	15	1	106	2.8
1980-1981	LOS ANGELES	41	47	111	.423	35	49	.714	29	0.7	23	0.6	21	1	130	3.2
1981-1982	WASH.-MILW.	14	27	78	.346	3	6	.500	13	0.9	18	1.3	11	1	57	4.1
NBA CAREER TOTALS		93	118	293	.403	53	71	.746	59	0.6	63	0.7	47	3	293	3.2
NBA PLAYOFF TOTALS		11	6	11	.545	4	4	1.000	5	0.5	4	0.4	5	0	16	1.5

Height	6-3
Weight	180
Born	12-6-56
College	UCLA

Horn, Ronald Leroy

SEASON	TEAM	G	FGM	FGA	PCT	FTM	FTA	PCT	REB	RPG	AST	APG	STL	BLK	PTS	PPG
1961-1962	ST. LOUIS	3	1	12	.083	1	2	.500	6	2.0	1	0.3	N/A	N/A	3	1.0
1962-1963	LOS ANGELES	28	27	82	.329	20	29	.690	71	2.5	10	0.4	N/A	N/A	74	2.6
1967-1968	DENVER (A)	1	0	2	.000	2	2	1.000	1	1.0	0	0.0	N/A	N/A	2	2.0
NBA CAREER TOTALS		31	28	94	.298	21	31	.677	77	2.5	11	0.4	N/A	N/A	77	2.5
NBA PLAYOFF TOTALS		7	4	12	.333	4	5	.800	11	1.6	2	0.3	N/A	N/A	12	1.7

Height	6-7
Weight	225
Born	5-24-38
College	Indiana

Horry, Robert

SEASON	TEAM	G	FGM	FGA	PCT	FTM	FTA	PCT	REB	RPG	AST	APG	STL	BLK	PTS	PPG
1992-1993	HOUSTON	79	323	682	.474	143	200	.715	392	5.0	191	2.4	80	83	801	10.1
1993-1994	HOUSTON	81	322	702	.459	115	157	.732	440	5.4	231	2.9	119	75	803	9.9
1994-1995	HOUSTON	64	240	537	.447	86	113	.761	324	5.1	216	3.4	94	76	652	10.2
1995-1996	HOUSTON	71	300	732	.410	111	143	.776	412	5.8	281	4.0	116	109	853	12.0
1996-1997	PHO.-L.A.	54	157	360	.436	60	90	.667	237	4.4	110	2.0	66	55	423	7.8
1997-1998	LOS ANGELES	72	200	420	.476	117	169	.692	542	7.5	163	2.3	112	94	536	7.4
NBA CAREER TOTALS		421	1542	3433	.449	632	872	.724	2347	5.6	1165	2.8	587	492	4068	9.7
NBA PLAYOFF TOTALS		87	331	735	.450	169	238	.710	547	6.3	273	3.1	130	96	957	11.0

Height	6-10
Weight	220
Born	8-25-70
College	Alabama

Hudson, Louis Clyde

SEASON	TEAM	G	FGM	FGA	PCT	FTM	FTA	PCT	REB	RPG	AST	APG	STL	BLK	PTS	PPG
1966-1967	ST. LOUIS	80	620	1328	.467	231	327	.706	435	5.4	95	1.2	N/A	N/A	1471	18.4
1967-1968	ST. LOUIS	46	227	500	.454	120	164	.732	193	4.2	65	1.4	N/A	N/A	574	12.5
1968-1969	ATLANTA	81	716	1455	.492	338	435	.777	533	6.6	216	2.7	N/A	N/A	1770	21.9
1969-1970	ATLANTA	80	830	1564	.531	371	450	.824	373	4.7	276	3.5	N/A	N/A	2031	25.4
1970-1971	ATLANTA	76	829	1713	.484	381	502	.759	386	5.1	257	3.4	N/A	N/A	2039	26.8
1971-1972	ATLANTA	77	775	1540	.503	349	430	.812	385	5.0	309	4.0	N/A	N/A	1899	24.7
1972-1973	ATLANTA	75	816	1710	.477	397	481	.825	467	6.2	258	3.4	N/A	N/A	2029	27.1
1973-1974	ATLANTA	65	678	1356	.500	295	353	.836	350	5.4	213	3.3	160	29	1651	25.4
1974-1975	ATLANTA	11	97	225	.431	48	57	.842	47	4.3	40	3.6	13	2	242	22.0
1975-1976	ATLANTA	81	569	1205	.472	237	291	.814	300	3.7	214	2.6	124	17	1375	17.0
1976-1977	ATLANTA	58	413	905	.456	142	169	.840	129	2.2	155	2.7	67	19	968	16.7
1977-1978	LOS ANGELES	82	493	992	.497	137	177	.774	188	2.3	193	2.4	94	14	1123	13.7
1978-1979	LOS ANGELES	78	329	636	.517	110	124	.887	140	1.8	141	1.8	58	17	768	9.8
NBA CAREER TOTALS		890	7392	15129	.489	3156	3960	.797	3926	4.4	2432	2.7	516	98	17940	20.2
NBA PLAYOFF TOTALS		61	519	1164	.446	262	326	.804	318	5.2	164	2.7	6	0	1300	21.3

Height	6-4
Weight	215
Born	7-11-44
College	Minnesota

Hundley, Rodney Clark

Height	6-4
Weight	185
Born	10-26-34
College	W Virginia

SEASON	TEAM	G	FGM	FGA	PCT	FTM	FTA	PCT	REB	RPG	AST	APG	STL	BLK	PTS	PPG
1957-1958	MINNEAPOLIS	65	174	548	.318	104	162	.642	186	2.9	121	1.9	N/A	N/A	452	7.0
1958-1959	MINNEAPOLIS	71	259	719	.360	164	218	.752	250	3.5	205	2.9	N/A	N/A	682	9.6
1959-1960	MINNEAPOLIS	73	365	1019	.358	203	273	.744	390	5.3	338	4.6	N/A	N/A	933	12.8
1960-1961	LOS ANGELES	79	323	921	.351	223	296	.753	289	3.7	350	4.4	N/A	N/A	869	11.0
1961-1962	LOS ANGELES	78	173	509	.340	83	127	.654	199	2.6	290	3.7	N/A	N/A	429	5.5
1962-1963	LOS ANGELES	65	88	262	.336	84	119	.706	106	1.6	151	2.3	N/A	N/A	260	4.0
NBA CAREER TOTALS		431	1382	3978	.347	861	1195	.721	1420	3.3	1455	3.3	N/A	N/A	3625	8.4
NBA PLAYOFF TOTALS		53	101	316	.320	68	95	.716	149	2.8	157	2.8	N/A	N/A	270	5.1

Imhoff, Darrall Tucker

Height	6-10
Weight	220
Born	11-11-38
College	California

SEASON	TEAM	G	FGM	FGA	PCT	FTM	FTA	PCT	REB	RPG	AST	APG	STL	BLK	PTS	PPG
1960-1961	NEW YORK	62	122	310	.394	49	96	.510	296	4.8	51	0.8	N/A	N/A	293	4.7
1961-1962	NEW YORK	76	186	482	.386	80	139	.576	470	6.2	82	1.1	N/A	N/A	452	5.9
1962-1963	DETROIT	45	48	153	.314	24	50	.480	155	3.4	28	0.6	N/A	N/A	120	2.7
1963-1964	DETROIT	58	104	251	.414	69	114	.605	283	4.9	56	1.0	N/A	N/A	277	4.8
1964-1965	LOS ANGELES	76	145	311	.466	88	154	.571	500	6.6	87	1.1	N/A	N/A	378	5.0
1965-1966	LOS ANGELES	77	151	337	.448	77	136	.566	509	6.6	113	1.5	N/A	N/A	379	4.9
1966-1967	LOS ANGELES	81	370	780	.474	127	207	.614	1080	13.3	222	2.7	N/A	N/A	867	10.7
1967-1968	LOS ANGELES	82	293	613	.478	177	286	.619	893	10.9	206	2.5	N/A	N/A	763	9.3
1968-1969	PHILADELPHIA	82	279	593	.470	194	325	.597	792	9.7	218	2.7	N/A	N/A	752	9.2
1969-1970	PHILADELPHIA	79	430	796	.540	215	331	.650	754	9.5	211	2.7	N/A	N/A	1075	13.6
1970-1971	CINCINNATI	34	119	258	.461	37	73	.507	233	6.9	79	2.3	N/A	N/A	275	8.1
1971-1972	CIN.-PORT.	49	52	132	.394	24	43	.558	134	2.7	52	1.1	N/A	N/A	128	2.6
NBA CAREER TOTALS		801	2299	5016	.458	1161	1954	.594	6099	7.6	1405	1.8	N/A	N/A	5759	7.2
NBA PLAYOFF TOTALS		54	139	291	.478	76	131	.580	442	8.2	101	1.9	N/A	N/A	354	6.6

Jackson, Anthony Eugene

Height	6-0
Weight	170
Born	1-17-58
College	Florida St

SEASON	TEAM	G	FGM	FGA	PCT	FTM	FTA	PCT	REB	RPG	AST	APG	STL	BLK	PTS	PPG
1980-1981	LOS ANGELES	2	1	3	.333	0	0	N/A	2	1.0	2	1.0	2	0	2	1.0
NBA CAREER TOTALS		2	1	3	.333	0	0	N/A	2	1.0	2	1.0	2	0	2	1.0

Johnson, Clayton H.

Height	6-4
Weight	175
Born	7-18-56
College	Missouri

SEASON	TEAM	G	FGM	FGA	PCT	FTM	FTA	PCT	REB	RPG	AST	APG	STL	BLK	PTS	PPG
1981-1982	LOS ANGELES	7	11	20	.550	3	6	.500	12	1.7	7	1.0	3	3	25	3.6
1982-1983	LOS ANGELES	48	53	135	.393	38	48	.792	69	1.4	24	0.5	22	4	144	3.0
1983-1984	SEATTLE	25	20	50	.400	14	22	.636	12	0.5	14	0.6	8	2	55	2.2
NBA CAREER TOTALS		80	84	205	.410	55	76	.724	93	1.2	45	0.6	33	9	224	2.8
NBA PLAYOFF TOTALS		17	11	20	.550	2	2	1.000	8	0.5	3	0.2	3	0	24	1.4

Johnson, Earvin "Magic"

SEASON	TEAM	G	FGM	FGA	PCT	FTM	FTA	PCT	REB	RPG	AST	APG	STL	BLK	PTS	PPG
1979-80	LOS ANGELES	77	503	949	.530	374	462	.810	596	7.7	563	7.3	187	41	1387	18.0
1980-81	LOS ANGELES	37	312	587	.532	171	225	.760	320	8.6	317	8.6	127	27	798	21.6
1981-82	LOS ANGELES	78	556	1036	.537	329	433	.760	751	9.6	743	9.5	208	34	1447	18.6
1982-83	LOS ANGELES	79	511	933	.548	304	380	.800	683	8.6	829	10.5	176	47	1326	16.8
1983-84	LOS ANGELES	67	441	780	.565	290	358	.810	491	7.3	875	13.1	150	49	1178	17.6
1984-85	LOS ANGELES	77	504	899	.561	391	464	.843	476	6.2	968	12.6	113	25	1406	18.3
1985-86	LOS ANGELES	72	483	918	.526	378	434	.871	426	5.9	907	12.6	113	16	1354	18.8
1986-87	LOS ANGELES	80	683	1308	.522	535	631	.848	504	6.3	977	12.2	138	36	1909	23.9
1987-88	LOS ANGELES	72	490	996	.492	417	489	.853	449	6.2	858	11.9	114	13	1408	19.6
1988-89	LOS ANGELES	77	579	1137	.509	513	563	.911	607	7.9	988	12.8	138	22	1730	22.5
1989-90	LOS ANGELES	79	546	1138	.480	567	637	.890	522	6.6	907	11.5	132	34	1765	22.3
1990-91	LOS ANGELES	79	466	976	.477	519	573	.906	551	7.0	989	12.5	102	17	1531	19.4
1991-92	LOS ANGELES	DID NOT PLAY — RETIRED.														
1992-93	LOS ANGELES	DID NOT PLAY — RETIRED.														
1993-94	LOS ANGELES	DID NOT PLAY — RETIRED.														
1994-95	LOS ANGELES	DID NOT PLAY — RETIRED.														
1995-96	LOS ANGELES	32	137	294	.466	172	201	.856	183	5.7	220	6.9	26	13	468	14.6
NBA CAREER TOTALS		906	6211	11951	.520	4960	5850	.848	6559	7.2	10141	11.2	1724	374	17707	19.5
NBA PLAYOFF TOTALS		190	1291	2552	.506	1068	1274	.838	1465	7.7	2346	12.3	358	64	3701	19.5

Height	6-9
Weight	220
Born	8-14-59
College	Mich St

Johnson, Ronald F.

SEASON	TEAM	G	FGM	FGA	PCT	FTM	FTA	PCT	REB	RPG	AST	APG	STL	BLK	PTS	PPG
1960-1961	DETROIT-L.A.	14	13	43	.302	11	17	.647	29	2.1	2	0.1	N/A	N/A	37	2.6
NBA CAREER TOTALS		14	13	43	.302	11	17	.647	29	2.1	2	0.1	N/A	N/A	37	2.6

Height	6-8
Weight	215
Born	7-20-38
College	Minnesota

Jolliff, Howard

SEASON	TEAM	G	FGM	FGA	PCT	FTM	FTA	PCT	REB	RPG	AST	APG	STL	BLK	PTS	PPG
1960-1961	LOS ANGELES	46	46	141	.326	11	23	.478	141	3.1	16	0.3	N/A	N/A	103	2.2
1961-1962	LOS ANGELES	64	104	253	.411	41	78	.526	383	6.0	76	1.2	N/A	N/A	249	3.9
1962-1963	LOS ANGELES	28	15	55	.273	6	9	.667	62	2.2	20	0.7	N/A	N/A	36	1.3
NBA CAREER TOTALS		138	165	449	.367	58	110	.527	586	4.2	112	0.8	N/A	N/A	388	2.8
NBA PLAYOFF TOTALS		13	8	22	.364	8	8	1.000	53	4.1	15	1.2	N/A	N/A	24	1.8

Height	6-7
Weight	220
Born	7-20-38
College	Ohio

Jones, Dwight E.

SEASON	TEAM	G	FGM	FGA	PCT	FTM	FTA	PCT	REB	RPG	AST	APG	STL	BLK	PTS	PPG
1973-1974	ATLANTA	74	238	502	.474	116	156	.744	454	6.1	86	1.2	29	64	592	8.0
1974-1975	ATLANTA	75	323	752	.430	132	183	.721	697	9.3	152	2.0	51	51	778	10.4
1975-1976	ATLANTA	66	251	542	.463	163	219	.744	524	7.9	83	1.3	52	61	665	10.1
1976-1977	HOUSTON	74	167	338	.494	101	126	.802	284	3.8	48	0.6	38	19	435	5.9
1977-1978	HOUSTON	82	346	777	.445	181	233	.777	641	7.8	109	1.3	77	39	873	10.6
1978-1979	HOUSTON	81	181	395	.458	96	132	.727	328	4.0	57	0.7	34	26	458	5.7
1979-1980	HOUSTON-CHICAGO	74	257	506	.508	146	201	.726	368	5.0	101	1.4	28	42	660	8.9
1980-1981	CHICAGO	81	245	507	.483	125	161	.776	401	5.0	99	1.2	40	36	615	7.6
1981-1982	CHICAGO	78	303	572	.530	172	238	.723	507	6.5	114	1.5	49	36	779	10.0
1982-1983	CHICAGO-L.A.	81	148	325	.455	79	123	.642	309	3.8	62	0.8	31	23	375	4.6
NBA CAREER TOTALS		766	2459	5216	.471	1311	1772	.740	4513	5.9	911	1.2	429	397	6230	8.1
NBA PLAYOFF TOTALS		27	69	153	.451	43	51	.843	134	5.0	29	1.1	15	10	181	6.7

Height	6-10
Weight	210
Born	2-27-52
College	Houston

Jones, Earl

SEASON	TEAM	G	FGM	FGA	PCT	FTM	FTA	PCT	REB	RPG	AST	APG	STL	BLK	PTS	PPG
1984-1985	LOS ANGELES	2	0	1	.000	0	0	N/A	0	0.0	0	0.0	0	0	0	0.0
1985-1986	MILWAUKEE	12	5	12	.417	3	4	.750	10	0.8	4	0.3	0	1	13	1.1
NBA CAREER TOTALS		14	5	13	.385	3	4	.750	10	0.7	4	0.3	0	1	13	0.9

Height	7-0
Weight	230
Born	1-13-61
Coll	Dist. of Columbia

Jones, Eddie

SEASON	TEAM	G	FGM	FGA	PCT	FTM	FTA	PCT	REB	RPG	AST	APG	STL	BLK	PTS	PPG
1994-1995	LOS ANGELES	64	342	744	.460	122	169	.722	249	3.9	128	2.0	131	41	897	14.0
1995-1996	LOS ANGELES	70	337	685	.492	136	184	.739	233	3.3	246	3.5	129	45	893	12.8
1996-1997	LOS ANGELES	80	473	1081	.438	276	337	.819	326	4.1	270	3.4	189	49	1374	17.2
1997-1998	LOS ANGELES	80	486	1005	.484	234	306	.765	302	3.7	246	3.1	160	55	1349	16.9
NBA CAREER TOTALS		294	1638	3515	.466	768	996	.771	1110	3.8	890	3.0	609	190	4513	15.3
NBA PLAYOFF TOTALS		36	159	349	.455	109	140	.778	135	3.7	87	2.4	51	35	478	13.2

Height	6-6
Weight	200
Born	10-20-71
College	Temple

Jordan, Edward Montgomery

SEASON	TEAM	G	FGM	FGA	PCT	FTM	FTA	PCT	REB	RPG	AST	APG	STL	BLK	PTS	PPG
1977-1978	CLEV.-N.J.	73	215	538	.400	131	167	.784	119	1.6	177	2.4	126	19	561	7.7
1978-1979	NEW JERSEY	82	401	960	.418	213	274	.777	215	2.6	365	4.5	201	40	1015	12.4
1979-1980	NEW JERSEY	82	437	1017	.430	201	258	.779	270	3.3	557	6.8	223	27	1087	13.3
1980-1981	N.J.-L.A.	74	150	352	.426	87	127	.685	98	1.3	241	3.3	98	8	393	5.3
1981-1982	LOS ANGELES	58	89	208	.428	43	54	.796	43	0.7	131	2.3	62	1	222	3.8
1982-1983	LOS ANGELES	35	40	132	.303	11	17	.647	26	0.7	80	2.3	31	1	94	2.7
1983-1984	PORT.-L.A.	16	17	49	.347	8	12	.667	17	1.1	44	2.8	25	0	42	2.6
NBA CAREER TOTALS		420	1349	3256	.414	694	909	.763	788	1.9	1595	3.8	766	96	3414	8.1
NBA PLAYOFF TOTALS		7	15	40	.375	8	9	.889	15	2.1	23	3.3	10	3	38	5.4

Height	6-1
Weight	170
Born	1-29-55
College	Rutgers

Jordan, Reginald

SEASON	TEAM	G	FGM	FGA	PCT	FTM	FTA	PCT	REB	RPG	AST	APG	STL	BLK	PTS	PPG
1993-1994	LOS ANGELES	23	44	103	.427	35	51	.686	67	2.9	26	1.1	14	5.	125	5.4
NBA CAREER TOTALS		23	44	103	.427	35	51	.686	67	2.9	26	1.1	14	5	125	5.4

Height	6-4
Weight	195
Born	1-26-68
Coll	New Mexico St

Kersey, Jerome

SEASON	TEAM	G	FGM	FGA	PCT	FTM	FTA	PCT	REB	RPG	AST	APG	STL	BLK	PTS	PPG
1984-1985	PORTLAND	77	178	372	.478	117	181	.646	206	2.7	63	0.8	49	29	473	6.1
1985-1986	PORTLAND	79	258	470	.549	156	229	.681	293	3.7	83	1.1	85	32	672	8.5
1986-1987	PORTLAND	82	373	733	.509	262	364	.720	496	6.0	194	2.4	122	77	1009	12.3
1987-1988	PORTLAND	79	611	1225	.499	291	396	.735	657	8.3	243	3.1	127	65	1516	19.2
1988-1989	PORTLAND	76	533	1137	.469	258	372	.694	629	8.3	243	3.2	137	84	1330	17.5
1989-1990	PORTLAND	82	519	1085	.478	269	390	.690	690	8.4	188	2.3	121	63	1310	16.0
1990-1991	PORTLAND	73	424	887	.478	232	327	.709	481	6.6	227	3.1	101	76	1084	14.8
1991-1992	PORTLAND	77	398	852	.467	174	262	.664	633	8.2	243	3.2	114	71	971	12.6
1992-1993	PORTLAND	65	281	642	.438	116	183	.634	406	6.2	121	1.9	80	41	686	10.6
1993-1994	PORTLAND	78	203	469	.433	101	135	.748	331	4.2	75	1.0	71	49	508	6.5
1994-1995	PORTLAND	63	203	489	.415	95	124	.766	256	4.1	82	1.3	52	35	508	8.1
1995-1996	GOLDEN STATE	76	205	500	.410	97	147	.660	363	4.8	114	1.5	91	45	510	6.7
1996-1997	LOS ANGELES	70	194	449	.432	71	118	.602	363	5.2	89	1.3	119	49	476	6.8
1997-1998	SEATTLE	37	97	233	.416	39	65	.600	135	3.6	44	1.2	52	14	234	6.3
NBA CAREER TOTALS		1014	4477	9543	.469	2278	3293	.692	5939	5.9	2009	2.0	1321	730	11287	11.3
NBA PLAYOFF TOTALS		105	568	1188	.478	343	472	.727	660	6.3	227	2.2	155	72	1480	14.1

Height	6-7
Weight	225
Born	6-26-62
College	Longwood

Keys, Randolph

SEASON	TEAM	G	FGM	FGA	PCT	FTM	FTA	PCT	REB	RPG	AST	APG	STL	BLK	PTS	PPG
1988-1989	CLEVELAND	42	74	172	.430	20	29	.690	56	1.3	19	0.5	12	6	169	4.0
1989-1990	CLEV.-CHA.	80	293	678	.432	101	140	.721	253	3.2	88	1.1	68	8	701	8.8
1990-1991	CHARLOTTE	44	59	145	.407	19	33	.576	100	2.3	18	0.4	22	15	140	3.2
1994-1995	LOS ANGELES	6	9	26	.346	2	2	1.000	17	2.8	2	0.3	1	2	20	3.3
NBA CAREER TOTALS		172	435	1021	.426	142	204	.696	426	2.5	127	0.7	103	31	1030	6.0
NBA PLAYOFF TOTALS		1	0	3	.000	0	0	N/A	3	3.0	1	1.0	0	0	0	0.0

Height	6-7
Weight	195
Born	4-19-66
College	S Mississippi

Killum, Earnest

SEASON	TEAM	G	FGM	FGA	PCT	FTM	FTA	PCT	REB	RPG	AST	APG	STL	BLK	PTS	PPG
1970-1971	LOS ANGELES	4	0	4	.000	1	1	1.000	2	0.5	0	0.0	N/A	N/A	1	0.3
NBA CAREER TOTALS		4	0	4	.000	1	1	1.000	2	0.5	0	0.0	N/A	N/A	1	0.3
NBA PLAYOFF TOTALS		2	1	1	1.000	2	3	.667	0	0.0	N/A	0.0	N/A	N/A	4	2.0

Height	6-3
Weight	185
Born	6-11-48
College	Stetson

King, Frankie

SEASON	TEAM	G	FGM	FGA	PCT	FTM	FTA	PCT	REB	RPG	AST	APG	STL	BLK	PTS	PPG
1995-1996	LOS ANGELES	6	3	11	.273	1	3	.333	2	0.3	2	0.3	2	0	7	1.2
1996-1997	PHILADELPHIA	7	7	17	.412	5	5	1.000	14	2.0	5	0.7	4	0	20	2.9
NBA CAREER TOTALS		13	10	28	.357	6	8	.750	16	1.2	7	0.5	6	0	27	2.1

Height	6-1
Weight	185
Born	6-6-72
College	W Carolina

King, James Leonard

SEASON	TEAM	G	FGM	FGA	PCT	FTM	FTA	PCT	REB	RPG	AST	APG	STL	BLK	PTS	PPG
1963-1964	LOS ANGELES	60	84	198	.424	66	101	.653	113	1.9	110	1.8	N/A	N/A	234	3.9
1964-1965	LOS ANGELES	77	184	469	.392	118	151	.781	214	2.8	178	2.3	N/A	N/A	486	6.3
1965-1966	LOS ANGELES	76	238	545	.437	94	115	.817	204	2.7	223	2.9	N/A	N/A	570	7.5
1966-1967	SAN FRANCISCO	67	286	685	.418	174	221	.787	319	4.8	240	3.6	N/A	N/A	746	11.1
1967-1968	SAN FRANCISCO	54	340	800	.425	217	268	.810	243	4.5	226	4.2	N/A	N/A	897	16.6
1968-1969	SAN FRANCISCO	46	137	394	.348	78	108	.722	120	2.6	123	2.7	N/A	N/A	352	7.7
1969-1970	S.F.-CIN.	34	53	129	.411	33	41	.805	62	1.8	52	1.5	N/A	N/A	139	4.1
1970-1971	CHICAGO	55	100	228	.439	64	79	.810	68	1.2	78	1.4	N/A	N/A	264	4.8
1971-1972	CHICAGO	73	162	356	.455	89	113	.788	81	1.1	101	1.4	N/A	N/A	413	5.7
1972-1973	CHICAGO	65	116	263	.441	44	52	.846	76	1.2	81	1.2	N/A	N/A	276	4.2
NBA CAREER TOTALS		607	1700	4067	.418	977	1249	.782	1500	2.5	1412	2.3	N/A	N/A	4377	7.2
NBA PLAYOFF TOTALS		73	246	564	.436	110	151	.728	246	3.4	182	2.5	N/A	N/A	602	8.2

Height	6-2
Weight	175
Born	2-7-41
College	Tulsa

Kleine, Joe

SEASON	TEAM	G	FGM	FGA	PCT	FTM	FTA	PCT	REB	RPG	AST	APG	STL	BLK	PTS	PPG
1985-1986	SACRAMENTO	80	160	344	.465	94	130	.723	373	4.7	46	0.6	24	34	414	5.2
1986-1987	SACRAMENTO	79	256	543	.471	110	140	.786	483	6.1	71	0.9	35	30	622	7.9
1987-1988	SACRAMENTO	82	324	686	.472	153	188	.814	579	7.1	93	1.1	28	59	801	9.8
1988-1989	SAC.-BOSTON	75	175	432	.405	134	152	.882	378	5.0	67	0.9	33	23	484	6.5
1989-1990	BOSTON	81	176	367	.480	83	100	.830	355	4.4	46	0.6	15	27	435	5.4
1990-1991	BOSTON	72	102	218	.468	54	69	.783	244	3.4	21	0.3	15	14	258	3.6
1991-1992	BOSTON	70	144	293	.491	34	48	.708	296	4.2	32	0.5	23	14	326	4.7
1992-1993	BOSTON	78	108	267	.404	41	58	.707	346	4.4	39	0.5	17	17	257	3.3
1993-1994	PHOENIX	74	125	256	.488	30	39	.769	193	2.6	45	0.6	14	19	285	3.9
1994-1995	PHOENIX	75	119	265	.449	42	49	.857	259	3.5	39	0.5	14	18	280	3.7
1995-1996	PHOENIX	56	71	169	.420	20	25	.800	132	2.4	44	0.8	13	6	164	2.9
1996-1997	PH.-L.A.-N.J.	59	69	170	.406	28	38	.737	203	3.4	35	0.6	17	18	168	2.8
1997-1998	CHICAGO	46	39	106	.368	15	18	.833	77	1.7	30	0.7	4	5	93	2.0
NBA CAREER TOTALS		937	1869	4116	.454	838	1054	.795	3918	4.2	608	0.6	252	284	4587	4.9
NBA PLAYOFF TOTALS		49	83	161	.516	23	29	.793	132	2.7	18	0.4	10	14	190	3.9

Height	7-0
Weight	270
Born	1-4-62
College	Arkansas

Knight, Travis

SEASON	TEAM	G	FGM	FGA	PCT	FTM	FTA	PCT	REB	RPG	AST	APG	STL	BLK	PTS	PPG
1996-1997	LOS ANGELES	71	140	275	.509	62	100	.620	319	4.5	39	0.5	31	58	342	4.8
1997-1998	BOSTON	74	193	438	.441	81	103	.786	365	4.9	104	1.4	54	82	482	6.5
NBA CAREER TOTALS		145	333	713	.467	143	203	.704	684	4.7	143	1.0	85	140	824	5.7
NBA PLAYOFF TOTALS		9	8	10	.800	3	4	.750	18	2.0	3	0.3	3	3	19	2.1

Height	7-0
Weight	235
Born	9-13-74
College	Connecticut

Krebs, James

SEASON	TEAM	G	FGM	FGA	PCT	FTM	FTA	PCT	REB	RPG	AST	APG	STL	BLK	PTS	PPG
1957-1958	MINNEAPOLIS	68	199	527	.378	135	176	.767	502	7.4	27	0.4	N/A	N/A	533	7.8
1958-1959	MINNEAPOLIS	72	271	679	.399	92	123	.748	491	6.8	50	0.7	N/A	N/A	634	8.8
1959-1960	MINNEAPOLIS	75	237	605	.392	98	136	.721	327	4.4	38	0.5	N/A	N/A	572	7.6
1960-1961	LOS ANGELES	75	271	692	.392	75	93	.806	456	6.1	68	0.9	N/A	N/A	617	8.2
1961-1962	LOS ANGELES	78	312	701	.445	156	208	.750	616	7.9	110	1.4	N/A	N/A	780	10.0
1962-1963	LOS ANGELES	79	272	627	.434	115	154	.747	502	6.4	87	1.1	N/A	N/A	659	8.3
1963-1964	LOS ANGELES	68	134	357	.375	65	85	.765	283	4.2	49	0.7	N/A	N/A	333	4.9
NBA CAREER TOTALS		515	1696	4188	.405	736	975	.755	3177	6.2	429	0.8	N/A	N/A	4128	8.0
NBA PLAYOFF TOTALS		62	127	341	.372	75	96	.781	348	5.6	53	0.9	N/A	N/A	329	5.3

Height	6-8
Weight	230
Born	9-8-35
College	SMU

Krystkowiak, Larry Brett

Height	6-9
Weight	240
Born	9-23-64
College	Montana

SEASON	TEAM	G	FGM	FGA	PCT	FTM	FTA	PCT	REB	RPG	AST	APG	STL	BLK	PTS	PPG
1986-1987	SAN ANTONIO	68	170	373	.456	110	148	.743	239	3.5	85	1.3	22	12	451	6.6
1987-1988	MILWAUKEE	50	128	266	.481	103	127	.811	231	4.6	50	1.0	18	8	359	7.2
1988-1989	MILWAUKEE	80	362	766	.473	289	351	.823	610	7.6	107	1.3	93	9	1017	12.7
1989-1990	MILWAUKEE	16	43	118	.364	26	33	.788	76	4.8	25	1.6	10	2	112	7.0
1990-1991	MILWAUKEE	DID NOT PLAY.... INJURED														
1991-1992	MILWAUKEE	79	293	660	.444	128	169	.757	429	5.4	114	1.4	54	12	714	9.0
1992-1993	UTAH	71	198	425	.466	117	147	.796	279	3.9	68	1.0	42	13	513	7.2
1993-1994	ORLANDO	34	71	148	.480	31	39	.795	123	3.6	35	1.0	14	4	173	5.1
1994-1995	CHICAGO	19	28	72	.389	27	30	.900	59	3.1	26	1.4	9	2	83	4.4
1996-1997	LOS ANGELES	3	1	2	.500	1	2	.500	5	1.7	3	1.0	2	0	3	1.0
NBA CAREER TOTALS		420	1294	2830	.457	832	1046	.795	2051	4.9	513	1.2	264	62	3425	8.2
NBA PLAYOFF TOTALS		20	50	122	.410	47	53	.887	109	5.5	30	1.5	10	3	147	7.4

Kupchak, Mitchell

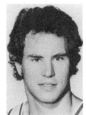

Height	6-9
Weight	230
Born	5-24-54
College	N Carolina

SEASON	TEAM	G	FGM	FGA	PCT	FTM	FTA	PCT	REB	RPG	AST	APG	STL	BLK	PTS	PPG
1976-1977	WASHINGTON	82	341	596	.572	170	246	.691	494	6.0	62	0.8	22	34	852	10.4
1977-1978	WASHINGTON	67	393	768	.512	280	402	.697	460	6.9	71	1.1	28	42	1066	15.9
1978-1979	WASHINGTON	66	369	685	.539	223	300	.743	430	6.5	88	1.3	23	23	961	14.6
1979-1980	WASHINGTON	40	67	160	.419	52	75	.693	105	2.6	16	0.4	8	8	186	4.7
1980-1981	WASHINGTON	82	392	747	.525	240	340	.706	569	6.9	62	0.8	36	26	1024	12.5
1981-1982	LOS ANGELES	26	153	267	.573	65	98	.663	210	8.1	33	1.3	12	10	371	14.3
1983-1984	LOS ANGELES	34	41	108	.380	22	34	.647	87	2.6	7	0.2	4	6	104	3.1
1984-1985	LOS ANGELES	58	123	244	.504	60	91	.659	184	3.2	21	0.4	19	20	306	5.3
1985-1986	LOS ANGELES	55	124	257	.482	84	112	.750	191	3.5	17	0.3	12	7	332	6.0
NBA CAREER TOTALS		510	2003	3832	.523	1196	1698	.704	2730	5.4	377	0.7	164	176	5202	10.2
NBA PLAYOFF TOTALS		68	202	426	.474	120	185	.649	321	4.7	44	0.6	13	15	524	7.7

Kupec, Charles J.

Height	6-6
Weight	220
Born	1-16-53
College	Michigan

SEASON	TEAM	G	FGM	FGA	PCT	FTM	FTA	PCT	REB	RPG	AST	APG	STL	BLK	PTS	PPG
1975-1976	LOS ANGELES	16	10	40	.250	7	11	.636	23	1.4	5	0.3	3	0	27	1.7
1976-1977	LOS ANGELES	82	153	342	.447	78	101	.772	199	2.4	53	0.6	18	4	384	4.7
1977-1978	HOUSTON	49	84	197	.426	27	33	.818	91	1.9	50	1.0	10	3	195	4.0
NBA CAREER TOTALS		147	247	579	.427	112	145	.772	313	2.1	108	0.7	31	7	606	4.1
NBA PLAYOFF TOTALS		11	8	18	.444	5	7	.714	16	1.5	4	0.4	3	0	21	1.9

Lamar, Dwight

Height	6-1
Weight	180
Born	4-7-51
College	SW Louisiana

SEASON	TEAM	G	FGM	FGA	PCT	FTM	FTA	PCT	REB	RPG	AST	APG	STL	BLK	PTS	PPG
1973-1974	SAN DIEGO (A)	84	686	1726	.397	272	350	.777	292	3.5	288	3.4	129	13	1713	20.4
1974-1975	SAN DIEGO (A)	77	667	1571	.425	247	315	.784	239	3.1	427	5.5	129	12	1606	20.9
1975-1976	S.D.-INDIANA (A)	41	277	668	.415	79	106	.745	116	2.8	171	4.2	42	2	657	16.0
1976-1977	LOS ANGELES	71	228	561	.406	46	68	.676	92	1.3	177	2.5	59	3	502	7.1
NBA CAREER TOTALS		71	228	561	.406	46	68	.676	92	1.3	177	2.5	59	3	502	7.1
NBA PLAYOFF TOTALS		10	12	41	.293	9	10	.900	9	0.9	14	1.4	3	0	33	3.3

Lamp, Jeffrey Alan

SEASON	TEAM	G	FGM	FGA	PCT	FTM	FTA	PCT	REB	RPG	AST	APG	STL	BLK	PTS	PPG
1981-1982	PORTLAND	54	100	196	.510	50	61	.820	64	1.2	28	0.5	16	1	250	4.6
1982-1983	PORTLAND	59	107	252	.425	42	52	.808	76	1.3	58	1.0	20	3	257	4.4
1983-1984	PORTLAND	64	128	261	.490	60	67	.896	63	1.0	51	0.8	22	4	318	5.0
1985-1986	MILW.-S.A.	74	245	514	.477	111	133	.835	200	2.7	117	1.6	39	4	608	8.2
1987-1988	LOS ANGELES	3	0	0	N/A	2	2	1.000	0	0.0	0	0.0	0	0	2	0.7
1988-1989	LOS ANGELES	37	27	69	.391	4	5	.800	34	0.9	15	0.4	8	2	60	1.6
NBA CAREER TOTALS		291	607	1292	.470	269	320	.841	437	1.5	269	0.9	105	14	1495	5.1
NBA PLAYOFF TOTALS		12	13	32	.406	1	2	.500	4	0.3	8	0.7	1	0	28	2.3

Height	6-6
Weight	195
Born	3-8-59
College	Virginia

Landsberger, Mark Walter

SEASON	TEAM	G	FGM	FGA	PCT	FTM	FTA	PCT	REB	RPG	AST	APG	STL	BLK	PTS	PPG
1977-1978	CHICAGO	62	127	251	.506	91	157	.580	301	4.9	41	0.7	21	6	345	5.6
1978-1979	CHICAGO	80	278	585	.475	91	194	.469	742	9.3	68	0.9	27	22	647	8.1
1979-1980	CHICAGO-L.A.	77	249	483	.516	116	222	.523	613	8.0	46	0.6	33	22	614	8.0
1980-1981	LOS ANGELES	69	164	327	.502	62	116	.534	377	5.5	27	0.4	19	6	390	5.7
1981-1982	LOS ANGELES	75	144	329	.438	33	65	.508	401	5.3	32	0.4	10	7	321	4.3
1982-1983	LOS ANGELES	39	43	102	.422	12	25	.480	128	3.3	12	0.3	8	4	98	2.5
1983-1984	ATLANTA	35	19	51	.373	15	26	.577	119	3.4	10	0.3	6	3	53	1.5
NBA CAREER TOTALS		437	1024	2128	.481	420	805	.522	2681	6.1	236	0.5	124	70	2468	5.6
NBA PLAYOFF TOTALS		41	42	114	.368	12	20	.600	151	3.7	7	0.2	4	4	96	2.3

Height	6-8
Weight	225
Born	5-21-55
College	Arizona St

Lantz, Stuart Burrell

SEASON	TEAM	G	FGM	FGA	PCT	FTM	FTA	PCT	REB	RPG	AST	APG	STL	BLK	PTS	PPG
1968-1969	SAN DIEGO	73	220	482	.456	129	167	.772	236	3.2	99	1.4	N/A	N/A	569	7.8
1969-1970	SAN DIEGO	82	455	1027	.443	278	361	.770	255	3.1	287	3.5	N/A	N/A	1188	14.5
1970-1971	SAN DIEGO	82	585	1305	.448	519	644	.806	406	5.0	344	4.2	N/A	N/A	1689	20.6
1971-1972	HOUSTON	81	557	1279	.435	387	462	.838	345	4.3	337	4.2	N/A	N/A	1501	18.5
1972-1973	DETROIT	51	185	455	.407	120	150	.800	172	3.4	138	2.7	N/A	N/A	490	9.6
1973-1974	DETROIT	50	154	361	.427	139	164	.848	113	2.3	97	1.9	38	3	447	8.9
1974-1975	N.O.-L.A.	75	228	561	.406	192	229	.838	194	2.6	188	2.5	56	12	648	8.6
1975-1976	LOS ANGELES	53	85	204	.417	80	89	.899	99	1.9	76	1.4	27	3	250	4.7
NBA CAREER TOTALS		547	2469	5674	.435	1844	2266	.814	1820	3.3	1566	2.9	121	18	6782	12.4
NBA PLAYOFF TOTALS		13	58	128	.453	49	59	.831	50	3.8	24	1.8	2	0	165	12.7

Height	6-3
Weight	180
Born	7-14-46
College	Nebraska

LaRusso, Rudolph

SEASON	TEAM	G	FGM	FGA	PCT	FTM	FTA	PCT	REB	RPG	AST	APG	STL	BLK	PTS	PPG
1959-1960	MINNEAPOLIS	71	355	913	.389	265	357	.742	679	9.6	83	1.2	N/A	N/A	975	13.7
1960-1961	LOS ANGELES	79	416	992	.419	323	409	.790	781	9.9	135	1.7	N/A	N/A	1155	14.6
1961-1962	LOS ANGELES	80	516	1108	.466	342	448	.763	828	10.4	179	2.2	N/A	N/A	1374	17.2
1962-1963	LOS ANGELES	75	321	761	.422	282	393	.718	747	10.0	187	2.5	N/A	N/A	924	12.3
1963-1964	LOS ANGELES	79	337	776	.434	298	397	.751	800	10.1	190	2.4	N/A	N/A	972	12.3
1964-1965	LOS ANGELES	77	381	827	.461	321	415	.773	725	9.4	198	2.6	N/A	N/A	1083	14.1
1965-1966	LOS ANGELES	76	410	897	.457	350	445	.787	660	8.7	165	2.2	N/A	N/A	1170	15.4
1966-1967	LOS ANGELES	45	211	509	.415	156	224	.696	351	7.8	78	1.7	N/A	N/A	578	12.8
1967-1968	SAN FRANCISCO	79	602	1389	.433	522	661	.790	741	9.4	182	2.3	N/A	N/A	1726	21.8
1968-1969	SAN FRANCISCO	75	553	1349	.410	444	559	.794	624	8.3	159	2.1	N/A	N/A	1550	20.7
NBA CAREER TOTALS		736	4102	9521	.431	3303	4308	.767	6936	9.4	1556	2.1	N/A	N/A	11507	15.6
NBA PLAYOFF TOTALS		93	467	1152	.405	410	546	.751	779	8.4	194	2.1	N/A	N/A	1344	14.5

Height	6-8
Weight	220
Born	11-11-37
College	Dartmouth

Lee, Alfred "Butch"

SEASON	TEAM	G	FGM	FGA	PCT	FTM	FTA	PCT	REB	RPG	AST	APG	STL	BLK	PTS	PPG
1978-1979	ATLANTA-CLEV.	82	290	634	.457	175	230	.761	126	1.5	295	3.6	86	1	755	9.2
1979-1980	CLEV.-L.A.	14	6	24	.250	6	8	.750	11	0.8	12	0.9	1	0	18	1.3
NBA CAREER TOTALS		96	296	658	.450	181	238	.761	137	1.4	307	3.2	87	1	773	8.1
NBA PLAYOFF TOTALS		3	0	0	N/A	2	2	1.000	1	0.3	N/A	0.0	0	0	2	0.7

Height	6-0
Weight	175
Born	12-5-56
College	Marquette

Leonard, William Robert

SEASON	TEAM	G	FGM	FGA	PCT	FTM	FTA	PCT	REB	RPG	AST	APG	STL	BLK	PTS	PPG
1956-1957	MINNEAPOLIS	72	303	867	.349	186	241	.772	220	3.1	169	2.3	N/A	N/A	792	11.0
1957-1958	MINNEAPOLIS	66	266	794	.335	205	268	.765	237	3.6	218	3.3	N/A	N/A	737	11.2
1958-1959	MINNEAPOLIS	58	206	552	.373	120	160	.750	178	3.1	186	3.2	N/A	N/A	532	9.2
1959-1960	MINNEAPOLIS	73	231	717	.322	136	193	.705	245	3.4	252	3.5	N/A	N/A	598	8.2
1960-1961	LOS ANGELES	55	61	207	.295	71	100	.710	70	1.3	81	1.5	N/A	N/A	193	3.5
1961-1962	CHICAGO	70	423	1128	.375	279	371	.752	199	2.8	378	5.4	N/A	N/A	1125	16.1
1962-1963	CHICAGO	32	84	245	.343	59	85	.694	68	2.1	143	4.5	N/A	N/A	227	7.1
NBA CAREER TOTALS		426	1574	4510	.349	1056	1418	.745	1217	2.9	1427	3.3	N/A	N/A	4204	9.9
NBA PLAYOFF TOTALS		34	130	364	.357	74	98	.755	90	2.6	165	4.9	N/A	N/A	334	9.8

Height	6-3
Weight	185
Born	2-15-32
College	Indiana

Lester, Ronnie

SEASON	TEAM	G	FGM	FGA	PCT	FTM	FTA	PCT	REB	RPG	AST	APG	STL	BLK	PTS	PPG
1980-1981	CHICAGO	8	10	24	.417	10	11	.909	6	0.8	7	0.9	2	0	30	3.8
1981-1982	CHICAGO	75	329	657	.501	208	256	.813	213	2.8	362	4.8	80	14	870	11.6
1982-1983	CHICAGO	65	202	446	.453	124	171	.725	172	2.6	332	5.1	51	6	528	8.1
1983-1984	CHICAGO	43	78	188	.415	75	87	.862	46	1.1	168	3.9	30	6	232	5.4
1984-1985	LOS ANGELES	32	34	82	.415	21	31	.677	26	0.8	80	2.5	15	3	89	2.8
1985-1986	LOS ANGELES	27	26	52	.500	15	19	.789	10	0.4	54	2.0	9	3	67	2.5
NBA CAREER TOTALS		250	679	1449	.469	453	575	.788	473	1.9	1003	4.0	187	32	1816	7.3
NBA PLAYOFF TOTALS		14	13	33	.394	12	16	.750	14	1.0	13	0.9	2	0	38	2.7

Height	6-2
Weight	175
Born	1-1-59
College	Iowa

Love, Stanley S.

SEASON	TEAM	G	FGM	FGA	PCT	FTM	FTA	PCT	REB	RPG	AST	APG	STL	BLK	PTS	PPG
1971-1972	BALTIMORE	74	242	536	.451	103	140	.736	338	4.6	52	0.7	N/A	N/A	587	7.9
1972-1973	BALTIMORE	72	190	436	.436	79	100	.790	300	4.2	46	0.6	N/A	N/A	459	6.4
1973-1974	LOS ANGELES	51	119	278	.428	49	64	.766	170	3.3	48	0.9	28	20	287	5.6
1974-1975	LOS ANGELES	30	85	194	.438	47	66	.712	97	3.2	26	0.9	16	13	217	7.2
1974-1975	SAN ANTONIO (A)	12	13	30	.433	3	4	.750	24	2.0	9	0.8	0	4	29	2.4
NBA CAREER TOTALS		227	636	1444	.440	278	370	.751	905	4.0	172	0.8	44	33	1550	6.8
NBA PLAYOFF TOTALS		7	3	10	.300	2	3	.667	10	1.4	2	0.3	1	0	8	1.1

Height	6-9
Weight	215
Born	4-9-49
College	Oregon

Lucas, Maurice D.

SEASON	TEAM	G	FGM	FGA	PCT	FTM	FTA	PCT	REB	RPG	AST	APG	STL	BLK	PTS	PPG
1974-1975	ST. LOUIS (A)	80	438	937	.467	180	229	.786	816	10.2	287	3.6	89	64	1058	13.2
1975-1976	ST. L.-KEN. (A)	86	620	1346	.461	217	283	.767	970	11.3	224	2.6	75	57	1460	17.0
1976-1977	PORTLAND	79	632	1357	.466	335	438	.765	899	11.4	229	2.9	83	56	1599	20.2
1977-1978	PORTLAND	68	453	989	.458	207	270	.767	621	9.1	173	2.5	61	56	1113	16.4
1978-1979	PORTLAND	69	568	1208	.470	270	345	.783	716	10.4	215	3.1	66	81	1406	20.4
1979-1980	PORT.-N.J.	63	371	813	.456	179	239	.749	537	8.5	208	3.3	42	62	923	14.7
1980-1981	NEW JERSEY	68	404	835	.484	191	254	.752	575	8.5	173	2.5	57	59	999	14.7
1981-1982	NEW YORK	80	505	1001	.504	253	349	.725	903	11.3	179	2.2	68	70	1263	15.8
1982-1983	PHOENIX	77	495	1045	.474	278	356	.781	799	10.4	219	2.8	56	43	1269	16.5
1983-1984	PHOENIX	75	451	908	.497	293	383	.765	725	9.7	203	2.7	55	39	1195	15.9
1984-1985	PHOENIX	63	346	727	.476	150	200	.750	557	8.8	145	2.3	39	17	842	13.4
1985-1986	LOS ANGELES	77	302	653	.462	180	230	.783	566	7.4	84	1.1	45	24	785	10.2
1986-1987	SEATTLE	63	175	388	.451	150	187	.802	307	4.9	65	1.0	34	21	500	7.9
1987-1988	PORTLAND	73	168	373	.450	109	148	.736	315	4.3	94	1.3	33	10	445	6.1
NBA CAREER TOTALS		855	4870	10297	.473	2595	3399	.763	7520	8.8	1987	2.3	639	538	12339	14.4
NBA PLAYOFF TOTALS		82	472	975	.484	215	289	.744	690	8.4	225	2.7	71	46	1159	14.1

Height	6-9
Weight	215
Born	2-18-52
College	Marquette

Lynch, George DeWitt III

SEASON	TEAM	G	FGM	FGA	PCT	FTM	FTA	PCT	REB	RPG	AST	APG	STL	BLK	PTS	PPG
1993-1994	LOS ANGELES	71	291	573	.508	99	166	.596	410	5.8	96	1.4	102	27	681	9.6
1994-1995	LOS ANGELES	56	138	295	.468	62	86	.721	184	3.3	62	1.1	51	10	341	6.1
1995-1996	LOS ANGELES	76	117	272	.430	53	80	.663	209	2.8	51	0.7	47	10	291	3.8
1996-1997	VANCOUVER	41	137	291	.471	60	97	.619	261	6.4	76	1.9	63	17	342	8.3
1997-1998	VANCOUVER	82	248	516	.481	111	158	.703	362	4.4	122	1.5	65	41	616	7.5
NBA CAREER TOTALS		326	931	1947	.478	385	587	.656	1426	4.4	407	1.2	328	105	2271	7.0
NBA PLAYOFF TOTALS		12	17	36	.472	13	20	.650	33	2.8	8	0.7	8	0	48	4.0

Height	6-8
Weight	220
Born	9-3-70
College	N Carolina

Lynn, Michael Edward

SEASON	TEAM	G	FGM	FGA	PCT	FTM	FTA	PCT	REB	RPG	AST	APG	STL	BLK	PTS	PPG
1969-1970	LOS ANGELES	44	44	133	.331	31	48	.646	64	1.5	30	0.7	N/A	N/A	119	2.7
1970-1971	BUFFALO	5	2	7	.286	3	3	1.000	4	0.8	1	0.2	N/A	N/A	7	1.4
NBA CAREER TOTALS		49	46	140	.329	34	51	.667	68	1.4	31	0.6	N/A	N/A	126	2.6
NBA PLAYOFF TOTALS		3	2	3	.667	0	0	N/A	2	0.7	1	0.3	N/A	N/A	4	1.3

Height	6-7
Weight	215
Born	11-25-45
College	UCLA

Mack, Oliver

SEASON	TEAM	G	FGM	FGA	PCT	FTM	FTA	PCT	REB	RPG	AST	APG	STL	BLK	PTS	PPG
1979-1980	L.A.-CHICAGO	50	98	199	.492	38	51	.745	71	1.4	53	1.1	24	3	234	4.7
1980-1981	CHICAGO-DALLAS	65	279	606	.460	80	125	.640	230	3.5	163	2.5	56	7	638	9.8
1981-1982	DALLAS	13	19	59	.322	6	8	.750	18	1.4	14	1.1	5	1	44	3.4
NBA CAREER TOTALS		**128**	**396**	**864**	**.458**	**124**	**184**	**.674**	**319**	**2.5**	**230**	**1.8**	**85**	**11**	**916**	**7.2**

Height 6-3
Weight 195
Born 6-6-57
College E Carolina

Matthews, Wesley Joel

SEASON	TEAM	G	FGM	FGA	PCT	FTM	FTA	PCT	REB	RPG	AST	APG	STL	BLK	PTS	PPG
1980-1981	WASH.-ATLANTA	79	385	779	.494	202	252	.802	139	1.8	411	5.2	107	17	977	12.4
1981-1982	ATLANTA	47	131	298	.440	60	79	.759	58	1.2	139	3.0	53	2	324	6.9
1982-1983	ATLANTA	64	171	424	.403	86	112	.768	91	1.4	248	3.9	80	8	442	6.9
1983-1984	ATLANTA-PHIL.	20	61	131	.466	27	36	.750	27	1.4	83	4.2	16	3	150	7.5
1984-1985	CHICAGO	78	191	386	.495	59	86	.684	67	0.9	354	4.5	73	12	443	5.7
1985-1986	SAN ANTONIO	75	320	603	.531	173	211	.820	131	1.7	476	6.3	87	32	817	10.9
1986-1987	LOS ANGELES	50	89	187	.476	29	36	.806	47	0.9	100	2.0	23	4	208	4.2
1987-1988	LOS ANGELES	61	114	248	.480	54	65	.831	66	1.3	138	2.7	25	3	289	6.7
1989-1990	ATLANTA	1	1	3	.333	2	2	1.000	0	0.0	5	5.0	0	0	4	4.0
NBA CAREER TOTALS		**465**	**1463**	**3059**	**.478**	**692**	**878**	**.788**	**626**	**1.3**	**1955**	**4.2**	**444**	**81**	**3854**	**7.9**
NBA PLAYOFF TOTALS		**38**	**68**	**141**	**.482**	**36**	**45**	**.800**	**18**	**0.5**	**66**	**1.7**	**14**	**2**	**179**	**4.8**

Height 6-1
Weight 170
Born 8-24-59
College Wisconsin

McAdoo, Robert Allen Jr.

SEASON	TEAM	G	FGM	FGA	PCT	FTM	FTA	PCT	REB	RPG	AST	APG	STL	BLK	PTS	PPG
1972-1973	BUFFALO	80	585	1293	.452	271	350	.774	728	9.1	139	1.7	N/A	N/A	1441	18.0
1973-1974	BUFFALO	74	901	1647	.547	459	579	.793	1117	15.1	170	2.3	88	246	2261	30.6
1974-1975	BUFFALO	82	1095	2138	.512	641	796	.805	1155	14.1	179	2.2	92	174	2831	34.5
1975-1976	BUFFALO	78	934	1918	.487	559	734	.762	965	12.4	315	4.0	93	160	2427	31.1
1976-1977	BUFFALO-N.Y.	72	740	1445	.512	381	516	.738	926	12.9	205	2.8	77	99	1861	25.8
1977-1978	NEW YORK	79	814	1564	.520	469	645	.727	1010	12.8	298	3.8	105	126	2097	26.5
1978-1979	N.Y.-BOSTON	60	596	1127	.529	295	450	.656	520	8.7	168	2.8	74	67	1487	24.8
1979-1980	DETROIT	58	492	1025	.480	235	322	.730	467	8.1	200	3.4	73	65	1222	21.1
1980-1981	DETROIT-N.J.	16	68	157	.433	29	41	.707	67	4.2	30	1.9	17	13	165	10.3
1981-1982	LOS ANGELES	41	151	330	.458	90	126	.714	159	3.9	32	0.8	22	36	392	9.6
1982-1983	LOS ANGELES	47	292	562	.520	119	163	.730	247	5.3	39	0.8	40	40	703	15.0
1983-1984	LOS ANGELES	70	352	748	.471	212	264	.803	289	4.1	74	1.1	42	50	916	13.1
1984-1985	LOS ANGELES	66	284	546	.520	122	162	.753	295	4.5	67	1.0	18	53	690	10.5
1985-1986	PHILADELPHIA	29	116	251	.462	62	81	.765	103	3.6	35	1.2	10	18	294	10.1
NBA CAREER TOTALS		**852**	**7420**	**14751**	**.503**	**3944**	**5229**	**.754**	**8048**	**9.4**	**1951**	**2.3**	**751**	**1147**	**18787**	**22.1**
NBA PLAYOFF TOTALS		**94**	**698**	**1423**	**.491**	**320**	**442**	**.724**	**711**	**7.6**	**127**	**1.4**	**72**	**151**	**1718**	**18.3**

Height 6-9
Weight 210
Born 9-15-51
College N Carolina

McCants, Melvin Lamont

SEASON	TEAM	G	FGM	FGA	PCT	FTM	FTA	PCT	REB	RPG	AST	APG	STL	BLK	PTS	PPG
1989-1990	LOS ANGELES	13	8	26	.308	6	8	.750	6	0.5	2	0.2	3	1	22	1.7
NBA CAREER TOTALS		13	8	26	.308	6	8	.750	6	0.5	2	0.2	3	1	22	1.7
NBA PLAYOFF TOTALS		2	0	0	N/A	0	0	N/A	0	0.0	N/A	0.0	0	0	0	0.0

Height	6-8
Weight	240
Born	8-19-67
College	Purdue

McCarter, Willie J

SEASON	TEAM	G	FGM	FGA	PCT	FTM	FTA	PCT	REB	RPG	AST	APG	STL	BLK	PTS	PPG
1969-1970	LOS ANGELES	40	132	349	.378	43	60	.717	83	2.1	93	2.3	N/A	N/A	307	7.7
1970-1971	LOS ANGELES	76	247	592	.417	46	77	.597	122	1.6	126	1.7	N/A	N/A	540	7.1
1971-1972	PORTLAND	39	103	257	.401	37	55	.673	43	1.1	85	2.2	N/A	N/A	243	6.2
NBA CAREER TOTALS		155	482	1198	.402	126	192	.656	248	1.6	304	2.0	N/A	N/A	1090	7.0
NBA PLAYOFF TOTALS		17	30	83	.361	2	7	.286	29	1.7	20	1.2	N/A	N/A	62	3.6

Height	6-3
Weight	175
Born	7-26-46
College	Drake

McCloud, George

SEASON	TEAM	G	FGM	FGA	PCT	FTM	FTA	PCT	REB	RPG	AST	APG	STL	BLK	PTS	PPG
1989-1990	INDIANA	44	45	144	.313	15	19	.789	42	1.0	45	1.0	19	3	118	2.7
1990-1991	INDIANA	74	131	351	.373	38	49	.776	118	1.6	150	2.0	40	11	343	4.6
1991-1992	INDIANA	51	128	313	.409	50	64	.781	132	2.6	116	2.3	26	11	338	6.6
1992-1993	INDIANA	78	216	525	.411	75	102	.735	205	2.6	192	2.5	53	11	565	7.2
1994-1995	DALLAS	42	144	328	.439	80	96	.833	147	3.5	53	1.3	23	9	402	9.6
1995-1996	DALLAS	79	530	1281	.414	180	224	.804	379	4.8	212	2.7	113	38	1497	18.9
1996-1997	DAL.-L.A.	64	238	578	.412	83	101	.822	179	2.8	109	1.7	61	8	658	10.3
1997-1998	PHOENIX	63	173	427	.405	39	51	.765	218	3.5	84	1.3	5.4	13	456	7.2
NBA CAREER TOTALS		495	1605	3947	.406	560	706	.793	1420	2.9	961	1.9	389	104	4377	8.8
NBA PLAYOFF TOTALS		11	36	78	.461	12	19	.632	33	3.0	28	2.5	7	3	101	9.2

Height	6-8
Weight	225
Born	5-27-67
College	Florida St

McDaniels, James Ronald

SEASON	TEAM	G	FGM	FGA	PCT	FTM	FTA	PCT	REB	RPG	AST	APG	STL	BLK	PTS	PPG
1971-1972	SEATTLE	12	51	123	.415	11	18	.611	82	6.8	9	0.8	N/A	N/A	113	9.4
1972-1973	SEATTLE	68	154	386	.399	70	100	.700	345	5.1	78	1.1	N/A	N/A	378	5.6
1973-1974	SEATTLE	27	63	173	.364	23	43	.535	128	4.7	24	0.9	7	15	149	5.5
1975-1976	LOS ANGELES	35	41	102	.402	9	9	1.000	74	2.1	15	0.4	4	10	91	2.6
1977-1978	BUFFALO	42	100	234	.427	36	42	.857	181	4.3	44	1.0	4	37	236	5.6
NBA CAREER TOTALS		184	409	1018	.402	149	212	.703	810	4.4	170	0.9	15	62	967	5.3

Height	6-11
Weight	230
Born	4-2-48
College	W Kentucky

McGee, Michael Ray

SEASON	TEAM	G	FGM	FGA	PCT	FTM	FTA	PCT	REB	RPG	AST	APG	STL	BLK	PTS	PPG
1981-1982	LOS ANGELES	39	80	172	.465	31	53	.585	49	1.3	16	0.4	18	3	191	4.9
1982-1983	LOS ANGELES	39	69	163	.423	17	23	.739	53	1.4	26	0.7	11	5	156	4.0
1983-1984	LOS ANGELES	77	347	584	.594	61	113	.540	193	2.5	81	1.1	49	6	757	9.8
1984-1985	LOS ANGELES	76	329	612	.538	94	160	.588	165	2.2	71	0.9	39	7	774	10.2
1985-1986	LOS ANGELES	71	252	544	.463	42	64	.656	140	2.0	83	1.2	53	7	587	8.3
1986-1987	ATLANTA	76	311	677	.459	80	137	.584	159	2.1	149	2.0	61	2	788	10.4
1987-1988	ATLANTA.-SAC.	48	223	530	.421	76	102	.745	128	2.7	71	1.5	52	6	575	12.0
1988-1989	NEW JERSEY	80	434	917	.473	77	144	.535	189	2.4	116	1.5	80	12	1038	13.0
1989-1990	PHOENIX	14	42	87	.483	10	21	.476	36	2.6	16	1.1	8	1	102	7.3
NBA CAREER TOTALS		520	2087	4286	.487	488	817	.597	1112	2.1	629	1.2	371	49	4968	9.6
NBA PLAYOFF TOTALS		68	201	400	.503	63	103	.612	109	1.6	55	0.8	23	3	486	7.1

Height	6-5
Weight	205
Born	7-29-59
College	Michigan

McGill, Bill

SEASON	TEAM	G	FGM	FGA	PCT	FTM	FTA	PCT	REB	RPG	AST	APG	STL	BLK	PTS	PPG
1962-1963	CHICAGO	60	181	353	.513	80	119	.672	161	2.7	38	0.6	N/A	N/A	442	7.4
1963-1964	BALT.-N.Y.	74	456	937	.487	204	282	.723	414	5.6	121	1.6	N/A	N/A	1116	15.1
1964-1965	ST. L.-L.A.	24	21	65	.323	13	017	.765	36	1.5	9	0.4	N/A	N/A	55	2.3
1968-1969	DENVER (A)	78	411	745	.552	180	264	.682	460	5.9	102	1.3	N/A	N/A	1002	12.8
1969-1970	PITT.-L.A.-DALLAS (A)	59	201	369	.545	77	108	.713	215	3.6	60	1.0	N/A	N/A	479	8.1
NBA CAREER TOTALS		158	658	1355	.486	297	418	.711	611	3.9	168	1.1	N/A	N/A	1613	10.2
NBA PLAYOFF TOTALS		5	5	9	.556	1	1	1.000	9	1.8	2	0.4	N/A	N/A	11	2.2

Height	6-9
Weight	225
Born	9-16-39
College	Utah

McKenna, Kevin Robert

SEASON	TEAM	G	FGM	FGA	PCT	FTM	FTA	PCT	REB	RPG	AST	APG	STL	BLK	PTS	PPG
1981-1982	LOS ANGELES	36	28	87	.322	11	17	.647	29	0.8	14	0.4	10	2	67	1.9
1983-1984	INDIANA	61	152	371	.410	80	98	.816	95	1.6	114	1.9	46	5	387	6.3
1984-1985	NEW JERSEY	29	61	134	.455	38	43	.884	49	1.7	58	2.0	30	7	165	5.7
1985-1986	WASHINGTON	30	61	166	.367	25	30	.833	36	1.2	23	0.8	29	2	174	5.8
1986-1987	NEW JERSEY	56	153	337	.454	43	57	.754	77	1.4	93	1.7	54	7	401	7.2
1987-1988	NEW JERSEY	31	43	109	.394	24	25	.960	31	1.0	40	1.3	15	2	126	4.1
NBA CAREER TOTALS		243	498	1204	.414	221	270	.819	317	1.3	342	1.4	184	25	1320	5.4
NBA PLAYOFF TOTALS		1	0	0	N/A	0	0	N/A	0	0.0	N/A	0.0	0	0	0	0.0

Height	6-5
Weight	195
Born	1-8-59
College	Creighton

McMillian, James M.

SEASON	TEAM	G	FGM	FGA	PCT	FTM	FTA	PCT	REB	RPG	AST	APG	STL	BLK	PTS	PPG
1970-1971	LOS ANGELES	81	289	629	.459	100	130	.769	330	4.1	133	1.6	N/A	N/A	678	8.4
1971-1972	LOS ANGELES	80	642	1331	.482	219	277	.791	522	6.5	209	2.6	N/A	N/A	1503	18.8
1972-1973	LOS ANGELES	81	655	1431	.458	223	264	.845	447	5.5	221	2.7	N/A	N/A	1533	18.9
1973-1974	BUFFALO	82	600	1214	.494	325	379	.858	610	7.4	256	3.1	129	26	1525	18.6
1974-1975	BUFFALO	62	347	695	.499	194	231	.840	385	6.2	156	2.5	69	15	888	14.3
1975-1976	BUFFALO	74	492	918	.536	188	219	.858	390	5.3	205	2.8	88	14	1172	15.8
1976-1977	NEW YORK	67	298	642	.464	67	86	.779	307	4.6	139	2.1	63	5	663	9.9
1977-1978	NEW YORK	81	288	623	.462	115	134	.858	289	3.6	205	2.5	76	17	691	8.5
1978-1979	PORTLAND	23	33	74	.446	17	21	.810	39	1.7	33	1.4	10	3	83	3.6
NBA CAREER TOTALS		631	3644	7557	.482	1448	1741	.832	3319	5.3	1557	2.5	435	80	8736	13.8
NBA PLAYOFF TOTALS		72	497	1101	.451	200	253	.791	377	5.2	137	1.9	36	7	1194	16.6

Height	6-5
Weight	225
Born	3-11-48
College	Columbia

McNamara, Mark Robert

SEASON	TEAM	G	FGM	FGA	PCT.	FTM	FTA	PCT	REB	RPG	AST	APG	STL	BLK	PTS	PPG
1982-1983	PHILADELPHIA	36	29	64	.453	20	45	.444	76	2.1	7	0.2	3	3	78	2.2
1983-1984	SAN ANTONIO	70	157	253	.621	74	157	.471	317	4.5	31	0.4	14	12	388	5.5
1984-1985	S.A.-K.C.	45	40	76	.526	32	62	.516	74	1.6	6	0.1	7	8	112	2.5
1986-1987	PHILADELPHIA	11	14	30	.467	7	19	.368	36	3.3	2	0.2	1	0	35	3.2
1987-1988	PHILADELPHIA	42	52	133	.391	48	66	.727	157	3.7	18	0.4	4	12	152	3.6
1988-1989	LOS ANGELES	39	32	64	.500	49	78	.628	100	2.6	10	0.3	4	3	113	2.9
1989-1990	LOS ANGELES	33	38	86	.442	26	40	.650	63	1.9	3	0.1	2	1	102	3.1
1990-1991	ORLANDO	2	0	1	.000	0	0	N/A	4	2.0	0	0.0	0	0	0	0.0
NBA CAREER TOTALS		278	362	707	.512	256	467	.548	827	3.0	77	0.3	35	39	980	3.5
NBA PLAYOFF TOTALS		8	5	9	.566	1	2	.500	4	0.5	N/A	0.0	0	0	11	1.4

Height	6-11
Weight	235
Born	6-8-59
College	Sta Clara

McNeill, Robert J.

SEASON	TEAM	G	FGM	FGA	PCT	FTM	FTA	PCT	REB	RPG	AST	APG	STL	BLK	PTS	PPG
1960-1961	NEW YORK	75	166	427	.389	105	126	.833	123	1.6	238	3.2	N/A	N/A	437	5.8
1961-1962	PHIL.-L.A.	50	56	136	.412	26	34	.765	56	1.1	89	1.8	N/A	N/A	138	2.8
NBA CAREER TOTALS		125	222	563	.394	131	160	.819	179	1.4	327	2.6	N/A	N/A	575	4.6
NBA PLAYOFF TOTALS		5	4	7	.571	1	2	.500	6	1.2	5	1.0	N/A	N/A	9	1.8

Height	6-1
Weight	180
Born	10-22-38
College	St. Joseph's

Meely, Cliff

SEASON	TEAM	G	FGM	FGA	PCT	FTM	FTA	PCT	REB	RPG	AST	APG	STL	BLK	PTS	PPG
1971-1972	HOUSTON	77	315	776	.406	133	197	.675	507	6.6	119	1.5	N/A	N/A	763	9.9
1972-1973	HOUSTON	82	268	657	.408	92	137	.672	496	6.0	91	1.1	N/A	N/A	628	7.7
1973-1974	HOUSTON	77	330	773	.427	90	140	.643	439	5.7	124	1.6	53	77	750	9.7
1974-1975	HOUSTON	48	156	349	.447	68	94	.723	164	3.4	45	0.9	21	21	380	7.9
1975-1976	HOUSTON-L.A.	34	52	132	.394	33	48	.688	97	2.9	19	0.6	14	8	137	4.0
NBA CAREER TOTALS		318	1121	2687	.417	416	616	.675	1703	5.4	398	1.3	88	106	2658	8.4

Height	7-2
Weight	302
Born	12-8-55
College	Mich St

Mikan, George Lawrence Jr.

SEASON	TEAM	G	FGM	FGA	PCT	FTM	FTA	PCT	REB	RPG	AST	APG	STL	BLK	PTS	PPG
1946-1947	CHICAGO (N)	25	147	N/A	N/A	119	164	.726	N/A	N/A	N/A	N/A	N/A	N/A	413	16.5
1947-1948	MINNEAPOLIS (N)	56	406	N/A	N/A	383	509	.752	N/A	N/A	N/A	N/A	N/A	N/A	1195	21.3
1948-1949	MINNEAPOLIS	60	583	1403	.416	532	689	.772	N/A	N/A	218	3.6	N/A	N/A	1698	28.3
1949-1950	MINNEAPOLIS	68	649	1595	.407	567	728	.779	N/A	N/A	197	2.9	N/A	N/A	1865	27.4
1950-1951	MINNEAPOLIS	68	678	1584	.428	576	717	.803	958	14.1	208	3.1	N/A	N/A	1932	28.4
1951-1952	MINNEAPOLIS	64	545	1414	.385	433	555	.780	866	13.5	194	3.0	N/A	N/A	1523	23.8
1952-1953	MINNEAPOLIS	70	500	1252	.399	442	567	.780	1007	14.4	201	2.9	N/A	N/A	1442	20.6
1953-1954	MINNEAPOLIS	72	441	1160	.380	424	546	.777	1028	14.3	174	2.4	N/A	N/A	1306	18.1
1955-1956	MINNEAPOLIS	37	148	375	.395	94	122	.770	308	8.3	53	1.4	N/A	N/A	390	10.5
NBA CAREER TOTALS		439	3544	8783	.404	3068	3924	.782	4167	13.4	1245	2.8	N/A	N/A	10156	23.1
NBA PLAYOFF TOTALS		70	563	1394	.404	554	705	.786	665	13.9	155	2.2	N/A	N/A	1680	24.0

Height	6-10
Weight	245
Born	6-18-24
College	DePaul

Mikkelsen, Arild Verner

| | Height | 6-7 |
| College | Hamline |

Height	6-7
Weight	230
Born	10-21-28
College	Hamline

SEASON	TEAM	G	FGM	FGA	PCT.	FTM	FTA	PCT	REB	RPG	AST	APG	STL	BLK	PTS	PPG
1949-1950	MINNEAPOLIS	68	288	722	.399	215	286	.752	N/A	N/A	123	1.8	N/A	N/A	791	11.6
1950-1951	MINNEAPOLIS	64	359	893	.402	186	275	.676	655	10.2	181	2.8	N/A	N/A	904	14.1
1951-1952	MINNEAPOLIS	66	363	866	.419	283	372	.761	681	10.3	180	2.7	N/A	N/A	1009	15.3
1952-1953	MINNEAPOLIS	70	378	868	.435	291	387	.752	654	9.3	148	2.1	N/A	N/A	1047	15.0
1953-1954	MINNEAPOLIS	72	288	771	.374	221	298	.742	615	8.5	119	1.7	N/A	N/A	797	11.1
1954-1955	MINNEAPOLIS	71	440	1043	.422	447	598	.747	722	10.2	145	2.0	N/A	N/A	1327	18.7
1955-1956	MINNEAPOLIS	72	317	821	.386	328	408	.804	608	8.4	173	2.4	N/A	N/A	962	13.4
1956-1957	MINNEAPOLIS	72	322	854	.377	342	424	.807	630	8.8	121	1.7	N/A	N/A	986	13.7
1957-1958	MINNEAPOLIS	72	439	1070	.410	370	471	.786	805	11.2	166	2.3	N/A	N/A	1248	17.3
1958-1959	MINNEAPOLIS	72	353	904	.390	286	355	.806	570	7.9	159	2.2	N/A	N/A	992	13.8
NBA CAREER TOTALS		699	3547	8812	.403	2969	3874	.766	5940	9.4	1515	2.2	N/A	N/A	10063	14.4
NBA PLAYOFF TOTALS		85	396	999	.396	349	446	.783	585	8.0	152	1.8	N/A	N/A	1141	13.4

Miller, Anthony

Height	6-9
Weight	255
Born	10-22-71
College	Mich St

SEASON	TEAM	G	FGM	FGA	PCT	FTM	FTA	PCT	REB	RPG	AST	APG	STL	BLK	PTS	PPG
1994-1995	LOS ANGELES	46	70	132	.530	47	76	.618	152	3.3	35	0.8	20	7	189	4.1
1995-1996	LOS ANGELES	27	15	35	.429	6	10	.600	25	0.9	4	0.1	4	1	36	1.3
1996-1997	ATLANTA	1	0	5	.000	0	0	N/A	7	7.0	0	0.0	0	0	0	0.0
1997-1998	ATLANTA	37	29	52	.558	21	39	.538	70	1.9	3	0.8	15	3	79	2.1
NBA CAREER TOTALS		111	114	224	.509	74	125	.592	254	2.3	42	0.4	24	39	304	2.7
NBA PLAYOFF TOTALS		8	3	10	.333	2	2	1.000	15	1.9	2	0.3	3	1	8	1.0

Mix, Steven Charles

Height	6-7
Weight	215
Born	12-30-47
College	Toledo

SEASON	TEAM	G	FGM	FGA	PCT	FTM	FTA	PCT	REB	RPG	AST	APG	STL	BLK	PTS	PPG
1969-1970	DETROIT	18	48	100	.480	23	39	.590	64	3.6	15	0.8	N/A	N/A	119	6.6
1970-1971	DETROIT	35	111	249	.446	68	89	.764	164	4.7	34	1.0	N/A	N/A	290	8.3
1971-1972	DETROIT	8	15	47	.319	7	12	.583	23	2.9	4	0.5	N/A	N/A	37	4.6
1973-1974	PHILADELPHIA	82	495	1042	.475	228	288	.792	864	10.5	152	1.9	212	37	1218	14.9
1974-1975	PHILADELPHIA	46	280	582	.481	159	205	.776	500	10.9	99	2.2	79	21	719	15.6
1975-1976	PHILADELPHIA	81	421	844	.499	287	351	.818	662	8.2	216	2.7	158	29	1129	13.9
1976-1977	PHILADELPHIA	75	288	551	.523	215	263	.817	376	5.0	152	2.0	90	20	791	10.5
1977-1978	PHILADELPHIA	82	291	560	.520	175	220	.795	297	3.6	174	2.1	87	3	757	9.2
1978-1979	PHILADELPHIA	74	265	493	.538	161	201	.801	293	4.0	121	1.6	57	16	691	9.3
1979-1980	PHILADELPHIA	81	363	703	.516	207	249	.831	290	3.6	149	1.8	67	9	937	11.6
1980-1981	PHILADELPHIA	72	288	575	.501	200	240	.833	264	3.7	114	1.6	59	18	776	10.8
1981-1982	PHILADELPHIA	75	202	399	.506	136	172	.791	225	3.0	93	1.2	42	17	541	7.2
1982-1983	MILW.-L.A.	58	137	283	.484	75	88	.852	137	2.4	70	1.2	33	3	350	6.0
NBA CAREER TOTALS		787	3204	6428	.498	1941	2417	.803	4159	5.3	1393	1.8	884	173	8355	10.6
NBA PLAYOFF TOTALS		89	244	494	.494	153	177	.864	248	2.8	137	1.5	65	13	642	7.2

Mueller, Erwin L.

SEASON	TEAM	G	FGM	FGA	PCT	FTM	FTA	PCT	REB	RPG	AST	APG	STL	BLK	PTS	PPG
1966-1967	CHICAGO	80	422	957	.441	171	260	.658	497	6.2	131	1.6	N/A	N/A	1015	12.7
1967-1968	CHICAGO-L.A.	74	223	489	.456	107	185	.578	389	5.3	154	2.1	N/A	N/A	553	7.5
1968-1969	CHICAGO-SEATTLE	78	144	384	.375	89	162	.549	297	3.8	186	2.4	N/A	N/A	377	4.8
1969-1970	SEATTLE-DETROIT	78	300	646	.464	189	263	.719	483	6.2	205	2.6	STL	N/A	789	10.1
1970-1971	DETROIT	52	126	309	.408	60	108	.556	223	4.3	113	2.2	N/A	N/A	312	6.0
1971-1972	DETROIT	42	68	197	.345	43	74	.581	147	3.5	57	1.4	N/A	N/A	179	4.3
1972-1973	DETROIT	21	9	31	.290	5	7	.714	14	0.7	7	0.3	N/A	N/A	23	1.1
NBA CAREER TOTALS		425	1292	3013	.429	664	1059	.627	2050	4.8	853	2.0	N/A	N/A	3248	7.6
NBA PLAYOFF TOTALS		17	28	85	.329	15	28	.536	68	4.0	27	1.6	N/A	N/A	71	4.2

Height	6-8
Weight	230
Born	3-12-44
Coll	San Francisco

Murphy, Allen

SEASON	TEAM	G	FGM	FGA	PCT	FTM	FTA	PCT	REB	RPG	AST	APG	STL	BLK	PTS	PPG
1976-1977	LOS ANGELES	2	1	5	.200	3	7	.429	4	2.0	0	0.0	0	0	5	2.5
NBA CAREER TOTALS		2	1	5	.200	3	7	.429	4	2.0	0	0	0	0	5	2.5

Height	6-5
Weight	190
Born	7-15-52
College	Louisville

Nash, Charles Francis

SEASON	TEAM	G	FGM	FGA	PCT	FTM	FTA	PCT	REB	RPG	AST	APG	STL	BLK	PTS	PPG
1964-1965	L.A.-S.F.	45	47	145	.324	43	52	.827	83	1.8	19	0.4	N/A	N/A	137	3.0
1967-1968	KENTUCKY (A)	39	106	305	.348	121	162	.747	190	4.9	46	1.2	N/A	N/A	333	8.5
NBA CAREER TOTALS		45	47	145	.324	43	52	.827	83	1.8	19	0.4	N/A	N/A	137	3.0
NBA PLAYOFF TOTALS		39	106	305	.348	121	162	.747	190	4.9	46	1.2	N/A	N/A	333	8.5

Height	6-6
Weight	220
Born	7-24-42
College	Kentucky

Nater, Swen Eric

SEASON	TEAM	G	FGM	FGA	PCT	FTM	FTA	PCT	REB	RPG	AST	APG	STL	BLK	PTS	PPG
1973-1974	VIR.-S.A. (A)	79	467	846	.552	180	254	.709	998	12.6	129	1.6	32	63	1114	14.1
1974-1975	SAN ANTONIO (A)	78	495	914	.542	185	246	.752	1279	16.4	97	1.2	43	87	1175	15.1
1975-1976	N.Y.-VIR. (A)	76	320	651	.492	108	155	.697	766	10.1	55	0.7	31	51	748	9.8
1976-1977	MILWAUKEE	72	383	725	.528	172	228	.754	865	12.0	108	1.5	54	51	938	13.0
1977-1978	BUFFALO	78	501	994	.504	208	272	.765	1029	13.2	216	2.8	40	47	1210	15.5
1978-1979	SAN DIEGO	79	357	627	.569	132	165	.800	701	8.9	140	1.8	38	29	846	10.7
1979-1980	SAN DIEGO	81	443	799	.554	196	273	.718	1216	15.0	233	2.9	45	37	1082	13.4
1980-1981	SAN DIEGO	82	517	935	.553	244	307	.795	1017	12.4	199	2.4	49	46	1278	15.6
1981-1982	SAN DIEGO	21	101	175	.577	59	79	.747	192	9.1	30	1.4	6	9	262	12.5
1982-1983	SAN DIEGO	7	6	20	.300	4	4	1.000	13	1.9	1	0.1	1	0	16	2.3
1983-1984	LOS ANGELES	69	124	253	.490	63	91	.692	264	3.8	27	0.4	25	7	311	4.5
NBA CAREER TOTALS		489	2432	4528	.537	1078	1419	.760	5297	10.8	954	2.0	258	226	5943	12.2
NBA PLAYOFF TOTALS		17	19	38	.500	20	26	.769	40	2.4	1	0.1	1	2	58	3.4

Height	6-11
Weight	250
Born	1-14-50
College	UCLA

Nelson, Donald Arvid

Height	6-6
Weight	210
Born	5-15-40
College	Iowa

SEASON	TEAM	G	FGM	FGA	PCT	FTM	FTA	PCT	REB	RPG	AST	APG	STL	BLK	PTS	PPG
1962-1963	CHICAGO	62	129	293	.440	161	221	.729	279	4.5	72	1.2	N/A	N/A	419	6.8
1963-1964	LOS ANGELES	80	135	323	.418	149	201	.741	323	4.0	76	1.0	N/A	N/A	419	5.2
1964-1965	LOS ANGELES	39	36	85	.424	20	26	.769	73	1.9	24	0.6	N/A	N/A	92	2.4
1965-1966	BOSTON	75	271	618	.439	223	326	.684	403	5.4	79	1.1	N/A	N/A	765	10.2
1966-1967	BOSTON	79	227	509	.446	141	190	.742	295	3.7	65	0.8	N/A	N/A	595	7.5
1967-1968	BOSTON	82	312	632	.494	195	268	.728	431	5.3	103	1.3	N/A	N/A	819	10.0
1968-1969	BOSTON	82	374	771	.485	201	259	.776	458	5.6	92	1.1	N/A	N/A	949	11.6
1969-1970	BOSTON	82	461	920	.501	337	435	.775	601	7.3	148	1.8	N/A	N/A	1259	15.4
1970-1971	BOSTON	82	412	881	.468	317	426	.744	565	6.9	153	1.9	N/A	N/A	1141	13.9
1971-1972	BOSTON	82	389	811	.480	356	452	.788	453	5.5	192	2.3	N/A	N/A	1134	13.8
1972-1973	BOSTON	72	309	649	.476	159	188	.846	315	4.4	102	1.4	N/A	N/A	777	10.8
1973-1974	BOSTON	82	364	717	.508	215	273	.788	345	4.2	162	2.0	19	13	943	11.5
1974-1975	BOSTON	79	423	785	.539	263	318	.827	469	5.9	181	2.3	32	15	1109	14.0
1975-1976	BOSTON	75	175	379	.462	127	161	.789	182	2.4	77	1.0	14	7	477	6.4
NBA CAREER TOTALS		1053	4017	8373	.480	2864	3744	.765	5192	4.9	1526	1.4	65	35	10898	10.3
NBA PLAYOFF TOTALS		150	585	1175	.498	407	498	.817	719	4.8	210	1.4	13	7	1577	10.5

Neumann, Johnny

Height	6-6
Weight	200
Born	9-11-51
College	Mississippi

SEASON	TEAM	G	FGM	FGA	PCT	FTM	FTA	PCT	REB	RPG	AST	APG	STL	BLK	PTS	PPG
1971-1972	MEMPHIS (A)	77	545	1328	.410	293	385	.761	322	4.2	147	1.9	N/A	N/A	1409	18.3
1972-1973	MEMPHIS (A)	79	605	1283	.472	329	423	.778	310	3.9	470	5.9	N/A	N/A	1548	19.6
1973-1974	MEMPHIS-UTAH (A)	87	482	1070	.450	166	215	.772	226	2.6	254	2.9	95	26	1148	13.2
1974-1975	VIR.-INDIANA (A)	52	186	445	.418	52	75	.693	89	1.7	135	2.6	26	11	445	8.6
1975-1976	VIR.-KEN. (A)	77	393	949	.414	151	189	.799	201	2.6	171	2.2	68	26	1008	13.1
1976-1977	BUFFALO-L.A.	63	161	397	.406	59	87	.678	72	1.1	141	2.2	31	10	381	6.0
1977-1978	INDIANA	20	35	86	.407	13	18	.722	14	0.7	27	1.4	6	1	83	4.2
NBA CAREER TOTALS		83	196	483	.406	72	105	.686	86	1.0	168	2.0	37	11	464	5.6
NBA PLAYOFF TOTALS		6	11	29	.379	2	4	.500	2	0.3	9	1.5	3	2	24	4.0

Nevitt, Charles Goodrich

Height	7-5
Weight	250
Born	6-13-59
College	N Carolina St

SEASON	TEAM	G	FGM	FGA	PCT	FTM	FTA	PCT	REB	RPG	AST	APG	STL	BLK	PTS	PPG
1982-1983	HOUSTON	6	11	15	.733	1	4	.250	17	2.8	0	0.0	1	12	23	3.8
1984-1985	LOS ANGELES	11	5	17	.294	2	8	.250	20	1.8	3	0.3	0	15	12	1.1
1985-1986	L.A.-DETROIT	29	15	43	.349	19	26	.731	32	1.1	7	0.2	4	19	49	1.7
1986-1987	DETROIT	41	31	63	.492	14	24	.583	83	2.0	4	0.1	7	30	76	1.9
1987-1988	DETROIT	17	7	21	.333	3	6	.500	18	1.1	0	0.0	1	5	17	1.0
1988-1989	HOUSTON	43	27	62	.435	11	16	.688	64	1.5	3	0.1	5	29	65	1.5
1989-1990	HOUSTON	3	2	2	1.000	0	0	N/A	3	1.0	1	0.3	0	1	4	1.3
1991-1992	CHICAGO	4	1	3	.333	0	0	N/A	1	0.3	1	0.3	0	0	2	0.5
1993-1994	SAN ANTONIO	1	0	0	N/A	3	6	.500	1	1.0	0	0.0	0	0	3	3.0
NBA CAREER TOTALS		155	99	226	.438	53	90	.589	239	1.5	19	0.1	18	111	251	1.6
NBA PLAYOFF TOTALS		16	5	16	.313	6	10	.600	16	1.0	1	0.1	4	9	16	1.0

Nixon, Norman Ellard

SEASON	TEAM	G	FGM	FGA	PCT	FTM	FTA	PCT	REB	RPG	AST	APG	STL	BLK	PTS	PPG
1977-1978	LOS ANGELES	81	496	998	.497	115	161	.714	239	3.0	553	6.8	138	7	1107	13.7
1978-1979	LOS ANGELES	82	623	1149	.542	158	204	.775	231	2.8	737	9.0	201	17	1404	17.1
1979-1980	LOS ANGELES	82	624	1209	.516	197	253	.779	229	2.8	642	7.8	147	14	1446	17.6
1980-1981	LOS ANGELES	79	576	1210	.476	196	252	.778	232	2.9	696	8.8	146	11	1350	17.1
1981-1982	LOS ANGELES	82	628	1274	.493	181	224	.808	176	2.1	652	8.0	132	7	1440	17.6
1982-1983	LOS ANGELES	79	533	1123	.475	125	168	.744	205	2.6	566	7.2	104	4	1191	15.1
1983-1984	SAN DIEGO	82	587	1270	.462	206	271	.760	203	2.5	914	11.1	94	4	1391	17.0
1984-1985	CLIPPERS	81	596	1281	.465	170	218	.780	218	2.7	711	8.8	95	4	1395	17.2
1985-1986	CLIPPERS	67	403	921	.438	131	162	.809	180	2.7	576	8.6	84	3	979	14.6
1988-1989	CLIPPERS	53	153	370	.414	48	65	.738	78	1.5	339	6.4	46	0	362	6.8
NBA CAREER TOTALS		768	5219	10805	.483	1527	1978	.772	1991	2.6	6386	8.3	1187	71	12065	15.7
NBA PLAYOFF TOTALS		58	440	921	.478	142	186	.763	195	3.4	465	8.0	89	8	1027	17.7

Height	6-2
Weight	175
Born	10-11-55
College	Duquesne

O'Neal, Shaquille

SEASON	TEAM	G	FGM	FGA	PCT	FTM	FTA	PCT	REB	RPG	AST	APG	STL	BLK	PTS	PPG
1992-1993	ORLANDO	81	733	1304	.562	427	721	.592	1122	13.9	152	1.9	60	286	1893	23.4
1993-1994	ORLANDO	81	953	1591	.599	471	850	.554	1072	13.2	195	2.4	76	231	2377	29.3
1994-1995	ORLANDO	79	930	1594	.583	455	854	.533	901	11.4	214	2.7	73	192	2315	29.3
1995-1996	ORLANDO	54	592	1033	.573	249	511	.487	596	11.0	155	2.9	34	115	1434	26.6
1996-1997	LOS ANGELES	51	552	991	.557	232	479	.484	640	12.5	159	3.1	46	147	1336	26.2
1997-1998	LOS ANGELES	60	670	1147	.584	359	681	.527	681	11.3	142	2.4	39	144	1699	28.3
NBA CAREER TOTALS		406	4430	7660	.578	2193	4096	.535	5012	12.3	1017	2.5	328	1115	11034	27.2
NBA PLAYOFF TOTALS		58	596	1030	.579	357	681	.524	637	11.0	199	3.4	41	115	1549	26.7

Height	7-1
Weight	315
Born	3-6-72
College	Louisiana St

Oldham, Jawann

SEASON	TEAM	G	FGM	FGA	PCT	FTM	FTA	PCT	REB	RPG	AST	APG	STL	BLK	PTS	PPG
1980-1981	DENVER	4	2	6	.333	0	0	N/A	5	1.3	0	0.0	0	2	4	1.0
1981-1982	HOUSTON	22	13	36	.361	8	14	.571	24	1.1	3	0.1	2	10	34	1.5
1982-1983	CHICAGO	16	31	58	.534	12	22	.545	47	2.9	5	0.3	5	13	74	4.6
1983-1984	CHICAGO	64	110	218	.505	39	66	.591	233	3.6	33	0.5	15	76	259	4.0
1984-1985	CHICAGO	63	89	192	.464	34	50	.680	236	3.7	31	0.5	11	127	212	3.4
1985-1986	CHICAGO	52	167	323	.517	53	91	.582	306	5.9	37	0.7	28	134	387	7.4
1986-1987	NEW YORK	44	71	174	.408	31	57	.544	179	4.1	19	0.4	22	71	173	3.9
1987-1988	SACRAMENTO	54	119	250	.476	59	87	.678	304	5.6	33	0.6	12	110	297	5.5
1989-1990	ORLANDO-L.A.	6	3	6	.500	3	7	.429	16	2.7	1	0.2	2	3	9	1.5
1990-1991	INDIANA	4	3	6	.500	0	0	N/A	3	0.8	0	0.0	0	0	6	1.5
NBA CAREER TOTALS		329	608	1269	.479	239	394	.607	1353	4.1	162	0.5	97	546	1455	4.4
NBA PLAYOFF TOTALS		5	7	16	.438	0	0	N/A	24	4.8	3	0.6	6	7	14	2.8

Height	7-0
Weight	220
Born	7-4-57
College	Seattle

Owens, Keith Kensel

SEASON	TEAM	G	FGM	FGA	PCT	FTM	FTA	PCT	REB	RPG	AST	APG	STL	BLK	PTS	PPG
1991-1992	LOS ANGELES	20	9	32	.281	8	10	.800	15	0.8	3	0.2	5	4	26	1.3
NBA CAREER TOTALS		20	9	32	.281	8	10	.800	15	0.8	3	0.2	5	4	26	1.3

Height	6-7
Weight	225
Born	5-31-69
College	UCLA

Patrick, Myles

SEASON	TEAM	G	FGM	FGA	PCT	FTM	FTA	PCT	REB	RPG	AST	APG	STL	BLK	PTS	PPG
1980-1981	LOS ANGELES	3	2	5	.400	1	2	.500	2	0.7	1	0.3	0	0	5	1.7
NBA CAREER TOTALS		3	2	5	.400	1	2	.500	2	0.7	1	0.3	0	0	5	1.7

Height	6-8
Weight	220
Born	11-16-54
College	Auburn

Peeler, Anthony Eugene

SEASON	TEAM	G	FGM	FGA	PCT	FTM	FTA	PCT	REB	RPG	AST	APG	STL	BLK	PTS	PPG
1992-1993	LOS ANGELES	77	297	634	.468	162	206	.786	179	2.3	166	2.2	60	14	802	10.4
1993-1994	LOS ANGELES	30	176	409	.430	57	71	.803	109	3.6	94	3.1	43	8	423	14.1
1994-1995	LOS ANGELES	73	285	659	.432	102	128	.797	168	2.3	122	1.7	52	13	756	10.4
1995-1996	LOS ANGELES	73	272	602	.452	61	86	.709	137	1.9	118	1.6	59	10	710	9.7
1996-1997	VANCOUVER	72	402	1011	.398	109	133	.820	247	3.4	256	3.6	105	17	1041	14.5
1997-1998	VANCOUVER-MINN.	38	190	420	.452	36	47	.766	123	3.2	137	3.6	61	6	469	12.3
NBA CAREER TOTALS		363	1622	3735	.434	527	671	.785	963	2.6	893	2.5	380	68	4201	11.6
NBA PLAYOFF TOTALS		18	72	183	.393	25	30	.833	74	4.1	46	2.5	26	5	198	11.0

Height	6-4
Weight	215
Born	11-25-69
College	Missouri

Perkins, Samuel Bruce

SEASON	TEAM	G	FGM	FGA	PCT	FTM	FTA	PCT	REB	RPG	AST	APG	STL	BLK	PTS	PPG
1984-1985	DALLAS	82	347	736	.471	200	244	.820	605	7.4	135	1.6	63	63	903	11.0
1985-1986	DALLAS	80	458	910	.503	307	377	.814	685	8.6	153	1.9	75	94	1234	15.4
1986-1987	DALLAS	80	461	957	.482	245	296	.828	616	7.7	146	1.8	109	77	1186	14.8
1987-1988	DALLAS	75	394	876	.450	273	332	.822	601	8.0	118	1.6	74	54	1066	14.2
1988-1989	DALLAS	78	445	959	.464	274	329	.833	688	8.8	127	1.6	76	92	1171	15.0
1989-1990	DALLAS	76	435	883	.493	330	424	.778	572	7.5	175	2.3	88	64	1206	15.9
1990-1991	LOS ANGELES	73	368	744	.495	229	279	.821	538	7.4	108	1.5	64	78	983	13.5
1991-1992	LOS ANGELES	63	361	803	.450	304	372	.817	556	8.8	141	2.2	64	62	1041	16.5
1992-1993	LAKERS-SEATTLE	79	381	799	.477	250	305	.820	524	6.6	156	2.0	60	82	1036	13.1
1993-1994	SEATTLE	81	341	779	.438	218	272	.801	366	4.5	111	1.4	67	31	999	12.3
1994-1995	SEATTLE	82	346	742	.466	215	269	.799	398	4.9	135	1.6	72	45	1043	12.7
1995-1996	SEATTLE	82	325	797	.408	191	241	.793	367	4.5	120	1.5	83	48	970	11.8
1996-1997	SEATTLE	81	290	661	.439	187	229	.817	300	3.7	103	1.3	69	49	889	11.0
1997-1998	SEATTLE	81	196	471	.416	101	128	.789	255	3.1	113	1.4	62	29	580	7.2
NBA CAREER TOTALS		1093	5148	11117	.463	3324	4097	.811	7071	6.5	1841	1.7	1026	868	14307	13.1
NBA PLAYOFF TOTALS		123	592	1309	.452	364	462	.787	821	6.7	225	1.8	112	113	1657	13.5

Height	6-9
Weight	255
Born	6-14-61
College	N Carolina

Price, James E.

SEASON	TEAM	G	FGM	FGA	PCT	FTM	FTA	PCT	REB	RPG	AST	APG	STL	BLK	PTS	PPG
1972-1973	LOS ANGELES	59	158	359	.440	60	73	.822	115	1.9	97	1.6	N/A	N/A	376	6.4
1973-1974	LOS ANGELES	82	538	1197	.449	187	234	.799	378	4.6	369	4.5	157	29	1263	15.4
1974-1975	L.A.-MILW.	50	317	717	.442	169	194	.871	198	4.0	286	5.7	111	24	803	16.1
1975-1976	MILWAUKEE	80	398	958	.415	141	166	.849	261	3.3	395	4.9	148	32	937	11.7
1976-1977	MILW.-BUFFALO-DENVER	81	253	567	.446	83	103	.806	231	2.9	261	3.2	128	20	589	7.3
1977-1978	DENVER-DETROIT	83	294	656	.448	135	169	.799	260	3.1	260	3.1	114	9	723	8.7
1978-1979	LOS ANGELES	75	171	344	.497	55	79	.696	123	1.6	218	2.9	66	12	397	5.3
NBA CAREER TOTALS		510	2129	4798	.444	830	1018	.815	1566	3.1	1886	3.7	724	126	5088	10.0
NBA PLAYOFF TOTALS		23	59	168	.351	20	32	.625	55	2.4	62	2.7	25	1	138	6.0

Height	6-2
Weight	195
Born	11-27-49
College	Louisville

Rambis, Darrell Kurt

SEASON	TEAM	G	FGM	FGA	PCT	FTM	FTA	PCT	REB	RPG	AST	APG	STL	BLK	PTS	PPG
1981-1982	LOS ANGELES	64	118	228	.518	59	117	.504	348	5.4	56	0.9	60	76	295	4.6
1982-1983	LOS ANGELES	78	235	413	.569	114	166	.687	531	6.8	90	1.2	105	63	584	7.5
1983-1984	LOS ANGELES	47	63	113	.558	42	66	.636	266	5.7	34	0.7	30	14	168	3.6
1984-1985	LOS ANGELES	82	181	327	.554	68	103	.660	528	6.4	69	0.8	82	47	430	5.2
1985-1986	LOS ANGELES	74	160	269	.595	88	122	.721	517	7.0	69	0.9	66	33	408	5.5
1986-1987	LOS ANGELES	78	163	313	.521	120	157	.764	453	5.8	63	0.8	74	41	446	5.7
1987-1988	LOS ANGELES	70	102	186	.548	73	93	.785	268	3.8	54	0.8	39	13	277	4.0
1988-1989	CHARLOTTE	75	325	627	.518	182	248	.734	703	9.4	159	2.1	100	57	832	11.1
1989-1990	CHA.-PHOENIX	74	190	373	.509	82	127	.646	525	7.1	135	1.8	100	37	462	6.2
1990-1991	PHOENIX	62	83	167	.497	60	85	.706	266	4.3	64	1.0	25	11	226	3.6
1991-1992	PHOENIX	28	38	82	.463	14	18	.778	106	3.8	37	1.3	12	14	90	3.2
1992-1993	PHOENIX-SAC.	72	67	129	.519	43	65	.662	227	3.2	53	0.7	43	18	177	2.5
1993-1994	LOS ANGELES	50	59	114	.518	46	71	.648	189	3.8	32	0.6	22	23	164	3.3
NBA CAREER TOTALS		854	1784	3341	.534	991	1438	.689	4927	5.8	915	1.1	758	447	4559	5.3
NBA PLAYOFF TOTALS		139	284	495	.574	151	215	.702	764	5.5	119	0.9	85	68	719	5.2

Height	6-8
Weight	215
Born	2-25-58
College	Santa Clara

Reed, Hubert F.

SEASON	TEAM	G	FGM	FGA	PCT	FTM	FTA	PCT	REB	RPG	AST	APG	STL	BLK	PTS	PPG
1958-1959	ST. LOUIS	65	136	317	.429	53	71	.746	317	4.9	32	0.5	N/A	N/A	325	5.0
1959-1960	ST. LOUIS-CIN.	71	270	601	.449	134	184	.728	614	8.6	69	1.0	N/A	N/A	674	9.5
1960-1961	CINCINATTI	75	156	364	.429	85	122	.697	367	4.9	69	0.9	N/A	N/A	397	5.3
1961-1962	CINCINATTI	80	203	460	.441	60	82	.732	440	5.5	53	0.7	N/A	N/A	466	5.8
1962-1963	CINCINATTI	80	199	427	.466	74	98	.755	398	5.0	83	1.0	N/A	N/A	472	5.9
1963-1964	LOS ANGELES	46	33	91	.363	10	15	.667	107	2.3	23	0.5	N/A	N/A	76	1.7
1964-1965	DETROIT	62	84	221	.380	40	58	.690	206	3.3	38	0.6	N/A	N/A	208	3.4
NBA CAREER TOTALS		479	1081	2481	.436	456	630	.724	2449	5.1	367	0.8	N/A	N/A	2618	5.5
NBA PLAYOFF TOTALS		21	43	106	.406	21	30	.700	103	4.9	16	0.8	N/A	N/A	107	5.1

Height	6-9
Weight	220
Born	10-4-36
College	Oklahoma City

Riley, Patrick James

Height	6-4
Weight	205
Born	3-20-45
College	Kentucky

SEASON	TEAM	G	FGM	FGA	PCT	FTM	FTA	PCT	REB	RPG	AST	APG	STL	BLK	PTS	PPG
1967-1968	SAN DIEGO	80	250	660	.379	128	202	.634	177	2.2	138	1.7	N/A	N/A	628	7.9
1968-1969	SAN DIEGO	56	202	498	.406	90	134	.672	112	2.0	136	2.4	N/A	N/A	494	8.8
1969-1970	SAN DIEGO	36	75	180	.417	40	55	.727	57	1.6	85	2.4	N/A	N/A	190	5.3
1970-1971	LOS ANGELES	54	105	254	.413	56	87	.644	54	1.0	72	1.3	N/A	N/A	266	4.9
1971-1972	LOS ANGELES	67	197	441	.447	55	74	.743	127	1.9	75	1.1	N/A	N/A	449	6.7
1972-1973	LOS ANGELES	55	167	390	.428	65	82	.793	65	1.2	81	1.5	N/A	N/A	399	7.3
1973-1974	LOS ANGELES	72	287	667	.430	110	144	.764	128	1.8	148	2.1	54	3	684	9.5
1974-1975	LOS ANGELES	46	219	523	.419	69	93	.742	85	1.8	121	2.6	36	4	507	11.0
1975-1976	L.A.-PHOENIX	62	117	301	.389	55	77	.714	50	0.8	57	0.9	22	6	289	4.7
NBA CAREER TOTALS		528	1619	3914	.414	668	948	.705	855	1.6	913	1.7	112	13	3906	7.4
NBA PLAYOFF TOTALS		44	111	297	.374	29	38	.763	66	1.5	52	1.2	4	0	251	5.7

Rivers, David Lee

Height	6-0
Weight	175
Born	1-20-65
College	Notre Dame

SEASON	TEAM	G	FGM	FGA	PCT	FTM	FTA	PCT	REB	RPG	AST	APG	STL	BLK	PTS	PPG
1988-1989	LOS ANGELES	47	49	122	.402	35	42	.833	43	0.9	106	2.3	23	9	134	2.9
1989-1990	CLIPPERS	52	80	197	.406	59	78	.756	85	1.6	155	3.0	31	0	219	4.2
1991-1992	CLIPPERS	15	10	30	.333	10	11	.909	19	1.3	21	1.4	7	1	30	2.0
NBA CAREER TOTALS		114	139	349	.398	104	131	.794	147	1.3	282	2.5	61	10	383	3.4
NBA PLAYOFF TOTALS		6	4	12	.333	7	8	.875	4	0.7	6	1.0	0	0	15	2.5

Roberson, Rick

Height	6-9
Weight	235
Born	7-7-47
College	Cincinnati

SEASON	TEAM	G	FGM	FGA	PCT	FTM	FTA	PCT	REB	RPG	AST	APG	STL	BLK	PTS	PPG
1969-1970	LOS ANGELES	74	262	586	.447	120	212	.566	672	9.1	92	1.2	N/A	N/A	644	8.7
1970-1971	LOS ANGELES	65	125	301	.415	88	143	.615	304	4.7	47	0.7	N/A	N/A	338	5.2
1971-1972	CLEVELAND	63	304	688	.442	215	366	.587	801	12.7	109	1.7	N/A	N/A	823	13.1
1972-1973	CLEVELAND	62	307	709	.433	167	290	.576	693	11.2	134	2.2	N/A	N/A	781	12.6
1973-1974	PORTLAND	69	364	797	.457	205	316	.649	701	10.2	133	1.9	65	55	933	13.5
1974-1975	NEW ORLEANS	16	48	108	.444	23	40	.575	118	7.4	23	1.4	7	8	119	7.4
1975-1976	KANSAS CITY	74	73	180	.406	42	103	.408	233	3.1	53	0.7	18	17	188	2.5
NBA CAREER TOTALS		423	1483	3369	.440	860	1470	.585	3522	8.3	591	1.4	90	80	3826	9.0
NBA PLAYOFF TOTALS		18	18	47	.383	10	17	.588	42	2.3	4	0.2	0	0	46	2.6

Roberts, Fred

SEASON	TEAM	G	FGM	FGA	PCT	FTM	FTA	PCT	REB	RPG	AST	APG	STL	BLK	PTS	PPG
1983-1984	SAN ANTONIO	79	214	399	.536	144	172	.837	304	3.8	98	1.2	52	38	573	7.3
1984-1985	S.A.-UTAH	74	208	418	.498	150	182	.824	186	2.5	87	1.2	28	22	567	7.7
1985-1986	UTAH	58	74	167	.443	67	87	.770	80	1.4	27	0.5	8	6	216	3.7
1986-1987	BOSTON	73	139	270	.515	124	153	.810	190	2.6	62	0.8	22	20	402	5.5
1987-1988	BOSTON	74	161	330	.488	128	165	.776	162	2.2	81	1.1	16	15	450	6.1
1988-1989	MILWAUKEE	71	155	319	.486	104	129	.806	209	2.9	66	0.9	36	23	417	5.9
1989-1990	MILWAUKEE	82	330	666	.496	195	249	.783	311	3.8	147	1.8	56	25	857	10.5
1990-1991	MILWAUKEE	82	357	670	.533	170	209	.813	281	3.4	135	1.6	63	29	888	10.8
1991-1992	MILWAUKEE	80	311	645	.482	128	171	.749	257	3.2	122	1.5	52	40	769	9.6
1992-1993	MILWAUKEE	79	226	428	.528	135	169	.799	237	3.0	118	1.5	57	27	599	7.6
1994-1995	CLEVELAND	21	28	72	.389	20	26	.769	34	1.6	8	0.4	6	3	80	3.8
1995-1996	LOS ANGELES	33	48	97	.495	22	28	.786	47	1.4	26	0.8	16	4	122	3.7
1996-1997	DALLAS	12	6	15	.400	10	14	.714	10	0.8	0	0.0	0	1	22	1.8
NBA CAREER TOTALS		818	2257	4496	.502	1397	1754	.796	2308	2.8	977	1.2	412	253	5962	7.3
NBA PLAYOFF TOTALS		67	148	299	.495	111	144	.771	140	2.1	57	0.9	23	12	407	6.1

Height	6-10
Weight	220
Born	8-14-60
College	BYU

Roberts, Marvin James

SEASON	TEAM	G	FGM	FGA	PCT	FTM	FTA	PCT	REB	RPG	AST	APG	STL	BLK	PTS	PPG
1971-1972	DENVER (A)	68	217	533	.407	86	120	.717	294	4.3	61	0.9	N/A	N/A	521	7.7
1972-1973	DENVER (A)	77	374	807	.463	201	255	.788	398	5.2	95	1.2	N/A	N/A	950	12.3
1973-1974	DENVER-CAR. (A)	74	266	598	.445	129	164	.787	371	5.0	119	1.6	47	7	662	8.9
1974-1975	KENTUCKY (A)	83	201	467	.430	127	164	.774	246	3.0	103	1.2	27	4	529	6.4
1975-1976	KEN.-VIR. (A)	72	259	621	.417	107	137	.781	236	3.3	120	1.7	36	8	625	8.7
1976-1977	LOS ANGELES	28	27	76	.355	4	6	.667	25	0.9	19	0.7	4	2	58	2.1
NBA CAREER TOTALS		28	27	76	.355	4	6	.667	25	0.9	19	0.7	4	2	58	2.1

Height	6-8
Weight	220
Born	1-29-50
College	Utah St

Robinson, Clifford Trent

SEASON	TEAM	G	FGM	FGA	PCT	FTM	FTA	PCT	REB	RPG	AST	APG	STL	BLK	PTS	PPG
1979-1980	NEW JERSEY	70	391	833	.469	168	242	.694	506	7.2	98	1.4	61	34	951	13.6
1980-1981	NEW JERSEY	63	525	1070	.491	178	248	.718	481	7.6	105	1.7	58	52	1229	19.5
1981-1982	K.C.-CLEV.	68	518	1143	.453	222	313	.709	609	9.0	120	1.8	88	103	1258	18.5
1982-1983	CLEVELAND	77	587	1230	.477	213	301	.708	856	11.1	145	1.9	61	58	1387	18.0
1983-1984	CLEVELAND	73	533	1185	.450	234	334	.701	753	10.3	185	2.5	51	32	1301	17.8
1984-1985	WASHINGTON	60	422	896	.471	158	213	.742	546	9.1	149	2.5	51	47	1003	16.7
1985-1986	WASHINGTON	78	595	1255	.474	269	353	.762	680	8.7	186	2.4	98	44	1460	18.7
1986-1987	PHILADELPHIA	55	338	729	.464	139	184	.755	307	5.6	89	1.6	86	30	815	14.8
1987-1988	PHILADELPHIA	62	483	1041	.464	210	293	.717	405	6.5	131	2.1	79	39	1178	19.0
1988-1989	PHILADELPHIA	14	90	187	.481	32	44	.727	75	5.4	32	2.3	17	2	212	15.1
1991-1992	LOS ANGELES	9	11	27	.407	7	8	.875	19	2.1	9	1.0	5	0	29	3.2
NBA CAREER TOTALS		629	4493	9596	.468	1830	2533	.722	5237	8.3	1249	2.0	655	441	10823	17.2
NBA PLAYOFF TOTALS		17	104	220	.473	42	66	.636	122	7.2	28	1.6	20	13	250	14.7

Height	6-9
Weight	220
Born	3-13-60
College	USC

Robinson, Flynn James

Height	6-1
Weight	190
Born	4-28-41
College	Wyoming

SEASON	TEAM	G	FGM	FGA	PCT	FTM	FTA	PCT	REB	RPG	AST	APG	STL	BLK	PTS	PPG
1966-1967	CINCINNATI	76	274	599	.457	120	154	.779	133	1.8	110	1.4	N/A	N/A	668	8.8
1967-1968	CIN.-CHICAGO	75	444	1010	.440	288	351	.821	272	3.6	219	2.9	N/A	N/A	1176	15.7
1968-1969	CHICAGO-MILW.	83	625	1442	.433	412	491	.839	306	3.7	377	4.5	N/A	N/A	1662	20.0
1969-1970	MILWAUKEE	81	663	1391	.477	439	489	.898	263	3.2	449	5.5	N/A	N/A	1765	21.8
1970-1971	CINCINATTI	71	374	817	.458	195	228	.855	143	2.0	138	1.9	N/A	N/A	943	13.3
1971-1972	LOS ANGELES	64	262	535	.490	111	129	.860	115	1.8	138	2.2	N/A	N/A	635	9.9
1972-1973	L.A.-BALT.	44	133	288	.462	32	39	.821	62	1.4	85	1.9	N/A	N/A	298	6.8
1973-1974	SAN DIEGO (A)	49	185	405	.457	52	68	.765	78	1.6	112	2.3	23	2	430	8.8
NBA CAREER TOTALS		494	2775	6082	.456	1597	1881	.849	1294	2.6	1516	3.1	23	2	7147	14.5
NBA PLAYOFF TOTALS		27	129	318	.406	70	88	.795	54	2.0	76	2.8	N/A	N/A	328	12.1

Robinson, Rumeal

Height	6-2
Weight	195
Born	11-13-66
College	Michigan

SEASON	TEAM	G	FGM	FGA	PCT	FTM	FTA	PCT	REB	RPG	AST	APG	STL	BLK	PTS	PPG
1990-1991	ATLANTA	47	108	242	.446	47	80	.588	71	1.5	132	2.8	32	8	265	5.6
1991-1992	ATLANTA	81	423	928	.456	175	275	.636	219	2.7	446	5.5	105	24	1055	13.0
1992-1993	NEW JERSEY	80	270	638	.423	112	195	.574	159	2.0	323	4.0	96	12	672	8.4
1993-1994	N.J.-CHAR.	31	55	152	.362	13	29	.448	32	1.0	63	2.0	18	3	131	4.2
1995-1996	PORTLAND	43	92	221	.416	33	51	.647	78	1.8	142	3.3	26	5	247	5.7
1996-1997	L.A.-PHO.-POR.	54	66	164	.402	26	35	.743	47	0.9	73	1.4	24	2	176	3.3
NBA CAREER TOTALS		336	1014	2345	.432	406	665	.611	606	1.8	1179	3.5	301	54	2546	7.6
NBA PLAYOFF TOTALS		16	32	78	.410	7	12	.583	16	1.0	44	2.8	10	0	77	4.8

Robisch, David George

Height	6-10
Weight	235
Born	12-22-49
College	Kansas

SEASON	TEAM	G	FGM	FGA	PCT	FTM	FTA	PCT	REB	RPG	AST	APG	STL	BLK	PTS	PPG
1971-1972	DENVER (A)	84	505	1138	.444	294	419	.702	804	9.6	201	2.4	N/A	N/A	1304	15.5
1972-1973	DENVER (A)	83	521	1010	.516	309	409	.756	744	9.0	170	2.0	N/A	N/A	1351	16.3
1973-1974	DENVER (A)	84	449	950	.473	318	411	.774	708	8.4	152	1.8	45	66	1216	14.5
1974-1975	DENVER (A)	84	392	779	.503	304	346	.879	503	6.0	153	1.8	46	48	1088	13.0
1975-1976	S.D.-INDIANA (A)	87	436	1033	.422	324	381	.850	794	9.1	166	1.9	71	59	1196	13.7
1976-1977	INDIANA	80	369	811	.455	213	256	.832	554	6.9	158	2.0	55	37	951	11.9
1977-1978	INDIANA-L.A.	78	177	430	.412	100	129	.775	352	4.5	88	1.1	39	29	454	5.8
1978-1979	LOS ANGELES	80	150	336	.446	86	115	.748	285	3.6	97	1.2	20	25	386	4.8
1979-1980	CLEVELAND	82	489	940	.520	277	329	.842	658	8.0	192	2.3	53	53	1255	15.3
1980-1981	CLEV.-DENVER	84	330	740	.446	200	247	.810	499	5.9	173	2.1	37	34	860	10.2
1981-1982	DENVER	12	48	106	.453	48	55	.873	63	5.3	32	2.7	3	4	144	12.0
1982-1983	DENVER	61	96	251	.382	92	118	.780	151	2.5	53	0.9	10	9	284	4.7
1983-1984	DENVER-S.A.-K.C.	31	35	96	.365	22	26	.846	58	1.9	20	0.6	3	2	92	3.0
NBA CAREER TOTALS		508	1694	3710	.457	1038	1275	.814	2620	5.2	813	1.6	220	193	4426	8.7
NBA PLAYOFF TOTALS		14	21	48	.438	7	11	.636	46	3.3	6	0.4	2	2	49	3.5

Roche, John Michael

SEASON	TEAM	G	FGM	FGA	PCT	FTM	FTA	PCT	REB	RPG	AST	APG	STL	BLK	PTS	PPG
1971-1972	NEW YORK (A)	82	403	859	.469	240	311	.772	172	2.1	259	3.2	N/A	N/A	1058	12.9
1972-1973	NEW YORK (A)	77	404	909	.444	265	347	.764	146	1.9	348	4.5	N/A	N/A	1107	14.4
1973-1974	N.Y.-KEN. (A)	84	397	829	.479	148	177	.836	122	1.5	363	4.3	57	15	978	11.6
1974-1975	KEN.-UTAH (A)	58	241	509	.473	85	106	.802	93	1.6	191	3.3	49	7	580	10.0
1975-1976	UTAH (A)	16	112	212	.528	31	41	.756	25	1.6	79	4.9	14	1	264	16.5
1975-1976	LOS ANGELES	15	3	14	.214	2	4	.500	3	0.2	6	0.4	0	0	8	0.5
1979-1980	DENVER	82	354	741	.478	175	202	.866	115	1.4	405	4.9	82	12	932	11.4
1980-1981	DENVER	26	82	179	.458	58	77	.753	37	1.4	140	5.4	17	8	231	8.9
1981-1982	DENVER	39	68	150	.453	28	38	.737	23	0.6	89	2.3	15	2	187	4.8
NBA CAREER TOTALS		162	507	1084	.468	263	321	.819	178	1.1	640	4.0	114	22	1358	8.4

Height	6-3
Weight	170
Born	9-26-49
College	S Carolina

Rooks, Sean

SEASON	TEAM	G	FGM	FGA	PCT	FTM	FTA	PCT	REB	RPG	AST	APG	STL	BLK	PTS	PPG
1992-1993	DALLAS	72	368	747	.493	234	389	.602	536	7.4	95	1.3	38	81	970	13.5
1993-1994	DALLAS	47	193	393	.491	150	210	.714	259	5.5	49	1.0	21	44	536	11.4
1994-1995	MINNESOTA	80	289	615	.470	290	381	.761	486	6.1	97	1.2	29	71	868	10.9
1995-1996	MINN.-ATL.	65	144	285	.505	135	202	.668	255	3.9	47	0.7	23	42	424	6.5
1996-1997	LOS ANGELES	69	87	185	.470	91	130	.700	163	2.4	42	0.6	17	38	265	3.8
1997-1998	LOS ANGELES	41	46	101	.455	47	79	.595	118	2.9	24	0.6	2	23	139	3.4
NBA CAREER TOTALS		374	1127	2326	.484	947	1391	.681	1817	4.9	354	0.9	130	299	3202	8.6
NBA PLAYOFF TOTALS		22	22	43	.512	19	29	.655	41	1.9	8	0.4	7	10	63	2.9

Height	6-10
Weight	260
Born	9-9-69
College	Arizona

Russell, Cazzie Lee, Jr.

SEASON	TEAM	G	FGM	FGA	PCT	FTM	FTA	PCT	REB	RPG	AST	APG	STL	BLK	PTS	PPG
1966-1967	NEW YORK	77	344	789	.436	179	228	.785	251	3.3	187	2.4	N/A	N/A	867	11.3
1967-1968	NEW YORK	82	551	1192	.462	282	349	.808	374	4.6	195	2.4	N/A	N/A	1384	16.9
1968-1969	NEW YORK	50	362	804	.450	191	240	.796	209	4.2	115	2.3	N/A	N/A	915	18.3
1969-1970	NEW YORK	78	385	773	.498	124	160	.775	236	3.0	135	1.7	N/A	N/A	894	11.5
1970-1971	NEW YORK	57	216	504	.429	92	119	.773	192	3.4	77	1.4	N/A	N/A	524	9.2
1971-1972	GOLDEN STATE	79	689	1514	.455	315	378	.833	428	5.4	248	3.1	N/A	N/A	1693	21.4
1972-1973	GOLDEN STATE	80	541	1182	.458	172	199	.864	350	4.4	187	2.3	N/A	N/A	1254	15.7
1973-1974	GOLDEN STATE	82	738	1531	.482	208	249	.835	353	4.3	192	2.3	54	17	1684	20.5
1974-1975	LOS ANGELES	40	264	580	.455	101	113	.894	115	2.9	109	2.7	27	2	629	15.7
1975-1976	LOS ANGELES	74	371	802	.463	132	148	.892	183	2.5	122	1.6	53	3	874	11.8
1976-1977	LOS ANGELES	82	578	1179	.490	188	219	.858	294	3.6	210	2.6	86	7	1344	16.4
1977-1978	CHICAGO	36	133	304	.438	49	57	.860	83	2.3	61	1.7	19	4	315	8.8
NBA CAREER TOTALS		817	5172	11154	.464	2033	2459	.827	3068	3.8	1838	2.2	239	33	12377	15.1
NBA PLAYOFF TOTALS		72	359	781	.460	134	154	.870	222	3.1	97	1.3	16	1	852	11.8

Height	6-5
Weight	220
Born	6-7-44
College	Michigan

Schayes, Daniel

Height	6-11
Weight	260
Born	5-10-59
College	Syracuse

SEASON	TEAM	G	FGM	FGA	PCT	FTM	FTA	PCT	REB	RPG	AST	APG	STL	BLK	PTS	PPG
1981-1982	UTAH	82	252	524	.481	140	185	.757	427	5.2	146	1.8	46	72	644	7.9
1982-1983	UTAH-DEN.	82	342	749	.457	228	295	.773	635	7.7	205	2.5	54	98	912	11.1
1983-1984	DENVER	82	183	371	.493	215	272	.790	433	5.3	91	1.1	32	60	581	7.1
1984-1985	DENVER	56	60	129	.465	79	97	.814	144	2.6	38	0.7	20	25	199	3.6
1985-1986	DENVER	80	221	440	.502	216	278	.777	439	5.5	79	1.0	42	63	658	8.2
1986-1987	DENVER	76	210	405	.519	229	294	.779	380	5.0	85	1.1	20	74	649	8.5
1987-1988	DENVER	81	361	668	.540	407	487	.836	662	8.2	106	1.3	62	92	1129	13.9
1988-1989	DENVER	76	317	607	.522	332	402	.826	500	6.6	105	1.4	42	81	969	12.8
1989-1990	DENVER	53	163	330	.494	225	264	.852	342	6.5	61	1.2	41	45	551	10.4
1990-1991	MILWAUKEE	82	298	597	.499	274	328	.835	535	6.5	98	1.2	55	61	870	10.6
1991-1992	MILWAUKEE	43	83	199	.417	74	96	.771	168	3.9	34	0.8	19	19	240	5.6
1992-1993	MILWAUKEE	70	105	263	.399	112	137	.818	249	3.6	78	1.1	36	36	322	4.6
1993-1994	MIL.-LOS ANGELES	36	28	84	.333	29	32	.906	79	2.2	13	0.4	10	10	85	2.4
1994-1995	PHOENIX	69	126	248	.508	50	69	.725	208	3.0	89	1.3	20	37	303	4.4
1995-1996	MIAMI	32	32	94	.340	37	46	.804	89	2.8	9	0.3	11	16	101	3.2
1996-1997	ORLANDO	45	47	120	.392	39	52	.750	125	2.8	14	0.3	15	16	133	3.0
1997-1998	ORLANDO	74	155	371	.418	96	119	.807	242	3.3	44	0.6	34	33	406	5.5
NBA CAREER TOTALS		1119	2983	6199	.481	2782	3453	.806	5657	5.1	1295	1.2	559	838	8752	7.8
NBA PLAYOFF TOTALS		68	189	364	.519	163	198	.823	331	4.9	76	1.1	26	47	541	8.0

Scott, Byron Antom

Height	6-4
Weight	220
Born	3-28-61
College	Arizona St

SEASON	TEAM	G	FGM	FGA	PCT.	FTM	FTA	PCT	REB	RPG	AST	APG	STL	BLK	PTS	PPG
1983-1984	LOS ANGELES	74	334	690	.484	112	139	.806	164	2.2	177	2.4	81	19	788	10.6
1984-1985	LOS ANGELES	81	541	1003	.539	187	228	.820	210	2.6	244	3.0	100	17	1295	16.0
1985-1986	LOS ANGELES	76	507	989	.513	138	176	.784	189	2.5	164	2.2	85	15	1174	15.4
1986-1987	LOS ANGELES	82	554	1134	.489	224	251	.892	286	3.5	281	3.4	125	18	1397	17.0
1987-1988	LOS ANGELES	81	710	1348	.527	272	317	.858	333	4.1	335	4.1	155	27	1754	21.7
1988-1989	LOS ANGELES	74	588	1198	.491	195	226	.863	302	4.1	231	3.1	114	27	1448	19.6
1989-1990	LOS ANGELES	77	472	1005	.470	160	209	.766	242	3.1	274	3.6	77	31	1197	15.5
1990-1991	LOS ANGELES	82	501	1051	.477	118	148	.797	246	3.0	177	2.2	95	21	1191	14.5
1991-1992	LOS ANGELES	82	460	1005	.458	244	291	.838	310	3.8	226	2.8	105	28	1218	14.9
1992-1993	LOS ANGELES	58	296	659	.449	156	184	.848	134	2.3	157	2.7	55	13	792	13.7
1993-1994	INDIANA	67	256	548	.467	157	195	.805	110	1.6	133	2.0	62	9	696	10.4
1994-1995	INDIANA	80	265	583	.455	193	227	.850	151	1.9	108	1.4	61	13	802	10.0
1995-1996	VANCOUVER	80	271	676	.401	203	243	.835	192	2.4	123	1.5	63	22	819	10.2
1996-1997	LOS ANGELES	79	163	379	.430	127	151	.841	118	1.5	999	1.3	46	16	526	6.7
NBA CAREER TOTALS		1073	5918	12268	.482	2486	2985	.833	2987	2.8	2729	2.5	1224	276	15097	14.1
NBA PLAYOFF TOTALS		183	934	1937	.482	449	548	.819	536	2.9	390	2.1	226	30	2451	18.0

Scott, Charles Thomas

Height	6-5
Weight	175
Born	12-15-48
College	N Carolina

SEASON	TEAM	G	FGM	FGA	PCT	FTM	FTA	PCT	REB	RPG	AST	APG	STL	BLK	PTS	PPG
1971-1972	PHOENIX	6	48	113	.425	17	21	.810	23	3.8	26	4.3	N/A	N/A	113	18.8
1972-1973	PHOENIX	81	806	1809	.446	436	556	.784	342	4.2	495	6.1	N/A	N/A	2048	25.3
1973-1974	PHOENIX	52	538	1171	.459	246	315	.781	222	4.3	271	5.2	99	22	1322	25.4
1974-1975	PHOENIX	69	703	1594	.441	274	351	.781	273	4.0	311	4.5	111	24	1680	24.3
1975-1976	BOSTON	82	588	1309	.449	267	335	.797	358	4.4	341	4.2	103	24	1443	17.6
1976-1977	BOSTON	43	326	734	.444	129	173	.746	191	4.4	196	4.6	60	12	781	18.2
1977-1978	BOSTON-L.A.	79	435	994	.438	194	260	.746	249	3.2	378	4.8	110	17	1064	13.5
1978-1979	DENVER	79	393	854	.460	161	215	.749	210	2.7	428	5.4	78	30	947	12.0
1979-1980	DENVER	69	276	688	.401	85	118	.720	166	2.4	250	3.6	47	23	639	9.3
NBA CAREER TOTALS		560	4113	9266	.444	1809	2344	.772	2034	3.6	2696	4.8	608	152	10037	17.9
NBA PLAYOFF TOTALS		33	195	494	.395	113	146	.774	141	4.3	133	4.0	40	12	503	15.2

Seals, Shea

SEASON	TEAM	G	FGM	FGA	PCT	FTM	FTA	PCT	REB	RPG	AST	APG	STL	BLK	PTS	PPG
1997-1998	LOS ANGELES	4	1	8	.125	2	4	.500	4	1.0	0	0.0	1	0	4	1.0
NBA CAREER TOTALS		4	1	8	.125	2	4	.500	4	1.0	0	0.0	1	0	4	1.0

Height	6-5
Weight	210
Born	8-26-75
College	Tulsa

Selvy, Franklin Delano

SEASON	TEAM	G	FGM	FGA	PCT	FTM	FTA	PCT	REB	RPG	AST	APG	STL	BLK	PTS	PPG
1954-1955	BALT.-MILW.	71	452	1195	.378	444	610	.728	394	5.5	245	3.5	N/A	N/A	1348	19.0
1955-1956	ST. LOUIS	17	67	183	.366	53	71	.746	54	3.2	35	2.1	N/A	N/A	187	11.0
1957-1958	ST. L.-MINN.	38	44	167	.263	47	77	.610	88	2.3	35	0.9	N/A	N/A	135	3.6
1958-1959	NEW YORK	68	233	605	.385	201	262	.767	248	3.6	96	1.4	N/A	N/A	667	9.8
1959-1960	SYR.-MINN.	62	205	521	.393	153	208	.736	175	2.8	111	1.8	N/A	N/A	563	9.1
1960-1961	LOS ANGELES	77	311	767	.405	210	279	.753	299	3.9	246	3.2	N/A	N/A	832	10.8
1961-1962	LOS ANGELES	79	433	1032	.420	298	404	.738	412	5.2	381	4.8	N/A	N/A	1164	14.7
1962-1963	LOS ANGELES	80	317	747	.424	192	269	.714	289	3.6	281	3.5	N/A	N/A	826	10.3
1963-1964	LOS ANGELES	73	160	423	.378	78	122	.639	139	1.9	149	2.0	N/A	N/A	398	5.5
NBA CAREER TOTALS		565	2222	5640	.394	1676	2302	.728	2098	3.7	1579	2.8	N/A	N/A	6120	10.8
NBA PLAYOFF TOTALS		52	219	554	.395	151	192	.786	226	4.3	189	3.6	N/A	N/A	589	11.3

Height	6-2
Weight	180
Born	11-9-32
College	Furman

Sims, Robert Antell Jr.

SEASON	TEAM	G	FGM	FGA	PCT	FTM	FTA	PCT	REB	RPG	AST	APG	STL	BLK	PTS	PPG
1961-1962	L.A.-ST. L.	65	193	491	.393	123	216	.569	183	2.8	154	2.4	N/A	N/A	509	7.8
NBA CAREER TOTALS		65	193	491	.393	123	216	.569	183	2.8	154	2.4	N/A	N/A	509	7.8

Height	6-5
Weight	220
Born	10-9-38
College	Pepperdine

Smith, Charles Anton

SEASON	TEAM	G	FGM	FGA	PCT	FTM	FTA	PCT	REB	RPG	AST	APG	STL	BLK	PTS	PPG
1990-1991	LOS ANGELES	64	97	220	.441	40	57	.702	71	1.1	135	2.1	28	12	234	3.7
1991-1992	LOS ANGELES	63	113	283	.399	49	75	.653	76	1.2	109	1.7	39	8	275	4.4
1992-1993	LOS ANGELES	55	133	275	.484	62	82	.756	87	1.6	63	1.1	50	7	330	6.0
1993-1994	LOS ANGELES	73	272	617	.441	85	119	.714	195	2.7	148	2.0	59	14	645	8.8
1994-1995	LOS ANGELES	61	132	309	.427	44	63	.698	107	1.8	102	1.7	46	7	340	5.6
1995-1996	PHOE.-MIA.	59	116	274	.423	28	46	.609	95	1.6	154	2.6	37	10	298	5.1
1996-1997	CHARLOTTE	69	138	337	.409	38	59	.644	94	1.4	150	2.2	48	19	346	5.0
NBA CAREER TOTALS		444	1001	2315	.432	346	501	.691	725	1.6	861	1.9	307	77	2468	5.6
NBA PLAYOFF TOTALS		27	34	81	.420	10	18	.556	21	0.8	22	0.8	11	1	87	3.2

Height	6-4
Weight	205
Born	6-14-68
College	Marquette

Smith, Elmore

SEASON	TEAM	G	FGM	FGA	PCT	FTM	FTA	PCT	REB	RPG	AST	APG	STL	BLK	PTS	PPG
1971-1972	BUFFALO	78	579	1275	.454	194	363	.534	1184	15.2	111	1.4	N/A	N/A	1352	17.3
1972-1973	BUFFALO	76	600	1244	.482	188	337	.558	946	12.4	192	2.5	N/A	N/A	1388	18.3
1973-1974	LOS ANGELES	81	434	949	.457	147	249	.590	906	11.2	150	1.9	71	393	1015	12.5
1974-1975	LOS ANGELES	74	346	702	.493	112	231	.485	810	10.9	145	2.0	84	216	804	10.9
1975-1976	MILWAUKEE	78	498	962	.518	222	351	.632	893	11.4	97	1.2	78	238	1218	15.6
1976-1977	MILW.-CLEV.	70	241	507	.475	117	213	.549	439	6.3	43	0.6	35	144	599	8.6
1977-1978	CLEVELAND	81	402	809	.497	205	309	.663	678	8.4	57	0.7	50	176	1009	12.5
1978-1979	CLEVELAND	24	69	130	.531	18	26	.692	106	4.4	13	0.5	7	16	156	6.5
NBA CAREER TOTALS		562	3169	6578	.482	1203	2079	.579	5962	10.6	808	1.4	325	1183	7541	13.4
NBA PLAYOFF TOTALS		13	86	172	.500	34	52	.654	118	9.1	8	0.6	17	25	206	15.8

Height	7-1
Weight	250
Born	5-9-49
College	Kentucky St

Smith, Robert Joseph

SEASON	TEAM	G	FGM	FGA	PCT	FTM	FTA	PCT	REB	RPG	AST	APG	STL	BLK	PTS	PPG
1959-1960	MINNEAPOLIS	10	13	54	.241	11	16	.688	33	3.3	14	1.4	N/A	N/A	37	3.7
1961-1962	LOS ANGELES	3	0	1	.000	0	0	N/A	0	0.0	0	0.0	N/A	N/A	0	0.0
NBA CAREER TOTALS		13	13	55	.236	11	16	.688	33	2.5	14	1.1	N/A	N/A	37	2.8

Height	6-4
Weight	190
Born	8-20-37
College	W Virginia

Smrek, Michael Frank

SEASON	TEAM	G	FGM	FGA	PCT	FTM	FTA	PCT	REB	RPG	AST	APG	STL	BLK	PTS	PPG
1985-1986	CHICAGO	38	46	122	.377	16	29	.552	110	2.9	19	0.5	6	23	108	2.8
1986-1987	LOS ANGELES	35	30	60	.500	16	25	.640	37	1.1	5	0.1	4	13	76	2.2
1987-1988	LOS ANGELES	48	44	103	.427	44	66	.667	85	1.8	8	0.2	7	42	132	2.8
1988-1989	SAN ANTONIO	43	72	153	.471	49	76	.645	129	3.0	12	0.3	13	58	193	4.5
1989-1990	GOLDEN STATE	13	10	24	.417	1	6	.167	34	2.6	1	0.1	4	11	21	1.6
1990-1991	G.S.-CLIPPERS	15	9	27	.333	6	12	.500	26	1.7	4	0.3	3	3	24	1.6
1991-1992	GOLDEN STATE	2	0	0	N/A	0	0	N/A	1	0.5	0	0.0	0	0	0	0.0
NBA CAREER TOTALS		194	211	489	.431	132	214	.617	422	2.2	49	0.3	37	150	554	2.9
NBA PLAYOFF TOTALS		21	3	16	.188	5	9	.556	13	0.6	N/A	0.0	1	10	11	0.5

Height	7-0
Weight	250
Born	8-31-62
College	Canisius

Sparrow, Rory Darnell

SEASON	TEAM	G	FGM	FGA	PCT	FTM	FTA	PCT	REB	RPG	AST	APG	STL	BLK	PTS	PPG
1980-1981	NEW JERSEY	15	22	63	.349	12	16	.750	18	1.2	32	2.1	13	3	56	3.7
1981-1982	ATLANTA	82	366	730	.501	124	148	.838	224	2.7	424	5.2	87	13	857	10.5
1982-1983	ATLANTA-N.Y.	81	392	810	.484	147	199	.739	230	2.8	397	4.9	107	5	936	11.6
1983-1984	NEW YORK	79	350	738	.474	108	131	.824	189	2.4	539	6.8	100	8	818	10.4
1984-1985	NEW YORK	79	326	662	.492	122	141	.865	169	2.1	557	7.1	81	9	781	9.9
1985-1986	NEW YORK	74	345	723	.477	101	127	.795	170	2.3	472	6.4	85	14	796	10.8
1986-1987	NEW YORK	80	263	590	.446	71	89	.798	115	1.4	432	5.4	67	6	608	7.6
1987-1988	N.Y.-CHICAGO	58	117	293	.399	24	33	.727	72	1.2	167	2.9	41	3	260	4.5
1988-1989	MIAMI	80	444	982	.452	94	107	.879	216	2.7	429	5.4	103	17	1000	12.5
1989-1990	MIAMI	82	210	510	.412	59	77	.766	138	1.7	298	3.6	49	4	487	5.9
1990-1991	SACRAMENTO	80	371	756	.491	58	83	.699	186	2.3	362	4.5	83	16	831	10.4
1991-1992	CHICAGO-LOS ANGELES	46	58	151	.384	8	13	.615	28	0.6	83	1.8	12	5	127	2.8
NBA CAREER TOTALS		836	3264	7008	.466	928	1164	.797	1755	2.1	4192	5.0	828	103	7557	9.0
NBA PLAYOFF TOTALS		30	100	240	.417	52	65	.800	51	1.7	161	5.4	26	1	257	8.6

Height	6-2
Weight	175
Born	6-12-58
College	Villanova

Spriggs, Larry Michael

SEASON	TEAM	G	FGM	FGA	PCT	FTM	FTA	PCT	REB	RPG	AST	APG	STL	BLK	PTS	PPG
1981-1982	HOUSTON	4	7	11	.636	0	2	.000	6	1.5	4	1.0	2	0	14	3.5
1982-1983	CHICAGO	9	8	20	.400	5	7	.714	9	1.0	3	0.3	1	2	21	2.3
1983-1984	LOS ANGELES	38	44	82	.537	36	50	.720	61	1.6	30	0.8	12	4	124	3.3
1984-1985	LOS ANGELES	75	194	354	.548	112	146	.767	227	3.0	132	1.8	47	13	500	6.7
1985-1986	LOS ANGELES	43	88	192	.458	38	49	.776	81	1.9	49	1.1	18	9	214	5.0
NBA CAREER TOTALS		169	341	659	.517	191	254	.752	384	2.3	218	1.3	80	28	873	5.2
NBA PLAYOFF TOTALS		30	55	106	.519	39	51	.765	68	2.3	40	1.3	5	6	149	5.0

Height	6-7
Weight	230
Born	9-8-59
College	Howard

Strong, Derek

SEASON	TEAM	G	FGM	FGA	PCT	FTM	FTA	PCT	REB	RPG	AST	APG	STL	BLK	PTS	PPG
1991-1992	WASHINGTON	1	0	4	.000	3	4	.750	5	5.0	1	1.0	0	0	3	3.0
1992-1993	MILWAUKEE	23	42	92	.457	68	85	.800	115	5.0	14	0.6	11	1	156	6.8
1993-1994	MILWAUKEE	67	141	341	.413	159	206	.772	281	4.2	48	0.7	38	14	444	6.6
1994-1995	BOSTON	70	149	329	.453	141	172	.820	375	5.4	44	0.6	24	13	441	6.3
1995-1996	LOS ANGELES	63	72	169	.426	69	85	.812	178	2.8	32	0.5	18	12	214	3.4
1996-1997	ORLANDO	82	262	586	.447	175	218	.803	519	6.3	73	0.9	47	20	699	8.5
1997-1998	ORLANDO	58	259	617	.420	218	279	.781	427	7.4	51	0.9	31	24	736	12.7
NBA CAREER TOTALS		364	925	2138	.433	833	1049	.794	1900	5.2	263	0.7	169	84	2693	7.4
NBA PLAYOFF TOTALS		9	25	52	.481	22	31	.710	74	8.2	7	0.8	5	3	72	8.0

Height	6-8
Weight	225
Born	2-9-68
College	Xavier

Tatum, William Earl

SEASON	TEAM	G	FGM	FGA	PCT	FTM	FTA	PCT	REB	RPG	AST	APG	STL	BLK	PTS	PPG
1976-1977	LOS ANGELES	68	283	607	.466	72	100	.720	236	3.5	118	1.7	85	22	638	9.4
1977-1978	L.A.-INDIANA	82	510	1087	.469	153	196	.781	295	3.6	296	3.6	140	40	1173	14.3
1978-1979	BOSTON-DETROIT	79	280	627	.447	52	71	.732	125	1.6	73	0.9	78	34	612	7.7
1979-1980	CLEVELAND	33	36	94	.383	11	19	.579	26	0.8	20	0.6	16	5	85	2.6
NBA CAREER TOTALS		262	1109	2415	.459	288	386	.746	682	2.6	507	1.9	319	101	2508	9.6
NBA PLAYOFF TOTALS		11	67	134	.500	16	24	.667	54	4.9	27	2.5	15	9	150	13.6

Height	6-4
Weight	185
Born	7-26-53
College	Marquette

Teagle, Terry Michael

SEASON	TEAM	G	FGM	FGA	PCT	FTM	FTA	PCT	REB	RPG	AST	APG	STL	BLK	PTS	PPG
1982-1983	HOUSTON	73	332	776	.428	87	125	.696	194	2.7	150	2.1	53	18	761	10.4
1983-1984	HOUSTON	68	148	315	.470	37	44	.841	78	1.1	63	0.9	13	4	340	5.0
1984-1985	DETROIT-G.S.	21	74	137	.540	25	35	.714	43	2.0	14	0.7	13	5	175	8.3
1985-1986	GOLDEN STATE	82	475	958	.496	211	265	.796	235	2.9	115	1.4	71	34	1165	14.2
1986-1987	GOLDEN STATE	82	370	808	.458	182	234	.778	175	2.1	105	1.3	68	13	922	11.2
1987-1988	GOLDEN STATE	47	248	546	.454	97	121	.802	81	1.7	61	1.3	32	4	594	12.6
1988-1989	GOLDEN STATE	66	409	859	.476	182	225	.809	263	4.0	96	1.5	79	17	1002	15.2
1989-1990	GOLDEN STATE	82	538	1122	.480	244	294	.830	367	4.5	155	1.9	91	15	1323	16.1
1990-1991	LOS ANGELES	82	335	757	.443	145	177	.819	181	2.2	82	1.0	31	8	815	9.9
1991-1992	LOS ANGELES	82	364	805	.452	151	197	.766	183	2.2	113	1.4	66	9	880	10.7
1992-1993	HOUSTON	2	2	7	.286	1	2	.500	3	1.5	2	1.0	0	0	5	2.5
NBA CAREER TOTALS		687	3295	7090	.465	1362	1719	.792	1803	2.6	956	1.4	517	127	7982	11.6
NBA PLAYOFF TOTALS		45	203	450	.451	89	114	.781	98	2.2	42	0.9	29	10	495	11.0

Height	6-5
Weight	195
Born	4-10-60
College	Baylor

Thomas, Irving

SEASON	TEAM	G	FGM	FGA	PCT	FTM	FTA	PCT	REB	RPG	AST	APG	STL	BLK	PTS	PPG
1990-1991	LOS ANGELES	26	17	50	.340	12	21	.571	31	1.2	10	0.4	4	1	46	1.8
NBA CAREER TOTALS		26	17	50	.340	12	21	.571	31	1.2	10	0.4	4	1	46	1.8
NBA PLAYOFF TOTALS		3	1	1	1.000	0	0	N/A	0	0.0	N/A	0.0	0	0	2	0.7

Height	6-9
Weight	230
Born	1-2-66
College	Florida St

Thompson, Mychal George

SEASON	TEAM	G	FGM	FGA	PCT	FTM	FTA	PCT	REB	RPG	AST	APG	STL	BLK	PTS	PPG
1978-1979	PORTLAND	73	460	938	.490	154	269	.572	604	8.3	176	2.4	67	134	1074	14.7
1980-1981	PORTLAND	79	569	1151	.494	207	323	.641	686	8.7	284	3.6	62	170	1345	17.0
1981-1982	PORTLAND	79	681	1303	.523	280	446	.628	921	11.7	319	4.0	69	107	1642	20.8
1982-1983	PORTLAND	80	505	1033	.489	249	401	.621	753	9.4	380	4.8	68	110	1259	15.7
1983-1984	PORTLAND	79	487	929	.524	266	399	.667	688	8.7	308	3.9	84	108	1240	15.7
1984-1985	PORTLAND	79	572	1111	.515	307	449	.684	618	7.8	205	2.6	78	104	1451	18.4
1985-1986	PORTLAND	82	503	1011	.498	198	309	.641	608	7.4	176	2.1	76	35	1204	14.7
1986-1987	S.A.-LOS ANGELES	82	359	797	.450	219	297	.737	412	5.0	115	1.4	45	71	938	11.4
1987-1988	LOS ANGELES	80	370	722	.512	185	292	.634	489	6.1	66	0.8	38	79	925	11.6
1988-1989	LOS ANGELES	80	291	521	.559	156	230	.678	467	5.8	48	0.6	58	59	738	9.2
1989-1990	LOS ANGELES	70	281	562	.500	144	204	.706	477	6.8	43	0.6	33	73	706	10.1
1990-1991	LOS ANGELES	72	113	228	.496	62	88	.705	228	3.2	21	0.3	23	23	288	4.0
NBA CAREER TOTALS		935	5191	10306	.504	2427	3707	.655	6951	7.4	2141	2.3	701	1073	12810	13.7
NBA PLAYOFF TOTALS		104	449	897	.501	234	361	.648	627	6.0	126	1.2	56	106	1132	10.9

Height	6-10
Weight	235
Born	1-30-55
College	Minnesota

Thompson, William Stansbury

SEASON	TEAM	G	FGM	FGA	PCT	FTM	FTA	PCT	REB	RPG	AST	APG	STL	BLK	PTS	PPG
1986-1987	LOS ANGELES	59	142	261	.544	48	74	.649	171	2.9	60	1.0	15	30	332	5.6
1987-1988	LOS ANGELES	9	3	13	.231	8	10	.800	9	1.0	1	0.1	1	0	14	1.6
1988-1989	MIAMI	79	349	716	.487	156	224	.696	572	7.2	176	2.2	56	105	854	10.8
1989-1990	MIAMI	79	375	727	.516	115	185	.622	551	7.0	166	2.1	54	89	867	11.0
1990-1991	MIAMI	73	205	411	.499	89	124	.718	312	4.3	111	1.5	32	48	499	6.8
1991-1992	GOLDEN STATE	1	0	0	N/A	0	0	N/A	0	0.0	0	0.0	0	0	0	0.0
NBA CAREER TOTALS		300	1074	2128	.505	416	617	.674	1615	5.4	514	1.7	158	272	2566	8.6
NBA PLAYOFF TOTALS		3	6	11	.545	2	2	1.000	6	2.0	2	0.7	4	0	14	4.7

Height	6-6
Weight	210
Born	8-30-62
College	Fresno St

Threatt, Sedale Eugene

SEASON	TEAM	G	FGM	FGA	PCT	FTM	FTA	PCT	REB	RPG	AST	APG	STL	BLK	PTS	PPG
1983-1984	PHILDELPHIA	45	62	148	.419	23	28	.821	40	0.9	41	0.9	13	2	148	3.3
1984-1985	PHILDELPHIA	82	188	416	.452	66	90	.733	99	1.2	175	2.1	80	16	446	5.4
1985-1986	PHILDELPHIA	70	310	684	.453	75	90	.833	121	1.7	193	2.8	93	5	696	9.9
1986-1987	PHIL.-CHICAGO	68	239	534	.448	95	119	.798	108	1.6	259	3.8	74	13	580	8.5
1987-1988	CHICAGO-SEATTLE	71	216	425	.508	57	71	.803	88	1.2	160	2.3	60	8	492	6.9
1988-1989	SEATTLE	63	235	476	.494	63	77	.818	117	1.9	238	3.8	83	4	544	8.6
1989-1990	SEATTLE	65	303	599	.506	130	157	.828	115	1.8	216	3.3	65	8	744	11.4
1990-1991	SEATTLE	80	433	835	.519	137	173	.792	99	1.2	273	3.4	113	8	1013	12.7
1991-1992	LOS ANGELES	82	509	1041	.489	202	243	.831	253	3.1	593	7.2	168	16	1240	15.1
1992-1993	LOS ANGELES	82	522	1028	.508	177	215	.823	273	3.3	564	6.9	142	11	1235	15.1
1993-1994	LOS ANGELES	81	411	852	.482	138	155	.890	153	1.9	344	4.2	110	19	965	11.9
1994-1995	LOS ANGELES	59	217	437	.497	88	111	.793	124	2.1	248	4.2	54	12	558	9.5
1995-1996	LOS ANGELES	82	241	526	.458	54	71	.761	95	1.2	269	3.3	68	11	596	7.3
1996-1997	HOUSTON	21	28	74	.378	6	8	.750	24	1.1	40	1.9	15	3	70	3.3
NBA CAREER TOTALS		951	3914	8075	.485	1311	1608	.815	1709	1.8	3613	3.8	1138	136	9327	9.8
NBA PLAYOFF TOTALS		70	251	555	.452	84	103	.816	110	1.6	252	3.6	73	7	607	8.7

Height	6-2
Weight	185
Born	9-10-61
College	W Va. Tech

Tolbert, Raymond Lee

SEASON	TEAM	G	FGM	FGA	PCT	FTM	FTA	PCT	REB	RPG	AST	APG	STL	BLK	PTS	PPG
1981-1982	N.J.-SEATTLE	64	100	202	.495	19	35	.543	126	2.0	33	0.5	12	15	219	3.4
1982-1983	SEATTLE-DETROIT	73	157	314	.500	52	103	.505	242	3.3	50	0.7	26	47	366	5.0
1983-1984	DETROIT	49	64	121	.529	23	45	.511	98	2.0	26	0.5	12	20	151	3.1
1987-1988	N.Y.-LOS ANGELES	25	35	69	.507	19	30	.633	55	2.2	10	0.4	8	5	89	3.6
1988-1989	ATLANTA	50	40	94	.426	23	37	.622	88	1.8	16	0.3	13	13	103	2.1
NBA CAREER TOTALS		261	396	800	.495	136	250	.544	609	2.3	135	0.5	71	100	928	3.6
NBA PLAYOFF TOTALS		5	3	5	.600	4	8	.500	5	1.0	1	0.2	4	0	10	2.0

Height	6-9
Weight	225
Born	9-10-58
College	Indiana

Trapp, John Quincy

SEASON	TEAM	G	FGM	FGA	PCT	FTM	FTA	PCT	REB	RPG	AST	APG	STL	BLK	PTS	PPG
1968-1969	SAN DIEGO	25	29	80	.363	19	29	.655	49	2.0	5	0.2	N/A	N/A	77	3.1
1969-1970	SAN DIEGO	70	185	434	.426	72	104	.692	309	4.4	49	0.7	N/A	N/A	442	6.3
1970-1971	SAN DIEGO	82	322	766	.420	142	188	.755	510	6.2	138	1.7	N/A	N/A	786	9.6
1971-1972	LOS ANGELES	58	139	314	.443	51	73	.699	180	3.1	42	0.7	N/A	N/A	329	5.7
1972-1973	L.A.-PHIL.	44	171	420	.407	90	122	.738	200	4.5	49	1.1	N/A	N/A	432	9.8
NBA CAREER TOTALS		279	846	2014	.420	374	516	.725	1248	4.5	283	1.0	N/A	N/A	2066	7.4
NBA PLAYOFF TOTALS		10	8	33	.242	4	7	.571	16	1.6	5	0.5	N/A	N/A	20	2.0

Height	6-7
Weight	215
Born	10-2-45
College	UNLV

Tresvant, John B.

Height	6-7
Weight	215
Born	11-6-39
College	Seattle

SEASON	TEAM	G	FGM	FGA	PCT	FTM	FTA	PCT	REB	RPG	AST	APG	STL	BLK	PTS	PPG
1964-1965	ST. LOUIS	4	4	11	.364	6	9	.667	18	4.5	6	1.5	N/A	N/A	14	3.5
1965-1966	ST. L.-DETROIT	61	171	400	.428	142	190	.747	364	6.0	72	1.2	N/A	N/A	484	7.9
1966-1967	DETROIT	68	256	585	.438	164	234	.701	483	7.1	88	1.3	N/A	N/A	676	9.9
1967-1968	DETROIT-CIN.	85	396	867	.457	250	384	.651	709	8.3	160	1.9	N/A	N/A	1042	12.3
1968-1969	CIN.-SEATTLE	77	380	820	.463	202	330	.612	686	8.9	166	2.2	N/A	N/A	962	12.5
1969-1970	SEATTLE-L.A.	69	264	595	.444	206	284	.725	425	6.2	112	1.6	N/A	N/A	734	10.6
1970-1971	L.A.-BALT.	75	202	436	.463	146	205	.712	382	5.1	86	1.1	N/A	N/A	550	7.3
1971-1972	BALTIMORE	65	162	360	.450	121	148	.818	323	5.0	83	1.3	N/A	N/A	445	6.8
1972-1973	BALTIMORE	55	85	182	.467	41	59	.695	156	2.8	33	0.6	N/A	N/A	211	3.8
NBA CAREER TOTALS		559	1920	4256	.451	1278	1843	.693	3546	6.3	806	1.4	N/A	N/A	5118	9.2
NBA PLAYOFF TOTALS		40	104	251	.414	66	95	.695	246	6.2	44	1.1	N/A	N/A	274	6.9

Turner, William R. III

Height	6-7
Weight	220
Born	2-18-44
College	Akron

SEASON	TEAM	G	FGM	FGA	PCT	FTM	FTA	PCT	REB	RPG	AST	APG	STL	BLK	PTS	PPG
1967-1968	SAN FRANCISCO	42	68	157	.433	36	60	.600	155	3.7	16	0.4	N/A	N/A	172	4.1
1968-1969	SAN FRANCISCO	79	222	535	.415	175	230	.761	380	4.8	67	0.8	N/A	N/A	619	7.8
1969-1970	S.F.-CIN.	72	197	468	.421	123	167	.737	304	4.2	43	0.6	N/A	N/A	517	7.2
1970-1971	SAN FRANCISCO	18	26	82	.317	13	20	.650	42	2.3	8	0.4	N/A	N/A	65	3.6
1971-1972	GOLDEN STATE	62	71	181	.392	40	53	.755	131	2.1	22	0.4	N/A	N/A	182	2.9
1972-1973	PORT.-L.A.	21	19	58	.328	4	7	.571	27	1.3	11	0.5	N/A	N/A	42	2.0
NBA CAREER TOTALS		294	603	1481	.407	391	537	.728	1039	3.5	167	0.6	N/A	N/A	1597	5.4
NBA PLAYOFF TOTALS		22	37	87	.425	22	31	.710	62	2.8	16	0.7	N/A	N/A	96	4.4

Van Exel, Nick

Height	6-1
Weight	190
Born	11-27-71
College	Cincinnati

SEASON	TEAM	G	FGM	FGA	PCT	FTM	FTA	PCT	REB	RPG	AST	APG	STL	BLK	PTS	PPG
1993-1994	LOS ANGELES	81	413	1049	.394	150	192	.781	238	02.9	466	5.8	85	8	1099	13.6
1994-1995	LOS ANGELES	80	165	1107	.420	235	300	.783	223	02.8	660	8.3	97	6	1348	16.9
1995-1996	LOS ANGELES	74	396	950	.417	163	204	.799	181	02.4	509	6.9	70	10	1099	14.9
1996-1997	LOS ANGELES	71	432	1075	.402	165	200	.825	226	02.9	672	8.5	75	10	1206	15.3
1997-1998	LOS ANGELES	64	311	743	.419	136	172	.791	194	442.0	6.9	64.0	3	6	881	13.8
NBA CAREER TOTALS		378	2017	4924	.409	849	1068	.795	1062	02.8	2749	7.3	391	40	5633	14.9
NBA PLAYOFF TOTALS		36	178	486	.366	112	146	.767	117	03.2	212	5.9	41	4	528	14.7

Vincent, Jay Fletcher

SEASON	TEAM	G	FGM	FGA	PCT	FTM	FTA	PCT	REB	RPG	AST	APG	STL	BLK	PTS	PPG
1981-1982	DALLAS	81	719	1448	.497	293	409	.716	565	7.0	176	2.2	89	21	1732	21.4
1982-1983	DALLAS	81	622	1272	.489	269	343	.784	592	7.3	212	2.6	70	45	1513	18.7
1983-1984	DALLAS	61	252	579	.435	168	215	.781	247	4.0	114	1.9	30	10	672	11.0
1984-1985	DALLAS	79	545	1138	.479	351	420	.836	704	8.9	169	2.1	48	22	1441	18.2
1985-1986	DALLAS	80	442	919	.481	222	274	.810	368	4.6	180	2.3	66	21	1106	13.8
1986-1987	WASHINGTON	51	274	613	.447	130	169	.769	210	4.1	85	1.7	40	17	678	13.3
1987-1988	DENVER	73	446	958	.466	231	287	.805	309	4.2	143	2.0	46	26	1124	15.4
1988-1989	DENVER-S.A.	29	104	257	.405	40	60	.667	110	3.8	27	0.9	6	4	249	8.6
1989-1990	PHIL.-LOS ANGELES	41	86	183	.470	41	49	.837	62	1.5	18	0.4	18	5	214	5.2
NBA CAREER TOTALS		576	3490	7367	.474	1745	2226	.784	3167	5.5	1124	2.0	413	171	8729	15.2
NBA PLAYOFF TOTALS		38	170	415	.410	150	174	.862	177	4.7	46	1.2	24	9	490	12.9

Height	6-8
Weight	220
Born	6-10-59
College	Mich St

Wagner, Milton, Jr.

SEASON	TEAM	G	FGM	FGA	PCT	FTM	FTA	PCT	REB	RPG	AST	APG	STL	BLK	PTS	PPG
1987-1988	LOS ANGELES	40	62	147	.422	26	29	.897	28	0.7	61	1.5	6	4	152	3.8
1990-1991	MIAMI	13	24	57	.421	9	11	.818	7	0.5	15	1.2	2	3	63	4.8
NBA CAREER TOTALS		53	86	204	.422	35	40	.875	35	0.7	76	1.4	8	7	215	4.1
NBA PLAYOFF TOTALS		5	2	5	.400	2	2	1.000	2	0.4	3	0.6	0	1	6	1.2

Height	6-5
Weight	185
Born	2-20-63
College	Louisville

Warner, Cornell

SEASON	TEAM	G	FGM	FGA	PCT	FTM	FTA	PCT	REB	RPG	AST	APG	STL	BLK	PTS	PPG
1970-1971	BUFFALO	65	156	376	.415	79	143	.552	452	7.0	53	0.8	N/A	N/A	391	6.0
1971-1972	BUFFALO	62	162	366	.443	58	78	.744	379	6.1	54	0.9	N/A	N/A	382	6.2
1972-1973	BUFFALO-CLEV.	72	174	421	.413	59	90	.656	522	7.3	72	1.0	N/A	N/A	407	5.7
1973-1974	CLEV.-MILW.	72	174	349	.499	85	114	.746	397	5.5	71	1.0	27	42	433	6.0
1974-1975	MILWAUKEE	79	248	541	.458	106	155	.684	812	10.3	127	1.6	49	54	602	7.6
1975-1976	LOS ANGELES	81	251	524	.479	89	128	.695	722	8.9	106	1.3	55	46	591	7.3
1976-1977	LOS ANGELES	14	25	53	.472	4	6	.667	69	4.9	11	0.8	1	2	54	3.9
NBA CAREER TOTALS		445	1190	2630	.452	480	714	.672	3353	7.5	494	1.1	132	144	2860	6.4
PLAYOFF CAREER		21	54	123	.439	13	19	.684	172	8.2	26	1.2	8	14	121	5.8

Height	6-9
Weight	225
Born	8-12-48
College	Jackson St

Washington, Kermit Alan

SEASON	TEAM	G	FGM	FGA	PCT	FTM	FTA	PCT	REB	RPG	AST	APG	STL	BLK	PTS	PPG
1973-1974	LOS ANGELES	45	73	151	.483	26	49	.531	147	3.3	19	0.4	21	18	172	3.8
1974-1975	LOS ANGELES	55	87	207	.420	72	122	.590	350	6.4	66	1.2	25	32	246	4.5
1975-1976	LOS ANGELES	36	39	90	.433	45	66	.682	165	4.6	20	0.6	11	26	123	3.4
1976-1977	LOS ANGELES	53	191	380	.503	132	187	.706	492	9.3	48	0.9	43	52	514	9.7
1977-1978	L.A.-BOSTON	57	247	507	.487	170	246	.691	614	10.8	72	1.3	47	64	664	11.6
1978-1979	SAN DIEGO	82	350	623	.562	227	330	.688	800	9.8	125	1.5	85	121	927	11.3
1979-1980	PORTLAND	80	421	761	.553	231	360	.642	842	10.5	167	2.1	73	131	1073	13.4
1980-1981	PORTLAND	73	325	571	.569	181	288	.628	686	9.4	149	2.0	85	86	831	11.4
1981-1982	PORTLAND	20	38	78	.487	24	41	.585	117	5.9	29	1.5	9	16	100	5.0
1987-1988	GOLDEN STATE	6	7	14	.500	2	2	1.000	19	3.2	0	0.0	4	4	16	2.7
NBA CAREER TOTALS		507	1778	3382	.526	1110	1691	.656	4232	8.3	695	1.4	403	550	4666	9.2
PLAYOFF CAREER		9	30	60	.500	12	17	.706	93	10.3	14	1.6	10	6	72	8.0

Height	6-8
Weight	230
Born	9-17-51
College	American Int

Wesley, Walter

Height	6-11
Weight	230
Born	1-25-45
College	Kansas

SEASON	TEAM	G	FGM	FGA	PCT	FTM	FTA	PCT	REB	RPG	AST	APG	STL	BLK	PTS	PPG
1966-1967	CINCINNATI	64	131	333	.393	52	123	.423	329	5.1	19	0.3	N/A	N/A	314	4.9
1967-1968	CINCINNATI	66	188	404	.465	76	152	.500	281	4.3	34	0.5	N/A	N/A	452	6.8
1968-1969	CINCINNATI	82	245	534	.459	134	207	.647	403	4.9	47	0.6	N/A	N/A	624	7.6
1969-1970	CHICAGO	72	270	648	.417	145	219	.662	455	6.3	68	0.9	N/A	N/A	685	9.5
1970-1971	CLEVELAND	82	565	1241	.455	325	473	.687	713	8.7	83	1.0	N/A	N/A	1455	17.7
1971-1972	CLEVELAND	82	412	1006	.410	196	291	.674	711	8.7	76	0.9	N/A	N/A	1020	12.4
1972-1973	CLEV.-PHOENIX	57	77	202	.381	26	46	.565	151	2.6	31	0.5	N/A	N/A	180	3.2
1973-1974	CAPITAL	39	71	151	.470	26	43	.605	136	3.5	14	0.4	9	20	168	4.3
1974-1975	PHIL.-MILW.	45	42	93	.452	16	27	.593	63	1.4	12	0.3	7	5	100	2.2
1975-1976	LOS ANGELES	1	1	2	.500	2	4	.500	1	1.0	1	1.0	0	0	4	4.0
NBA CAREER TOTALS		590	2002	4614	.434	998	1585	.630	3243	5.5	385	0.7	16	25	5002	8.5
NBA PLAYOFF TOTALS		8	18	41	.439	6	12	.500	28	3.5	2	0.3	0	0	42	5.3

West, Jerry Alan

Height	6-2
Weight	180
Born	5-28-38
College	W Virginia

SEASON	TEAM	G	FGM	FGA	PCT	FTM	FTA	PCT	REB	RPG	AST	APG	STL	BLK	PTS	PPG
1960-1961	LOS ANGELES	79	529	1264	.419	331	497	.666	611	7.7	333	4.2	N/A	N/A	1389	17.6
1961-1962	LOS ANGELES	75	799	1795	.445	712	926	.769	591	7.9	402	5.4	N/A	N/A	2310	30.8
1962-1963	LOS ANGELES	55	559	1213	.461	371	477	.778	384	7.0	307	5.6	N/A	N/A	1489	27.1
1963-1964	LOS ANGELES	72	740	1529	.484	584	702	.832	443	6.2	403	5.6	N/A	N/A	2064	28.7
1964-1965	LOS ANGELES	74	822	1655	.497	648	789	.821	447	6.0	364	4.9	N/A	N/A	2292	31.0
1965-1966	LOS ANGELES	79	818	1731	.473	840	977	.860	562	7.1	480	6.1	N/A	N/A	2476	31.3
1966-1967	LOS ANGELES	66	645	1389	.464	602	686	.878	392	5.9	447	6.8	N/A	N/A	1892	28.7
1967-1968	LOS ANGELES	51	476	926	.514	391	482	.811	294	5.8	310	6.1	N/A	N/A	1343	26.3
1968-1969	LOS ANGELES	61	545	1156	.471	490	597	.821	262	4.3	423	6.9	N/A	N/A	1580	25.9
1969-1970	LOS ANGELES	74	831	1673	.497	647	785	.824	338	4.6	554	7.5	N/A	N/A	2309	31.2
1970-1971	LOS ANGELES	69	667	1351	.494	525	631	.832	320	4.6	655	9.5	N/A	N/A	1859	26.9
1971-1972	LOS ANGELES	77	735	1540	.477	515	633	.814	327	4.2	747	9.7	N/A	N/A	1985	25.8
1972-1973	LOS ANGELES	69	618	1291	.479	339	421	.805	289	4.2	607	8.8	N/A	N/A	1575	22.8
1973-1974	LOS ANGELES	31	232	519	.447	165	198	.833	116	3.7	206	6.6	81	23	629	20.3
NBA CAREER TOTALS		932	9016	19032	.474	7160	8801	.814	5376	5.8	6238	6.7	81	23	25192	27.0
NBA PLAYOFF TOTALS		153	1622	3460	.469	1213	1506	.805	855	5.6	970	6.3	0	0	4457	29.1

Wetzel, John Francis

Height	6-5
Weight	190
Born	10-22-44
College	Virginia Tech

SEASON	TEAM	G	FGM	FGA	PCT	FTM	FTA	PCT	REB	RPG	AST	APG	STL	BLK	PTS	PPG
1967-1968	LOS ANGELES	38	52	119	.437	35	46	.761	84	2.2	51	1.3	N/A	N/A	139	3.7
1970-1971	PHOENIX	70	124	288	.431	83	101	.822	153	2.2	114	1.6	N/A	N/A	331	4.7
1971-1972	PHOENIX	51	31	82	.378	24	30	.800	65	1.3	56	1.1	N/A	N/A	86	1.7
1972-1973	ATLANTA	28	42	94	.447	14	17	.824	58	2.1	39	1.4	N/A	N/A	98	3.5
1973-1974	ATLANTA	70	107	252	.425	41	57	.719	170	2.4	138	2.0	73	19	255	3.6
1974-1975	ATLANTA	63	87	204	.426	68	77	.883	114	1.8	77	1.2	51	8	242	3.8
1975-1976	PHOENIX	37	22	46	.478	20	24	.833	38	1.0	19	0.5	9	3	64	1.7
NBA CAREER TOTALS		357	465	1085	.429	285	352	.810	682	1.9	494	1.4	133	30	1215	3.4
PLAYOFF CAREER		5	3	7	.429	2	2	1.000	4	0.8	4	0.8	0	0	8	1.6

Wiley, Eugene

SEASON	TEAM	G	FGM	FGA	PCT	FTM	FTA	PCT	REB	RPG	AST	APG	STL	BLK	PTS	PPG
1962-1963	LOS ANGELES	75	109	236	.462	23	68	.338	504	6.7	40	0.5	N/A	N/A	241	3.2
1963-1964	LOS ANGELES	78	146	273	.535	45	75	.600	510	6.5	44	0.6	N/A	N/A	337	4.3
1964-1965	LOS ANGELES	80	175	376	.465	56	111	.505	690	8.6	105	1.3	N/A	N/A	406	5.1
1965-1966	LOS ANGELES	67	123	289	.426	43	76	.566	490	7.3	63	0.9	N/A	N/A	289	4.3
1967-1968	OAKLAND-DALLAS (A)	9	7	20	.350	4	8	.500	20	2.2	2	0.2	N/A	N/A	18	2.0
NBA CAREER TOTALS		300	553	1174	.471	167	330	.506	2194	7.3	252	0.8	N/A	N/A	1273	4.2
PLAYOFF CAREER		27	52	103	.505	16	37	.432	272	10.1	34	1.3	N/A	N/A	120	4.4

Height	6-10
Weight	220
Born	11-12-37
College	Wichita St

Wilkes, Jamaal Abdul-Lateef

SEASON	TEAM	G	FGM	FGA	PCT.	FTM	FTA	PCT	REB	RPG	AST	APG	STL	BLK	PTS	PPG
1974-1975	GOLDEN STATE	82	502	1135	.442	160	218	.734	671	8.2	183	2.2	107	22	1164	14.2
1975-1976	GOLDEN STATE	82	617	1334	.463	227	294	.772	720	8.8	167	2.0	102	31	1461	17.8
1976-1977	GOLDEN STATE	76	548	1147	.478	247	310	.797	578	7.6	211	2.8	127	16	1343	17.7
1977-1978	LOS ANGELES	51	277	630	.440	106	148	.716	380	7.5	182	3.6	77	22	660	12.9
1978-1979	LOS ANGELES	82	626	1242	.504	272	362	.751	609	7.4	227	2.8	134	27	1524	18.6
1979-1980	LOS ANGELES	82	726	1358	.535	189	234	.808	525	6.4	250	3.0	129	28	1644	20.0
1980-1981	LOS ANGELES	81	786	1495	.526	254	335	.758	435	5.4	235	2.9	121	29	1827	22.6
1981-1982	LOS ANGELES	82	744	1417	.525	246	336	.732	393	4.8	143	1.7	89	24	1734	21.1
1982-1983	LOS ANGELES	80	684	1290	.530	203	268	.757	343	4.3	182	2.3	65	17	1571	19.6
1983-1984	LOS ANGELES	75	542	1055	.514	208	280	.743	340	4.5	214	2.9	72	41	1294	17.3
1984-1985	LOS ANGELES	42	148	303	.488	51	66	.773	94	2.2	41	1.0	19	3	347	8.3
1985-1986	CLIPPERS	13	26	65	.400	22	27	.815	29	2.2	15	1.2	7	2	75	5.8
NBA CAREER TOTALS		828	6226	12471	.499	2185	2878	.759	5117	6.2	2050	2.5	1049	262	14644	17.7
PLAYOFF CAREER		113	785	1689	.465	250	344	.727	718	6.4	246	2.2	137	53	1820	16.1

Height	6-6
Weight	190
Born	5-2-53
College	UCLA

Williams, Ronald Robert

SEASON	TEAM	G	FGM	FGA	PCT	FTM	FTA	PCT	REB	RPG	AST	APG	STL	BLK	PTS	PPG
1968-1969	SAN FRANCISCO	75	238	567	.420	109	142	.768	178	2.4	247	3.3	N/A	N/A	585	7.8
1969-1970	SAN FRANCISCO	80	452	1046	.432	277	337	.822	190	2.4	424	5.3	N/A	N/A	1181	14.8
1970-1971	SAN FRANCISCO	82	426	977	.436	331	392	.844	244	3.0	480	5.9	N/A	N/A	1183	14.4
1971-1972	GOLDEN STATE	80	291	614	.474	195	234	.833	147	1.8	308	3.9	N/A	N/A	777	9.7
1972-1973	GOLDEN STATE	73	180	409	.440	75	83	.904	81	1.1	114	1.6	N/A	N/A	435	6.0
1973-1974	MILWAUKEE	71	192	393	.489	60	68	.882	69	1.0	153	2.2	49	2	444	6.3
1974-1975	MILWAUKEE	46	62	165	.376	24	29	.828	43	0.9	71	1.5	23	2	148	3.2
1975-1976	LOS ANGELES	9	17	43	.395	10	13	.769	19	2.1	21	2.3	3	0	44	4.9
NBA CAREER TOTALS		516	1858	4214	.441	1081	1298	.833	971	1.9	1818	3.5	75	4	4797	9.3
PLAYOFF CAREER		32	104	248	.419	52	59	.881	57	1.8	94	2.9	9	3	260	8.1

Height	6-3
Weight	190
Born	9-24-44
College	W Virginia

Wilson, Trevor

SEASON	TEAM	G	FGM	FGA	PCT	FTM	FTA	PCT	REB	RPG	AST	APG	STL	BLK	PTS	PPG
1990-1991	ATLANTA	25	21	70	.300	13	26	.500	40	1.6	11	0.4	5	1	55	2.2
1993-1994	LOS ANGELES-SAC.	57	187	388	.482	92	166	.554	273	4.8	72	1.3	38	11	466	8.2
TOTAL CAREER		82	208	458	.454	105	192	.547	313	3.8	83	1.0	43	12	521	6.4

Height	6-8
Weight	210
Born	3-16-68
College	UCLA

Winters, Brian Joseph

SEASON	TEAM	G	FGM	FGA	PCT	FTM	FTA	PCT	REB	RPG	AST	APG	SSTL	BLK	PTS	PPG
1974-1975	LOS ANGELES	68	359	810	.443	76	92	.826	138	2.0	195	2.9	74	18	794	11.7
1975-1976	MILWAUKEE	78	618	1333	.464	180	217	.829	249	3.2	366	4.7	124	25	1416	18.2
1976-1977	MILWAUKEE	78	652	1308	.498	205	242	.847	231	3.0	337	4.3	114	29	1509	19.3
1977-1978	MILWAUKEE	80	674	1457	.463	246	293	.840	250	3.1	393	4.9	124	27	1594	19.9
1978-1979	MILWAUKEE	79	662	1343	.493	237	277	.856	177	2.2	383	4.8	83	40	1561	19.8
1979-1980	MILWAUKEE	80	535	1116	.479	184	214	.860	223	2.8	362	4.5	101	28	1292	16.2
1980-1981	MILWAUKEE	69	331	697	.475	119	137	.869	140	2.0	229	3.3	70	10	799	11.6
1981-1982	MILWAUKEE	61	404	806	.501	123	156	.788	170	2.8	253	4.1	57	9	967	15.9
1982-1983	MILWAUKEE	57	255	587	.434	73	85	.859	110	1.9	156	2.7	45	4	605	10.6
NBA CAREER TOTALS		650	4490	9457	.475	1443	1713	.842	1688	2.6	2674	4.1	792	190	10537	16.2
PLAYOFF CAREER		41	269	549	.490	80	99	.808	118	2.9	192	4.7	52	16	637	15.5

Height	6-4
Weight	185
Born	3-1-52
College	S. Carolina

Woolridge, Orlando Vernada

SEASON	TEAM	G	FGM	FGA	PCT	FTM	FTA	PCT	REB	RPG	AST	APG	STL	BLK	PTS	PPG
1981-1982	CHICAGO	75	202	394	.513	144	206	.699	227	3.0	81	1.1	23	24	548	7.3
1982-1983	CHICAGO	57	361	622	.580	217	340	.638	298	5.2	97	1.7	38	44	939	16.5
1983-1984	CHICAGO	75	570	1086	.525	303	424	.715	369	4.9	136	1.8	71	60	1444	19.3
1984-1985	CHICAGO	77	679	1225	.554	409	521	.785	435	5.6	135	1.8	58	38	1767	22.9
1985-1986	CHICAGO	70	540	1090	.495	364	462	.788	350	5.0	213	3.0	49	47	1448	20.7
1986-1987	NEW JERSEY	75	556	1067	.521	438	564	.777	367	4.9	261	3.5	54	86	1551	20.7
1987-1988	NEW JERSEY	19	110	247	.445	92	130	.708	91	4.8	71	3.7	13	20	312	16.4
1988-1989	LOS ANGELES	74	231	494	.468	253	343	.738	270	3.6	58	0.8	30	65	715	9.7
1989-1990	LOS ANGELES	62	306	550	.556	176	240	.733	185	3.0	96	1.5	39	46	788	12.7
1990-1991	DENVER	53	490	983	.498	350	439	.797	361	6.8	119	2.2	69	23	1330	25.1
1991-1992	DETROIT	82	452	907	.498	241	353	.683	260	3.2	88	1.1	41	33	1146	14.0
1992-1993	DETROIT-MILW.	58	289	599	.482	120	177	.678	185	3.2	115	2.0	27	27	698	12.0
1993-1994	PHILADELPHIA	74	364	773	.471	208	302	.689	298	4.0	139	1.9	41	56	937	12.7
NBA CAREER TOTALS		851	5150	10037	.513	3315	4501	.737	3696	4.3	1609	1.9	553	569	13623	16.0
NBA PLAYOFF TOTALS		36	161	327	.492	106	148	.716	130	3.6	42	1.2	20	26	428	11.9

Height	6-9
Weight	215
Born	12-16-59
College	Notre Dame

Worthy, James

SEASON	TEAM	G	FGM	FGA	PCT.	FTM	FTA	PCT	REB	RPG	AST	APG	STL	BLK	PTS	PPG
1982-1983	LOS ANGELES	77	447	772	.579	138	221	.624	399	5.2	132	1.7	91	64	1033	13.4
1983-1984	LOS ANGELES	82	495	890	.556	195	257	.759	515	6.3	207	2.5	77	70	1185	14.5
1984-1985	LOS ANGELES	80	610	1066	.572	190	245	.776	511	6.4	201	2.5	87	67	1410	17.6
1985-1986	LOS ANGELES	75	629	1086	.579	242	314	.771	387	5.2	201	2.7	82	77	1500	20.0
1986-1987	LOS ANGELES	82	651	1207	.539	292	389	.751	466	5.7	226	2.8	108	83	1594	19.4
1987-1988	LOS ANGELES	75	617	1161	.531	242	304	.796	374	5.0	289	3.9	72	55	1478	19.7
1988-1989	LOS ANGELES	81	702	1282	.548	251	321	.782	489	6.0	288	3.6	108	56	1657	20.5
1989-1990	LOS ANGELES	80	711	1298	.548	248	317	.782	478	6.0	288	3.6	99	49	1685	21.1
1990-1991	LOS ANGELES	78	716	1455	.492	212	266	.797	356	4.6	275	3.5	104	35	1670	21.4
1991-1992	LOS ANGELES	54	450	1007	.447	166	204	.814	305	5.6	252	4.7	76	23	1075	19.9
1992-1993	LOS ANGELES	82	510	1142	.447	171	211	.810	247	3.0	278	3.4	92	27	1221	14.9
1993-1994	LOS ANGELES	80	340	838	.406	100	135	.741	181	2.3	154	1.9	45	18	812	10.2
NBA CAREER TOTALS		926	6878	13204	.521	2447	3184	.769	4708	5.1	2791	3.0	1041	624	16320	17.6
NBA PLAYOFF TOTALS		143	1267	2329	.544	474	652	.727	747	5.2	463	3.2	177	96	3022	21.1

Height	6-9
Weight	225
Born	2-17-61
College	N Carolina

Yates, Wayne E.

SEASON	TEAM	G	FGM	FGA	PCT	FTM	FTA	PCT	REB	RPG	AST	APG	STL	BLK	PTS	PPG
1961-1962	LOS ANGELES	37	31	105	.295	10	22	.455	94	2.5	16	0.4	N/A	N/A	72	1.9
NBA CAREER TOTALS		37	31	105	.295	10	22	.455	94	2.5	16	0.4	N/A	N/A	72	1.9
NBA PLAYOFF TOTALS		4	3	8	.375	1	2	.500	5	1.3	1	0.3	N/A	N/A	7	1.8

Height	6-8
Weight	235
Born	11-7-37
College	Memphis St

YEAR-BY-YEAR
TEAM PERFORMANCES

MINNESOTA 1948-49

2ND WESTERN DIVISION; NBA CHAMPIONS

PLAYER	G	FGM	FGA	PCT	FTM	FTA	PCT	AST	PTS	PPG
GEORGE MIKAN	60	583	1403	.416	532	689	.772	218	1698	28.3
JIM POLLARD	53	314	792	.396	156	227	.687	142	784	14.8
HERM SCHAEFER	58	214	572	.374	174	213	.817	185	602	10.4
DON CARLSON	55	211	632	.334	86	130	.662	170	508	9.2
ARNIE FERRIN	47	130	378	.344	85	128	.664	76	345	7.3
TONY JAROS	59	132	385	.343	79	110	.718	58	343	5.8
JACK DWAN	60	121	380	.318	34	69	.493	129	276	4.6
DONNIE FORMAN	44	68	231	.294	43	67	.642	74	179	4.1
JOHNNY JORGENSEN	48	41	114	.360	24	33	.727	33	106	2.2
EARL GARDNER	50	38	101	.376	13	28	.464	19	89	1.8
MIKE BLOOM	24	13	92	.141	29	40	.725	15	55	2.3
EDWIN KACHAN	19	16	42	.381	15	22	.682	12	47	2.5
DONALD SMITH	8	2	13	.154	2	3	.667	2	6	0.8
JACK TINGLE	2	1	6	.167	0	0	N/A	1	2	1.0
RAY ELLEFSON	3	1	5	.200	0	0	N/A	0	2	0.7

NBA PLAYOFFS

FIRST ROUND
DEF. CHICAGO, 2-0

SECOND ROUND
DEF. ROCHESTER, 2-0

FINALS
DEF. WASHINGTON, 4-2

TEAM LEADERS

SCORING
MIKAN 28.3

ASSISTS
MIKAN 3.6

REBOUNDS
N/A . . . . N/A

FIELD GOAL PCT.
MIKAN 416

FREE THROW PCT
SCHAEFER 809

MINUTES PLAYED
N/A . . . . N/A

LEAGUE AWARDS

ALL-NBA TEAM
MIKAN, POLLARD, FIRST TEAM

MINNESOTA 1949-50

1ST CENTRAL DIVISION; NBA CHAMPIONS

PLAYER	G	FGM	FGA	PCT	FTM	FTA	PCT	AST	PTS	PPG
GEORGE MIKAN	68	649	1595	.407	567	728	.779	197	1865	27.4
JIM POLLARD	66	394	1140	.346	185	242	.764	252	973	14.7
VERN MIKKELSEN	68	288	722	.399	215	286	.752	123	791	11.6
ARNIE FERRIN	63	132	396	.333	76	109	.697	95	340	5.4
HERM SCHAEFER	65	122	314	.389	86	101	.851	203	330	5.1
BOB HARRISON	66	125	348	.359	50	74	.676	131	300	4.5
SLATER MARTIN	67	106	302	.351	59	93	.634	148	271	4.0
DON CARLSON	57	99	290	.341	69	95	.726	76	267	4.7
TONY JAROS	61	84	*289	.291	72	96	.750	60	240	3.9
BILLY HASSETT	42	38	145	.262	35	67	.522	69	111	2.6
BUD GRANT	35	42	115	.365	7	17	.412	19	91	2.6
LEFTY WALTHER	22	32	80	.400	11	21	.524	10	75	3.4
GENE STUMP	23	27	95	.284	7	14	.500	23	61	2.7
NORMIE GLICK	1	1	1	1.000	0	0	.N/A	1	2	2.0

NBA PLAYOFFS

FIRST ROUND
DEF. CHICAGO, 2-0

SECOND ROUND
DEF. FT. WAYNE, 2-0

THIRD ROUND
DEF. ANDERSON, 2-0

FINALS
DEF. SYRACUSE, 4-2

TEAM LEADERS

SCORING
MIKAN 27.4

ASSISTS
POLLARD 3.8

REBOUNDS
N/A . . . . N/A

FIELD GOAL PCT.
MIKAN 407

FREE THROW PCT
MIKAN 779

MINUTES PLAYED
N/A . . . . N/A

LEAGUE AWARDS

ALL-NBA TEAM
MIKAN, POLLARD, FIRST TEAM

MINNESOTA 1950-51
1ST WESTERN DIVISION

REGULAR SEASON RECORD
44-24

PLAYER	G	FGM	FGA	PCT	FTM	FTA	PCT	AST	PTS	PPG
GEORGE MIKAN	68	678	1584	.428	576	717	.803	208	1932	28.4
VERN MIKKELSEN	64	359	893	.402	186	275	.676	181	904	14.1
JIM POLLARD	54	256	728	.352	117	156	.750	184	629	11.6
SLATER MARTIN	68	227	627	.362	121	177	.684	235	575	8.5
BOB HARRISON	68	150	432	.347	101	128	.789	195	401	5.9
ARNIE FERRIN	68	119	373	.319	114	164	.695	107	352	5.2
KEVIN O'SHEA	63	87	267	.326	97	134	.724	100	271	4.3
TONY JAROS	63	88	287	.307	65	103	.631	72	241	3.8
BUD GRANT	61	53	184	.288	52	83	.627	71	158	2.6
JOE HUTTON	60	59	180	.328	29	43	.674	53	147	2.5

NBA PLAYOFFS

FIRST ROUND

FIRST ROUND
DEF. INDIANAPOLIS, 2-1
SECOND ROUND
LOST TO ROCHESTER, 1-3

TEAM LEADERS

SCORING
MIKAN 28.4

ASSISTS
MIKAN 4.4

REBOUNDS
MIKAN 14.1

FIELD GOAL PCT.
MIKAN 428

FREE THROW PCT
MIKAN 803

MINUTES PLAYED
N/A . . . . N/A

LEAGUE AWARDS

ALL-NBA TEAM
MIKAN, FIRST TEAM
MIKKELSEN, SECOND TEAM

ALL-STAR TEAM
MIKAN
MIKKELSEN
POLLARD

MINNESOTA 1951-52
2ND WESTERN DIVISION; NBA CHAMPIONS

REGULAR SEASON RECORD
40-26

PLAYER	G	FGM	FGA	PCT	FTM	FTA	PCT	AST	PTS	PPG
GEORGE MIKAN	64	545	1414	.385	433	555	.780	194	1523	23.8
VERN MICKELSEN	66	363	866	.419	283	372	.761	180	1009	15.3
JIM POLLARD	65	411	1155	.356	183	260	.704	234	1005	15.5
SLATER MARTIN	66	237	632	.375	142	190	.747	249	616	9.3
FRANK SAUL	64	157	436	.360	119	153	.778	147	433	6.8
BOB HARRISON	65	156	487	.320	89	124	.718	188	401	6.2
HOWIE SCHULTZ	66	89	315	.283	90	119	.756	102	268	4.1
WHITEY SKOOG	35	102	296	.345	30	38	.789	60	234	6.7
LEW HITCH	61	77	215	.358	63	94	.670	50	217	3.6
JOE HUTTON	60	53	158	.335	49	70	.700	62	155	2.6
JOHN PITCH	9	1	10	.100	3	6	.500	2	5	0.6

NBA PLAYOFFS

FIRST ROUND
DEF. INDIANAPOLIS, 2-0
SECONDROUND
DEF. ROCHESTER, 3-1
FINALS
DEF. NEW YORK, 4-3

TEAM LEADERS

SCORING
MIKAN 23.8

ASSISTS
MARTIN 3.8

REBOUNDS
MIKAN 13.5

FIELD GOAL PCT.
MIKKELSEN 419

FREE THROW PCT
MIKAN 780

MINUTES PLAYED
MIKAN 40.2

LEAGUE AWARDS

ALL-NBA TEAM
MIKAN, FIRST TEAM
MIKKELSEN, POLLARD, SECOND TEAM

ALL-STAR TEAM
MIKAN
MIKKELSEN
POLLARD

MINNESOTA 1952-53
1ST WESTERN DIVISION; NBA CHAMPIONS

REGULAR SEASON RECORD
48-22

PLAYER	G	FGM	FGA	PCT	FTM	FTA	PCT	AST	PT	PPG
GEORGE MIKAN	70	500	1252	.399	442	567	.780	201	1442	20.6
VERN MIKKELSEN	70	378	868	.435	291	387	.752	148	1047	15.0
JIM POLLARD	66	333	933	.357	193	251	.769	231	859	13.0
SLATER MARTIN	70	260	634	.410	224	287	.780	250	744	10.6
FRANK SAUL	70	187	471	.397	142	200	.710	110	516	7.4
BOB HARRISON	70	195	518	.376	107	165	.648	160	497	7.1
JIM HOLSTEIN	66	98	274	.358	70	105	.667	74	266	4.0
LEW HITCH	70	89	255	.349	83	136	.610	66	261	3.7
WHITEY SKOOG	68	102	264	.386	46	61	.754	82	250	3.7
HOWIE SCHULTZ	40	24	90	.267	43	62	.694	29	91	2.3

NBA PLAYOFFS

FIRST ROUND
DEF. INDIANAPOLIS, 2-0

SECOND ROUND
DEF. FT. WAYNE, 3-2

FINALS
DEF. NEW YORK, 4-1

TEAM LEADERS

SCORING
MIKAN 20.6

ASSISTS
MARTIN 3.6

REBOUNDS
MIKAN 14.4

FIELD GOAL PCT.
MIKKELSEN 498

FREE THROW PCT
MARTIN 780

MINUTES PLAYED
MIKAN 37.9

LEAGUE AWARDS

ALL-NBA TEAM
MIKAN, FIRST TEAM
MIKKELSEN, SECOND TEAM

MINNESOTA 1953-54
1ST WESTERN DIVISION; NBA CHAMPIONS

REGULAR SEASON RECORD
46-26

PLAYER	G	FGM	FGA	PCT	FTM	FTA	PCT	AST	PTS	PPG
GEORGE MIKAN	72	441	1160	.380	424	546	.777	174	1306	18.1
JIM POLLARD	71	326	882	.370	179	230	.778	214	831	11.7
VERN MIKKELSEN	72	288	771	.374	221	298	.742	119	797	11.1
SLATER MARTIN	69	254	654	.388	176	243	.724	253	684	9.9
CLYDE LOVELLETTE	72	237	560	.423	114	164	.695	51	588	8.2
WHITEY SKOOG	71	212	530	.400	72	97	.742	179	496	7.0
FRANK SAUL	71	162	467	.347	128	170	.753	139	452	6.4
DICK SCHNITTKER	71	122	307	.397	86	132	.652	59	330	4.6
JIM HOLSTEIN	70	88	288	.306	64	112	.571	79	240	3.4

NBA PLAYOFFS

FIRST ROUND
DEF. ROCHESTER, 1-0

SECOND ROUND
DEF. FT. WAYNE, 1-0

THIRD ROUND
DEF. ROCHESTER, 2-1

FINALS
DEF. SYRACUSE, 4-3

TEAM LEADERS

SCORING
MIKAN 18.1

ASSISTS
MARTIN 3.7

REBOUNDS
MIKAN 14.3

FIELD GOAL PCT.
LOVELLETTE 423

FREE THROW PCT
MIKAN 777

MINUTES PLAYED
POLLARD 35.0

LEAGUE AWARDS

ALL-NBA TEAM
MIKAN, FIRST TEAM
POLLARD, SECOND TEAM

ALL-STAR TEAM
MIKAN
POLLARD

MINNESOTA 1954-55
2ND WESTERN DIVISION

REGULAR SEASON RECORD
40-32

PLAYER	G	FGM	FGA	PCT	FTM	FTA	PCT	AST	PTS	PPG
VERN MIKKELSEN	71	440	1043	.422	447	598	.747	145	1327	18.7
CLYDE LOVELLETTE	70	519	1192	.435	273	398	.686	100	1311	18.7
SLATER MARTIN	72	350	919	.381	276	359	.769	427	976	13.6
WHITEY SKOOG	72	330	836	.395	125	155	.806	251	785	10.9
DICK SCHNITTKER	72	226	583	.388	298	362	.823	114	750	10.4
JIM POLLARD	63	265	749	.354	151	186	.812	160	681	10.8
LEW HITCH	74	167	417	.400	115	169	.680	125	449	6.1
ED KALAFAT	72	118	375	.315	111	168	.661	75	347	4.8
JIM HOLSTEIN	62	107	330	.324	67	94	.713	58	281	4.5
DON SUNDERLAGE	45	33	133	.248	48	73	.658	37	114	2.5
ROBERT CARNEY	19	24	64	.375	21	40	.525	16	69	3.6

NBA PLAYOFFS

FIRST ROUND
DEF. ROCHESTER, 2-1

SECOND ROUND
LOST TO FT. WAYNE, 1-3

TEAM LEADERS

SCORING
MIKKELSEN 18.7

ASSISTS
MARTIN 5.9

REBOUNDS
LOVELLETTE 11.5

FIELD GOAL PCT.
LOVELLETTE 498

FREE THROW PCT
SCHNITTKER 823

MINUTES PLAYED
MARTIN 38.7

LEAGUE AWARDS

ALL-NBA TEAM
MIKKELSEN, MARTIN, SECOND TEAM

ALL-STAR TEAM
MIKKELSEN
POLLARD

MINNESOTA 1955-56
3RD WESTERN DIVISION

REGULAR SEASON RECORD
33-39

PLAYER	G	FGM	FGA	PCT	FTM	FTA	PCT	AST	PTS	PPG
CLYDE LOVELLETTE	71	594	1370	.434	338	469	.721	164	1526	21.5
VERN MIKKELSEN	72	317	821	.386	328	408	.804	173	962	13.4
SLATER MARTIN	72	309	863	.358	329	395	.833	445	947	13.2
WHITEY SKOOG	72	340	854	.398	155	193	.803	255	835	11.6
DICK SCHNITTKER	72	254	647	.393	304	355	.856	142	812	11.3
ED KALAFAT	72	194	540	.359	186	252	.738	130	574	8.0
GEORGE MIKAN	37	148	375	.395	94	122	.770	53	390	10.5
DICK GARMAKER	68	138	373	.370	112	139	.806	104	388	5.7
CHARLES MENCEL	69	120	375	.320	78	96	.813	132	318	4.6
LEW HITCH	69	94	235	.400	100	132	.758	77	288	4.2
BOB WILLIAMS	20	21	46	.457	24	45	.533	7	66	3.3
JOHNNY HORAN	19	12	42	.286	10	11	.909	2	34	1.8
RON FEIREISEL	10	8	28	.286	14	16	.875	6	30	3.0

NBA PLAYOFFS

FIRST ROUND
LOST TO ST. LOUIS, 1-2

TEAM LEADERS

SCORING
LOVELLETTE 21.5

ASSISTS
MARTIN 6.2

REBOUNDS
LOVELLETTE 14.0

FIELD GOAL PCT.
LOVELLETTE 434

FREE THROW PCT
SCHNITTKER 856

MINUTES PLAYED
LOVELLETTE 35.5

LEAGUE AWARDS

ALL-NBA TEAM
LOVELLETTE, MARTIN, SECOND TEAM

ALL-STAR TEAM
MIKKELSEN

MINNESOTA 1956-57
2ND WESTERN DIVISION

REGULAR
SEASON RECORD
34-38

PLAYER	G	FGM	FGA	PCT	FTM	FTA	PCT	AST	PTS	PPG
CLYDE LOVELLETTE	69	574	1348	.426	286	399	.717	139	1434	20.8
DICK GARMAKER	72	406	1015	.400	365	435	.839	190	1177	16.3
VERN MIKKELSEN	72	322	854	.377	342	424	.807	121	986	13.7
BOB LEONARD	72	303	867	.349	186	241	.772	169	792	11.0
WALTER DUKES	71	228	626	.364	264	383	.689	54	720	10.1
CHARLES MENCEL	72	243	688	.353	179	240	.746	201	665	9.2
ED KALAFAT	65	178	507	.351	197	298	.661	105	553	8.5
JIM PAXSON	71	138	485	.285	170	236	.720	86	446	6.3
DICK SCHNITTKER	70	113	351	.322	160	193	.829	52	386	5.5
WHITEY SKOOG	23	78	220	.355	44	47	.936	76	200	8.7
BOB WILLIAMS	4	1	4	.250	2	3	.667	0	4	1.0

NBA PLAYOFFS

FIRST ROUND
DEF. FT. WAYNE, 2-0

SECOND ROUND
LOST TO ST. LOUIS, 0-3

TEAM LEADERS

SCORING
LOVELLETTE 20.8

ASSISTS
GARMAKER 2.6

REBOUNDS
LOVELLETTE 13.4

FIELD GOAL PCT.
LOVELLETTE 426

FREE THROW PCT
GARMAKER 839

MINUTES PLAYED
LOVELLETTE 36.1

LEAGUE AWARDS

ALL-NBA TEAM
GARMAKER, SECOND TEAM

ALL-STAR TEAM
MIKKELSEN

MINNESOTA 1957-58
4TH WESTERN DIVISION

REGULAR
SEASON RECORD
19-53

PLAYER	G	FGM	FGA	PCT	FTM	FTA	PCT	AST	PTS	PPG
VERN MIKKELSEN	72	439	1070	.410	370	471	.786	166	1248	17.3
LARRY FOUST	72	391	982	.398	428	566	.756	108	1210	16.8
DICK GARMAKER	68	390	988	.395	314	411	.764	183	1094	16.1
BOB LEONARD	66	266	794	.335	205	268	.765	218	737	11.2
ED FLEMING	72	226	655	.345	181	255	.710	139	633	8.8
JIM KREBS	68	199	527	.378	135	176	.767	27	533	7.8
WALTER DEVLIN	70	170	489	.348	133	172	.773	167	473	6.8
DICK SCHNITTKER	50	128	357	.359	201	237	.848	71	457	9.1
ROD HUNDLEY	65	174	548	.318	104	162	.642	121	452	7.0
BO ERIAS	18	59	170	.347	30	.47	638	26	148	8.2
FRANK SELVY	38	44	167	.263	47	77	.610	35	135	3.6
MCCOY INGRAM	24	27	103	.262	13	28	.464	20	67	2.8
BOB BURROW	14	22	70	.314	11	33	.333	6	55	3.9
GEORGE BROWN	1	0	2	.000	1	2	.500	0	1	1.0

NBA PLAYOFFS

DID NOT ADVANCE TO PLAYOFFS

TEAM LEADERS

SCORING
MIKKELSEN 17.3

ASSISTS
LEONARD 3.3

REBOUNDS
FOUST 12.2

FIELD GOAL PCT.
MIKKELSEN 410

FREE THROW PCT
SCHNITTKER 848

MINUTES PLAYED
MIKKELSEN 33.3

LEAGUE AWARDS

NONE

MINNESOTA 1958-59
2ND WESTERN DIVISION; NBA FINALISTS

REGULAR
SEASON RECORD
33-39

PLAYER	G	FGM	FGA	PCT	FTM	FTA	PCT	AST	PTS	PPG
ELGIN BAYLOR	70	605	1482	.408	532	685	.777	287	1742	24.9
VERN MIKKELSEN	72	353	904	.390	286	355	.806	159	992	13.8
DICK GARMAKER	72	350	885	.395	284	368	.772	211	984	13.7
LARRY FOUST	72	301	771	.390	280	366	.765	91	882	12.3
ROD HUNDLEY	71	259	719	.360	164	218	.752	205	682	9.6
JIM KREBS	72	271	679	.399	92	123	.748	50	634	8.8
BOB LEONARD	58	206	552	.373	120	160	.750	186	532	9.2
ED FLEMING	71	192	419	.458	137	190	.721	89	521	7.3
BOO ELLIS	72	163	379	.430	102	144	.708	59	428	5.9
STEVE HAMILTON	67	109	294	.371	74	109	.679	36	292	4.4

NBA PLAYOFFS

FIRST ROUND
DEF. DETROIT, 2-1

SECOND ROUND
DEF. ST. LOUIS, 4-2

FINALS
LOST TO BOSTON, 0-4

TEAM LEADERS

SCORING
BAYLOR 24.9

ASSISTS
BAYLOR 4.1

REBOUNDS
BAYLOR 15.0

FIELD GOAL PCT.
BAYLOR 408

FREE THROW PCT
MIKKELSEN 839

MINUTES PLAYED
BAYLOR 40.8

LEAGUE AWARDS

ALL-NBA TEAM
BAYLOR, FIRST TEAM

ROOKIE OF THE YEAR
ELGIN BAYLOR

ALL-STAR TEAM
BAYLOR

MINNESOTA 1959-60
3RD WESTERN DIVISION

REGULAR
SEASON RECORD
25-50

PLAYER	G	FGM	FGA	PCT	FTM	FTA	PCT	AST	PTS	PPG
ELGIN BAYLOR	70	755	1781	.424	564	770	.732	243	2074	29.6
RUDY LARUSSO	71	355	913	.389	265	357	.742	83	975	13.7
ROD HUNDLEY	73	365	1019	.358	203	273	.744	338	933	12.8
BOB LEONARD	73	231	717	.322	136	193	.705	252	598	8.2
JIM KREBS	75	237	605	.392	98	136	.721	38	572	7.6
FRANK SELVY	62	205	521	.393	153	208	.736	111	563	9.1
TOM HAWKINS	69	220	579	.380	106	164	.646	54	546	7.9
RAY FELIX	47	136	355	.383	70	112	.625	23	342	7.3
BOO ELLIS	46	64	185	.346	51	76	.671	27	179	3.9
ED FLEMING	27	59	141	.418	53	69	.768	38	171	6.3
CHARLIE SHARE	41	59	151	.391	53	80	.663	62	171	4.2
RON SOBIE	16	37	108	.343	31	37	.838	21	105	6.6
STEVE HAMILTON	15	29	77	.377	18	23	.783	7	76	5.1
BOBBY SMITH	10	13	54	.241	11	16	.688	14	37	3.7
NICK MANTIS	10	10	39	.256	1	2	.500	9	21	2.1

NBA PLAYOFFS

FIRST ROUND
DEF. DETROIT, 2-0

SECOND ROUND
LOST TO ST. LOUIS, 3-4

TEAM LEADERS

SCORING
BAYLOR 29.6

ASSISTS
HUNDLEY 4.6

REBOUNDS
BAYLOR 16.4

FIELD GOAL PCT.
BAYLOR 424

FREE THROW PCT
HUNDLEY 744

MINUTES PLAYED
BAYLOR 41.0

LEAGUE AWARDS

ALL-NBA TEAM
BAYLOR, FIRST TEAM

ALL-STAR TEAM
BAYLOR

LOS ANGELES 1960-61

2ND WESTERN DIVISION

REGULAR SEASON RECORD
36-43

PLAYER	G	FGM	FGA	PCT	FTM	FTA	PCT	AST	PTS	PPG
ELGIN BAYLOR	73	931	2166	.430	676	863	.783	371	2538	34.8
JERRY WEST	79	529	1264	.419	331	497	.666	333	1389	17.6
RUDY LARUSSO	79	416	992	.419	323	409	.790	135	1155	14.6
ROD HUNDLEY	79	323	921	.351	223	296	.753	350	869	11.0
FRANK SELVY	77	311	767	.405	210	279	.753	246	832	10.8
TOM HAWKINS	78	310	719	.431	140	235	.596	88	760	9.7
JIM KREBS	75	271	692	.392	75	93	.806	68	617	8.2
RAY FELIX	78	189	508	.372	135	193	.699	37	513	6.6
BOB LEONARD	55	61	207	.295	71	100	.710	81	193	3.5
HOWIE JOLLIFF	46	46	141	.326	11	23	.478	16	103	2.2
RON JOHNSON	14	13	43	.302	11	17	.647	2	37	2.6
GARY ALCORN	20	12	40	.300	7	8	.875	2	31	1.6

NBA PLAYOFFS

FIRST ROUND
DEF. DETROIT, 3-2

SECOND ROUND
LOST TO ST. LOUIS, 3-4

TEAM LEADERS

SCORING
BAYLOR 34.8

ASSISTS
BAYLOR 5.1

REBOUNDS
BAYLOR 19.8

FIELD GOAL PCT.
HAWKINS 431

FREE THROW PCT
LARUSSO 790

MINUTES PLAYED
BAYLOR 42.9

LEAGUE AWARDS

ALL-NBA TEAM
BAYLOR, FIRST TEAM

ALL-STAR TEAM
BAYLOR
WEST
HUNDLEY

LOS ANGELES 1961-62

1ST WESTERN DIVISION; NBA FINALISTS

REGULAR SEASON RECORD
54-26

PLAYER	G	FGM	FGA	PCT	FTM	FTA	PCT	AST	PTS	PPG
JERRY WEST	75	799	1795	.445	712	926	.769	402	2310	30.8
ELGIN BAYLOR	48	680	1588	.428	476	631	.754	222	1836	38.3
RUDY LARUSSO	80	516	1108	.466	342	448	.763	179	1374	17.2
FRANK SELVY	79	433	1032	.420	298	404	.738	381	1164	14.7
JIM KREBS	78	312	701	.445	156	208	.750	110	780	10.0
TOM HAWKINS	79	289	704	.411	143	222	.644	95	721	9.1
RAY FELIX	80	171	398	.430	90	130	.692	55	432	5.4
ROD HUNDLEY	78	173	509	.340	83	127	.654	290	429	5.5
HOWIE JOLLIFF	64	104	253	.411	41	78	.526	76	249	3.9
BOB MCNEILL	50	56	136	.412	26	34	.765	89	138	2.8
WAYNE YATES	37	31	105	.295	10	22	.455	16	72	1.9
BOBBY SMITH	3	0	1	.000	0	0	N/A	0	0	0.0

NBA PLAYOFFS

FIRST ROUND
BYE

SECOND ROUND
DEF. DETROIT, 4-2

FINALS
LOST TO BOSTON, 3-4

TEAM LEADERS

SCORING
WEST 30.8

ASSISTS
WEST 5.4

REBOUNDS
BAYLOR 18.6

FIELD GOAL PCT.
LARUSSO 466

FREE THROW PCT
WEST 769

MINUTES PLAYED
WEST 41.2

LEAGUE AWARDS

ALL-NBA TEAM
BAYLOR, WEST, FIRST TEAM

ALL-STAR TEAM
BAYLOR
WEST
SELVY
LARUSSO

LOS ANGELES 1962-63
1ST WESTERN DIVISION; NBA FINALISTS

REGULAR
SEASON RECORD
53-27

PLAYER	G	FGM	FGA	PCT	FTM	FTA	PCT	AST	PTS	
ELGIN BAYLOR	80	1029	2273	.453	661	790	.837	386	2719	34.0
JERRY WEST	55	559	1213	.461	371	477	.778	307	1489	27.1
DICK BARNETT	80	547	1162	.471	343	421	.815	224	1437	18.0
RUDY LARUSSO	75	321	761	.422	282	393	.718	187	924	12.3
FRANK SELVY	80	317	747	.424	192	269	.714	281	826	10.3
JIM KREBS	79	272	627	.434	115	154	.747	87	659	8.3
LEROY ELLIS	80	222	530	.419	133	202	.658	46	577	7.2
ROD HUNDLEY	65	88	262	.336	84	119	.706	151	260	4.0
GENE WILEY	75	109	236	.462	23	68	.338	40	241	3.2
RON HORN	28	27	82	.329	20	29	.690	10	74	2.6
HOWIE JOLLIFF	28	15	55	.273	6	9	.667	20	36	1.3

NBA PLAYOFFS

FIRST ROUND
BYE

SECOND ROUND
DEF. ST. LOUIS, 4-3

FINALS
LOST TO BOSTON, 2-4

TEAM LEADERS

SCORING
BAYLOR 34.0

ASSISTS
BAYLOR 4.8

REBOUNDS
BAYLOR 14.3

FIELD GOAL PCT.
BARNETT 471

FREE THROW PCT
BAYLOR 837

MINUTES PLAYED
BAYLOR 42.1

LEAGUE AWARDS

ALL-NBA TEAM
BAYLOR, WEST, FIRST TEAM

ALL-STAR TEAM
BAYLOR
WEST
LARUSSO

LOS ANGELES 1963-64
3RD WESTERN DIVISION

REGULAR
SEASON RECORD
42-38

PLAYER	G	FGM	FGA	PCT	FTM	FTA	PCT	AST	PTS	PPG
JERRY WEST	72	740	1529	.484	584	702	.832	403	2064	28.7
ELGIN BAYLOR	78	756	1778	.425	471	586	.804	347	1983	25.4
DICK BARNETT	78	541	1197	.452	351	454	.773	238	1433	18.4
RUDY LARUSSO	79	337	776	.434	298	397	.751	190	972	12.3
LEROY ELLIS	78	200	473	.423	112	170	.659	41	512	6.6
DON NELSON	80	135	323	.418	149	201	.741	76	419	5.2
FRANK SELVY	73	160	423	.378	78	122	.639	149	398	5.5
GENE WILEY	78	146	273	.535	45	75	.600	44	337	4.3
JIM KREBS	68	134	357	.375	65	85	.765	49	333	4.9
JIM KING	60	84	198	.424	66	101	.653	110	234	3.9
HUB REED	46	33	91	.363	10	15	.667	23	76	1.7
MEL GIBSON	8	6	20	.300	1	2	.500	6	13	1.6

NBA PLAYOFFS

FIRST ROUND
LOST TO ST. LOUIS, 2-3

TEAM LEADERS

SCORING
WEST 28.7

ASSISTS
WEST 5.6

REBOUNDS
BAYLOR 12.0

FIELD GOAL PCT.
WEST 484

FREE THROW PCT
WEST 832

MINUTES PLAYED
BAYLOR 40.6

LEAGUE AWARDS

ALL-NBA TEAM
BAYLOR, WEST, FIRST TEAM

ALL-STAR TEAM
BAYLOR
WEST

LOS ANGELES 1964-65
1ST WESTERN DIVISION; NBA FINALISTS

REGULAR
SEASON RECORD
49-31

PLAYER	G	FGM	FGA	PCT	FTM	FTA	PCT	AST	PTS	PPG
JERRY WEST	74	822	1655	.497	648	789	.821	364	2292	31.0
ELGIN BAYLOR	74	763	1903	.401	483	610	.792	280	2009	27.1
RUDY LARUSSO	77	381	827	.461	321	415	.773	198	1083	14.1
DICK BARNETT	74	375	908	.413	270	338	.799	159	1020	13.8
LEROY ELLIS	80	311	700	.444	198	284	.697	49	820	10.3
JIM KING	77	184	469	.392	118	151	.781	178	486	6.3
GENE WILEY	80	175	376	.465	56	111	.505	105	406	5.1
DARRALL IMHOFF	76	145	311	.466	88	154	.571	87	378	5.0
WALT HAZZARD	66	117	306	.382	46	71	.648	140	280	4.2
DON NELSON	39	36	85	.424	20	26	.769	24	92	2.4
COTTON NASH	25	14	57	.246	25	32	.781	10	53	2.1
BILL MCGILL	8	7	20	.350	1	1	1.000	3	15	1.9
JERRY GROTE	11	6	11	.545	2	2	1.000	4	14	1.3

NBA PLAYOFFS

FIRST ROUND
BYE

SECOND ROUND
DEF. BALTIMORE, 4-2

FINALS
LOST TO BOSTON, 1-4

TEAM LEADERS

SCORING
WEST 31.0

ASSISTS
WEST 4.9

REBOUNDS
BAYLOR 12.8

FIELD GOAL PCT.
WEST 497

FREE THROW PCT
WEST 821

MINUTES PLAYED
WEST 41.4

LEAGUE AWARDS

ALL-NBA TEAM
BAYLOR, WEST, FIRST TEAM

ALL-STAR TEAM
BAYLOR
WEST

LOS ANGELES 1965-66
1ST WESTERN DIVISION; NBA FINALISTS

REGULAR
SEASON RECORD
45-35

PLAYER	G	FGM	FGA	PCT	FTM	FTA	PCT	AST	PTS	
JERRY WEST	79	818	1731	.473	840	977	.860	480	2476	31.3
RUDY LARUSSO	76	410	897	.457	350	445	.787	165	1170	15.4
WALT HAZZARD	80	458	1003	.457	182	257	.708	393	1098	13.7
ELGIN BAYLOR	65	415	1034	.401	249	337	.739	224	1079	16.6
LEROY ELLIS	80	393	927	.424	186	256	.727	74	972	12.2
BOB BOOZER	78	365	754	.484	225	289	.779	87	955	12.2
JIM KING	76	238	545	.437	94	115	.817	223	570	7.5
GAIL GOODRICH	65	203	503	.404	103	149	.691	103	509	7.8
DARRALL IMHOFF	77	151	337	.448	77	136	.566	113	379	4.9
GENE WILEY	67	123	289	.426	43	76	.566	63	289	4.3
JOHN FAIRCHILD	30	23	89	.258	14	20	.700	11	60	2.0

NBA PLAYOFFS

FIRST ROUND
BYE

SECOND ROUND
DEF. ST. LOUIS, 4-3

FINALS
LOST TO BOSTON, 3-4

TEAM LEADERS

SCORING
WEST 31.3

ASSISTS
WEST 6.1

REBOUNDS
ELLIS 9.2

FIELD GOAL PCT.
BOOZER 484

FREE THROW PCT
WEST 860

MINUTES PLAYED
WEST 40.7

LEAGUE AWARDS

ALL-NBA TEAM
WEST, FIRST TEAM

ALL-STAR TEAM
WEST
LARUSSO

LOS ANGELES 1966-67

3RD WESTERN DIVISION

REGULAR
SEASON RECORD
36-45

PLAYER	G	FGM	FGA	PCT	FTM	FTA	PCT	AST	PTS	PPG
JERRY WEST	66	645	1389	.464	602	686	.878	447	1892	28.7
ELGIN BAYLOR	70	711	1658	.429	440	541	.813	215	1862	26.6
GAIL GOODRICH	77	352	776	.454	253	337	.751	210	957	12.4
DARRALL IMHOFF	81	370	780	.474	127	207	.614	222	867	10.7
ARCHIE CLARK	76	331	732	.452	136	192	.708	205	798	10.5
WALT HAZZARD	79	301	706	.426	129	177	.729	323	731	9.3
TOM HAWKINS	76	275	572	.481	82	173	.474	83	632	8.3
RUDY LARUSSO	45	211	509	.415	156	224	696	78	578	12.8
JIM BARNES	80	217	497	.437	128	187	.684	47	562	7.0
JERRY CHAMBERS	68	224	496	.452	68	93	.731	44	516	7.6
MEL COUNTS	31	112	252	.444	40	54	.741	22	264	8.5
JOHN BLOCK	22	20	52	.385	24	34	.706	5	64	2.9
HANK FINKEL	27	17	47	.362	7	12	.583	5	41	1.5

NBA PLAYOFFS

FIRST ROUND
LOST TO S.F., 0-3

TEAM LEADERS

SCORING
WEST 28.7

ASSISTS
WEST 6.8

REBOUNDS
IMHOFF 13.3

FIELD GOAL PCT.
HAWKINS 481

FREE THROW PCT
WEST. 878

MINUTES PLAYED
IMHOFF 33.6

LEAGUE AWARDS

ALL-NBA TEAM
BAYLOR, WEST, FIRST TEAM

ALL-STAR TEAM
BAYLOR
WEST
IMHOFF

LOS ANGELES 1967-68

2ND WESTERN DIVISION; NBA FINALISTS

REGULAR
SEASON RECORD
52-30

PLAYER	G	FGM	FGA	PCT	FTM	FTA	PCT	AST	PTS	PPG
ELGIN BAYLOR	77	757	1709	.443	488	621	.786	355	2002	26.0
ARCHIE CLARK	81	628	1309	.480	356	481	.740	353	1612	19.9
JERRY WEST	51	476	926	.514	391	482	.811	310	1343	26.3
GAIL GOODRICH	79	395	812	.486	302	392	.770	205	1092	13.8
MEL COUNTS	82	384	808	.475	190	254	.748	139	958	11.7
TOM HAWKINS	78	389	779	.499	125	229	.546	117	903	11.6
DARRALL IMHOFF	82	293	613	.478	177	286	.619	206	763	9.3
FREDDIE CRAWFORD	38	159	330	.482	74	120	.617	95	392	10.3
ERWIN MUELLER	39	132	254	.520	61	103	.592	78	325	8.3
JIM BARNES	42	101	235	.430	59	88	.670	27	261	6.2
JOHN WETZEL	38	52	119	.437	35	46	.761	51	139	3.7
DENNIS HAMILTON	44	54	108	.500	13	13	1.000	30	121	2.8
CLIFF ANDERSON	18	7	29	.241	12	28	.429	17	26	1.4

NBA PLAYOFFS

FIRST ROUND
DEF. ST. LOUIS, 4-2

SECOND ROUND
DEF. CHICAGO, 4-1

THIRD ROUND
DEF. S.F., 4-0

FINALS
LOST TO BOSTON, 2-4

TEAM LEADERS

SCORING
BAYLOR 26.0

ASSISTS
BAYLOR 4.6

REBOUNDS
BAYLOR 12.2

FIELD GOAL PCT.
WEST. 514

FREE THROW PCT
WEST. 811

MINUTES PLAYED
CLARK 37.5

LEAGUE AWARDS

ALL-NBA TEAM
BAYLOR, FIRST TEAM
WEST, SECOND TEAM

ALL-STAR TEAM
BAYLOR
WEST
CLARK

LOS ANGELES 1968-69

1ST WESTERN DIVISION; NBA FINALISTS

REGULAR SEASON RECORD
55-27

PLAYER	G	FGM	FGA	PCT	FTM	FTA	PCT	AST	PTS	PPG
ELGIN BAYLOR	76	730	1632	.447	421	567	.743	408	1881	24.8
WILT CHAMBERLAIN	81	641	1099	.583	382	857	.446	366	1664	20.5
JERRY WEST	61	545	1156	.471	490	597	.821	423	1580	25.9
MEL COUNTS	77	390	867	.450	178	221	.805	109	958	12.4
JOHNNY EGAN	82	246	597	.412	204	240	.850	215	696	8.5
KEITH ERICKSON	77	264	629	.420	120	175	.686	194	648	8.4
BILL HEWITT	75	239	528	.453	61	106	.575	76	539	7.2
TOM HAWKINS	74	230	461	.499	62	151	.411	81	522	7.1
FREDDIE CRAWFORD	81	211	454	.465	83	154	.539	154	505	6.2
CLIFF ANDERSON	35	44	108	.407	47	82	.573	31	135	3.9
JAY CARTY	28	34	89	.382	8	11	.727	11	76	2.7

NBA PLAYOFFS

FIRST ROUND
DEF. S.F., 4-2

THIRD ROUND
DEF. ATLANTA, 4-1

FINALS
LOST TO BOSTON, 3-4

TEAM LEADERS

SCORING
BAYLOR 24.8

ASSISTS
WEST 6.9

REBOUNDS
CHAMBERLAIN 21.1

FIELD GOAL PCT.
CHAMBERLAIN 583

FREE THROW PCT
EGAN 850

MINUTES PLAYED
CHAMBERLAIN 45.3

LEAGUE AWARDS

ALL-NBA TEAM
BAYLOR, FIRST TEAM
WEST, SECOND TEAM

PLAYOFFS MVP
WEST

ALL-STAR TEAM
BAYLOR
WEST
CHAMBERLAIN

ALL-ROOKIE TEAM
HEWITT

LOS ANGELES 1969-70

2ND WESTERN DIVISION; NBA FINALISTS

REGULAR SEASON RECORD
46-36

PLAYER	G	FGM	FGA	PCT	FTM	FTA	PCT	AST	PTS	PPG
JERRY WEST	74	831	1673	.497	647	785	.824	554	2309	31.2
WILT CHAMBERLAIN	12	129	227	.568	70	157	.446	49	328	27.3
ELGIN BAYLOR	54	511	1051	.486	276	357	.773	292	1298	24.0
HAPPY HAIRSTON	55	426	870	.490	281	350	.803	110	1133	20.6
MEL COUNTS	81	434	1017	.427	156	201	.776	160	1024	12.6
DICK GARRETT	73	354	816	.434	138	162	.852	180	846	11.6
KEITH ERICKSON	68	258	563	.458	91	122	.746	209	607	8.9
RICK ROBERSON	74	262	586	.447	120	212	.566	92	644	8.7
WILLIE MCCARTER	40	132	349	.378	43	60	.717	93	307	7.7
JOHNNY EGAN	72	215	491	.438	99	121	.818	216	529	7.3
JOHN TRESVANT	20	47	88	.534	23	35	.657	17	117	5.9
BILL HEWITT	20	25	88	.284	16	31	.516	28	66	3.3
MIKE LYNN	44	44	133	.331	31	48	.646	30	119	2.7

NBA PLAYOFFS

FIRST ROUND
DEF. PHOENIX, 4-3

SECOND ROUND
DEF. ATLANTA, 4-3

FINALS
LOST TO NEW YORK, 3-4

TEAM LEADERS

SCORING
WEST 31.2

ASSISTS
WEST 7.5

REBOUNDS
HAIRSTON 12.3

FIELD GOAL PCT.
WEST 497

FREE THROW PCT
WEST 824

MINUTES PLAYED
WEST 42.0

LEAGUE AWARDS

ALL-NBA TEAM
WEST, FIRST TEAM

ALL-STAR TEAM
BAYLOR
WEST

LOS ANGELES 1970-71

1ST PACIFIC DIVISION

REGULAR SEASON RECORD
48-34

PLAYER	G	FGM	FGA	PCT	FTM	FTA	PCT	AST	PTS	PPG
JERRY WEST	69	667	1351	.494	525	631	.832	655	1859	26.9
WILT CHAMBERLAIN	82	668	1226	.545	360	669	.538	352	1696	20.7
HAPPY HAIRSTON	80	574	1233	.466	337	431	.782	168	1485	18.6
GAIL GOODRICH	79	558	1174	.475	264	343	.770	380	1380	17.5
KEITH ERICKSON	73	369	783	.471	85	112	.759	223	823	11.3
ELGIN BAYLOR	2	8	19	.421	4	6	.667	2	20	10.0
JIM MCMILLIAN	81	289	629	.459	100	130	.769	133	678	8.4
WILLIE MCCARTER	76	247	592	.417	46	77	.597	126	540	7.1
JOHN TRESVANT	8	18	35	.514	7	10	.700	10	43	5.4
RICK ROBERSON	65	125	301	.415	88	143	.615	47	338	5.2
PAT RILEY	54	105	254	.413	56	87	.644	72	266	4.9
FRED HETZEL	59	111	256	.434	60	77	.779	37	282	4.8
ERNIE KILLUM	4	0	4	.000	1	1	1.000	0	1	0.3

NBA PLAYOFFS

FIRST ROUND
DEF. CHICAGO, 4-3

THIRD ROUND
LOST TO MILWAUKEE, 1-4

TEAM LEADERS

SCORING
WEST 26.9

ASSISTS
WEST 9.5

REBOUNDS
CHAMBERLAIN 18.2

FIELD GOAL PCT.
CHAMBERLAIN 545

FREE THROW PCT
WEST 832

MINUTES PLAYED
CHAMBERLAIN 44.3

LEAGUE AWARDS

ALL-NBA TEAM
WEST, FIRST TEAM

ALL-STAR TEAM
WEST
CHAMBERLAIN

LOS ANGELES 1971-72

1ST PACIFIC DIVISION; NBA CHAMPIONS

REGULAR SEASON RECORD
69-13

PLAYER	G	FGM	FGA	PCT	FTM	FTA	PCT	AST	PTS	PPG
GAIL GOODRICH	82	826	1695	.487	475	559	.850	365	2127	25.9
JERRY WEST	77	735	1540	.477	515	633	.814	747	1985	25.8
JIM MCMILLIAN	80	642	1331	.482	219	277	.791	209	1503	18.8
WILT CHAMBERLAIN	82	496	764	.649	221	524	.422	329	1213	14.8
HAPPY HAIRSTON	80	368	798	.461	311	399	.779	193	1047	13.1
ELGIN BAYLOR	9	42	97	.433	22	27	.815	18	106	11.8
FLYNN ROBINSON	64	262	535	.490	111	129	.860	138	635	9.9
PAT RILEY	67	197	441	.447	55	74	.743	75	449	6.7
JOHN TRAPP	58	139	314	.443	51	73	.699	42	329	5.7
KEITH ERICKSON	15	40	83	.482	6	7	.857	35	86	5.7
LEROY ELLIS	74	138	300	.460	66	95	.695	46	342	4.6
JIM CLEAMONS	38	35	100	.350	28	36	.778	35	98	2.6

NBA PLAYOFFS

FIRST ROUND
DEF. CHICAGO, 4-0

SECOND ROUND
DEF. MILWAUKEE, 4-2

FINALS
DEF. NEW YORK, 4-1

TEAM LEADERS

SCORING
GOODRICH 25.9

ASSISTS
WEST 9.7

REBOUNDS
CHAMBERLAIN 19.2

FIELD GOAL PCT.
CHAMBERLAIN 649

FREE THROW PCT
GOODRICH 850

MINUTES PLAYED
CHAMBERLAIN 42.3

LEAGUE AWARDS

ALL-NBA TEAM
WEST, FIRST TEAM
CHAMBERLAIN, SECOND TEAM

PLAYOFFS MVP
CHAMBERLAIN

COACH OF THE YEAR
BILL SHARMAN

ALL-STAR TEAM
WEST
CHAMBERLAIN
GOODRICH

LOS ANGELES 1972-73

1ST PACIFIC DIVISION; NBA FINALISTS

REGULAR SEASON RECORD
60-22

PLAYER	G	FGM	FGA	PCT	FTM	FTA	PCT	AST	PTS	PPG
GAIL GOODRICH	76	750	1615	.464	314	374	.840	332	1814	23.9
JERRY WEST	69	618	1291	.479	339	421	.805	607	1575	22.8
JIM MCMILLIAN	81	655	1431	.458	223	264	.845	221	1533	18.9
HAPPY HAIRSTON	28	158	328	.482	140	178	.787	68	456	16.3
WILT CHAMBERLAIN	82	426	586	.727	232	455	.510	365	1084	13.2
BILL BRIDGES	72	286	597	.479	133	190	.700	196	705	9.8
KEITH ERICKSON	76	299	696	.430	89	110	.809	242	687	9.0
PAT RILEY	55	167	390	.428	65	82	.793	81	399	7.3
JIM PRICE	59	158	359	.440	60	73	.822	97	376	6.4
FLYNN ROBINSON	6	14	28	.500	6	8	.750	8	34	5.7
MEL COUNTS	59	127	278	.457	39	58	.672	62	293	5.0
TRAVIS GRANT	33	51	116	.440	23	26	.885	7	125	3.8
LEROY ELLIS	10	11	40	.275	4	5	.800	3	26	2.6
JOHN TRAPP	5	3	12	.250	7	10	.700	21	13	2.6
BILL TURNER	19	17	52	.327	4	7	.571	11	38	2.0
ROGER BROWN	1	0	0	N/A	1	3	.333	0	1	1.0

NBA PLAYOFFS

FIRST ROUND
DEF. CHICAGO, 4-3OND

SECOND ROUND
DEF. GOLDEN STATE, 4-1

FINALS
LOST TO NEW YORK, 1-4

TEAM LEADERS

SCORING
GOODRICH 23.9

ASSISTS
WEST 8.8

REBOUNDS
CHAMBERLAIN 18.6

FIELD GOAL PCT.
CHAMBERLAIN 727

FREE THROW PCT
MCMILLIAN 845

MINUTES PLAYED
CHAMBERLAIN 43.2

LEAGUE AWARDS

ALL-NBA TEAM
WEST, FIRST TEAM

ALL-STAR TEAM
WEST
CHAMBERLAIN
GOODRICH

ALL-ROOKIE TEAM
PRICE

LOS ANGELES 1973-74

1ST PACIFIC DIVISION

REGULAR SEASON RECORD
47-35

PLAYER	G	FGM	FGA	PCT	FTM	FTA	PCT	AST	PTS	PPG
GAIL GOODRICH	82	784	1773	.442	508	588	.864	427	2076	25.3
JERRY WEST	31	232	519	.447	165	198	.833	206	629	20.3
JIM PRICE	82	538	1197	.449	187	234	.799	369	1263	15.4
HAPPY HARISTON	77	385	759	.507	343	445	.771	208	1113	14.5
CONNIE HAWKINS	71	368	733	.502	173	224	.772	379	909	12.8
ELMORE SMITH	81	434	949	.457	147	249	.590	150	1015	12.5
PAT RILEY	72	287	667	.430	110	144	.764	148	684	9.5
BILL BRIDGES	65	216	513	.421	116	164	.707	148	548	8.4
STAN LOVE	51	119	278	.428	49	64	.766	48	287	5.6
KERMIT WASHINGTON	45	73	151	.483	26	49	.531	19	172	3.8
MEL COUNTS	45	61	167	.365	24	33	.727	54	146	3.2
NATE HAWTHORNE	33	38	93	.409	30	48	.625	23	106	3.2
TRAVIS GRANT	3	1	4	.250	1	3	.333	0	3	1.0

NBA PLAYOFFS

FIRST ROUND
LOST TO MILWAUKEE, 1-4

TEAM LEADERS

SCORING
GOODRICH 25.3

ASSISTS
GOODRICH 5.2

REBOUNDS
HAIRSTON 13.5

FIELD GOAL PCT.
HAIRSTON 507

FREE THROW PCT
GOODRICH 864

MINUTES PLAYED
GOODRICH 37.3

LEAGUE AWARDS

ALL-NBA TEAM
GOODRICH, FIRST TEAM

ALL-STAR TEAM
GOODRICH

LOS ANGELES 1974-75
5TH PACIFIC DIVISION

REGULAR SEASON RECORD
30-52

PLAYER	G	FGM	FGA	PCT	FTM	FTA	PCT	AST	PTS	PPG
GAIL GOODRICH	72	656	1429	.459	318	378	.841	420	1630	22.6
JIM PRICE	9	75	167	.449	41	45	.911	63	191	21.2
LUCIUS ALLEN	56	443	1006	.440	207	269	.770	319	1093	19.5
CAZZIE RUSSELL	40	264	580	.455	101	113	.894	109	629	15.7
BRIAN WINTERS	68	359	810	.443	76	92	.826	195	794	11.7
PAT RILEY	46	219	523	.419	69	93	.742	121	507	11.0
ELMORE SMITH	74	346	702	.493	112	231	.485	145	804	10.9
HAPPY HAIRSTON	74	271	536	.506	217	271	.801	173	759	10.3
STU LANTZ	56	189	446	.424	145	176	.824	158	523	9.3
CONNIE HAWKINS	43	139	324	.429	68	99	.687	120	346	8.0
STAN LOVE	30	85	194	.438	47	66	.712	26	217	7.2
ZELMO BEATY	69	136	310	.439	108	135	.800	74	380	5.5
CORKY CALHOUN	57	120	286	.420	44	62	.710	75	284	5.0
KERMIT WASHINGTON	55	87	207	.420	72	122	.590	66	246	4.5
BILL BRIDGES	17	20	57	.351	16	30	.533	27	56	3.3

NBA PLAYOFFS
DID NOT ADVANCE TO SEASON PLAYOFFS

TEAM LEADERS
SCORING
GOODRICH 22.6
ASSISTS
GOODRICH 5.8
REBOUNDS
HAIRSTON 12.6
FIELD GOAL PCT.
HAIRSTON 506
FREE THROW PCT
GOODRICH 841
MINUTES PLAYED
GOODRICH 37.1

LEAGUE AWARDS
ALL-STAR TEAM
GOODRICH
ALL-ROOKIE TEAM
WINTERS

LOS ANGELES 1975-76
4TH PACIFIC DIVISION

REGULAR SEASON RECORD
40-42

PLAYER	G	FGM	FGA	PCT	FTM	FTA	PCT	AST	PTS	PPG
KAREEM ABDUL JABBAR	82	914	1728	.529	447	636	.703	413	2275	27.7
GAIL GOODRICH	75	583	1321	.441	293	346	.847	421	1459	19.5
LUCIUS ALLEN	76	461	1004	.459	197	254	.776	357	1119	14.7
CAZZIE RUSSELL	74	371	802	.463	132	148	.892	122	874	11.8
DONNIE FREEMAN	64	263	606	.434	163	199	.819	171	689	10.8
DON FORD	76	311	710	.438	104	139	.748	111	726	9.6
CORNELL WARNER	81	251	524	.479	89	128	.695	106	591	7.3
PAT RILEY	2	5	13	.385	1	3	.333	0	11	5.5
CORKY CALHOUN	76	172	368	.467	65	83	.783	85	409	5.4
RON WILLIAMS	9	17	43	.395	10	13	.769	21	44	4.9
STU LANTZ	53	85	204	.417	80	89	.899	76	250	4.7
WALT WESLEY	1	1	2	.500	2	4	.500	1	4	4.0
KERMIT WASHINGTON	36	39	90	.433	45	66	.682	20	123	3.4
CLIFF MEELY	20	20	51	.392	24	32	.750	9	64	3.2
JIM MCDANIELS	35	41	102	.402	9	9	1.000	15	91	2.6
C.J. KUPEC	16	10	40	.250	7	11	.636	5	27	1.7
JOHN ROCHE	15	3	14	.214	2	4	.500	6	8	0.5

NBA PLAYOFFS
DID NOT ADVANCE TO SEASON PLAYOFFS

TEAM LEADERS
SCORING
ABDUL-JABBAR 27.7
ASSISTS
GOODRICH 5.6
REBOUNDS
ABDUL-JABBAR 16.9
FIELD GOAL PCT.
ABDUL-JABBAR 529
FREE THROW PCT
RUSSELL 892
MINUTES PLAYED
ABDUL-JABBAR 41.2

LEAGUE AWARDS
ALL-NBA TEAM
ABDUL-JABBAR, FIRST TEAM
SEASON MVP
ABDUL-JABBAR
ALL-STAR TEAM
ABDUL-JABBAR

LOS ANGELES 1976-77

1ST PACIFIC DIVISION

REGULAR SEASON RECORD
53-29

PLAYER	G	FGM	FGA	PCT	FTM	FTA	PCT	AST	PTS	PPG
KAREEM ABDUL-JABBAR	82	888	1533	.579	376	536	.701	319	2152	26.2
CAZZIE RUSSELL	82	578	1179	.490	188	219	.858	210	1344	16.4
LUCIUS ALLEN	472	1035		.456	195	252	.774	405	1139	14.6
KERMIT WASHINGTON	53	191	380	.503	132	187	.706	48	514	9.7
EARL TATUM	68	283	607	.466	72	100	.720	118	638	9.4
MACK CALVIN	12	27	82	.329	41	48	.854	21	95	7.9
DON FORD	82	262	570	.460	73	102	.716	133	597	7.3
BO LAMAR	71	228	561	.406	46	68	.676	177	502	7.1
TOM ABERNETHY	70	169	349	.484	101	134	.754	98	439	6.3
DON CHANEY	81	213	522	.408	70	94	.745	308	496	6.1
JOHNNY NEUMANN	59	146	363	.402	54	81	.667	137	346	5.9
C.J. KUPEC	82	153	342	.447	78	101	.772	53	384	4.7
CORNELL WARNER	14	25	53	.472	4	6	.667	11	54	3.9
ALLEN MURPHY	2	1	5	.200	3	7	.429	0	5	2.5
MARV ROBERTS	28	27	76	.355	4	6	.667	19	58	2.1

NBA PLAYOFFS

FIRST ROUND
DEF. GOLDEN STATE, 4-3

SECOND ROUND
LOST TO PORTLAND, 0-4

TEAM LEADERS

SCORING
ABDUL-JABBAR 26.2

ASSISTS
ALLEN. 5.2

REBOUNDS
ABDUL-JABBAR 13.3

FIELD GOAL PCT.
ABDUL-JABBAR. 579

FREE THROW PCT
RUSSELL. 862

MINUTES PLAYED
ABDUL-JABBAR 36.8

LEAGUE AWARDS

ALL-NBA TEAM
ABDUL-JABBAR, FIRST TEAM

SEASON MVP
ABDUL-JABBAR

ALL-STAR TEAM
ABDUL-JABBAR

LOS ANGELES 1977-78

4TH PACIFIC DIVISION

REGULAR SEASON RECORD
45-37

PLAYER	G	FGM	FGA	PCT	FTM	FTA	PCT	AST	PTS	PPG
KAAREEM ABDUL-JABBAR	62	663	1205	.550	274	350	.783	269	1600	25.8
ADRIAN DANTLEY	56	377	725	.520	334	417	.801	188	1088	19.4
JAMES EDWARDS	25	145	316	.459	80	125	.640	29	370	14.8
EARL TATUM	25	153	314	.487	45	59	.763	70	351	14.0
LOU HUDSON	82	493	992	.497	137	177	.774	193	1123	13.7
NORM NIXON	81	496	998	.497	115	161	.714	553	1107	13.7
JAMAAL WILKES	51	277	630	.440	106	148	.716	182	660	12.9
CHARLIE SCOTT	48	225	509	.442	110	142	.775	235	560	11.7
KERMIT WASHINGTON	25	110	244	.451	68	110	.618	30	288	11.5
DON FORD	79	272	576	.472	68	90	.756	142	612	7.7
TOM ABERNETHY	73	201	404	.498	91	111	.820	101	493	6.8
KENNY CARR	52	134	302	.444	55	85	.647	26	323	6.2
DAVE ROBISCH	55	104	249	.418	50	65	.769	40	258	4.7
ERNIE DIGREGORIO	25	41	100	.410	16	20	.800	71	98	3.9
DON CHANEY	9	13	36	.361	5	6	.833	17	31	3.4
BRAD DAVIS	33	30	72	.417	22	29	.759	83	82	2.5

NBA PLAYOFFS

FIRST ROUND
LOST TO SEATTLE, 1-2

TEAM LEADERS

SCORING
ABDUL-JABBAR 25.8

ASSISTS
NIXON 6.8

REBOUNDS
ABDUL-JABBAR 12.9

FIELD GOAL PCT.
ABDUL-JABBAR. 550

FREE THROW PCT
DANTLEY. 801

MINUTES PLAYED
NIXON 34.3

LEAGUE AWARDS

ALL-NBA TEAM
ABDUL-JABBAR, SECOND TEAM

ALL-ROOKIE TEAM
NIXON

LOS ANGELES 1978-79
3RD PACIFIC DIVISION

REGULAR
SEASON RECORD
47-35

PLAYER	G	FGM	FGA	PCT	FTM	FTA	PCT	AST	PTS	PPG
KAREEM ABDUL-JABBAR	80	777	1347	.577	349	474	.736	431	1903	23.8
JAMAAL WILKES	82	626	1242	.504	272	362	.751	227	1524	18.6
ADRIAN DANTLEY	60	374	733	.510	292	342	.854	138	1040	17.3
NORM NIXON	82	623	1149	.542	158	204	.775	737	1404	17.1
LOU HUDSON	78	329	636	.517	110	124	.887	141	768	9.8
RON BOONE	82	259	569	.455	90	104	.865	154	608	7.4
KENNY CARR	72	225	450	.500	83	137	.606	60	533	7.4
DON FORD	79	228	450	.507	72	89	.809	101	528	6.7
JIM PRICE	75	171	344	.497	55	79	.696	218	397	5.3
DAVE ROBISCH	80	150	336	.446	86	115	.748	97	386	4.8
BRAD DAVIS	5	8	11	.727	3	4	.750	9	19	3.8
RON CARTER	46	54	124	.435	36	54	.667	25	144	3.1
MICHAEL COOPER	3	3	6	.500	0	0	N/A	0	6	2.0

NBA PLAYOFFS

FIRST ROUND
DEF. DENVER, 2-1

SECOND ROUND
LOST TO SEATTLE, 1-4

TEAM LEADERS

SCORING
ABDUL-JABBAR 23.8

ASSISTS
NIXON 9.0

REBOUNDS
ABDUL-JABBAR 12.8

FIELD GOAL PCT.
ABDUL-JABBAR. 577

FREE THROW PCT
DANTLEY. 854

MINUTES PLAYED
ABDUL-JABBAR 39.5

LEAGUE AWARDS

ALL-NBA TEAM
ABDUL-JABBAR, SECOND TEAM

ALL-STAR TEAM
ABDUL-JABBAR

LOS ANGELES 1979-80
1ST PACIFIC DIVISION; NBA CHAMPIONS

REGULAR
SEASON RECORD
60-22

PLAYER	G	FGM	FGA	PCT	FTM	FTA	PCT	AST	PTS	PPG
KAREEM ABDUL-JABBAR	82	835	1383	.604	364	476	.765	371	2034	24.8
JAMAAL WILKES	82	726	1358	.535	189	234	.808	250	1644	20.0
MAGIC JOHNSON	77	503	949	.530	374	462	.810	563	1387	18.0
NORM NIXON	82	624	1209	.516	197	253	.779	642	1446	17.6
JIM CHONES	82	372	760	.489	125	169	.740	151	869	10.6
SPENCER HAYWOOD	76	288	591	.487	159	206	.772	93	736	9.7
MICHAEL COOPER	82	303	578	.524	111	143	.776	221	722	8.8
MARK LANDSBERGER	23	66	137	.482	29	56	.518	14	161	7.0
RON BOONE	6	14	40	.350	6	7	.857	7	34	5.7
KENNY CARR	5	7	16	.438	2	2	1.000	1	16	3.2
DON FORD	52	66	130	.508	23	28	.821	36	155	3.0
BRAD HOLLAND	38	44	104	.423	15	16	.938	22	106	2.8
MARTY BYRNES	32	25	50	.500	13	15	.867	13	63	2.0
OLLIE MACK	27	21	50	.420	9	18	.500	20	51	1.9
BUTCH LEE	11	4	13	.308	6	7	.857	9	14	1.3

NBA PLAYOFFS

FIRST ROUND
DEF. PHOENIX, 4-1

SECOND ROUND
DEF. SEATTLE, 4-1

FINALS
DEF. PHILADELPHIA, 4-2

TEAM LEADERS

SCORING
ABDUL-JABBAR 24.8

ASSISTS
NIXON 8.0

REBOUNDS
ABDUL-JABBAR 10.8

FIELD GOAL PCT.
ABDUL-JABBAR. 604

FREE THROW PCT
E. JOHNSON 810

MINUTES PLAYED
NIXON 39.4

LEAGUE AWARDS

ALL-NBA TEAM
ABDUL-JABBAR, FIRST TEAM

SEASON MVP
ABDUL-JABBAR

PLAYOFFS MVP
E. JOHNSON

ALL-STAR TEAM
ABDUL-JABBAR
E. JOHNSON

ALL-ROOKIE TEAM
E. JOHNSON

LOS ANGELES 1980-81
2ND PACIFIC DIVISION

REGULAR SEASON RECORD
54-28

PLAYER	G	FGM	FGA	PCT	FTM	FTA	PCT	AST	PTS	PPG
KAREEM ABDUL-JABBAR	80	836	1457	.574	423	552	.766	272	2095	26.2
JAMAAL WILKES	81	786	1495	.526	254	335	.758	235	1827	22.6
MAGIC JOHNSON	37	312	587	.532	171	225	.760	317	798	21.6
NORM NIXON	79	576	1210	.476	196	252	.778	696	1350	17.1
JIM CHONES	82	378	751	.503	126	193	.653	153	882	10.8
MICHAEL COOPER	81	321	654	.491	117	149	.785	332	763	9.4
MARK LANDSBERGER	69	164	327	.502	62	116	.534	27	390	5.7
BUTCH CARTER	54	114	247	.462	70	95	.737	52	301	5.6
EDDIE JORDAN	60	120	279	.430	63	95	.663	195	306	5.1
BRAD HOLLAND	41	47	111	.423	35	49	.714	23	130	3.2
JIM BREWER	78	107	197	.543	15	40	.375	55	229	2.9
ALAN HARDY	22	22	59	.373	7	10	.700	3	51	2.3
MYLES PATRICK	3	2	5	.400	1	2	.500	1	5	1.7
TONY JACKSON	2	1	3	.333	0	0	N/A	2	2	1.0

NBA PLAYOFFS
FIRST ROUND
LOST TO HOUSTON, 1-2

TEAM LEADERS
SCORING
ABDUL-JABBAR 26.2
ASSISTS
NIXON 8.8
REBOUNDS
ABDUL-JABBAR 10.3
FIELD GOAL PCT.
ABDUL-JABBAR 573
FREE THROW PCT
M. COOPER 785
MINUTES PLAYED
WILKES 37.3

LEAGUE AWARDS
ALL-NBA TEAM
ABDUL-JABBAR, FIRST TEAM
ALL-STAR TEAM
ABDUL-JABBAR
WILKES

LOS ANGELES 1981-82
1ST PACIFIC DIVISION; NBA CHAMPIONS

REGULAR SEASON RECORD
57-25

PLAYER	G	FGM	FGA	PCT	FTM	FTA	PCT	AST	PTS	PPG
KAREEM ABDUL-JABBAR	76	753	1301	.579	312	442	.706	225	1818	23.9
JAMAAL WILKES	82	744	1417	.525	246	336	.732	143	1734	21.1
MAGIC JOHNSON	78	556	1036	.537	329	433	.760	743	1447	18.6
NORM NIXON	82	628	1274	.493	181	224	.808	652	1440	17.6
MITCH KUPCHAK	26	153	267	.573	65	98	.663	33	371	14.3
MICHAEL COOPER	76	383	741	.517	139	171	.813	230	907	11.9
BOB MCADOO	41	151	330	.458	90	126	.714	32	392	9.6
MIKE MCGEE	39	80	172	.465	31	53	.585	16	191	4.9
KURT RAMBIS	64	118	228	.518	59	117	.504	56	295	4.6
MARK LANDSBERGER	75	144	329	.438	33	65	.508	32	321	4.3
EDDIE JORDAN	58	89	208	.428	43	54	.796	131	222	3.8
CLAY JOHNSON	7	11	20	.550	3	6	.500	7	25	3.6
JIM BREWER	71	81	175	.463	7	19	.368	42	170	2.4
KEVIN MCKENNA	36	28	87	.322	11	17	.647	14	67	1.9

NBA PLAYOFFS
FIRST ROUND
DEF. PHOENIX, 4-0
SECOND ROUND
DEF. SAN ANTONIO, 4-0
FINALS
DEF. PHILADELPHIA, 4-2

TEAM LEADERS
SCORING
ABDUL-JABBAR 23.9
ASSISTS
NIXON 9.5
REBOUNDS
E. JOHNSON 9.6
FIELD GOAL PCT.
ABDUL-JABBAR 579
FREE THROW PCT
M. COOPER 813
MINUTES PLAYED
WILKES 38.7

LEAGUE AWARDS
ALL-NBA TEAM
E. JOHNSON, SECOND TEAM
PLAYOFFS MVP
E. JOHNSON
ALL-STAR TEAM
ABDUL-JABBAR
E. JOHNSON
NIXON

LOS ANGELES 1982-83

1ST PACIFIC DIVISION; NBA FINALISTS

REGULAR SEASON RECORD
58-24

PLAYER	G	FGM	FGA	PCT	FTM	FTA	PCT	AST	PTS	PPG
KAREEM ADBUL-JABBAR	79	722	1228	.588	278	371	.749	200	1722	21.8
JAMAAL WILKES	80	684	1290	.530	203	268	.757	182	1571	19.6
MAGIC JOHNSON	79	511	933	.548	304	380	.800	829	1326	16.8
NORM NIXON	79	533	1123	.475	125	168	.744	566	1191	15.1
BOB MCADOO	47	292	562	.520	119	163	.730	39	703	15.0
JAMES WORTHY	77	447	772	.579	138	221	.624	132	1033	13.4
STEVE MIX	1	4	10	.400	1	1	1.000	2	9	9.0
MICHAEL COOPER	82	266	497	.535	102	130	.785	315	639	7.8
KURT RAMBIS	78	235	413	.569	114	166	.687	90	584	7.5
DWIGHT JONES	32	62	132	.470	32	48	.667	22	156	4.9
MIKE MCGEE	39	69	163	.423	17	23	.739	26	156	4.0
CLAY JOHNSON	48	53	135	.393	38	48	.792	24	144	3.0
EDDIE JORDAN	35	40	132	.303	11	17	.647	80	94	2.7
MARK LANDSBERGER	39	43	102	.422	12	25	.480	12	98	2.5
BILLY RAY BATES	4	2	16	.125	1	2	.500	0	5	1.3
JOE COOPER	2	1	4	.250	0	0	N/A	0	2	1.0

NBA PLAYOFFS

FIRST ROUND
DEF. PORTLAND, 4-1

SECOND ROUND
DEF. SAN ANTONIO, 4-2

FINALS
LOST TO PHILADELPHIA, 0-4

TEAM LEADERS

SCORING
ABDUL-JABBAR 21.8

ASSISTS
E. JOHNSON 10.5

REBOUNDS
E. JOHNSON 8.6

FIELD GOAL PCT
ABDUL-JABBAR 558

FREE THROW PCT
E. JOHNSON 800

MINUTES PLAYED
E. JOHNSON 36.8

LEAGUE AWARDS

ALL-NBA TEAM
E. JOHNSON, FIRST TEAM
ABDUL-JABBAR, SECOND TEAM

ALL-STAR TEAM
ABDUL-JABBAR
E. JOHNSON
WILKES

ALL-ROOKIE TEAM
WORTHY

LOS ANGELES 1983-84

1ST PACIFIC DIVISION; NBA FINALISTS

REGULAR SEASON RECORD
54-28

PLAYER	G	FGM	FGA	PCT	FTM	FTA	PCT	AST	PTS	PPG
KAREEM ABDUL-JABBAR	80	716	1238	.578	285	394	.723	211	1717	21.5
MAGIC JOHNSON	67	441	780	.565	290	358	.810	875	1178	17.6
JAMAAL WILKES	75	542	1055	.514	208	280	.743	214	1294	17.3
JAMES WORTHY	82	495	890	.556	195	257	.759	207	1185	14.5
BOB MCADOO	70	352	748	.471	212	264	.803	74	916	13.1
BYRON SCOTT	74	334	690	.484	112	139	.806	177	788	10.6
MIKE MCGEE	77	347	584	.594	61	113	.540	81	757	9.8
MICHAEL COOPER	82	273	549	.497	155	185	.838	482	739	9.0
CALVIN GARRETT	41	78	152	.513	30	39	.769	31	188	4.6
SWEN NATER	69	124	253	.490	63	91	.692	27	311	4.5
KURT RAMBIS	47	63	113	.558	42	66	.636	34	168	3.6
LARRY SPRIGGS	38	44	82	.537	36	50	.720	30	124	3.3
MITCH KUPCHAK	34	41	108	.380	22	34	.647	7	104	3.1
EDDIE JORDAN	3	4	8	.500	1	2	.500	5	9	3.0

NBA PLAYOFFS

FIRST ROUND
DEF. KANSAS CITY, 3-0

SECOND ROUND
DEF. DALLAS, 4-1

THIRD ROUND
DEF. PHOENIX, 4-2

FINALS
LOST TO BOSTON, 3-4

TEAM LEADERS

SCORING
ABDUL-JABBAR 21.5

ASSISTS
E. JOHNSON 13.1

REBOUNDS
ABDUL-JABBAR 7.3

FIELD GOAL PCT.
MCGEE 594

FREE THROW PCT
M. COOPER 838

MINUTES PLAYED
ABDUL-JABBAR 32.8

LEAGUE AWARDS

ALL-NBA TEAM
ABDUL-JABBAR, E. JOHNSON, FIRST TEAM

ALL-STAR TEAM
ABDUL-JABBAR
E. JOHNSON

ALL-ROOKIE TEAM
B. SCOTT

LOS ANGELES 1984-85

1ST PACIFIC DIVISION; NBA CHAMPIONS

REGULAR SEASON RECORD 62-20

PLAYER	G	FGM	FGA	PCT	FTM	FTA	PCT	AST	PTS	PPG
KAREEM ABDUL-JABBAR	79	723	1207	.599	289	395	.732	249	1735	22.0
MAGIC JOHNSON	77	504	899	.561	391	464	.843	968	1406	18.3
JAMES WORTHY	80	610	1066	.572	190	245	.776	201	1410	17.6
BYRON SCOTT	81	541	1003	.539	187	228	.820	244	1295	16.0
BOB MCADOO	66	284	546	.520	122	162	.753	67	690	10.5
MIKE MCGEE	76	329	612	.538	94	160	.588	71	774	10.2
MICHAEL COOPER	82	276	593	.465	115	133	.865	429	702	8.6
JAMAAL WILKES	42	148	303	.488	51	66	.773	41	347	8.3
LARRY SPRIGGS	75	194	354	.548	112	146	.767	132	500	6.7
MITCH KUPCHAK	58	123	244	.504	60	91	.659	21	306	5.3
KURT RAMBIS	82	181	327	.554	68	103	.660	69	430	5.2
RONNIE LESTER	32	34	82	.415	21	31	.677	80	89	2.8
CHUCK NEVITT	11	5	17	.294	2	8	.250	3	12	1.1
EARL JONES	2	0	1	.000	0	0	N/A	0	0	0.0

NBA PLAYOFFS

FIRST ROUND DEF. PHOENIX, 3-0
SECOND ROUND DEF. PORTLAND, 4-1
THIRD ROUND DEF. DENVER, 4-1
FINALS DEF. BOSTON, 4-2

TEAM LEADERS

SCORING ABDUL-JABBAR 22.0
ASSISTS E. JOHNSON 12.6
REBOUNDS ABDUL-JABBAR 7.9
FIELD GOAL PCT. ABDUL-JABBAR 599
FREE THROW PCT M. COOPER 865
MINUTES PLAYED E. JOHNSON 36.1

LEAGUE AWARDS

ALL-NBA TEAM E. JOHNSON, FIRST TEAM ABDUL-JABBAR, SECOND TEAM
PLAYOFFS MVP ABDUL-JABBAR
ALL-STAR TEAM ABDUL-JABBAR E. JOHNSON

LOS ANGELES 1985-86

1ST PACIFIC DIVISION

REGULAR SEASON RECORD 62-20

PLAYER	G	FGM	FGA	PCT	FTM	FTA	PCT	AST	PTS	PPG
KAREEM ABDUL-JABBBAR	79	755	1338	.564	336	439	.765	280	1846	23.4
JAMES WORTHY	75	629	1086	.579	242	314	.771	201	1500	20.0
MAGIC JOHNSON	72	483	918	.526	378	434	.871	907	1354	18.8
BYRON SCOTT	76	507	989	.513	138	176	.784	164	1174	15.4
MAURICE LUCAS	77	302	653	.462	180	230	.783	84	785	10.2
MICHAEL COOPER	82	274	606	.452	147	170	.865	466	758	9.2
MIKE MCGEE	71	252	544	.463	42	64	.656	83	587	8.3
PETUR GUDMUNDSSON	8	20	37	.541	18	27	.667	3	58	7.3
A.C. GREEN	82	209	388	.539	102	167	.611	54	521	6.4
MITCH KUPCHAK	55	124	257	.482	84	112	.750	17	332	6.0
KURT RAMBIS	74	160	269	.595	88	122	.721	69	408	5.5
LARRY SPRIGGS	43	88	192	.458	38	49	.776	49	214	5.0
JEROME HENDERSON	1	2	3	.667	0	0	N/A	0	4	4.0
RONNIE LESTER	27	26	52	.500	15	19	.789	54	67	2.5
CHUCK NEVITT	4	3	11	.273	4	6	.667	2	10	2.5

NBA PLAYOFFS

FIRST ROUND DEF. SAN ANTONIO, 3-0
SECOND ROUND DEF. DALLAS, 4-2
THIRD ROUND LOST TO HOUSTON, 1-4

TEAM LEADERS

SCORING ABDUL-JABBAR . . . . . . : 23.4
ASSISTS E. JOHNSON 12.6
REBOUNDS LUCAS 7.4
FIELD GOAL PCT. WORTHY 579
FREE THROW PCT E. JOHNSON 871
MINUTES PLAYED ABDUL-JABBAR 33.3

LEAGUE AWARDS

ALL-NBA TEAM ABDUL-JABBAR, E. JOHNSON, FIRST TEAM
ALL-STAR TEAM ABDUL-JABBAR E. JOHNSON WORTHY

LOS ANGELES 1986-87

1ST PACIFIC DIVISION; NBA CHAMPIONS

PLAYER	G	FGM	FGA	PCT	FTM	FTA	PCT	AST	PTS	PPG
MAGIC JOHNSON	80	683	1308	.522	535	631	.848	977	1909	23.9
JAMES WORTHY	82	651	1207	.539	292	389	.751	226	1594	19.4
KAREEM ABDUL-JABBAR	78	560	993	.564	245	343	.714	203	1366	17.5
BYRON SCOTT	82	554	1134	.489	224	251	.892	281	1397	17.0
A.C. GREEN	79	316	587	.538	220	282	.780	84	852	10.8
MICHAEL COOPER	82	322	736	.438	126	148	.851	373	859	10.5
MYCHAL THOMPSON	33	129	269	.480	75	101	.743	28	333	10.1
KURT RAMBIS	78	163	313	.521	120	157	.764	63	446	5.7
BILLY THOMPSON	59	142	261	.544	48	74	.649	60	332	5.6
ADRIAN BRANCH	32	48	96	.500	42	54	.778	16	138	4.3
WES MATTHEWS	50	89	187	.476	29	36	.806	100	208	4.2
FRANK BRICKOWSKI	37	53	94	.564	40	59	.678	12	146	3.9
MIKE SMREK	35	30	60	.500	16	25	.640	5	76	2.2

NBA PLAYOFFS

FIRST ROUND
DEF. DENVER, 3-0

SECOND ROUND
DEF. GOLDEN STATE, 4-1

THIRD ROUND
DEF. SEATTLE, 4-0

FINALS
DEF. BOSTON, 4-2

TEAM LEADERS

SCORING
E. JOHNSON 23.9

ASSISTS
E. JOHNSON 12.2

REBOUNDS
GREEN 7.8

FIELD GOAL PCT.
ABDUL-JABBAR 564

FREE THROW PCT
B. SCOTT 892

MINUTES PLAYED
E. JOHNSON 36.3

LEAGUE AWARDS

ALL-NBA TEAM
E. JOHNSON, FIRST TEAM

SEASON MVP
E. JOHNSON

PLAYOFFS MVP
E. JOHNSON

DEFENSIVE PLAYER OF THE YEAR
M. COOPER

ALL-STAR TEAM
ABDUL-JABBAR
E. JOHNSON
WORTHY

LOS ANGELES 1987-88

1ST PACIFIC DIVISION; NBA CHAMPIONS

PLAYER	G	FGM	FGA	PCT	FTM	FTA	PCT	AST	PTS	PPG
BYRON SCOTT	81	710	1348	.527	272	317	.858	335	1754	21.7
JAMES WORTHY	75	617	1161	.531	242	304	.796	289	1478	19.7
MAGIC JOHNSON	72	490	996	.492	417	489	.853	858	1408	19.6
KAREEM ABDUL-JABBAR	80	480	903	.532	205	269	.762	135	1165	14.6
MYCHAL THOMPSON	80	370	722	.512	185	292	.634	66	925	11.6
A.C. GREEN	82	322	640	.503	293	379	.773	93	937	11.4
TONY CAMPBELL	13	57	101	.564	28	39	.718	15	143	11.0
MICHAEL COOPER	61	189	482	.392	97	113	.858	289	532	8.7
WES MATTHEWS	51	114	248	.460	54	65	.831	138	289	5.7
KURT RAMBIS	70	102	186	.548	73	93	.785	54	277	4.0
MILT WAGNER	40	62	147	.422	26	29	.897	61	152	3.8
RAY TOLBERT	14	16	28	.571	10	13	.769	5	42	3.0
MIKE SMERK	48	44	103	.427	44	66	.667	8	132	2.8
BILLY THOMPSON	9	3	13	.231	8	10	.800	1	14	1.6
JEFF LAMP	3	0	0	N/A	2	2	1.000	0	2	0.7

NBA PLAYOFFS

FIRST ROUND
DEF. SAN ANTONIO, 3-0

SECOND ROUND
DEF. UTAH, 4-3

THIRD ROUND
DEF. DALLAS, 4-3

FINALS
DEF. DETROIT, 4-3

TEAM LEADERS

SCORING
B. SCOTT. 21.7

ASSISTS
E. JOHNSON 11.9

REBOUNDS
GREEN 8.7

FIELD GOAL PCT.
ABDUL-JABBAR 532

FREE THROW PCT
B. SCOTT 858

MINUTES PLAYED
B. SCOTT. 37.6

LEAGUE AWARDS

ALL-NBA TEAM
E. JOHNSON, FIRST TEAM

PLAYOFFS MVP
WORTHY

ALL-STAR TEAM
ABDUL-JABBAR
E. JOHNSON
WORTHY

LOS ANGELES 1988-89

1ST PACIFIC DIVISION; NBA FINALISTS

REGULAR
SEASON RECORD
57-25

PLAYER	G	FGM	FGA	PCT	FTM	FTA	PCT	AST	PTS	PPG
MAGIC JOHNSON	77	579	1137	.509	513	563	.911	988	1730	22.5
JAMES WORTHY	81	702	1282	.548	251	321	.782	288	1657	20.5
BYRON SCOTT	74	588	1198	.491	195	226	.863	231	1448	19.6
A.C. GREEN	82	401	758	.529	282	359	.786	103	1088	13.3
KAREEM ABDUL-JABBAR	74	313	659	.475	122	165	.739	74	748	10.1
ORLANDO WOOLRIDGE	74	231	494	.468	253	343	.738	58	715	9.7
MYCHAL THOMPSON	80	291	521	.559	156	230	.678	48	738	9.2
MICHAEL COOPER	80	213	494	.431	81	93	.871	314	587	7.3
TONY CAMPBELL	63	158	345	.458	70	83	.843	47	388	6.2
DAVID RIVERS	47	49	122	.402	35	42	.833	106	134	2.9
MARK MCNAMARA	39	32	64	.500	49	78	.628	10	113	2.9
JEFF LAMP	37	27	69	.391	4	5	.800	15	60	1.6

NBA PLAYOFFS

FIRST ROUND
DEF. PORTLAND, 3-0

SECOND ROUND
DEF. SEATTLE, 4-0

THIRD ROUND
DEF. PHOENIX, 4-0

FINALS
LOST TO DETROIT, 0-4

TEAM LEADERS

SCORING
E. JOHNSON 22.5

ASSISTS
E. JOHNSON 12.8

REBOUNDS
GREEN 9.0

FIELD GOAL PCT.
WORTHY 548

FREE THROW PCT
E. JOHNSON 911

MINUTES PLAYED
WORTHY 36.5

LEAGUE AWARDS

ALL-NBA TEAM
E. JOHNSON, FIRST TEAM

SEASON MVP
E. JOHNSON

ALL-STAR TEAM
ABDUL-JABBAR
E. JOHNSON
WORTHY

LOS ANGELES 1989-90

1ST PACIFIC DIVISION

REGULAR
SEASON RECORD
63-19

PLAYER	G	FGM	FGA	PCT	FTM	FTA	PCT	AST	PTS	PPG
MAGIC JOHNSON	79	546	1138	.480	567	637	.890	907	1765	22.3
JAMES WORTHY	80	711	1298	.548	248	317	.782	288	1685	21.1
BYRON SCOTT	77	472	1005	.470	160	209	.766	274	1197	15.5
A.C. GREEN	82	385	806	.478	278	370	.751	90	1061	12.9
ORLANDO WOOLRIDGE	62	306	550	.556	176	240	.733	96	788	12.7
MYCHAL THOMPSON	70	281	562	.500	144	204	.706	43	706	10.1
VLADE DIVAC	82	274	549	.499	153	216	.708	75	701	8.5
MICHAEL COOPER	80	191	493	.387	83	94	.883	215	515	6.4
LARRY DREW	80	170	383	.444	46	60	.767	217	418	5.2
JAY VINCENT	24	41	78	.526	8	12	.667	10	90	3.8
MARK MCNAMARA	33	38	86	.442	26	40	.650	3	102	3.1
MEL MCCANTS	13	8	26	.308	6	8	.750	2	22	1.7
JAWANN OLDHAM	3	2	3	.667	1	2	.500	1	5	1.7
STEVE BUCKNALL	18	9	33	.273	5	6	.833	10	23	1.3
MIKE HIGGINS	6	0	0	N/A	1	2	.500	1	1	0.2

NBA PLAYOFFS

FIRST ROUND
DEF. HOUSTON, 3-1

SECOND ROUND
LOST TO PHOENIX, 1-4

TEAM LEADERS

SCORING
E. JOHNSON 22.3

ASSISTS
E. JOHNSON 11.5

REBOUNDS
GREEN 8.7

FIELD GOAL PCT.
WOOLRIDGE 556

FREE THROW PCT
E. JOHNSON 890

MINUTES PLAYED
WORTHY 37.0

LEAGUE AWARDS

ALL-NBA TEAM
E. JOHNSON, FIRST TEAM
WORTHY, THIRD TEAM

SEASON MVP
E. JOHNSON

COACH OF THE YEAR
PAT RILEY

ALL-STAR TEAM
GREEN
E. JOHNSON
WORTHY

ALL-ROOKIE TEAM
DIVAC

Los Angeles 1990-91
2ND PACIFIC DIVISION; NBA FINALISTS

REGULAR SEASON RECORD
58-24

PLAYER	G	FGM	FGA	PCT	FTM	FTA	PCT	AST	PTS	PPG
JAMES WORTHY	78	716	1455	.492	212	266	.797	275	1670	21.4
MAGIC JOHNSON	79	466	976	.477	519	573	.906	989	1531	19.4
BYRON SCOTT	82	501	1051	.477	118	148	.797	177	1191	14.5
SAM PERKINS	73	368	744	.495	229	279	.821	108	983	13.5
VLADE DIVAC	82	360	637	.565	196	279	.703	92	921	11.2
TERRY TEAGLE	82	335	757	.443	145	177	.819	82	815	9.9
A.C. GREEN	82	258	542	.476	223	302	.738	71	750	9.1
MYCHAL THOMPSON	72	113	228	.496	62	88	.705	21	288	4.0
TONY SMITH	64	97	220	.441	40	57	.702	135	234	3.7
LARRY DREW	48	54	125	.432	17	22	.773	118	139	2.9
ELDEN CAMPBELL	52	56	123	.455	32	49	.653	10	144	2.8
IRVING THOMAS	26	17	50	.340	12	21	.571	10	46	1.8
TONY BROWN	7	2	3	.667	0	0	N/A	3	5	0.7

NBA PLAYOFFS

FIRST ROUND
DEF. HOUSTON, 3-0

SECOND ROUND
DEF. GOLDEN STATE, 4-1

THIRD ROUND
DEF. PORTLAND, 4-2

FINALS
LOST TO CHICAGO, 1-4

TEAM LEADERS

SCORING
WORTHY 21.4

ASSISTS
E. JOHNSON 12.5

REBOUNDS
DIVAC 8.1

FIELD GOAL PCT.
DIVAC 565

FREE THROW PCT
E. JOHNSON 906

MINUTES PLAYED
WORTHY 38.6

LEAGUE AWARDS

ALL-NBA TEAM
E. JOHNSON, FIRST TEAM
WORTHY, THIRD TEAM

ALL-STAR TEAM
E. JOHNSON
WORTHY

Los Angeles 1991-92
6TH PACIFIC DIVISION

REGULAR SEASON RECORD
43-39

PLAYER	G	FGM	FGA	PCT	FTM	FTA	PCT	AST	PTS	PPG
JAMES WORTHY	54	450	1007	.447	166	204	.814	252	1075	19.9
SAM PERKINS	63	361	803	.450	304	372	.817	141	1041	16.5
SEDALE THREATT	82	509	1041	.489	202	243	.831	593	1240	15.1
BYRON SCOTT	82	460	1005	.458	244	291	.838	226	1218	14.9
A.C. GREEN	82	382	803	.476	340	457	.744	117	1116	13.6
VLADE DIVAC	36	157	317	.495	86	112	.768	60	405	11.3
TERRY TEAGLE	82	364	805	.452	151	197	.766	113	880	10.7
ELDEN CAMPBELL	81	220	491	.448	138	223	.619	59	578	7.1
TONY SMITH	63	113	283	.399	49	75	.653	109	275	4.4
CHUCKY BROWN	36	55	118	.466	25	41	.610	23	135	3.8
CLIFF ROBINSON	9	11	27	.407	7	8	.875	9	29	3.2
RORY SPARROW	42	57	143	.399	8	13	.615	79	124	3.0
JACK HALEY	49	31	84	.369	14	29	.483	7	76	1.6
DEMETRIUS CALIP	7	4	18	.222	2	3	.667	12	11	1.6
KEITH OWENS	20	9	32	.281	8	10	.800	3	26	1.3

NBA PLAYOFFS

FIRST ROUND
LOST TO PORTLAND, 1-3

TEAM LEADERS

SCORING
WORTHY 19.9

ASSISTS
THREATT 7.2

REBOUNDS
GREEN 9.3

FIELD GOAL PCT.
THREATT 489

FREE THROW PCT
B. SCOTT 838

MINUTES PLAYED
THREATT 37.4

LEAGUE AWARDS

ALL-STAR TEAM
E. JOHNSON
WORTHY

LOS ANGELES 1992-93
5TH PACIFIC DIVISION

REGULAR SEASON RECORD
39-43

PLAYER	G	FGM	FGA	PCT	FTM	FTA	PCT	AST	PTS	PPG
SEDALE THREATT	82	522	1028	.508	177	215	.823	564	1235	15.1
JAMES WORTHY	82	510	1142	.447	171	211	.810	278	1221	14.9
BYRON SCOTT	58	296	659	.449	156	184	.848	157	792	13.7
SAM PERKINS	49	242	527	.459	184	222	.829	128	673	13.7
A.C. GREEN	82	379	706	.537	277	375	.739	116	1051	12.8
VLADE DIVAC	82	397	819	.485	235	341	.689	232	1050	12.8
ANTHONY PEELER	77	297	634	.468	162	206	.786	166	802	10.4
ELDEN CAMPBELL	79	238	520	.458	130	204	.637	48	606	7.7
JAMES EDWARDS	52	122	270	.452	84	118	.712	41	328	6.3
DOUG CHRISTIE	23	45	106	.425	50	66	.758	53	142	6.2
TONY SMITH	55	133	275	.484	62	82	.756	63	330	6.0
BENOIT BENJAMIN	28	52	108	.481	22	37	.595	10	126	4.5
DUANE COOPER	65	62	158	.392	25	35	.714	150	156	2.4
ALEX BLACKWELL	27	14	42	.333	6	8	.750	7	34	1.3

NBA PLAYOFFS
FIRST ROUND
LOST TO PHOENIX, 2-3

LEAGUE AWARDS
NONE

TEAM LEADERS
SCORING
THREATT............15.1
ASSISTS
THREATT 6.9
REBOUNDS
DIVAC...............8.9
FIELD GOAL PCT.
GREEN..............537
FREE THROW PCT
B. SCOTT............848
MINUTES PLAYED
THREATT............35.3

LOS ANGELES 1993-94
5TH PACIFIC DIVISION

REGULAR SEASON RECORD
33-49

PLAYER	G	FGM	FGA	PCT	FTM	FTA	PCT	AST	PTS	PPG
VLADE DIVAC	79	453	895	.506	208	303	.686	307	1123	14.2
ANTHONY PEELER	30	176	409	.430	57	71	.803	94	423	14.1
NICK VAN EXEL	81	413	1049	.394	150	192	.781	466	1099	13.6
ELDEN CAMPBELL	76	373	808	.462	188	273	.689	86	934	12.3
SEDALE THREATT	81	411	852	.482	138	155	.890	344	965	11.9
DOUG CHRISTIE	65	244	562	.434	145	208	.697	136	671	10.3
JAMES WORTHY	80	340	838	.406	100	135	.741	154	812	10.2
TREVOR WILSON	5	19	39	.487	13	25	.520	12	51	10.2
GEORGE LYNCH	71	291	573	.508	99	166	.596	96	681	9.6
SAM BOWIE	25	75	172	.436	72	83	.867	47	223	8.9
TONY SMITH	73	272	617	.441	85	119	.714	148	645	8.8
REGGIE JORDAN	23	44	103	.427	35	51	.686	26	125	5.4
JAMES EDWARDS	45	78	168	.464	54	79	.684	22	210	4.7
KURT RAMBIS	50	59	114	.518	46	71	.648	32	164	3.3
DAN SCHAYES	13	14	38	.368	8	10	.800	8	36	2.8
ANTONIO HARVEY	27	29	79	.367	12	26	.462	5	70	2.6

NBA PLAYOFFS
DID NOT ADVANCE TO SEASON PLAYOFFS

LEAGUE AWARDS
ALL-ROOKIE TEAM
VAN EXEL, SECOND TEAM

TEAM LEADERS
SCORING
DIVAC..............14.2
ASSISTS
VAN EXEL............5.8
REBOUNDS
DIVAC..............10.8
FIELD GOAL PCT.
LYNCH..............508
FREE THROW PCT
THREATT 890
MINUTES PLAYED
VAN EXEL...........33.3

LOS ANGELES 1994-95

3RD PACIFIC DIVISION

REGULAR SEASON RECORD
48-34

PLAYER	G	FGM	FGA	PCT	FTM	FTA	PCT	AST	PTS	PPG
CEDRIC CEBALLOS	58	497	977	.509	209	292	.716	105	1261	21.7
NICK VAN EXEL	80	465	1107	.420	235	300	.783	660	1348	16.9
VLADE DIVAC	80	485	957	.507	297	382	.777	329	1277	16.0
EDDIE JONES	64	342	744	.460	122	169	.722	128	897	14.0
ELDEN CAMPBELL	73	360	785	.459	193	290	.666	92	913	12.5
ANTHONY PEELER	73	285	659	.432	102	128	.797	122	756	10.4
SEDALE THREATT	59	217	437	.497	88	111	.793	248	558	9.5
LLOYD DANIELS	25	71	182	.390	20	25	.800	36	185	7.4
GEORGE LYNCH	56	138	295	.468	62	86	.721	62	341	6.1
TONY SMITH	61	132	309	.427	44	63	.698	102	340	5.6
SAM BOWIE	67	118	267	.442	68	89	.764	118	306	4.6
ANTHONY MILLER	46	70	132	.530	47	76	.618	35	189	4.1
RANDOLPH KEYS	6	9	26	.346	2	2	1.000	2	20	3.3
ANTONIO HARVEY	59	77	176	.438	24	45	.533	23	179	3.0
KURT RAMBIS	26	18	35	.514	8	12	.667	16	44	1.7
LESTER CONNER	2	0	0	N/A	2	2	1.000	0	2	1.0

NBA PLAYOFFS

FIRST ROUND
DEF. SEATTLE, 3-1

SECOND ROUND
LOST TO SAN ANTONIO, 2-4

TEAM LEADERS

SCORING
CEBALLOS. 21.7

ASSISTS
VAN EXEL. 8.3

REBOUNDS
DIVAC. 10.4

FIELD GOAL PCT.
CEBALLOS 509

FREE THROW PCT
PEELER 797

MINUTES PLAYED
VAN EXEL. 36.8

LEAGUE AWARDS

COACH OF THE YEAR
DEL HARRIS

ALL-STAR TEAM
CEBALLOS

ALL-ROOKIE TEAM
E. JONES

LOS ANGELES 1995-96

2ND PACIFIC DIVISION

REGULAR SEASON RECORD
53-29

PLAYER	G	FGM	FGA	PCT	FTM	FTA	PCT	AST	PTS	PPG
CEDRIC CEBALLOS	78	638	1203	.530	329	409	.804	119	1656	21.2
NICK VAN EXEL	74	396	950	.417	163	204	.799	509	1099	14.9
MAGIC JOHNSON	32	137	294	.466	172	201	.856	220	468	14.6
ELDEN CAMPBELL	82	447	888	.503	249	349	.713	181	1143	13.9
VLADE DIVAC	79	414	807	.513	189	295	.641	261	1020	12.9
EDDIE JONES	70	337	685	.492	136	184	.739	246	893	12.8
ANTHONY PEELER	73	272	602	.452	61	86	.709	118	710	9.7
SEDALE THREATT	82	241	526	.458	54	71	.761	269	596	7.3
GEORGE LYNCH	76	117	272	.430	53	80	.663	51	291	3.8
FRED ROBERTS	33	48	97	.495	22	28	.786	26	122	3.7
DEREK STRONG	63	72	169	.426	69	85	.812	32	214	3.4
CORIE BLOUNT	57	79	167	.473	25	44	.568	42	183	3.2
ANTHONY MILLER	27	15	35	.429	6	10	.600	4	36	1.3
FRANKIE KING	6	3	11	.273	1	3	.333	2	7	1.2

NBA PLAYOFFS

FIRST ROUND
LOST TO HOUSTON, 1-3

TEAM LEADERS

SCORING
CEBALLOS. 21.2

ASSISTS
VAN EXEL. 6.9

REBOUNDS
DIVAC. 8.6

FIELD GOAL PCT.
CEBALLOS 530

FREE THROW PCT
E. JOHNSON 856

MINUTES PLAYED
E. CAMPBELL 32.9

LEAGUE AWARDS

NONE

LOS ANGELES 1996-97

2ND PACIFIC DIVISION

REGULAR SEASON RECORD
56-26

PLAYER	G	FGM	FGA	PCT	FTM	FTA	PCT	AST	PTS	PPG
SHAQUILLE O'NEAL	51	552	991	.557	232	479	.484	159	1336	26.2
EDDIE JONES	80	473	1081	.438	276	337	.819	270	1374	17.2
NICK VAN EXEL	79	432	1075	.402	165	200	.825	672	1206	15.3
ELDEN CAMPBELL	77	442	942	.469	263	370	.711	126	1148	14.9
CEDRIC CEBALLOS	8	34	83	.410	13	15	.867	15	86	10.8
GEORGE MCCLOUD	23	34	96	.354	6	9	.667	17	95	4.1
ROBERT HORRY	22	75	165	.455	28	40	.700	56	203	9.2
KOBE BRYANT	71	176	422	.417	136	166	.819	91	539	7.6
JEROME KERSEY	70	194	449	.432	71	118	.602	89	476	6.8
BYRON SCOTT	79	163	379	.430	127	151	.841	99	526	6.7
TRAVIS KNIGHT	71	140	275	.509	62	100	.620	39	342	4.8
CORIE BLOUNT	58	92	179	.514	56	83	.675	35	241	4.2
DEREK FISHER	80	104	262	.397	79	120	.658	119	309	3.9
SEAN ROOKS	69	87	185	.470	91	130	.700	42	265	3.8
RUMEAL ROBINSON	15	17	48	.354	5	8	.625	13	45	3.0
LARRY KRYSTKOWIAK	3	1	2	.500	2	2	.500	3	3	1.0
JOE KLEIN	8	2	8	.250	2	2	1.000	0	6	0.8

NBA PLAYOFFS

FIRST ROUND
DEF. PORTLAND, 3-1

SECOND ROUND
LOST TO UTAH, 1-4

TEAM LEADERS

SCORING
O'NEAL. 26.2

ASSISTS
VAN EXEL. 8.5

REBOUNDS
O'NEAL. 12.5

FIELD GOAL PCT.
O'NEAL 557

FREE THROW PCT
B. SCOTT 841

MINUTES PLAYED
E. JONES 37.5

LEAGUE AWARDS

ALL-NBA TEAM
O'NEAL, THIRD TEAM

ALL-STAR TEAM
O'NEAL
E. JONES

ALL-ROOKIE TEAM
KNIGHT, BRYANT, SECOND TEAM

LOS ANGELES 1997-98

2ND PACIFIC DIVISION

REGULAR SEASON RECORD
61-21

PLAYER	G	FGM	FGA	PCT	FTM	FTA	PCT	AST	PTS	PPG
SHAQUILLE O'NEAL	80	670	1147	.584	359	681	.527	142	1699	28.3
EDDIE JONES	80	486	1005	.484	234	306	.765	246	1349	16.9
KOBE BRYANT	79	391	913	.428	363	457	.794	199	1220	15.4
NICK VAN EXEL	64	311	743	.419	136	172	.791	442	881	13.8
RICK FOX	82	363	771	.471	171	230	.743	276	983	12.0
ELDEN CAMPBELL	81	289	624	.463	237	342	.693	78	816	10.1
ROBERT HORRY	72	200	420	.476	117	169	.692	163	536	7.4
DEREK FISHER	82	164	378	.434	115	152	.757	333	474	5.8
MARIO BENNETT	45	80	135	.593	16	44	.364	18	177	3.9
CORIE BLOUNT	70	107	187	.572	39	78	.500	37	253	3.6
SEAN ROOKS	41	46	101	.455	47	79	.595	24	139	3.4
JON BARRY	49	38	104	.365	27	29	.931	51	121	2.5
SHEA SEALS	4	1	8	.125	2	4	.500	0	4	1.0

NBA PLAYOFFS

FIRST ROUND
DEF. PORTLAND, 3-1

SECOND ROUND
DEF. SEATTLE, 4-1

THIRD ROUND
LOST TO UTAH, 0-4

TEAM LEADERS

SCORING
O'NEAL. 28.3

ASSISTS
VAN EXEL. 6.9

REBOUNDS
O'NEAL. 11.4

FIELD GOAL PCT.
O'NEAL 584

FREE THROW PCT
BRYANT. 794

MINUTES PLAYED
E. JONES 36.4

LEAGUE AWARDS

ALL-NBA TEAM
O'NEAL, FIRST TEAM

ALL-STAR TEAM
VAN EXEL
BRYANT
E. JONES
O'NEAL

ACKNOWLEDGEMENTS

Any book is the sum total of a lot of effort by a lot of people. But none requires more effort by more people than an encyclopedia, which, by its nature, requires enough information to cover every aspect of a subject.

This encyclopedia was the brainchild of Carla Lazzareschi of Los Angeles Times Books. She conceived it, she put together the staff that has produced it and she has shepherded it through a process made more difficult by a demanding deadline.

She deserves special praise, but much must also be heaped on Mike James, who, along with help from Steve Horn, diligently edited the book, and Chuck Nigash and Jason Mooshigian, who artistically combined the words and pictures into a highly attractive package. A grateful nod to Allen Martinet of BAM Graphics for helping to keep track of the many photos.

Special thanks to Paul Singleton of The Times library, who was never too busy to somehow find players and facts long forgotten.

To long-time Laker photographer Wen Roberts for generously making available his vast, impressive files. To Laker public relations director John Black for the use of his office and his research material, and to Michael Uhlenkamp, Raymond Ridder and Matt Fleer of the Laker office.

Many thanks also to Gary Alcorn, the Associated Press, Lou Baumeister, Elgin Baylor, Bill Bertka, Thomas Bonk, Jerry Buss, Russell Carter and the Washington Post, Mitch Chortkoff, Ralph Cipriano and the Philadelphia Inquirer, Michael Cooper, the Dallas Morning News, Mike Downey, Bill Dwyre, Helene Elliott, Mal Florence, Abigail Goldman, Gail Goodrich, Ted Green, Dan Hafner, John Hall, Randy Harvey, Tommy Hawkins, Chick Hearn, Tommy Heinsohn, Mark Heisler, Scott Howard-Cooper, Hot Rod Hundley, Rudy LaRusso, Mary Lou Liebich, Dr. Steve Lombardo, the Los Angeles Times library, Peter May and the Boston Globe, Robin Mayper, Mike McGraw and the Chicago Daily Herald, Sam McManis, George Mikan, the National Basketball Assn., Frank O'Neill, Norm Nixon, the Orange County Register, Scott Ostler, Jim Perzik, PhillySport magazine, Bill Plaschke, Larry Pruner and the Vancouver Sun, Patrick Reusse and the Minneapolis Star Tribune, Jim Rhode, Pat Riley, Dick Scanlon and the Ledger, Fred Schaus, Peter Schmuck, Bill Sharman, Owen Slot and the Independent (London), the Sporting News, Bob Steiner, Donald Sterling, Susan Stratton, Gary Vitti, Henry Weinstein, Jerry West and Mel Zikes.

Thanks to the following authors for their valuable contributions:

Winnin' Times, Scott Ostler and Steve Springer, Macmillan Publishing Co., New York, 1986.
My Life, Magic Johnson with William Novak, Random House, New York, 1992.
Giant Steps, Kareem Abdul-Jabbar and Peter Knobler, Bantam Books, Inc., New York, 1983.
Kareem, Kareem Abdul-Jabbar with Mignon McCarthy, Warner Books, New York, 1990.
Showtime, Inside the Lakers' Breakthrough Season, Pat Riley, Warner Books, Inc., New York, 1988.
The History of the Lakers, Stew Thornley, Nodin Press, Minneapolis, 1989.

And finally, my gratitude to Earvin Johnson and Lon Rosen for their heartfelt contributions to this book.

- STEVE SPRINGER